"I immediately went to my nurse manager after I failed the NCLEX® and she referred me to ATI. I was able to discover the areas I was weak in, and focused on those areas in the review modules and online assessments.

I was much more prepared the second time around!"

Terim Richards
Nursing student

Danielle Platt

Nurse Manager • Children's Mercy Hospital • Kansas City, MO

"The year our hospital did not use the ATI program, we experienced a 15% decrease in the NCLEX® pass rates. We reinstated the ATI program the following year and had a 90% success rate."

"As a manager, I have witnessed graduate nurses fail the NCLEX® and the devastating effects it has on their morale. Once the nurses started using ATI, it was amazing to see the confidence they had in themselves and their ability to go forward and take the NCLEX® exam."

Mary Moss

Associate Dean of Nursing - Service and Health Division • Mid-State Technical College • Wisconsin Rapids, WI

"I like that ATI lets students know what to expect from the NCLEX®, helps them plan their study time and tells them what to do in the days and weeks before the exam. It is different from most of the NCLEX® review books on the market."

Editor

Jeanne Wissmann, PhD, RN, CNE
Director Nursing Curriculum and Educational Services
Assessment Technologies Institute®, LLC

Associate Editors

Janine Stomboly, BSN, RN
Curriculum Director of PN Assessments

Kristen M. Lawler, MBA
Director of Development

Brant L. Stacy, BS Journalism
Product Developer

Advisory Reviewers

Lisa Easterby, MSN, RN

Important Notice to the Reader of this Publication

Preface

Overview

The overall goal of this Assessment Technologies Institute®, LLC (ATI) Content Mastery Series module is to provide nursing students with an additional resource for the focused review of "Maternal Newborn Nursing" content relevant to NCLEX-RN® preparation and entry level nursing practice. Content within this review module is provided in a key point plus rationale format in order to focus recall and application of relevant content. Unit and chapter selections are reflective of the maternal newborn-relevant content categories and content explanations of the NCLEX-RN® test plan, the ATI "Maternal Newborn Nursing" assessment test plans, and standard nursing curricular content. Each chapter begins with an overview of some of the topic-relevant nursing activities outlined by the NCLEX-RN® test plan in an effort to guide the learner's review and application of chapter content.

Contributors

ATI would like to extend appreciation to the nurse educators and nurse specialists who contributed chapters for this review module. The name of each contributor is noted in the chapter byline. We would also like to thank those talented individuals who reviewed, edited, and developed this module. In the summer and fall of 2005, two focus groups of committed nurse educators gave invaluable input and feedback regarding the format and purposes of review modules. Their input and ideas were instrumental to the development of this review module and we are very appreciative. Additionally, we would like to recognize and extend appreciation to the multiple nursing students and educators who have contacted us in the past year with comments and ideas regarding the content of this review module. And finally, we want to recognize and express appreciation to all of the contributors, reviewers, production developers, and editors of previous editions of this Content Mastery Series module.

Suggestions for Effective Utilization

Δ   As a review of NCLEX-RN®-relevant maternal newborn nursing content in developing and assessing your readiness for NCLEX-RN®.

Δ   As a focused review resource based on the results of an ATI "Maternal Newborn Nursing" or RN Comprehensive Predictor assessment. "Topics to Review" identified upon completion of these assessments can be used to focus your efforts to a review of content within specific chapter(s) of this review module. For example, an identified "Topic to Review" of "Complications of Pregnancy: Spontaneous Abortion" suggests that a review of Chapter 8 "Complications of Pregnancy" and completion of the application exercises at the end of the chapter would be helpful.

Δ   To foster long-term recall and development of an ability to apply knowledge to a variety of situations, learners are encouraged to take a comprehensive approach to topic review. Using this review module along with other resources (class notes, course textbooks, nursing reference texts, instructors, ATI DVD series), consider exploration of topics, addressing questions such as:

- What are priorities in the nursing care of clients in each of the phases of pregnancy and childbirth—antepartum, intrapartum, and postpartum?

- Identify the various contraceptive methods and procedures to prevent conception. What are the benefits, risks, and nursing instructions for each?

- What are common risk factors for infertility? What is the nurse's role in assessment, genetic counseling, and associated therapeutic and diagnostic procedures?

- What are the normal physiological changes of pregnancy? What body system changes should the nurse expect to see during the nursing assessment of pregnant clients?

- What is the recommended weight gain for each trimester of pregnancy and complications that can occur from excessive or poor weight gain? What type of client teaching should the nurse provide regarding nutrients and vitamins?

- Identify the physical discomforts of pregnancy and client instruction to promote relaxation and comfort.

- How can the nurse provide culturally sensitive nursing care when planning, providing, and evaluating perinatal care?

- Identify potential complications of each trimester of pregnancy? For each complication, what are the risk factors, appropriate nursing assessments, signs and symptoms, diagnostic and therapeutic procedures, and nursing interventions to prevent and/or respond appropriately to complications of pregnancy?

- What are the normal stages of fetal growth and development? What risk factors can negatively impact fetal development and lead to fetal and neonatal complications?

- Identify the various antepartum diagnostic tests and procedures performed to assure maternal and fetal well-being? What are the indications, potential complications, and nursing implications for each test or procedure?

- Identify the common birthing methods and the premise of each.

- What are the normal processes, mechanisms, stages, and phases of labor and birth?

- What maternal and fetal assessments does the nurse perform throughout the stages of labor and birth? What are the parameters for assessment frequency (high-risk versus low-risk to mother/fetus) to monitor maternal and fetal well-being? Identify the indications for use, advantages and disadvantages, potential complications, and nursing implications for each?

- Identify complications of labor and birth, maternal and/or fetal nursing assessments, signs and symptoms, possible causes, and nursing interventions.

- Identify the diagnostic and therapeutic procedures to assist with the complications of labor and birth. What are indications for use, potential complications, and nursing implications for each?

- Identify sources of intrapartal pain and factors that influence the client's perception of pain. What are pharmacologic and nonpharmacologic pain management methods for labor and birth? Identify the advantages, disadvantages, potential complications, and nursing implications of each.

- What normal physiological changes should the nurse expect to observe when assessing a postpartum client? Identify potential postpartum complications, signs and symptoms to observe for during assessment, and nursing interventions for each.

- What should the nurse teach the client about self-care during the postpartum period regarding comfort measures and prevention of postpartum complications?

- What are the normal phases of maternal, paternal, and sibling psychosocial adaptation to the integration of the newborn into the family? What are appropriate nursing assessments and interventions to assess/facilitate bonding?

- What nursing assessments should be performed to assure the newborn is adjusting to extrauterine life? What are normal assessment parameters and deviations from the norm? What are the nursing implications for management of each neonatal complication?

- What is the appropriate frequency of feedings and caloric intake to provide adequate neonatal nutrition? What are proper breastfeeding and bottle feeding techniques and the proper method of storing expressed breast milk?

- What are the nursing assessments and interventions, including client/parent teaching regarding circumcision care, to promote healing and to prevent circumcision complications?

- Identify client learning needs and nursing interventions to teach the correct use of infant car seats and appropriate care of the newborn. What are methods to evaluate the effectiveness of client/parent learning?

Δ   Complete application exercises at the end of each chapter after a review of the topic. Answer questions fully and note rationales for answers. Complete exercises initially without looking for the answers within the chapter or consulting the answer key. Use these exercises as an opportunity to assess your readiness to apply knowledge. When reviewing the answer key, in addition to identifying the correct answer, examine why you missed or answered correctly each item—was it related to ability to recall?, recognition of a common testing principle?, or perhaps attention to key words?

Feedback

All feedback is welcome – suggestions for improvement, reports of mistakes (small or large), and testimonials of effectiveness. Please address feedback to: comments@atitesting.com

Table of Contents

Unit 1   Antepartum

Chapter 1:   Reproductive Cycle: Contraception and Conception
Contributor: Brenda R. French, MSN, RN

NCLEX-RN® Connections:

Learning Objective: Review and apply knowledge within **"Reproductive Cycle: Contraception and Conception"** in readiness for performance of the following nursing activities as outlined by the NCLEX-RN® test plan:

     Δ   Assess and support the client's need and preferences for contraception.

     Δ   Recognize contraindications to the client's chosen contraceptive method.

     Δ   Provide information on genetic counseling as appropriate.

     Δ   Provide the client/family/significant other with support throughout the client's infertility assessment.

Key Points

     Δ   Contraception is the prevention of conception or impregnation.

     Δ   Conception is the union of a man's sperm and a woman's ovum.

     Δ   Infertility is defined as a lack of conception despite unprotected sexual intercourse for at least 12 months.

Key Factors

     Δ   Genetic counseling may be recommended by the primary care provider if there is a family history of birth defects. The age of the mother may also play a role in this decision with a maternal age less than 16 years old or older than 35 years being a risk factor.

     Δ   Prenatal assessment of genetic disorders (e.g., chorionic villus sampling, percutaneous umbilical blood sampling, and amniocentesis) can pose potential risks to the fetus.

     Δ   Common factors in infertility include decreased sperm production, ovulation disorders, tubal occlusions, and endometriosis.

Δ   Partners that experience infertility may experience stress related to:

  •   Physical inability to conceive.

  •   Expense.

  •   Impact on the couple's relationship.

  •   Lack of family support.

Δ   Use of medications to treat female infertility increases the risk of multiple births by more than 25%.

Therapeutic and Diagnostic Procedures and Nursing Interventions

Infertility Procedures

Δ   **Pelvic examination** – an assessment for vaginal or uterine anomalies. The nurse should position the client on the exam table and have equipment and supplies prepared for the primary care provider.

Δ   **Hysterosalpingography** – an outpatient radiological procedure where dye is used to assess patency of fallopian tubes. The nurse should obtain the client's history of allergies to iodine and seafood.

Δ   **Hysteroscopy** – a radiographic procedure where the uterus is examined for evidence of defect, distortion, or scar tissue that might impair successful impregnation.

Δ   **Laparoscopy** – a procedure where gas insufflation is used to visualize internal organs and may cause postprocedural pain. General anesthesia is required for this procedure.

Δ   **Semen collection** – a procedure in which semen is collected from the man in a sterile collection device for evaluation and analysis. In 40% of couples who are infertile, inability to conceive is due to male infertility. Therefore, this infertility test is a preferred starting point in evaluating a couple in order to rule out male infertility. It is less costly and invasive compared to female infertility testing.

Contraception Procedures

Δ   **Vasectomy** – the cutting of the vas deferens in the male as a form of permanent sterilization. The nurse should reinforce the need for alternate forms of birth control for approximately 20 ejaculations or 1 week to several months to allow all of the sperm to clear the vas deferens postprocedure to assure complete male infertility.

Δ   **Tubal ligation (salpingectomy)** – the cutting, burning, or blocking of the fallopian tubes to prevent the ovum from being fertilized by the sperm.

Δ   **Hysterectomy** – the surgical removal of the uterus. Removal may be partial (removal of uterus only) or complete (removal of uterus and bilateral fallopian tubes and ovaries).

Assessments and Nursing Interventions

Assessment: Contraception

Δ   The nurse assesses the need/desire for contraception

Δ   **BRAIDED** is an acronym for informed consent with contraception:

- **B**enefits (information about advantages)

- **R**isks (information about disadvantages)

- **A**lternatives (information about other methods available)

- **I**nquiries (opportunity for the client to ask questions)

- **D**ecisions (opportunity for the client to decide or change mind)

- **E**xplanations (information about the selected method and how to use it)

- **D**ocumentation (information given and client's understanding of the information)

Δ   The client's preference for contraception is considered. The decision may be individual. Examples of decisions include: woman – birth control pill; man – condom. Sexual partners often make a joint decision regarding their desired preference (e.g., vasectomy or tubal ligation). Postpartum discharge instructions should include the discussion of future contraceptive plans.

Δ   Expected outcomes for family planning methods consist of preventing pregnancy until the desired time.

Δ   Nurses need to support clients in making the decision that is best for their individualized situations.

Nursing Interventions: Contraception

Natural Family Planning Methods	
Abstinence – abstaining from having sexual intercourse eliminates the possibility of sperm entering the woman's vagina.	
Client Instruction	• Refrain from sexual intercourse. This method can be associated with saying "no," but can also incorporate saying "yes" to other gratifying sexual activities such as affectionate touching, communication, holding hands, kissing, massage, and oral and manual stimulation.
Advantages	• Most effective method of birth control. • Abstinence during fertile periods (rhythm method) can be used but requires an understanding of the menstrual cycle and fertility awareness. • Can eliminate the risk of sexually transmitted infections if there is no genitalia contact.

Disadvantages	• Requires self-control.
Risks/possible complications/ contraindications	• If complete abstinence is maintained there are no risks.

Coitus interruptus (withdrawal) – man withdraws penis from vagina prior to ejaculation.

Client Instruction	• Be aware of leakage of any fluids from the penis.
Advantages	• Possible choice for monogamous couples with no other option for birth control, such as those opposed to birth control due to religious conviction.
Disadvantages	• Most ineffective method of contraception. • No protection against sexually transmitted infection.
Risks/possible complications/ contraindications	• Depends on the man's ability to control ejaculation. Adolescent boys frequently lack control to make this an effective method. • Leakage of fluid containing spermatozoa prior to ejaculation can be deposited in vagina.

Calendar method (Rhythm method) - A woman records her menstrual cycle, calculates the fertile period based on assumption that ovulation occurs roughly 14 days before the onset of the next menstrual cycle, and avoids intercourse during that time. Also taken into account is the timing of intercourse with this method because sperm are viable for 48 to 120 hr and the ovum is viable for 24 hr.

Client Instruction	• Accurately record the number of days in each cycle counting from the first day of menses for a period of 6 months. • The start of the fertile period is approximated by subtracting 18 days from the number of days in the shortest cycle. • The end of the fertile period is established by subtracting 11 days from the number of days of the longest cycle. For example: ◊ Shortest cycle, 26 – 18 = 8th day ◊ Longest cycle, 30 – 11 = 19th day ◊ Fertile period is days 8 through 19. • Refrain from intercourse during these days to avoid contraception.
Advantages	• Most useful as an adjunct to basal body temperature or cervical mucus method. • Inexpensive.

Disadvantages	• Not a very reliable technique. • Requires accurate record keeping. • Requires compliance by both partners in regards to abstinence during fertile periods.
Risks/possible complications/ contraindications	• Various factors can affect and change the time of ovulation and cause unpredictable menstrual cycles. • Risk of pregnancy.

Basal body temperature (BBT) – temperature will drop prior to ovulation. This can be used to facilitate conception or be used as a natural contraceptive.

Client Instruction	• The woman is instructed to measure oral temperature prior to getting out of bed each morning to monitor ovulation.
Advantages	• Inexpensive, convenient, and no side effects.
Disadvantages	• BBT reliability can be influenced by many variables that can cause inaccurate interpretation of temperature changes, such as stress, fatigue, illness, alcohol, and warmth or coolness of sleeping environment.
Risks/possible complications/ contraindications	• Possible complication is unwanted pregnancy.

Billings method (cervical mucus method) – fertility awareness method based on ovulation. Ovulation occurs approximately 14 days prior to the next menstrual cycle, which is when the woman is fertile. Following ovulation, the cervical mucus becomes thick and sticky under the influence of estrogen and progesterone to allow for sperm viability and motility. The mucus's ability to stretch between the fingers is greatest at the time of ovulation. This is known as **spinnbarkeit sign.**

Client Instruction	• Engage in good handwashing prior to and following assessment. • Begin examining mucus from the last day of the menstrual cycle. • Obtained from the vaginal introitus. It is not necessary to reach into the vagina to the cervix.
Advantages	• The woman can become knowledgeable in recognizing her own mucus characteristics at ovulation and self-evaluation can be very accurate. • Self-evaluation of cervical mucus can also be diagnostically helpful in determining the start of ovulation while breastfeeding, in noting the commencement of menopause, and in planning a desired pregnancy.

Disadvantages	• Some women may be uncomfortable with touching their genitals and mucus and will find this method objectionable.
Risks/possible complications/ contraindications	• Assessment of cervical mucus characteristics may be inaccurate if mucus is mixed with semen, contraceptive jellies or foams, or discharge from infections. • Do not douche prior to assessment.

Condoms – a thin flexible sheath worn on the penis during intercourse to prevent semen from entering the uterus.

Client Instruction	• Man places condom on his erect penis, leaving an empty space at the tip for a sperm reservoir. • Following ejaculation, the man withdraws his penis from the woman's vagina while holding condom rim to prevent any semen spillage to vulva or vaginal area. • May be used in conjunction with spermicidal gel or cream to increase effectiveness.
Advantages	• Protects against sexually transmitted infection and involves the male in the birth control method.
Disadvantages	• High rate of noncompliance. • May reduce spontaneity of intercourse. • Penis must be erect to apply condom. • Withdrawal of penis while still erect can interfere with sexual intercourse.
Risks/possible complications/ contraindications	• Condoms can rupture or leak and have a one-time usage creating a replacement cost. • Condoms made of latex should not be worn by those who are sensitive or allergic to latex. • Only water-soluble lubricants should be used with latex condoms to avoid condom breakage.

Barrier Methods

Diaphragm and spermicide – a dome-shaped cup with a flexible rim made of latex or rubber that fits snugly over the cervix with spermicidal cream or gel placed into the dome and around the rim.

Client Instruction	• Female client has to be fitted with diaphragm properly by a primary care provider. • The client must be refitted by the primary care provider every 2 years, if there is a 7 kg (15 lb) weight change, full-term pregnancy, or second-term abortion. • Requires proper insertion and removal. Prior to coitus, the diaphragm is inserted vaginally over the cervix with spermicidal jelly or cream that is applied to the cervical side of the dome and around the rim. The diaphragm must remain in place at least 6 hr after coitus. • More spermicide must be reapplied with each act of coitus. • Empty bladder prior to diaphragm insertion.
Advantages	• Barrier method eliminates surgery and gives a woman more control over contraception.
Disadvantages	• Diaphragms are inconvenient, interfere with spontaneity, and require reapplication of spermicidal gel, cream, or foam with each act of coitus to be effective.
Risks/possible complications/ contraindications	• Diaphragm is not recommended for clients who have a history of toxic shock syndrome (TSS) or frequent, recurrent urinary tract infections. • TSS is caused by a bacterial infection. Signs and symptoms include high fever, a faint feeling and drop in blood pressure, watery diarrhea, headache, and muscle aches. • Proper handwashing aids in prevention of TSS as well as removing diaphragm promptly at 6 hr following coitus.

Combined oral contraceptives – hormonal contraception containing estrogen and progestin, which acts by suppressing ovulation, thickening the cervical mucus to block semen, and altering the uterine decidua to prevent implantation.

Client Instruction	• Medication requires a prescription and follow-up appointments with the primary care provider. • Medication requires consistent and proper use to be effective. • Client is instructed in observing for side effects and danger signs of medication. Signs include chest pain, shortness of breath, leg pain from a possible clot, headache, or eye problems from a cerebrovascular accident, or hypertension. • In the event of a client missing a dose, the nurse should instruct the client that if 1 pill is missed, take 1 as soon as possible; if 2 or 3 pills are missed, instruct the client to follow the manufacturer's instructions. Instruct the client on the use of alternative forms of contraception or abstinence in order to prevent pregnancy until regular dosing is resumed.
Advantages	• Highly effective if taken correctly and consistently. • Medication can alleviate dysmenorrhea by decreasing menstrual flow and menstrual cramps. • Reduces acne.
Disadvantages	• Oral contraceptives do not protect against sexually transmitted infection. • Birth control pills can increase the risk of thromboses, breast tenderness, scant or missed menstruation, stroke, nausea, headaches, hormone-dependent cancers, and can be teratogenic. • Exacerbates conditions affected by fluid retention such as migraine, epilepsy, asthma, kidney, or heart disease.
Risks/possible complications/ contraindications	• Women with a history of blood clots, stroke, cardiac problems, breast or estrogen-related cancers, pregnancy, or smoking (if over 35 years of age), are advised not to take oral contraceptive medications. • Oral contraceptive effectiveness decreases when taking medications that affect liver enzymes such as anticonvulsants and some antibiotics.

Hormonal Methods

Minipill – oral progestins that provide the same action as combined oral contraceptives.	
Client Instruction	• The client should take the pill at the same time daily to ensure effectiveness secondary to a low dose of progestin. • The client cannot miss a pill. • The client may need another form of birth control during the first month of use to prevent pregnancy.
Advantages	• Minipill has fewer side effects when compared to combination oral birth control pills.
Disadvantages	• Less effective in suppressing ovulation than combined oral contraceptives. • Pill increases occurrence of ovarian cysts. • Pill does not protect against sexually transmitted infection. • Users frequently report breakthrough, irregular, vaginal bleeding. • Increases appetite.
Risks/possible complications/ contraindications	• Oral contraceptive effectiveness decreases when taking medications that affect liver enzymes such as anticonvulsants and some antibiotics.

Emergency oral contraceptive – morning after pill.	
Client Instruction	• Pill is taken within 72 hr after unprotected coitus. • Primary care provider or nurse will recommend an over-the-counter antiemetic to be taken 1 hr prior to each dose to counteract the side effects of nausea that can occur with high doses of estrogen and progestin. • Advise the woman to be evaluated for pregnancy, if menstruation does not begin within 21 days. • The nurse should provide client counseling on contraception and modification of risky sexual behaviors.
Advantages	• Pill is not taken on a regular basis.
Disadvantages	• Nausea • Does not provide long-term contraception.
Risks/possible complications/ contraindications	• Contraindicated if a client is pregnant or has undiagnosed abnormal vaginal bleeding.

Transdermal contraceptive patch – contains norelgestromin (progesterone) and ethinyl estradiol, which is delivered at continuous levels through the skin into subcutaneous tissue.

Client Instruction	• Client applies the patch to dry skin overlying subcutaneous tissue in areas of buttock, abdomen, upper arm, or torso, excluding breast area. • Requires patch replacement once a week. • Patch is applied the same day of the week for 3 weeks with no application of the patch on the fourth week.
Advantages	• Maintains consistent blood levels of hormone. • Avoids liver metabolism of medication since it is not absorbed in the gastrointestinal tract. • Decreases risk of forgetting daily pill.
Disadvantages	• Patch does not protect against sexually transmitted infection. • Poses same side effects as oral contraceptives.
Risks/possible complications/ contraindications	• Same as those of oral contraceptives. • Avoid application of patch to skin rashes or lesions.

Injectable progestins (Depo-Provera) – an intramuscular injection given to a female client every 11 to 13 weeks.

Client Instruction	• Start of injections should be during the first 5 days of the client's menstrual cycle and every 11 to 13 weeks thereafter. • Advise the client to keep follow-up appointments.
Advantages	• Very effective and only requires four injections per year. • Does not impair lactation.
Disadvantages	• Can prolong amenorrhea or uterine bleeding. • Increases risk of thromboembolism. • Depo-Provera does not protect against sexually transmitted infection.
Risks/possible complications/ contraindications	• Nurse should avoid massaging injection site following administration to avoid accelerating medication absorption, which will shorten the duration of medication's effectiveness.

Implantable progestin levonorgestrel (Norplant) – requires a minor surgical procedure to subdermally implant or remove 6 Silastic capsules containing levonorgestrel on the inner aspect of the upper arm.

Client instruction	• Avoid trauma to the area of implantation.
Advantages	• Effective continuous contraception for 5 years. • Reversible.
Disadvantages	• Levonorgestrel can cause irregular menstrual bleeding. • Levonorgestrel does not protect against sexually transmitted infection.
Risks/possible complications/ contraindications	• Condoms should be used to protect against sexually transmitted infections.

Intrauterine Methods

Intrauterine device (IUD) – a chemically active T-shaped device inserted through the woman's cervix and placed in the uterus by the primary care provider. Releases a chemical substance that damages sperm in transit to the uterine tubes and prevents fertilization.

Client Instruction	• Device must be monitored monthly by the client after menstruation to assure the presence of the small string that hangs from the device into the upper part of the vagina to rule out migration or expulsion of the device.
Advantages	• IUD can maintain effectiveness for 1 to 10 years. • Contraception can be reversed. • Does not interfere with spontaneity
Disadvantages	• IUD can increase the risk of pelvic inflammatory disease, uterine perforation, or ectopic pregnancy. • Client should report to primary care provider late or abnormal spotting or bleeding, abdominal pain or pain with intercourse, abnormal or foul-smelling vaginal discharge, fever, chills, a change in string length, or if IUD cannot be located. • IUD does not protect from sexually transmitted infection.
Risks/possible complications/ contraindications	• Contraindicated in women who have not had a least one child or are not in a monogamous relationship. • Can cause irregular menstrual bleeding. • There is a risk of bacterial vaginosis, uterine perforation, or uterine expulsion.

Surgical Methods

Female sterilization (bilateral tubal ligation) – a surgical procedure requiring anesthesia that may be local or general.

Client Instruction	• Client is to take nothing by mouth after midnight preceding surgery.
Advantages	• Permanent contraception. • Sexual function is unaffected.
Disadvantages	• A surgical procedure carrying risks related to anesthesia complications, infection, hemorrhage, or trauma. • Considered irreversible in the event the client desires conception.
Risks/possible complications/ contraindications	• Risk of ectopic pregnancy, if pregnancy occurs.

Male sterilization (vasectomy) – a surgical procedure consisting of ligation and severance of the vas deferens.

Client Instruction	• Following the procedure, scrotal support and moderate activity for a couple of days is recommended to reduce discomfort. • Sterility is delayed until the proximal portion of the vas deferens is cleared of all remaining sperm (approximately 20 ejaculations). • Alternate forms of birth control must be used until the vas deferens is cleared of sperm. • Follow-up is important for sperm count.
Advantages	• A vasectomy is a permanent contraceptive method. • Procedure is short, safe and simple. • Sexual function is not impaired.
Disadvantages	• Requires surgery. • Considered irreversible in the event the client desires conception.
Risks/possible complications/ contraindications	• Complications are rare, but may include bleeding, infection, and anesthesia reaction.

Assessments: Genetic Counseling

Δ   Identify clients in need of genetic counseling. For example, a client who has either a sickle cell trait or sickle cell anemia, or a client over the age of 35. Make referrals to genetic specialists as necessary.

Δ   Provide and clarify information pertaining to the risk of or the occurrence of genetic disorders within a family preceding, during, and following a genetic counseling session.

Nursing Interventions: Genetic Counseling

Δ   Assist in the construction of family medical histories of several generations.

Δ   Provide emotional support. Client responses vary and include denial, anger, grief, guilt, and self blame.

Δ   Make referrals to support groups and provide follow-up.

Assessments: Infertility

Δ   **Age** – over 35 years of age might have an effect on fertility.

Δ   **Duration of infertility** – more than 1 year of coitus without contraceptives.

Δ   **Obstetric history** – past episodes of spontaneous abortions.

Δ   **Gynecologic history** – abnormal uterine contours or any history of disorders that might contribute to the formation of scar tissue that can cause blockage of ovum or sperm.

Δ   **Medical history** – atypical secondary sexual characteristic such as abnormal body fat distribution or hair growth indicative of an endocrine disorder.

Δ   **Surgical history** – particularly pelvic and abdominal procedures.

Δ   **Sexual history** – intercourse frequency, number of partners across the lifespan, and any history of sexually transmitted infections.

Δ   **Occupational/environmental exposure risk assessment** – exposure to hazardous teratogenic materials in the home or at place of employment.

Nursing Interventions: Supporting Clients Experiencing Infertility

Δ   Encourage couples to express and discuss their feelings.

Δ   Monitor for side effects associated with medications to treat female and male infertility.

Δ   Provide information regarding assisted reproductive therapies (e.g., in vitro fertilization and embryo transfer, intrafallopian gamete transfer, surrogate parenting, and reproductive alternatives such as adoption).

Δ   Make referrals to support groups.

Primary Reference:

Lowdermilk, D. L. & Perry, S. E. (2004). *Maternity & women's health care* (8th ed.). St. Louis, MO: Mosby.

Additional Resources:

Hogan, M., Glazebrook, R. (2003). *Maternal-newborn nursing reviews & rationales*. Upper Saddle River, NJ: Pearson Education, Inc.

Ladewig, P., London, M., & Davidson, M. (2006). *Contemporary maternal-newborn nursing care* (6th ed.). Upper Saddle River, NJ: Pearson Education, Inc.

Nordenberg, T. (1997, April). Protecting against unintended pregnancy: A guide to contraceptive choices. *FDA Consumer Magazine*. Retrieved August 9, 2006, from http://www.fda.gov/fdac/features/1997/397_baby.html.

Chapter 1: Reproductive Cycle: Contraception and Conception

Application Exercises

Scenario: A 19-year-old mother of a 4-week-old newborn arrives at the primary care provider's office for a postpartum visit. The nurse discusses the possible birth control options with this client.

1. Which of the following is most likely the best contraception option for this client?

    A. Birth control pills

    B. Condoms

    C. Diaphragm

    D. Depo-Provera injections

2. Explain why a bilateral tubal ligation would not be a good option for this client.

3. A 40-year-old woman who is pregnant for the third time is concerned about the possibility of having a child born with Down syndrome. What are the advantages of genetic counseling for this client?

4. A couple arrives at the clinic to discuss how they will begin their infertility assessment. Which of the following statements made by the nurse gives an appropriate understanding of the infertility assessment process? Which of the following are inappropriate responses made by the nurse?

    A. "Infertility assessments are very expensive and your insurance may not cover the cost."

    B. "It is usually the woman who is 'having trouble,' so the man doesn't have to be involved."

    C. "The man is the easiest to assess and the primary care provider will usually begin there."

    D. "Think about adopting first because there are so many babies that need good homes."

5. A nurse is instructing a client who has been prescribed oral contraceptives about danger signs. The nurse evaluates that the client understands the teaching regarding side effects if the client states the need to report

    A. reduced menstrual flow or amenorrhea.

    B. weight gain or breast tenderness.

    C. chest pain or shortness of breath.

    D. mild hypertension or headaches.

Chapter 1: Reproductive Cycle: Contraception and Conception

Application Exercises Answer Key

Scenario: A 19-year-old mother of a 4-week-old newborn arrives at the primary care provider's office for a postpartum visit. The nurse discusses the possible birth control options with this client.

1. Which of the following is most likely the best contraception option for this client?

      A. Birth control pills

      B. Condoms

      C. Diaphragm

      D. Depo-Provera injections

The client should be advised of the effectiveness rate of each. Birth control pills taken daily or Depo-Provera injections taken every 3 months are both good options for the client because both are reversible forms of contraception. The Depo-Provera injection however has an additional benefit of reducing the occurrence of noncompliance and missed doses, requiring only 4 injections annually. Condoms and/or a diaphragm should not be a primary choice because of the high rate of noncompliance and incorrect application and insertion respectively. However, if used concurrently with the Depo-Provera injections, condoms could offer some protection against sexually transmitted infections.

2. Explain why a bilateral tubal ligation would not be a good option for this client.

The client is 19 years old and a tubal ligation would not be an option because it is considered a permanent form of sterilization. Most state Medicaid plans will not cover this expense unless the client is older.

3. A 40-year-old woman who is pregnant for the third time is concerned about the possibility of having a child born with Down syndrome. What are the advantages of genetic counseling for this client?

A specialist will be available to discuss the client's concerns. Arrangements can be made to follow up with testing to determine if the client has genetic issues. The client should be informed that the testing requires a chorionic villus sampling or an amniocentesis to make a definite diagnosis. These tests could potentially pose a risk to the fetus.

4. A couple arrives at the clinic to discuss how they will begin their infertility assessment. Which of the following statements made by the nurse gives an appropriate understanding of the infertility assessment process? Which of the following are inappropriate responses made by the nurse?

   A. "Infertility assessments are very expensive and your insurance may not cover the cost."
   B. "It is usually the woman who is 'having trouble,' so the man doesn't have to be involved."
   C. **"The man is the easiest to assess and the primary care provider will usually begin there."**
   D. "Think about adopting first because there are so many babies that need good homes."

Option A is incorrect because although an infertility assessment can be very expensive, it is inappropriate to say at this time because this is the couple's initial visit. Option B is incorrect because it is almost evenly divided as to which partner the infertility issue may rest with. However, conceiving a child is a partnership, and both partners should support one another. Option C is correct since assessment of the male involves a noninvasive specimen exam. Option D is incorrect. Adoption may be an option for this couple after they have investigated having their own biological child.

5. A nurse is instructing a client who has been prescribed oral contraceptives about danger signs. The nurse evaluates that the client understands the teaching regarding side effects if the client states the need to report

        A. reduced menstrual flow or amenorrhea.

        B. weight gain or breast tenderness.

        C. chest pain or shortness of breath.

        D. mild hypertension or headaches.

Chest pain or shortness of breath may be indicative of a pulmonary embolus or myocardial infarction. Options A, B, and D are all common side effects of oral contraceptives which usually subside after a few months of use or can be alleviated by switching to an alternative brand.

Unit 1   Antepartum

Chapter 2:   Fetal Development
                Contributor: Brenda French, MSN, RN

⟳ NCLEX-RN® Connections:

Learning Objective: Review and apply knowledge within "**Fetal Development**" in readiness for performance of the following nursing activities as outlined by the NCLEX-RN® test plan:

Δ   Compare the developing fetus's physical development to the norm for the developmental stage.

Δ   Identify and report deviations from expected fetal growth and development.

📖 Key Points

Δ   **Gestation** begins with conception (fertilization with union of sperm and egg) and continues throughout birth and pregnancy.

Δ   **Fertilization** is the union of the egg and the sperm to form the zygote, which then begins a rapid series of cell divisions separating into the **trophoblast** (outer layer giving rise to the placenta) and the **embryoblast** (inner core giving rise to the embryo) while traveling down the fallopian tube toward the uterus.

   •   **Sex determination** takes place at the time of fertilization and is dependent on whether the spermatozoon that penetrates the ovum carries an X factor (female) or a Y factor (male).

Δ   **Implantation** of the **zygote** into the endometrium of the **uterus** (usually at the uterine fundus in normal implantation) happens between 6 and 10 days after conception.

   •   **Decidua** is the term applied to the uterine endometrium after implantation of the zygote.

Δ   **Chorionic villi** are fingerlike projections that develop out of the trophoblast (developing placenta) and extend into the maternal blood vessels of the decidua. This is where oxygen and nutrients are obtained and carbon dioxide and waste products are disposed.

Δ   **Intrauterine development** encompasses three stages: ovum or preembryonic, embryo, and fetus.

Δ   The **ovum stage** (conception to day 14) is the stage encompassing cellular replication (morula), blastocyst formation, and the differentiation into three primary germ layers of cells (endoderm/entoderm, mesoderm, and ectoderm) from which all fetal tissues and organs will originate.

Δ   The **embryo stage** (day 15 to 8 weeks) is the most critical. All organs and external features are developed during this stage. During this stage, the embryo is at the greatest risk from teratogens (harmful agents that cause fetal malformations). Pregnant women need to avoid exposure to large groups of people during the first trimester to decrease their exposure to infections. Handwashing is an important intervention that a pregnant woman can take to decrease the risk of contracting infectious organisms.

•   During the embryo stage, most of the organ systems and external structures develop and are formed from the primary germ layers.

Layers of the Embryo		
Endoderm or entoderm	Mesoderm	Ectoderm
The inner-most layer of cells in the developing embryo that gives rise to the internal organs such as the intestines, epithelium of the respiratory tract, and other organs.	Middle layer of cells in the developing embryo that gives rise to the connective tissue, bone marrow, muscles, blood, lymph tissue, epithelial tissue, and bones and teeth.	Outer layer of cells in the developing embryo that gives rise to skin, nails, hair, glands, and central and peripheral nervous systems

Δ   The **fetal stage** is when the fetus becomes recognizable as a human. This stage lasts from 9 weeks until the completion of pregnancy.

Δ   With modern technology, viability is now possible at 20 weeks (fetal weight of 500 g or more). Extrauterine survival generally depends on the oxygenation capabilities of the fetus's lungs and its central nervous system function. After 32 weeks, sufficient surfactant is present and alveoli are developed enough to provide a fetus with a good chance of survival.

Fetal Stages of Development	
4 weeks	Fetal heart begins to beat Body flexed C-shaped with arm and leg buds present
8 weeks	All body organs formed First indication of musculoskeletal ossification
8 to 12 weeks	Fetal heart rate can be heard using a Doppler
12 weeks	The sex of the fetus can be determined Blood forming in marrow Kidneys able to secrete urine

16 weeks	Face looks human Meconium is present in bowel Heart muscle well-developed Sensory organs differentiated
20 weeks	Primitive respiratory movements begin Heartbeat can be heard with fetoscope Quickening (fetal movement) occurs Brain grossly formed Vernix caseosa (protective, cheese-like coating on skin) and lanugo (fine, downy hair)
24 weeks	Body lean, but well-proportioned Lecithin (respiratory marker) begins to appear in amniotic fluids Ability to hear
28 weeks	Brown fat present Eyes begin to open and close Weak suck reflex
32 weeks	Subcutaneous fat collecting Fetus has fingernails and toenails Sense of taste present Aware of sounds outside the mother's body
38+ weeks	Skin pink, body rounded, lanugo on shoulders and upper body only, vernix caseosa scant Fetus receives antibodies from mother

Δ   The fetus has specialized circulatory pathways. Four specialized structures shunt blood away from the lungs and liver.

◊   **Ductus arteriosus** – connects the pulmonary artery with the aorta allowing blood to bypass the lungs.

◊   **Foramen ovale** – an intra-atrial opening that shunts blood from the right to the left atria of the heart.

◊   **Ductus venosus** – shunts blood from the umbilical vein to the inferior vena cava allowing most of the blood to bypass the liver.

◊   The **placenta** produces the hormones needed to maintain pregnancy and performs the metabolic functions of respiration, nutrition, excretion, and storage. Maternal oxygen diffuses across the placenta into the fetal blood, and carbon dioxide diffuses from the fetal blood across the placenta into the maternal blood. In this way, the placenta acts as the lungs for the fetus.

◊ **Amniotic fluid** suspends the embryo/fetus and serves:

- ° To maintain a constant body temperature of the fetus.

- ° As a source of oral fluid and a repository for waste.

- ° As a cushion for the fetus to prevent injury.

- ° To allow fetal movement for musculoskeletal development.

- ° To prevent the amnion (inner membrane of the placenta) from adhering to the fetus.

- ° To prevent umbilical cord compression.

◊ The **umbilical cord** contains **two umbilical arteries** that carry **deoxygenated blood** from the fetus to the placenta and **one umbilical vein** that supplies the embryo with **oxygen** and nutrients from the placenta (maternal blood supply). **Wharton's jelly** is a thick substance that surrounds the umbilical cord acting as a physical buffer to prevent pressure on the vein and arteries in the cord from interfering with fetal circulation.

Key Factors

Δ **Risk factors** that can **negatively impact fetal development** and lead to fetal and neonatal complications include:

- **Preterm labor,** which can lead to fetal respiratory distress syndrome.

- **Premature rupture of membranes,** which can lead to fetal infection.

- **Ectopic pregnancy,** which leads to the inevitable loss of the fetus and possible rupture of the fallopian tube.

- **Polyhydramnios,** which can lead to fetal congenital anomalies and abnormal fetal presentation.

- **Oligohydramnios,** which can lead to intrauterine fetal death, fetal cord compression, and intrauterine growth restriction (IUGR).

- **Nuchal cord,** which can lead to fetal asphyxia.

- **Maternal diabetes,** which can lead to a large for gestational age fetus or neonate.

- **Rh or ABO isoimmunization,** which can lead to a fetal hemolytic disorder (erythroblastosis fetalis).

- Maternal age greater than 35, which increases the risk of chromosomal abnormalities.

- **Teratogenic effects in utero,** such as exposure to maternal substance abuse, alcohol consumption, chemicals, radiation exposure, and/or infections, which can lead to congenital anomalies and/or fetal or neonatal death.

- **Smoking,** which can lead to IUGR.

- **Poor nutrition,** which can lead to congenital anomalies such as neural tube defects (folic acid deficiency) and IUGR.

- **Multifetal pregnancy** (twins) result from dizygotic embryos (two ova, fraternal) or a monozygotic embryo (splitting of one zygote, identical). Twin pregnancy can result in abnormal attachment of the placenta to the uterus, an incomplete splitting of the monozygote, tangling of umbilical cords, circulatory problems, and IUGR.

- **Multifetal pregnancies** (three or more fetuses) are on the rise because of the use of fertility medications and in vitro fertilization. Multifetal pregnancy can restrict blood flow available for each fetus and restrict uterine cavity space available for fetal growth resulting in IUGR.

- **Uteroplacental insufficiency** bears a significant threat for **fetal intrauterine growth restriction**, **fetal distress**, various types of **neonatal morbidity**, and intrauterine **fetal death**.

- **Postterm pregnancy** can result in perinatal hypoxia and acidosis from decreased perfusion of the aging placenta or a macrosomic neonate if the placenta continues to provide adequate oxygenation and nutrition.

Therapeutic and Diagnostic Procedures

Δ   **Abdominal and transvaginal ultrasound** can be used to assess fetal growth and development (fetal tissues, organs, fluids, and bones) and fetal maturity.

Δ   **Biophysical profile** is used to assess amniotic fluid volume index, fetal breathing movements, body movements, fetal muscle tone, and fetal heart reactivity.

Δ   **Amniocentesis** can be used to assess for genetic abnormalities or fetal lung maturity.

NANDA Nursing Diagnoses

Δ   Delayed growth and development of the fetus related to substance abuse, infection, maternal age, or maternal malnutrition

Δ   Risk for disproportionate growth related to maternal diabetes or postterm pregnancy

Δ   Risk for sudden infant death syndrome related to intrauterine growth restriction or premature birth

Δ   Ineffective thermoregulation of fetus related to oligohydramnios

Nursing Assessments and Interventions

Δ   **Nursing assessments** of **fetal development** include:

- Monitoring fetal heart rate pattern (normal rate 110 to 160 beats/min).

- Measuring fundal height to assess fetal growth.

- Assessing risk factors (e.g., genetic, nutritional, age, behavioral factors).

Δ   **Nursing interventions** pertaining to **fetal development** include:

- Recording fetal kick counts.

    ◊   Instruct the mother to perform fetal kick counts daily.

        °   She should be given instructions regarding the method of counting fetal movements (e.g., 2 to 3 times a day, noting how many movements in 60 min), the importance of fetal movement, and how to record the count.

- Providing client education regarding fetal development and the importance of abstaining from behaviors harmful to the fetus.

    ◊   Less than 3 movements in 1 hr should be reported to the primary care provider.

(For further discussion pertaining to diagnostic and therapeutic procedures and nursing assessments and interventions for fetal assessment refer to chapter 7, Antepartum: Diagnostic Interventions, and chapter 11, Fetal Assessment During Labor.)

Complications

Δ   Complications of fetal development include:

- **Genetic abnormalities** related to defective genes, transmissible inherited disorders, chromosome anomalies, and ABO incompatibility. Abnormal genetic factors may result in spontaneous abortion.

- **Congenital anomalies** are malformations of the fetus that are present at birth.

- **Intrauterine growth restriction** is the failure of the fetus to grow at the expected rate.

- **Macrosomic (large for gestational age)** refers to a fetus or neonate larger than normal for age.

- **Fetal or neonatal death.**

Δ   Monitoring for abnormal diagnostic fetal assessments (e.g., decreased fetal movements, abnormal fetal heart rate patterns, abnormally excessive or inadequate fetal growth for duration of pregnancy).

Δ   Encouraging early and ongoing assessment of fetal health and adherence to primary care provider's recommendations and prescriptions.

Primary Reference:

Lowdermilk, D. L. & Perry, S. E. (2004). *Maternity & women's health care* (8th ed.). St. Louis, MO: Mosby.

Additional Resources:

Ladewig, P., London, M., & Davidson, M. (2006). *Contemporary maternal-newborn nursing care.* Upper Saddle River, NJ: Pearson Education, Inc.

NANDA International (2004). *NANDA nursing diagnoses: Definitions and classification 2005-2006.* Philadelphia: NANDA.

Chapter 2: Fetal Development

Application Exercises

1. A client who is pregnant for the first time and at 12 weeks gestation is concerned that her fetus is not growing normally. She states, "I have not felt the baby move yet." Which of the following responses by the nurse is most appropriate?

    A. "I will need to report this to your primary care provider immediately."

    B. "Fetal movement is usually felt for the first time around the 20th week."

    C. "It is not unusual to have no fetal movement until labor begins."

    D. "If you have not felt the fetus move by the 22nd week, we will need to perform an amniocentesis."

2. A woman in her 8th week of pregnancy comes to the clinic for her first prenatal visit. She states that she has experienced no problems and has decided not to come for care unless she needs it. Which of the following responses by the nurse best emphasizes the importance of first trimester prenatal care?

    A. "The first 3 months of pregnancy is the most critical time in fetal development."

    B. "We recommend that all clients come in for prenatal visits as often as medical insurance will cover it."

    C. "Your primary care provider needs to meet with you at least twice prior to admitting you for labor and delivery."

    D. "Most clients do not realize they are pregnant until about the 28th week."

3. Teratogens pose the greatest nongenetic risk to the fetus during the first trimester. List examples of teratogenic factors. What advice should a nurse give a pregnant client on avoiding these factors?

4. Identical twins or a monozygotic pregnancy

    A. are contained in a single amniotic sac.

    B. may be of the same or different genders.

    C. result from fertilization of one ovum.

    D. are commonly due to the use of fertility medications.

5. The amniotic fluid surrounding the fetus in utero functions to

    A. maintain a constant body temperature of the fetus.

    B. promote adherence of the placenta to the uterus.

    C. reduce excessive fetal movement in the uterus.

    D. allow exchange of oxygen, nutrients, and waste.

6. The umbilical cord contains which of the following blood vessels?

    A. One artery and one vein

    B. Two arteries and two veins

    C. One vein and two arteries

    D. Two veins and one artery

7. The shunt that allows most of the blood that enters the right atrium to flow directly into the left atrium is referred to as the

    A. ductus arteriosus.

    B. foramen ovale.

    C. pulmonary artery.

    D. ductus venosus.

8. All major organ systems are present by the end of gestational week

    A. 4.

    B. 8.

    C. 12.

    D. 16.

Chapter 2: Fetal Development

Application Exercises Answer Key

1. A client who is pregnant for the first time and 12 weeks gestation is concerned that her fetus is not growing normally. She states, "I have not felt the baby move yet." Which of the following responses by the nurse is most appropriate?

   A. "I will need to report this to your primary care provider immediately."

   B. "Fetal movement is usually felt for the first time around the 20th week."

   C. "It is not unusual to have no fetal movement until labor begins."

   D. "If you have not felt the fetus move by the 22nd week, we will need to perform an amniocentesis."

   Quickening is the first maternal perception of fetal movement commonly felt as a fluttering feeling. It occurs approximately between the 16th and 20th weeks of gestation. Usually closer to the 20th week.

2. A woman in her 8th week of pregnancy comes to the clinic for her first prenatal visit. She states that she has experienced no problems and has decided not to come for care unless she needs it. Which of the following responses by the nurse best emphasizes the importance of first trimester prenatal care?

   A. "The first 3 months of pregnancy is the most critical time in fetal development."

   B. "We recommend that all clients come in for prenatal visits as often as medical insurance will cover it."

   C. "Your primary care provider needs to meet with you at least twice prior to admitting you for labor and delivery."

   D. "Most clients do not realize they are pregnant until about the 28th week."

   The first 3 months (first trimester) of pregnancy is a critical period in fetal development. During this time, internal organs are developing and the fetus is at an increased risk from teratogens that can cause fetal anomalies.

3. Teratogens pose the greatest nongenetic risk to the fetus during the first trimester. List examples of teratogenic factors? What advice should a nurse give a pregnant client on avoiding these factors?

    Δ   **Radiation**

    Δ   **Alcohol**

    Δ   **Tobacco**

    Δ   **Drugs**

    Δ   **Viruses or bacteria**

The primary way to eliminate the risks mentioned above is to avoid them. Pregnant women should not smoke or drink alcohol. Prescription and over-the-counter medications should not be taken unless they have been approved by the provider. This includes vitamins, herbal, and complementary alternatives. Pregnant women need to avoid exposure to large groups of people during the first trimester. This will decrease their exposure to infections. Handwashing is an important intervention a pregnant woman can take to decrease the risk of coming in contact with infectious organisms.

4. Identical twins or a monozygotic pregnancy

    A. are contained in a single amniotic sac.

    B. may be of the same or different genders.

    C. result from fertilization of one ovum.

    D. are commonly due to the use of fertility medications.

Multifetal pregnancy of identical twins results from the splitting of one zygote (monozygotic) with the zygote being formed from the fertilization of one ovum. Monozygotic twins are the same gender. There can be one or two amniotic sacs. Multifetal pregnancies (three or more fetuses) are on the rise because of the use of fertility medications and in vitro fertilization.

5. The amniotic fluid surrounding the fetus in utero functions to

   A. maintain a constant body temperature of the fetus.
   B. promote adherence of the placenta to the uterus.
   C. reduce excessive fetal movement in the uterus.
   D. allow exchange of oxygen, nutrients, and waste.

   Amniotic fluid serves to maintain a constant temperature surrounding the fetus, is a source of oral fluid and a repository for waste, is a cushion for the fetus to prevent injury, allows fetal movement for musculoskeletal development, prevents amnion from adhering to the fetus, and prevents umbilical cord compression.

6. The umbilical cord contains which of the following blood vessels?

   A. One artery and one vein
   B. Two arteries and two veins
   C. One vein and two arteries
   D. Two veins and one artery

   The umbilical cord contains two umbilical arteries that carry deoxygenated blood from the fetus to the placenta and one umbilical vein that supplies the embryo with oxygen and nutrients from the placenta (maternal blood supply).

7. The shunt that allows most of the blood that enters the right atrium to flow directly into the left atrium is referred to as the

   A. ductus arteriosus.
   B. foramen ovale.
   C. pulmonary artery.
   D. ductus venosus.

   The ductus arteriosus connects the pulmonary artery with the aorta allowing blood to bypass the lungs. The foramen ovale is an intra-atrial opening that shunts blood from the right to the left atria of the heart. The pulmonary artery is not a shunt. The ductus venosus shunts blood from the umbilical vein to the inferior vena cava allowing most of the blood to bypass the liver.

8. All major organ systems are present by the end of gestational week

    A. 4.

    B. 8.

    C. 12.

    D. 16.

All body organs are formed by 8 weeks gestation.

Unit 1   Antepartum

Chapter 3:   Normal Physiological Changes of Pregnancy
Contributor: Brenda French, MSN, RN

NCLEX-RN® Connections:

Learning Objective: Review and apply knowledge within "**Normal Physiological Changes of Pregnancy**" in readiness for performance of the following nursing activities as outlined by the NCLEX-RN® test plan:

Δ   Calculate expected delivery dates.

Δ   Assess the physiological status of the pregnant client and occurrence of body image changes expected with pregnancy.

Δ   Evaluate the client's acceptance of expected body image changes with pregnancy.

Δ   Assess the client/family/significant others' response (emotional, psychosocial) to the pregnancy.

Key Points

Δ   Signs and symptoms of pregnancy are usually divided into three groups:

- **Presumptive signs** – changes experienced by the woman that make her think that she might be pregnant. These changes may be subjective symptoms or objective signs.

- **Probable signs** – changes observed by an examiner that make the examiner suspect a woman is pregnant. These changes are primarily related to physical changes of the uterus.

- **Positive signs** – signs that can only be explained by pregnancy.

Presumptive and probable signs can be caused by physiological factors other than pregnancy (e.g., peristalsis, pelvic congestion, and tumors).

Presumptive signs	Probable signs	Positive signs
• Amenorrhea • Nausea and vomiting • Fatigue • Urinary frequency • Breast changes • **Quickening** – slight fluttering movements of the fetus felt by a woman, usually between 16 to 20 weeks gestation. • Uterine enlargement • Linea nigra • Chloasma (mask of pregnancy) • Striae gravidarum • Darkened areola	• Abdominal enlargement related to changes in uterine size, shape, and position. • Cervical changes • **Hegar's sign** – softening and compressibility of lower uterus. • **Chadwick's sign** – deepened violet-bluish color of vaginal mucosa secondary to increased vascularity of the area. • **Goodell's sign** – softening of cervical tip. • **Ballottement** – rebound of unengaged fetus • **Braxton Hicks contractions** – false contractions, painless, irregular, and usually relieved by walking. • Positive pregnancy test • Fetal outline felt by examiner	• Fetal heart sounds • Fetal movement palpated by an experienced examiner • Visualization of fetus by ultrasound

Δ **Calculation of Delivery Date**

- **Nägele's rule** – take the first day of the last menstrual cycle, subtract 3 months, and add 7 days and 1 year.

  ◊ Remember to take into account how many days there are in each particular month when adding 7 days.

- **McDonald's method** – measure uterine fundal height in centimeters from the symphysis pubis to the top of the uterine fundus (between 18 to 30 weeks gestation age). The calculations are as follows:

  ◊ The gestational age is estimated to be equal to the fundal height.

- **Gravidity** – number of pregnancies.

  ◊ **Nulligravida** – a woman who has never been pregnant.

  ◊ **Primigravida** – a woman in her first pregnancy.

  ◊ **Multigravida** – a woman who has had two or more pregnancies.

  ◊ **Parity** – number of pregnancies in which the fetus or fetuses reach viability (approximately 20 to 24 weeks or fetal weight of more than 500 g [2 lb]) regardless of whether the fetus is born alive or not.

    ° **Nullipara** – no pregnancy beyond the stage of viability.

    ° **Primipara** – has completed one pregnancy to stage of viability.

    ° **Multipara** – has completed two or more pregnancies to stage of viability.

  ◊ **GTPAL acronym**

    ° **G**ravidity

    ° **T**erm births (38 weeks or more)

    ° **P**reterm births (from viability up to 37 weeks)

    ° **A**bortions/miscarriages (prior to viability)

    ° **L**iving children

Key Factors

Δ **Physiological Status of Pregnant Client**

- **Reproductive** – uterus increases in size and changes shape and position. Ovulation and menses cease during pregnancy.

- **Cardiovascular** – cardiac output and blood volume increase to meet the greater metabolic needs. Heart rate increases during pregnancy.

- **Respiratory** – maternal oxygen needs increase. During the last trimester, the size of the chest may enlarge to allow for lung expansion as the uterus pushes upward.

- **Musculoskeletal** – body alterations and weight increase necessitate an adjustment in posture. Pelvic joints relax.

- **Gastrointestinal** – nausea and vomiting may be due to hormonal changes and/or an increase of pressure within the abdominal cavity as the pregnant client's stomach and intestines are displaced within the abdomen.

- **Renal** – filtration rate increases during pregnancy secondary to the influence of pregnancy hormones and an increase in blood volume and metabolic demands. Urinary frequency is common during pregnancy.

- **Endocrine** – placenta becomes an endocrine organ that produces large amounts of human chorionic gonadotropin, progesterone, estrogen, human placental lactogen, and prostaglandins. Hormones are very active during pregnancy and function to maintain pregnancy and prepare the body for delivery.

Δ **Body Image Changes:**

- Due to the physical changes as well as the psychological changes that occur during pregnancy, the pregnant woman requires support from her primary care provider and her family members.

- In the first trimester of pregnancy, physiological changes are not very obvious. Many women look forward to the changes so that pregnancy will be more noticeable.

- During the second trimester there are rapid physical changes. The most obvious is the enlargement of the abdomen and breasts. There is also an increase in size and skin changes such as stretch marks and hyperpigmentation of the face (chloasma). The physical changes can also affect a woman's mobility. She may find herself losing her balance and feeling back or leg discomfort and fatigue. All of these factors may lead to a negative body image. The client may make statements of resentment toward the pregnancy and express anxiousness for the pregnancy to be over soon.

Therapeutic and Diagnostic Procedures and Nursing Interventions

Δ **Serum and Urine Pregnancy Tests**

- Serum and urine tests assess for the presence of **human chorionic gonadotropin** (hCG), the earliest biochemical marker for pregnancy. Human chorionic gonadotropin can be detected 6 to 11 days in serum and 26 days in urine after conception following implantation.

- Production of hCG begins with implantation, peaks at about 60 to 70 days of gestation, and then declines until around 140 days of pregnancy, when it begins to gradually increase until term.

- Higher levels of hCG can indicate multifetal pregnancy, ectopic pregnancy, hydatidiform mole (gestational trophoblastic disease) or a genetic abnormality such as Down syndrome).

- Some medications (e.g., anticonvulsants, diuretics, tranquilizers) can cause false positive or false negative pregnancy results.

- Urine samples should be first-voided morning specimens.

Assessments, Nursing Diagnoses, and Nursing Interventions

Δ   **Expected Vital Signs**

- Blood pressure remains within the prepregnancy range during the first trimester.

- Blood pressure decreases 5 to 10 mm Hg for both the diastolic and the systolic during the second trimester.

- Blood pressure should return to the prepregnancy baseline range after approximately 20 weeks gestation.

- Position of the pregnant woman may also affect the blood pressure. In the supine position, the blood pressure may appear to be lower due to the weight and pressure of the gravid uterus on the vena cava decreasing venous blood flow to the heart. Maternal hypotension and fetal hypoxia can occur. This is referred to as **supine hypotensive syndrome** or **supine vena cava syndrome**. Signs and symptoms include dizziness, lightheadedness, and pale, clammy skin. Encourage the client to engage in maternal positioning on the left lateral side, semi-Fowler's position, or, if supine, with a wedge placed under one hip to alleviate pressure to the vena cava.

- Pulse increases 10 to 15 beats/min around 20 weeks gestation and remains elevated throughout the remainder of the pregnancy.

- Respirations increase by 1 to 2/min. Respiratory changes in pregnancy are related to the elevation of the diaphragm by as much as 4 cm and changes to the chest wall to facilitate increased maternal oxygen demands. Some shortness of breath may be noted.

Δ   **Expected Physical Assessment Findings**

- Fetal heart tones are heard at a normal baseline rate of 110 to 160 beats/min with reassuring fetal heart rate accelerations noted indicating an intact fetal central nervous system.

- Heart changes in size and shape with resulting cardiac hypertrophy to accommodate increased blood volume and increased cardiac output. Heart sounds during pregnancy also change to reflect the increase in blood volume with a more distinguishable splitting of S_1 and S_2, with S_3 more easily heard after 20 weeks. Murmurs may also be auscultated. Heart size and shape returns to normal shortly after delivery.

- Uterine size changes from a uterine weight of 50 to 1,000 g (0.1 to 3 lb). By 36 weeks gestation, the top of the uterus, the fundus, will reach the xiphoid process. This may cause the pregnant client to experience shortness of breath as the uterus pushes against the diaphragm.

- Cervical changes are obvious because of the color change. The cervix becomes a purplish-blue color that extends into the vagina and labia. This is known as **Chadwick's sign**. The cervix markedly softens in consistency, which is referred to as **Goodell's sign**.

- Breast changes occur due to hormones secreted during pregnancy. The breasts increase in size and the areolas take on a darkened pigmentation.

- Skin changes:

    ◊ **Chloasma** – mask of pregnancy (pigmentation increases on the face).

    ◊ **Linea nigra** – dark line of pigmentation from the umbilicus extending to the pubic area.

    ◊ **Striae gravidarum** – stretch marks most notably found on the abdomen and thighs.

NANDA Nursing Diagnosis

Δ   Disturbed body image disturbance related to negative feelings about body

Interventions That May Assist the Client:

Δ   Offer acknowledgement and encouragement of the client in the sharing of feelings regarding the pregnancy by providing an atmosphere free of judgment.

Δ   Discuss with the client the expected physiological changes and a possible timeline for a return to the prepregnant state.

Δ   Assist the client in setting goals for the postpartum period in regard to self-care and newborn care.

Δ   Refer the client to counseling if the body image concerns begin to have a negative impact on the pregnancy.

Δ   Provide education about the expected physiological and psychosocial changes. Common discomforts of pregnancy and ways to resolve those discomforts can be reviewed during prenatal visits.

Complications and Nursing Implications

Δ   The client should be encouraged to keep all follow-up appointments and to contact the primary care provider immediately if there is any bleeding, leakage of fluid, or contractions at any time during the pregnancy.

Primary Reference:

Lowdermilk, D. L. & Perry, S. E. (2004). *Maternity & women's health care* (8th ed.). St. Louis, MO: Mosby.

Additional Resources:

Ladewig, P., London, M., & Davidson, M. (2006). *Contemporary maternal-newborn nursing care* (6th ed.). Upper Saddle River NJ: Pearson Education, Inc.

McKinney, E., Ashwill, J., Murray, S., James, S., Gorrie, T., & Droske, S. (2000). *Maternal-child nursing*. New York. W.B. Saunders Company.

NANDA International (2004). *NANDA nursing diagnoses: Definitions and classification 2005-2006*. Philadelphia: NANDA.

Chapter 3: Normal Physiological Changes of Pregnancy

Application Exercises

Scenario: A client presents to the clinic for a pregnancy test. She states that her last menstrual period was on 12-01-06. The result of the test is positive. She has been pregnant two other times, delivered twins at term who are now 2 years old, and had one miscarriage at 8 weeks.

    1. When is the client's expected date of delivery or confinement (EDC)?

    2. Identify the client's obstetrical history using the GTPAL method.

Scenario: An 18-year-old G1P0 client is upset about recent body changes that have occurred since she last visited her primary care provider. She has gained a total of 16 kg (35 lb), her face has dark pigmentation, and she has a dark line extending down from her umbilicus. She tells the nurse she is going on a diet because the baby is not due for another month and she does not want to be fat the rest of her life.

    3. What could the nurse say to provide emotional support to this client?

    4. What are some possible causes of the body image changes she is experiencing?

    5. A nurse understands that a client is demonstrating probable signs of pregnancy when which of the following signs are observed by a primary care provider? (Select all that apply.)

       _____   A. Chloasma

       _____   B. Goodell's sign

       _____   C. Ballottement

       _____   D. Chadwick's sign

       _____   E. Quickening

6. During a prenatal visit, the primary care provider notes that the client's cervix has a purplish-blue color. The client questions the nurse as to why this is. Which of the following responses by the nurse is most appropriate?

    A. "Increased vascularity of the area will occur during pregnancy."

    B. "Decreased vascularity of the area will occur during pregnancy."

    C. "This finding is within normal limits whether you are pregnant or not."

    D. "This is an abnormal finding suggestive of pathology."

7. The following are probable and presumptive signs of pregnancy. Match each sign nomenclature with its correct explanation.

Hegar's sign	A. mask of pregnancy (pigmentation increases on the face)
Chadwick's sign	B. slight fluttering movements of fetus felt by woman
Goodell's sign	C. deepened violet-bluish color of vaginal mucosa secondary to increased vascularity of the area
Ballottement	D. dark line of pigmentation from the umbilicus to the pubic area
Braxton Hicks	E. softening and compressibility of the lower uterus
Quickening	F. painless, irregular contractions that are usually relieved with walking
Chloasma	G. softening of cervical tip
Linea nigra	H. stretch marks most often found on the abdomen and thighs
Striae gravidarum	I. rebound of unengaged fetus

Chapter 3: Normal Physiological Changes of Pregnancy

Application Exercises Answer Key

Scenario: A client presents to the clinic for a pregnancy test. She states that her last menstrual period was on 12-01-06. The result of the test is positive. She has been pregnant two other times, delivered twins at term who are now 2 years old, and had one miscarriage at 8 weeks.

1. When is the client's expected date of delivery or confinement (EDC)?

   12-01-06 minus 3 months, plus 7 days and 1 year = EDC is Sept. 8, 2007.

2. Identify the client's obstetrical history using the GTPAL method.

   G 3 T 1 P 0 A 1 L 2

   G 3 – the client has been pregnant twice and is currently pregnant; T 1 – the client delivered twins at term (one term delivery); P 0 – the client has had no preterm deliveries; A 1 – the client has had one miscarriage; L 2 – the client has two living children

Scenario: An 18-year-old G1P0 client is upset about recent body changes that have occurred since she last visited her primary care provider. She has gained a total of 16 kg (35 lb), her face has dark pigmentation, and she has a dark line extending down from her umbilicus. She tells the nurse she is going on a diet because the baby is not due for another month and she does not want to be fat the rest of her life.

3. What could the nurse say to provide emotional support to this client?

   Pregnancy is not a time to diet. Encourage the client to consider her food choices. Suggest a daily exercise regime such as walking. Walking may help to elevate the client's depressed mood. Hyperpigmentation of the face is normal and will fade. The increase in breast size is also normal and will also decrease after the birth of the infant. The client may want to consider purchasing new bras and a nursing bra if she plans to breastfeed.

4. What are some possible causes of the body image changes she is experiencing?

Weight gain could be due to the fetus, placenta, and amniotic fluid, and maybe some overeating.

5. A nurse understands that a client is demonstrating probable signs of pregnancy when which of the following signs are observed by a primary care provider? (Select all that apply.)

_____ A. Chloasma
__X__ **B. Goodell's sign**
__X__ **C. Ballottement**
__X__ **D. Chadwick's sign**
_____ E. Quickening

Chloasma and quickening are presumptive signs of pregnancy.

6. During a prenatal visit, the primary care provider notes that the client's cervix has a purplish-blue color. The client questions the nurse as to why this is. Which of the following responses by the nurse is most appropriate?

A. "Increased vascularity of the area will occur during pregnancy."
B. "Decreased vascularity of the area will occur during pregnancy."
C. "This finding is within normal limits whether you are pregnant or not."
D. "This is an abnormal finding suggestive of pathology."

During pregnancy, venous congestion occurs as a result of increased vascularity of the area. This finding is only normal during pregnancy and is not indicative of pathology.

7. The following are probable and presumptive signs of pregnancy. Match each sign nomenclature with its correct explanation.

Hegar's sign   A. mask of pregnancy (pigmentation increases on the face)

Chadwick's sign   B. slight fluttering movements of fetus felt by woman

Goodell's sign   C. deepened violet-bluish color of vaginal mucosa secondary to increased vascularity of the area

Ballottement   D. dark line of pigmentation from the umbilicus to the pubic area

Braxton Hicks   E. softening and compressibility of the lower uterus

Quickening   F. painless, irregular contractions that are usually relieved with walking

Chloasma   G. softening of cervical tip

Linea nigra   H. stretch marks most often found on the abdomen and thighs

Striae gravidarum   I. rebound of unengaged fetus

Hegar's sign (E)   **Quickening (B)**

Chadwick's sign (C)   **Chloasma (A)**

Goodell's sign (G)   **Linea nigra (D)**

Ballottement (I)   **Striae gravidarum (H)**

Braxton Hicks (F)

Unit 1   Antepartum

Chapter 4:   Nutrition and Pregnancy
Contributor: Brenda French, MSN, RN

⟳ NCLEX-RN® Connections:

Learning Objective: Review and apply knowledge within "**Nutrition and Pregnancy**" in readiness for performance of the following nursing activities as outlined by the NCLEX-RN® test plan:

Δ   Evaluate nutritional status of the client during pregnancy.

Δ   Evaluate the client's weight in accordance with nutritional goals.

Δ   Provide a diet based on nutritional needs during pregnancy, considering a client's preferences.

Δ   Provide client's nutritional supplements as needed during pregnancy.

📖 Key Points

Δ   Recommended weight gain during pregnancy is usually 11 to 14 kg (25 to 35 lb). The general rule is that clients should gain 1 to 2 kg (3 to 4 lb) during the first trimester and after that, a weight gain of approximately 0.5 kg (1 lb) per week for the last two trimesters.

Δ   Excessive weight gain can lead to **macrosomia** and labor complications.

Δ   Poor weight gain may result in low birth weight of the newborn.

Δ   Pregnancy is never a good time to engage in a weight loss program.

Δ   A 300 daily calorie increase is recommended for pregnancy. If breastfeeding during the postpartum period, a 200 to 500 daily caloric increase is sufficient.

Δ   Increasing protein intake is essential to basic growth. Also, increasing the intake of foods high in **folic acid** is crucial for neurological development and prevention of neural tube defects. Foods high in folic acid include leafy vegetables, dried peas and beans, seeds, and orange juice. Breads, cereals, and other grains are fortified with folic acid.

Δ **Iron** supplements are often added to the prenatal plan to facilitate an increase of the maternal red blood cell mass. Iron is best absorbed between meals and when given with a good source of vitamin C. Milk and caffeine interfere with the absorption of iron supplements. Good food sources of iron include beef liver, red meats, fish, poultry, dried peas and beans, and fortified cereals and breads

Δ **Calcium**, which is important to a developing fetus, is involved in bone and teeth formation.

- Good sources of calcium include milk, calcium-fortified soy milk, fortified orange juice, nuts, legumes, and dark green leafy vegetables.

- Daily recommendation is 1,000 mg daily for pregnant and nonpregnant women over the age of 19, and 1,300 mg for those under 19 years of age.

Δ Caffeine intake should be limited to 300 mg daily. The equivalent of 500 to 750 mL of coffee daily may increase the risk of a **spontaneous abortion** or **fetal intrauterine growth restriction**.

Δ A well-balanced diet is important during pregnancy.

Δ Urine output should be no less than 30 mL/hr.

Key Factors

Δ Factors that may influence nutritional choices include:

- Culture.

- Age.

- Education.

Δ **Nutritional Risk Factors**

- Socioeconomic issues such as low income

  ◊ **Women Infants and Children** programs are federally available programs for pregnant women and their children (up to 5 years old).

- Teenagers may have poor nutritional habits (e.g., a diet low in vitamins and protein, not taking prescribed iron supplements).

- Vegetarians may have low protein, calcium, iron, zinc, and vitamin B_{12}.

- Nausea and vomiting during pregnancy

- Anemia

- Eating disorders such as anorexia nervosa or bulimia

- Pregnant clients diagnosed with the appetite disorder **pica** (craving to eat nonfood substances such as dirt or red clay). This disorder may diminish the amount of nutritional foods taken in.

Therapeutic and Diagnostic Procedures and Nursing Interventions

Δ   Nutrition-related laboratory tests to assess for anemia including **hemoglobin** and **hematocrit**.

- Blood volume and composition expand to meet increased metabolic needs.

- Plasma increase exceeds red blood cell increase. Therefore, normal pregnancy hemoglobin and hematocrit lower-end parameters are decreased.

- Nonpregnant parameters

  ◊   Hemoglobin 12 to 16 g/dL

  ◊   Hematocrit 36 to 47%

- Pregnant parameters

  ◊   Hemoglobin 10.5 to 11 to 16 g/dL

  ◊   Hematocrit 32 to 47%

Assessments, Nursing Diagnoses, and Nursing Interventions

Δ   **Diet History**

- Subjective data based on what the client self-reports

  ◊   Journal

  ◊   Daily food sheets

  ◊   Questionnaires

- Objective data based on measurable information

  ◊   Client weight on first prenatal visit and follow-up visits

  ◊   Laboratory reports such as Hgb and iron levels

Δ   **Calorie Count**

- Client will first record everything eaten. Then the nurse, dietician, or client can identify the caloric value of each item. Often, this count gives a better objective finding of the nutritional status of the intake.

Nursing Care Plan for a Pregnant Client			
NANDA	**Expected outcomes:**	**Interventions:**	**Evaluation of the plan:**
• Altered nutrition: Less than body requirements related to the lack of education regarding the importance of nutrition during pregnancy as evidenced by limiting calories so she won't "get fat"	• The client will consume the recommended dietary allowances/ nutrients during her pregnancy.	• The nurse will assess the client's dietary journal on the next prenatal visit. • The nurse will provide educational materials regarding nutritional benefits to the mother and her newborn. • The nurse will provide encouragement and answer questions that the client has regarding her dietary plans. • The nurse will weigh the client and monitor for signs of inadequate weight gain. • The nurse will make a referral if needed.	• Is there adequate weight gain? • Is the client compliant with the nursing plan of care?

Special diet recommendations based on pregnancy complications

Δ **Hyperemesis gravidarum** – persistent nausea and vomiting during early pregnancy resulting in dehydration, weight loss, and possible electrolyte imbalances.

• Treatment for hyperemesis gravidarum includes:

◊ Nothing by mouth.

◊ Intravenous fluids.

◊ Controlling nausea and vomiting.

◊ Slowly progressing to small feedings as tolerated by the client. In severe cases, tube feedings may be needed.

Δ **Pregnancy-induced hypertension (PIH)** – a blood pressure elevation to 140/90 mm Hg, a systolic increase of 30 mm Hg, or a diastolic increase of 15 mm Hg above the client's baseline. Other symptoms include edema and protein in the urine. PIH can range from mild to severe forms leading to seizure and/or coma.

• Treatment for PIH includes:

◊ Monitoring the client's vital signs frequently, especially blood pressure.

◊ Assessing for edema and recording daily weights.

◊ Checking for protein in the client's urine and encouraging the client to adopt a diet high in protein.

◊ Monitoring the client's intake and output using a Foley catheter if necessary.

◊ Assessing the client's neurological functions including deep tendon reflexes, headache, and level of consciousness.

◊ Restricting all the client's activities and adhering to bed rest.

◊ Administering the medication of choice, **magnesium sulfate**, to prevent seizures. This medication is also a central nervous system depressant and should be monitored closely.

◊ **Calcium gluconate** is the antidote in the event of magnesium sulfate toxicity. Signs of magnesium sulfate toxicity are evidenced by respirations less than 12/min, loss of deep tendon reflexes, and a decreased urinary output of less than 30 cc/hr.

◊ If condition worsens, a cesarean birth may be prescribed.

Δ **Gestational diabetes** – diabetes that first occurs during pregnancy.

• Treatment for gestational diabetes includes:

◊ Restricting dietary intake of calories and carbohydrates.

◊ Educating the client on monitoring blood glucose and diet management.

◊ Educating the client on signs and symptoms of hypoglycemia and hyperglycemia with careful monitoring of fetus for macrosomia.

◊ Administering insulin to the client for glucose control if needed. Oral hypoglycemics are contraindicated due to possible teratogenic effects.

Δ **Anemia** – hemoglobin below 10.5 to 11 g/dL, hematocrit below 32% to 33% during pregnancy.

• Treatment for anemia includes:

◊ Educating the client regarding foods that are **rich in iron** such as meat, poultry, and fish. Iron supplements may be prescribed.

◊ Educating the client regarding **vitamin C food sources** such as green vegetables, citrus fruits, and potatoes. Vitamin C will **aid in the absorption of iron.**

◊ Teaching the client about problems with **constipation** and **darkened stools related** to **iron supplementation**.

Postpartum Nutritional Plan

Δ **Lactating women's nutritional plans should include instructions to:**

- Increase caloric intake.

- Increase oral fluids.

- Increase protein intake.

- Avoid alcohol and caffeine.

- Avoid food substances that are not agreeing with the newborn.

Δ **Non-breastfeeding women's nutritional plans should include:**

- Resuming previous diet plan.

- Adhering to a recommended well-balanced diet.

Primary Reference:

Lowdermilk, D. L. & Perry, S. E. (2004). *Maternity & women's health care* (8th ed.). St. Louis, MO: Mosby.

Additional Resources:

McKinney, E., Ashwill, J., Murray, S., James, S., Gorrie, T., & Droske, S. (2000). *Maternal-child nursing*. New York. W.B. Saunders Company.

NANDA International (2004). *NANDA nursing diagnoses: Definitions and classification 2005-2006*. Philadelphia: NANDA.

Chapter 4: Nutrition and Pregnancy

Application Exercises

1. A nurse working in a prenatal clinic is providing education to a client who is pregnant. The client does not like milk. What is a good source of calcium that the nurse can recommend to the client?

    A. Dark green leafy vegetables

    B. Deep red or orange vegetables

    C. Citrus fruits and juices

    D. Meat, poultry, and fish

2. Which of the following clients should the nurse be concerned about regarding weight gain?

    A. A client who has gained 1.8 kg (4 lb) and is in her first trimester.

    B. A client who has gained 11.3 kg (25) lb and is in her third trimester.

    C. A client who has gained 6.8 kg (15 lb) and is in her first trimester.

    D. A client who has gained 9.1 kg (20 lb) and is in her second trimester.

3. A prenatal nurse recommends folic acid supplements to a pregnant client. Which of the following defects can occur in the fetus or neonate as a result of folic acid deficiency?

    A. Iron deficiency anemia

    B. Poor bone formation

    C. Macrosomic fetus

    D. Neural tube defect

4. A breastfeeding mother should increase her calories per day by

    A. 100 to 300.

    B. 300 to 500.

    C. 500 to 700.

    D. 700 to 900.

5. A client who is pregnant is diagnosed with iron deficiency anemia and has been prescribed iron supplements. The nurse should advise the client to take the iron supplements with which of the following?

       A. Ice water

       B. Low-fat or whole milk

       C. Tea or coffee

       D. Orange juice

Chapter 4: Nutrition and Pregnancy

Application Exercises Answer Key

1. A nurse working in a prenatal clinic is providing education to a client who is pregnant. The client does not like milk. What is a good source of calcium that the nurse can recommend to the client?

   A. Dark green leafy vegetables
   B. Deep red or orange vegetables
   C. Citrus fruits and juices
   D. Meat, poultry, and fish

   Pregnant women need calcium, but it does not have to be obtained by consuming milk. Calcium is very important to a developing fetus. It is involved in bone and teeth formation. Good sources of calcium include calcium-fortified orange juice, nuts, legumes, and low oxalate, dark green, leafy vegetables. Clients can also try calcium-fortified soy milk.

2. Which of the following clients should the nurse be concerned about regarding weight gain?

   A. A client who has gained 1.8 kg (4 lb) and is in her first trimester.
   B. A client who has gained 11.3 kg (25 lb) and is in her third trimester.
   C. A client who has gained 6.8 kg (15 lb) and is in her first trimester.
   D. A client who has gained 9.1 kg (20 lb) and is in her second trimester.

   A client who has gained 15 lb in her first trimester has gained too much weight. Recommended weight gain during pregnancy is usually 11 to 14 kg (25 to 35 lb). The general rule is that clients should gain 1 to 2 kg (3 to 4 lb) during the first trimester and after that a weight gain of approximately 0.5 kg (1 lb) per week for the last two trimesters. Excessive weight gain can lead to a difficult labor. The fetus tends to be larger, and this may lead to shoulder dystocia or cephalopelvic disproportion. A cesarean birth may be required. After the birth, a client will usually lose approximately 5 kg (12 lb) immediately.

3. A prenatal nurse recommends folic acid supplements to a pregnant client. Which of the following defects can occur in the fetus or neonate as a result of folic acid deficiency?

        A. Iron deficiency anemia

        B. Poor bone formation

        C. Macrosomic fetus

        D. Neural tube defect

Folic acid supplements are recommended to prevent neural tube defects in the fetus. Evidence-based practice research has proven that an inadequate intake of folic acid has been associated with neural tube defects. It is recommended that all women of childbearing age take this supplement. Excellent food sources of folic acid are fresh green leafy vegetables, liver, peanuts, cereals, and whole-grain breads. Iron deficiency anemia can occur as a result of a lack of iron-rich sources of food such as meat, chicken, and fish. Calcium deficiency can result in poor teeth and bone formation. Maternal obesity can lead to a macrosomic fetus.

4. A breastfeeding mother should increase her calories per day by

        A. 100 to 300.

        B. 300 to 500.

        C. 500 to 700.

        D. 700 to 900.

If a client is breastfeeding, a 300 to 500 daily caloric increase is sufficient.

5. A client who is pregnant is diagnosed with iron deficiency anemia and has been prescribed iron supplements. The nurse should advise the client to take the iron supplements with which of the following?

        A. Ice water

        B. Low-fat or whole milk

        C. Tea or coffee

        D. Orange juice

Orange juice contains vitamin C, which aids in the absorption of iron. Milk and caffeine interfere with iron absorption. Also, caffeine intake from tea and coffee should be limited to 300 mg daily because caffeine increases the risk of a spontaneous abortion or fetal intrauterine growth restriction. Water will not help the absorption of iron, but drinking plenty of water should be encouraged to prevent constipation, which is a side effect of iron supplements.

Unit 1   Antepartum

Chapter 5:   Perinatal Cultural Awareness

Contributors: Janine Stomboly, BSN, RN
Brenda French, MSN, RN

↻ NCLEX-RN® Connections:

Learning Objective: Review and apply knowledge within "**Perinatal Cultural Awareness**" in readiness for performance of the following nursing activities as outlined by the NCLEX-RN® test plan:

Δ   Assess the importance of the client's culture/ethnicity when planning/providing/evaluating perinatal care.

Δ   Recognize the client's cultural background/practices.

Δ   Provide written teaching materials in client's language.

Δ   Assign appropriate interpreters to assist in helping the client/family/significant others' understand perinatal care.

Δ   Provide culturally-competent care.

Δ   Recognize cultural differences in the client's perception of and response to labor pain.

📖 Key Points

Δ   **Culture** is defined as the values, beliefs, and practices of a particular group that incorporates attitudes and customs learned through socialization with others. Culture includes language, communication style, traditions, religions, art, music, dress, health beliefs, and health practices.

  •   **Ethnicity** has an influence on culture and is the bond or kinship a person feels with his or her country of birth or place of ancestral origin. Ethnicity exists regardless of whether or not a person has ever lived outside the United States.

Δ   The movement is toward **eliminating acultural nursing care** (care that avoids concern for cultural differences), which is the traditional tendency to treat all clients as though no cultural differences exist.

Δ **Culturally-competent nursing** is care that respects and is compatible with each client's culture and shows respect for the values and beliefs of others. A nurse who is culturally sensitive incorporates a client's cultural preferences into the prenatal care situation as much as possible.

Δ The United States' **predominant culture is Anglicized or English-based**, with a general cultural tendency to:

- **Freely express** positive and negative feelings.

- Prefer **direct eye contact** when communicating.

- **Address** people in a **casual manner**.

- Prefer a **strong handshake** as a way of greeting.

- **Include fathers** in **childbirth classes**, **labor**, and **birth**.

Δ There are **four major subcultures** in the United States. An awareness of **general communication patterns** among these **subcultures** can assist a nurse in providing quality nursing care. A nurse should keep in mind that there are variations among individuals and not to stereotype.

- **Native Americans** are those who are of Indian nations found in North America including Eskimos and Aleuts.

  ◊ Native Americans are **generally private, hesitate in sharing personal information**, and consider impatience disrespectful. Therefore, a nurse should be patient in awaiting responses to questions.

  ◊ Native Americans believe **no person has the right to speak for another** and may refuse to comment on a family member's behalf.

  ◊ Native Americans generally believe **lingering eye contact is an invasion of privacy and disrespectful.**

  ◊ When making introductions, Native Americans may interpret the custom of a strong handshake as offensive and prefer a light passing of the hands.

  ◊ **Stoicism** of the woman is **encouraged** during labor and birth.

  ◊ **Fathers may be absent during the delivery but present at other times**, such as naming the infant. The nurse should not assume there is no father figure if the father is not present during labor and delivery.

  ◊ **Female family and friends attend to the client during labor and delivery**.

  ◊ Some families **may want the placenta returned**. Ask if they do and who should receive it.

- **African Americans** are those whose ancestral origin resides in Africa.

  ◊ African Americans generally **hesitate to give more information than what is asked for** when in a health care environment. Therefore, a nurse should follow up thoroughly with open-ended questions.

  ◊ **Communication style** is **frequently loud** and **animated** with **lots of body movement**.

  ◊ African Americans are **comfortable** with **close personal space** with friends and family.

  ◊ Sustained **eye contact varies dependent upon generation**. Older adults should not be looked directly in the eyes. Older adults make fleeting direct eye contact.

  ◊ Expressions of pain are usually open and public.

  ◊ **Fathers are frequently active participants in labor and delivery.**

  ◊ Traditionally, female attendants frequently accompany the laboring client.

- **Latinos** are those who can trace their ethnic origin to Latin or South America.

  ◊ Latinos are generally **comfortable sitting close** to interviewers.

  ◊ "Evil eye" (placing a bad omen or curse) can be given to a child if the child is admired and the admirer does not touch the child.

  ◊ **Latinos consider direct eye contact** as **attentive** and **respectful.** Looking away may be a sign of dishonesty. Mexican Americans, though, may interpret prolonged **staring** as **confrontational** and intimidating.

  ◊ Latino men are generally protective and authoritarian regarding women and children, and expect to be consulted in decision making.

  ◊ **Latino fathers**, especially the older generation, **may prefer to not play an active role in the labor and birthing process.** They prefer to observe or wait outside. Women participate in coaching, but the husband expects to be informed.

  ◊ Latino women are generally vocal and active during labor and birth and **prefer** to **keep** their **body covered**.

- **Asian Americans** are those who descend from China, Japan, Korea, the Philippines, Thailand, Cambodia, Laos, and Vietnam.

  ◊ Asian Americans generally respond with **brief factual answers**. They **do not openly disagree** with authority figures (for example, primary care providers and nurses) so they may conceal their noncompliance.

  ◊ Asian Americans believe **prolonged lingering eye contact** is an **invasion** of **privacy** and **disrespectful**.

◊ Asian Americans feel **more comfortable** with the nurse **at more than an arm's length away** in distance.

◊ Many Asians consider the **head** to be **sacred** and it **can only be touched by close relatives**.

◊ Many believe that the **area between a woman's waist and knees** is **especially private** and should not be touched by any male other than the woman's husband.

◊ Asians **tend to control their emotions and expressions of physical discomfort**.

◊ Do not address Asian Americans by the first name initially unless told to do so.

◊ **Modesty is important**.

◊ Female family members are usually present at the birth. **The father and other male family members usually do not participate in birthing classes or the labor and delivery**. However, the younger generation who have been acculturated by American culture might.

Δ It is imperative for a nurse to remember that **diversity exists within cultural groups** and take care **not to stereotype** (fixed attitudes about all people who share a common characteristic).

Δ It is essential for a nurse to examine his or her own cultural beliefs and **take care not to exhibit behaviors of ethnocentrism** (belief that one's own ethnicity and culture are superior to all others).

 Nursing Assessments

Δ To provide **culturally-competent care**, a perinatal nurse should attempt to **collect data** about the **unique characteristics of a client's culture**. Data includes:

• **Language** (as well as English proficiency) **and communication style**.

◊ Eye contact

◊ Body space and distance

◊ Touch

◊ Emotional expression

• **Hygiene practices.**

• **Feelings about modesty.**

◊ Ask the client whether the gender of her caregiver is of concern.

- **Special clothing or ornamentation.**

  ◊ For example, certain Mexican women wear a cord beneath their breasts and knotted over the umbilicus because they believe it prevents morning sickness and ensures a safe birth.

- **Religion and religious practices.**

  ◊ For example, Muslim fathers whisper a prayer in the neonate's ear immediately after birth and shave the infant's head.

- **Rituals surrounding birth**.

  ◊ Ask the client if there are certain practices she expects to follow while she is pregnant.

  ◊ Ask the client if there are any activities she cannot do while pregnant.

- **Family and gender roles**

  ◊ Ask the client about who she expects/wants to provide labor support during the birthing process. Inquire about the degree of involvement to be expected from her partner, mother, or other female support persons.

- **Proper forms of greeting and showing respect.**

- **Food habits and dietary restrictions.**

  ◊ Ask the client whether there are certain foods she is expected to eat or avoid while she is pregnant. Determine whether she is lactose intolerant. Examples include:

    ° Some Asian cultures permit their pregnant women to eat only warm foods.

    ° Some Muslims may eat only halal meats and those of Jewish heritage may eat only kosher foods. Many Muslim and Jewish people do not eat pork.

- **Methods for making decisions.**

- **Health beliefs and illness practices.**

  ◊ Ask the client about expectations regarding newborn care (for example, breastfeeding preferences, circumcision, use of belly bands on umbilicus, use of herbs to increase milk flow, and the use of olive or castor oil to stimulate passage of meconium). Examples include:

    ° In some cultures, a primary care provider is not needed during pregnancy because it is considered a healthy state.

    ° Some Mexicans may believe that a pregnant woman should not witness an eclipse because it may cause a cleft palate in the newborn.

    ° Many Native Americans and Asians encourage pregnant women to be active and walk.

      °   Filipinos may commonly believe that any activity is dangerous and others take over the work for the pregnant and postpartum woman.

      °   Some Latinos believe that sexual activity during pregnancy helps keep the birth canal lubricated.

      °   Some Vietnamese prohibit sexual intercourse during pregnancy because of a belief that it can harm the mother and fetus.

NANDA Nursing Diagnoses

Δ   Acute discomfort related to cultural differences in the communication of pain

Δ   Coping: readiness for enhanced family related to anticipation of newborn

Δ   Anxiety/fear related to cultural differences of caregivers and clients

Δ   Communication: impaired related to cultural differences

Nursing Interventions

Δ   **Culturally-sensitive nursing interventions** of the **perinatal client and family** include:

- Working with a **knowledgeable interpreter** to provide information and answer questions as needed. Explain all procedures carefully to the client and ensure understanding.

- **Addressing** the **client as she prefers**. This may be formal or informal.

- Use of **culturally sensitive communication techniques** such as sitting or standing in the client's **cultural comfort zone** and making **appropriate eye contact.**

- **Respecting** the **client's food preferences** and helping her plan an adequate prenatal diet. Refer the client to a dietitian if needed.

- Providing a **female caregiver if** that is **desired**.

- **Respecting** the **client's decision regarding support person** involvement and avoid imposing personal values or expectations.

- **Honoring** the **client's health beliefs and practices** and providing for requested preferences unless practices are contraindicated because of safety. For example, avoid removing medals or clothing that hold **religious or symbolic meaning**. If they must be removed, keep them safe and return them as soon as possible.

- Apologize if cultural traditions or beliefs are violated.

Primary Reference:

Lowdermilk, D. L. & Perry, S. E. (2004). *Maternity & women's health care* (8th ed.). St. Louis, MO: Mosby.

Additional Resources:

Hogan, M., & Glazebrook, R. (2003). *Maternal-newborn nursing.* Upper Saddle River, NJ: Pearson Education, Inc.

Ladewig, P., London, M., & Davidson, M. (2006). *Contemporary maternal-newborn nursing care.* (6th ed.). Upper Saddle River, NJ: Pearson Education, Inc.

Lipson, J. G., & Dibble, S. L. (2005). *Culture and clinical care* (2nd ed.). San Francisco, CA: The Regents, University of California.

NANDA International (2004). *NANDA nursing diagnoses: Definitions and classification 2005-2006.* Philadelphia: NANDA.

Timby, B. K. (2004). *Fundamental skills and concepts in patient care* (8th ed.). Philadelphia: Lippincott Williams and Wilkins.

Chapter 5: Perinatal Cultural Awareness

Application Exercises

1. Which of the following food preferences would most likely be selected from the menu by an Asian client who is postpartum?

   A. Gelatin

   B. Ice cream

   C. Broth

   D. Fruit

2. When making staffing assignments on a labor and delivery unit, the charge nurse would consider that which of the following laboring clients would most likely object to a male nurse?

   A. African American

   B. Native American

   C. Asian American

   D. Anglo American

3. A client who is Latino is in labor and the father to be is refusing to come into the labor and delivery room. The nursing student assisting in the care believes he should participate in the birth and repeatedly urges the father to come into the labor and delivery room even though he keeps refusing. This nursing student is exhibiting

   A. cultural sensitivity.

   B. ethnocentrism.

   C. encouragement.

   D. discouragement.

4. A postpartum client who is Filipino is bottle feeding and does not want to feed her infant. She also prefers to let her mother or sisters, who are always present, or the nurse, provide all of the care for the infant. She does hold the infant occasionally, but mostly prefers to sleep. The nurse should

   A. notify social services of the risk for neglect.

   B. be concerned about parent-infant bonding.

   C. insist that the client provide infant care.

   D. know that this is the cultural norm.

5. True or False: A client who is Native American and in active labor states that she wants to keep the placenta. Every effort should be made by the nurse to accommodate this request.

Chapter 5: Perinatal Cultural Awareness

Application Exercises Answer Key

1. Which of the following food preferences would most likely be selected from the menu by an Asian client who is postpartum?

   A. Gelatin

   B. Ice cream

   C. Broth

   D. Fruit

   Broth would be the food item of choice because many Asians believe that pregnant and postpartum women should only have warm food.

2. When making staffing assignments on a labor and delivery unit, the charge nurse would consider that which of the following laboring clients would most likely object to a male nurse?

   A. African American

   B. Native American

   C. Asian American

   D. Anglo American

   Culturally, an Asian American woman would most likely object to a male nurse. Many Asians believe that the area between a woman's waist and knees is especially private and should not be touched by any other man than the woman's husband. Modesty is very important in Asian cultures.

3. A client who is Latino is in labor and the father to be is refusing to come into the labor and delivery room. The nursing student assisting in the care believes he should participate in the birth and repeatedly urges the father to come into the labor and delivery room even though he keeps refusing. This nursing student is exhibiting

    A. cultural sensitivity.

    B. ethnocentrism.

    C. encouragement.

    D. discouragement.

Ethnocentrism is the belief that one's own ethnicity or cultural values are superior to all others. For this nursing student to impose her own cultural values upon the family and insist that the father participate would exhibit ethnocentrism not encouragement. The culturally sensitive nurse should respect the client and her family's cultural preference.

4. A postpartum client who is Filipino is bottle feeding and does not want to feed her infant. She also prefers to let her mother or sisters, who are always present, or the nurse, provide all of the care for the infant. She does hold the infant occasionally, but mostly prefers to sleep. The nurse should

    A. notify social services of the risk for neglect.

    B. be concerned about parent-infant bonding.

    C. insist that the client provide infant care.

    D. know that this is the cultural norm.

Generally, this is the cultural norm for Filipinos. Filipinos believe that any activity is dangerous for the pregnant or postpartum woman, and others take over the work for her. Therefore, social services does not need to be notified. To insist that the client provide infant care would be culturally insensitive and ethnocentric. The client is holding the infant occasionally when not sleeping, so there does appear to be some parent-infant bonding occurring. The client's family is also bonding with the infant.

5. True or False: A client who is Native American and in active labor states that she wants to keep the placenta. Every effort should be made by the nurse to accommodate this request.

True: This is culturally appropriate for Native Americans. Native Americans may want to take the placenta with them after the birth. The nurse should ask if they want the placenta and who should receive it and make arrangements.

Unit 1　　　Antepartum

Chapter 6:　　Prenatal and Childbirth Education
Contributors: Brenda French, MSN, RN
　　　　　　 Lisa M. Easterby, RN, MSN

↻ **NCLEX-RN® Connections:**

> **Learning Objective:** Review and apply knowledge within **"Prenatal and Childbirth Education"** in readiness for performance of the following nursing activities as outlined by the NCLEX-RN® test plan:
>
> Δ　Select the appropriate teaching approach and utilize teaching principles when providing prenatal and childbirth instruction.
>
> Δ　Instruct clients on ways to promote prenatal health and evaluate the client's understanding of the information provided.

📖 Key Points

Δ　**Prenatal** education encompasses a great deal of information provided to a client who is pregnant. Major areas of focus include assisting the client in **self-care** of the **discomforts of pregnancy**, promoting a **safe outcome** to **pregnancy,** and fostering **positive feelings** by the pregnant woman and her family **regarding** the **childbearing** experience.

Δ　**Nurses** play an **integral role** in **assessing** the client's **current knowledge**, **previous pregnancies,** and **birthing experiences.** Nurses provide anticipatory **teaching** to the pregnant woman and her family about:

- **Physical** and **emotional changes during pregnancy** and **interventions** that can be implemented to provide relief.

- **Danger signs** and **symptoms** to report to the primary care provider.

- Various **birthing options** available to enhance the birthing process.

Δ　The **greatest period** of **danger** to the **developing fetus** for incurring structural anomalies from intrauterine environmental hazards occurs between day 15 to 18 weeks from conception.

Δ Preconception and prenatal education should **stress healthy behaviors** that promote the health of the pregnant woman and her fetus.

- Clients should be instructed to **avoid** all **over-the-counter medications**, supplements, and prescriptive medications unless the obstetrician who is supervising their care has knowledge of this practice.

- **Alcohol** (birth defects) and **tobacco** (low birth weight) are **contraindicated** in pregnancy.

- **Substance abuse** of any kind is to be **avoided during pregnancy** and during **lactation**.

Δ **Components** of **childbirth education** may include early prenatal care, preparation for birth, pain management, complications of pregnancy and delivery, sibling and grandparent classes, breastfeeding, and newborn care.

Δ **Birth plans** can be verbal or written agreements that describe what the pregnant woman wishes to occur during labor and delivery.

Nursing Assessments

Δ **Nursing assessment** in **prenatal care** includes obtaining information regarding:

- **Reproductive** and **obstetrical history** (e.g., contraception use, gynecological diagnoses, and obstetrical difficulties).

- **Medical history**, including the woman's immune status (e.g., rubella and hepatitis B).

- **Family history**, such as genetic disorders.

- Any recent or current illnesses or **infections.**

- **Current medications**, including substance abuse and alcohol consumption. The nurse should display a **nonjudgmental**, **matter-of-fact demeanor** when interviewing the client **regarding substance abuse** and observe for signs and symptoms such as lack of grooming.

- **Psychosocial history** (e.g., client's emotional response to pregnancy, teenage pregnancy, spouse, support system, history of depression, domestic violence issues).

- Any **hazardous environmental exposures.**

- Current **exercise** and **diet** habits.

Δ The **nurse** should **ascertain** what the **client's goals** are for the **birthing process**. The nurse should discuss various birthing methods, such as Lamaze, and pain control options (e.g., epidural, natural childbirth).

NANDA Nursing Diagnoses

Δ   Deficient knowledge related to common discomforts of pregnancy and relief measures as well as signs of pregnancy complications

Δ   Anxiety related to deficient knowledge regarding psychological and physical changes of pregnancy

Nursing Interventions

Δ   Anticipatory **prenatal education topics** should be reviewed with the client by the nurse **based** on the **client's current knowledge** and **previous pregnancy** and **birth experiences**. The adult learner's readiness to learn is enhanced when the nurse provides teaching during the appropriate trimester based on learning needs. Utilizing a variety of educational methods, such as pamphlets and videos, and then having the client reverbalize and demonstrate learned topics will ensure that learning has taken place. Topics by trimester include:

- **First Trimester**
  - ◊   **Physical** and **psychosocial changes**
  - ◊   Common **discomforts of pregnancy** and **measures to provide relief**
  - ◊   **Lifestyle**: exercise/stress/nutrition, sex, dental care, over-the-counter and prescription medications, tobacco, alcohol, substance abuse (discuss strategies to decrease or discontinue use), and sexually transmitted infections (encourage safe sexual practices)
  - ◊   Possible **complications** and **signs to report**
  - ◊   Choosing an obstetrician
  - ◊   Fetal growth and development
  - ◊   Prenatal exercise
  - ◊   Expected laboratory testing

- **Second Trimester**
  - ◊   Planning to breast or bottle feed
  - ◊   **Common discomforts** and **relief measures**
  - ◊   Lifestyle: sex and pregnancy, rest and relaxation, posture, body mechanics, clothing, seat belt safety, and travel
  - ◊   Fetal movement
  - ◊   **Complications** (e.g., preterm labor, gestational hypertension, gestational diabetes mellitus, premature rupture of membranes)
  - ◊   **Childbirth preparation**

- **Third Trimester**
  - ◊ Childbirth preparations include:
    - ° **Birth plan.**
    - ° **Breathing** and **relaxation** techniques (e.g., **deep cleansing breaths** at one-half the usual respiratory rate during contractions can **promote relaxation** of the **abdominal muscles,** which **lessens** the **discomfort** of **uterine contractions**).
    - ° **Decisions about pain management** during labor and birth (e.g., natural childbirth, epidural).
    - ° Signs and symptoms of labor.
    - ° Labor process.
    - ° Infant care.
    - ° Postpartum care.
  - ◊ **Fetal movement/kick counts** to ascertain fetal well-being. The client should be instructed to count and record fetal movements or kicks daily.
    - ° It is recommended that mothers count fetal activity 2 or 3 times a day for 60 min each time. **Fetal movements of less than 3 in/hr** or **movements that cease entirely for 12 hr indicate a need for further evaluation**.
  - ◊ **Diagnostic testing** for fetal well-being (e.g., nonstress test, biophysical profile, ultrasound, and contraction stress test. *(For information, refer to chapter 7, Antepartum: Diagnostic Interventions)*

Δ **Maternal adaptation** to **pregnancy** and the attainment of the maternal role – whereby the idea of pregnancy is accepted and assimilated into the client's way of life – includes hormonal and psychological aspects.

- **Emotional lability** is experienced by many women with unpredictable mood changes and increased irritability, tearfulness, and anger alternating with feelings of joy and cheerfulness with little or no provocation. This all may result from profound hormonal changes.

- A feeling of **ambivalence** about the pregnancy, which is a normal response, may occur early in the pregnancy resolving before the third trimester. It consists of conflicting feelings (e.g., joy, pleasure, sorrow, hostility) about the pregnancy. These feelings can occur simultaneously whether the pregnancy was planned or not.

Δ **Common Discomforts of Pregnancy**

- **Nausea and vomiting** may occur during the first trimester. The client should eat crackers or dry toast one half to 1 hr before rising in the morning to relieve discomfort. Instruct the client to avoid an empty stomach, spicy, greasy, or gas-forming foods. Encourage the client to drink fluids between meals.

- **Breast tenderness** may occur during the first trimester. The client should wear a bra that provides adequate support.

- **Urinary frequency** may occur during the first and third trimesters. The client should empty her bladder frequently, limit fluid intake before bedtime, wear perineal pads, and perform Kegel exercises (alternate tightening and relaxation of pubococcygeal muscles) to reduce stress incontinence (leakage of urine with coughing and sneezing).

- **Urinary tract infections (UTI)** are **common during pregnancy** because of renal changes and the vaginal flora becoming more alkaline.

  ◊ UTI risks can be decreased by encouraging the client to **wipe** the perineal area from **front to back** after voiding; using soft, absorbent, white, **unscented toilet** tissue; avoiding bubble baths; wearing **cotton underpants**; avoiding tight-fitting pants; and consuming **plenty of water** (eight glasses per day).

  ◊ **Yogurt** and **acidophilus milk** help to prevent urinary tract and vaginal infections by acidifying the pH of urine and the vaginal flora. Cranberry juice lowers the pH of urine and aids in UTI prevention or treatment.

  ◊ The client should **urinate before** and **after intercourse** to flush bacteria from the urethra that can be introduced during intercourse.

  ◊ Advise the client to urinate as soon as the urge occurs because retaining urine provides an environment for bacterial multiplication.

  ◊ Advise the client to **notify her primary care provider** if her **urine** is **malodorous** or contains **blood** or **pus**.

- **Fatigue** may occur during the first and third trimesters. The client should learn to engage in frequent rest periods.

- **Heartburn** is possible during the second and third trimesters due to the stomach displacement by the enlarging uterus and a slowing of the gastrointestinal tract motility and digestion brought about by increased progesterone levels. The client should eat small frequent meals, not allow the stomach to get too empty or too full, sit up for 30 min after meals, and check with her primary care provider prior to using any over-the-counter antacids.

- **Constipation** is possible during the second and third trimesters. The client should be encouraged to drink plenty of fluids, eat a diet high in fiber, and exercise regularly.

- **Hemorrhoids** may occur during the second and third trimesters. A warm sitz bath or witch hazel pads applied to the area will help relieve discomfort.

- **Backaches** are possible during the second and third trimesters. The client should exercise regularly, perform pelvic tilt exercises (alternately arching and straightening the back), utilize proper body mechanics using the legs to lift rather than the back, maintain good posture, and lie with legs slightly elevated.

- **Shortness of breath** and **dyspnea** occur in 60% of pregnant women related to the diaphragm being elevated about 4 cm by the enlarging of the uterus. This limits diaphragm expansion on inspiration. The client should maintain good posture, sleep with extra pillows, avoid overloading the stomach, and contact her primary care provider if symptoms worsen.

- **Leg cramps** are a possible symptom in the third trimester due to the compression of lower extremity nerves and blood vessels by the enlarging uterus. This can result in poor peripheral circulation as well as an imbalance in the calcium/phosphorus ratio. Homans' sign should be checked and if it is negative, the client should extend the affected leg keeping the knee straight and dorsiflexing the foot (toes toward head). Massaging and applying heat over the affected muscle or a foot massage while the leg is extended can help relieve cramping. The client can hold onto the back of a chair and lean forward with one leg in front and one leg behind. The client's diet and calcium intake should also be evaluated. The client should notify her primary care provider if frequent cramping occurs.

- **Varicose veins** and **lower extremity edema** can occur during the second and third trimesters. The client should rest with her legs elevated, avoid constricting clothing, wear support hose, avoid sitting or standing in one position for extended periods of time, and not sit with her legs crossed at the knees. The client should drink adequate fluids for the natural diuretic effect and exercise moderately with frequent walking to stimulate venous return.

- **Gingivitis**, **nasal stuffiness**, and **epistaxis** (nosebleed) can occur as a result of elevated estrogen levels causing an increased vascularity and proliferation of connective tissue. The client should gently brush her teeth, observe good dental hygiene, use a humidifier, and use normal saline nose drops or spray.

- **Braxton-Hicks contractions** (intensification of contractions in preparation for the work of labor) may occur during the third trimester. Inform the client that a change of position and walking should cause contractions to subside. If contractions increase in intensity and frequency (true contractions) with regularity producing cervical changes, the client should notify her primary care provider.

- **Supine hypotension** occurs when a woman lies on her back and the weight of the gravid uterus compresses her ascending vena cava. This reduces blood supply to the fetus. The client may experience feelings of lightheadedness and faintness. Teach the client to lie in a side-lying or semi-sitting position with her knees slightly flexed.

Δ **Exercise during pregnancy** yields positive benefits and should consist of 30 min of **moderate exercise daily** if not medically or obstetrically contraindicated.

- Consider decreasing weight-bearing exercises (e.g., jogging, running).

- Avoid high-risk activities (e.g., mountain climbing, sky diving).

- Engage in exercise such as walking and/or swimming.

- Maintain ability to converse easily during exercise to keep exercise level within safe limits.

- Avoid becoming overheated and exercising for an extended period of time.

- Avoid the use of hot tubs or saunas.

- Drink plenty of water.

Δ **Danger signs during pregnancy** that indicate potentially dangerous situations should be reported to the primary care provider immediately if experienced by the client. Danger signs include:

- Gush of fluid from the vagina (rupture of amniotic fluid) prior to 37 weeks gestation.

- Vaginal bleeding (placental problems such as abruption or previa).

- Abdominal pain (premature labor, abruptio placenta, or ectopic pregnancy).

- Persistent vomiting (hyperemesis gravidarum).

- Severe headaches (pregnancy-induced hypertension).

- Elevated temperature (infection, urinary tract infection).

- Dysuria (urinary tract infection).

- Blurred vision (pregnancy-induced hypertension).

- Edema of face and hands (pregnancy-induced hypertension).

- Epigastric pain (pregnancy-induced hypertension).

- Concurrent occurrence of flushed dry skin, fruity breath, rapid breathing, increased thirst and urination, and headache (hyperglycemia).

- Concurrent occurrence of clammy pale skin, weakness, tremors, irritability, and lightheadedness (hypoglycemia).

Δ During the client's second trimester, the nurse should begin to present and review various options of birthing methods, assist the client in making an informed decision regarding her birth plan, and encouraging her to schedule childbirth preparation classes.

Δ Common birthing methods prepare a pregnant woman, decrease her anxiety during labor and birth, and provide education about maternal relaxation techniques and partner support during the birthing process.

- **Dick-Read method** – refers to "**childbirth without fear**." Uses controlled breathing and conscious and progressive relaxation of different muscle groups throughout the entire body. This method instructs a woman to relax completely between contractions and keep all muscles except the uterus relaxed during contractions.

- **Lamaze** – focuses on **partner-coached breathing** techniques and **relaxation** with the woman panting and using **outside focal points** during labor.

- **Leboyer** – not a method of childbirth preparation. It is an approach to birth that **centers** on the **responses** and **needs of** the **infant** and is referred to as "birth without violence." **Environmental variables** are stressed to ease the transition of the infant from the uterus to the external environment (e.g., dim lights, soft voices, warm birthing room). Water births are based on this method.

- **Bradley – stresses** the **partner's involvement as the birthing coach.** This method uses abdominal breathing techniques, focuses on the laboring woman's body, and promotes general relaxation with an emphasis on **natural childbirth.**

Primary Reference:

Lowdermilk, D. L. & Perry, S. E. (2004). *Maternity & women's health care* (8th ed.). St. Louis, MO: Mosby.

Additional Resources:

Hogan, M., & Glazebrook, R. (2003). *Maternal-newborn nursing.* Upper Saddle River, NJ: Pearson Education, Inc.

Ladewig, P., London, M., & Davidson, M. (2006). *Contemporary maternal-newborn nursing care.* Upper Saddle River, NJ: Pearson Education, Inc.

McKinney, E., Ashwill, J., Murray, S., James, S., Gorrie, T., & Droske, S. (2000). *Maternal-child nursing.* New York: W.B. Saunders Company.

NANDA International (2004). *NANDA nursing diagnoses: Definitions and classification 2005-2006.* Philadelphia: NANDA.

Chapter 6: Prenatal and Childbirth Education

Application Exercises

1. A nurse is teaching a group of women who are pregnant about measures to relieve backache during pregnancy. The nurse should teach the women which of the following? (Select all that apply.)

   _____ Avoid any lifting.
   _____ Perform Kegel exercises twice a day.
   _____ Perform the pelvic rock exercise every day.
   _____ Use good body mechanics.
   _____ Avoid constrictive clothing.

2. A nurse is teaching a group of clients who are pregnant about risk factors to avoid during pregnancy. The nurse determines that a client needs further instruction when the client states,

   A. "I can have a drink of wine with dinner."
   B. "I should not take over-the-counter medications without checking with my primary care provider first."
   C. "Smoking is a major cause of low birth weight in babies."
   D. "Signs of infection should be reported to my primary care provider promptly."

3. A client who is 8 weeks pregnant tells the nurse that she isn't sure she is happy about being pregnant. The nurse best responds to the client by stating,

   A. "I will inform the primary care provider that you are having these feelings."
   B. "It is normal to have feelings of ambivalence during the first trimester."
   C. "You should be happy that you are going to bring new life into the world."
   D. "I am going to make an appointment with the psychiatrist for you to discuss these thoughts."

4. "Birth without fear" refers to which of the following birthing methods?

   A. Leboyer
   B. Lamaze
   C. Dick-Read
   D. Bradley

5. Which of the following birthing methods places emphasis on natural childbirth?

    A. Leboyer
    B. Lamaze
    C. Dick-Read
    D. Bradley

6. A client who is pregnant should promptly report which of the following symptoms to the primary care provider?

    A. Vaginal bleeding
    B. Swelling of the ankles
    C. Heartburn after eating
    D. Faintness when lying on back

7. A client who is pregnant reports heartburn occurring frequently after her evening meal. What is the most appropriate recommendation for the nurse to make to this client?

    A. "Lie on your right side for half an hour after eating your evening meal."
    B. "Eat most of your day's intake at your midday meal rather than evening."
    C. "Sit up for approximately half an hour after eating your meal."
    D. "Eat larger meals less frequently rather than frequent small meals."

8. A client who is 7 weeks pregnant is experiencing nausea and vomiting in the morning. The nurse in the prenatal clinic provides teaching that should include which of the following?

    A. Eat crackers or plain toast before getting out of bed.
    B. Eat a piece of buttered toast before getting out of bed.
    C. Skip breakfast and eat lunch after nausea has subsided.
    D. Eat a large supper to prevent an empty stomach in the morning.

9. A nurse in the prenatal clinic is providing instruction to a client with lower extremity edema who reports leg cramps. Which of the following should be included in the instruction?

    A. Eliminate calcium and phosphorus from the diet.
    B. Extend the affected leg straight and point the toes.
    C. Lean forward holding onto back of chair with one leg in front and one leg behind.
    D. Bend the leg at the knee while massaging the calf muscle.

Chapter 6: Prenatal and Childbirth Education

Application Exercises Answer Key

1. A nurse is teaching a group of women who are pregnant about measures to relieve backache during pregnancy. The nurse should teach the women which of the following? (Select all that apply.)

_____	Avoid any lifting.
_____	Perform Kegel exercises twice a day.
__X__	**Perform the pelvic rock exercise every day.**
__X__	**Use good body mechanics.**
_____	Avoid constrictive clothing.

The pelvic rock or tilt exercises stretch out the muscles of the lower back and help relieve lower back pain. Good body mechanics will help prevent injury to the back that can occur from using incorrect muscles. Lifting can be done, but use the knees to lift rather than the back. Kegel exercises are done to strengthen the perineal muscles. Avoiding constrictive clothing will help prevent vaginitis, heat rash, or varicoses.

2. A nurse is teaching a group of clients who are pregnant about risk factors to avoid during pregnancy. The nurse determines that a client needs further instruction when the client states,

    A. **"I can have a drink of wine with dinner."**

    B. "I should not take over-the-counter medications without checking with my primary care provider first."

    C. "Smoking is a major cause of low birth weight in babies."

    D. "Signs of infection should be reported to my primary care provider promptly."

No alcohol should be consumed during pregnancy. All medications should be approved with the primary care provider. Signs of infection or any concerns should be reported to the primary care provider. Smoking is a major cause of low birth weight infants.

3. A client who is 8 weeks pregnant tells the nurse that she isn't sure she is happy about being pregnant. The nurse best responds to the client by stating,

> A. "I will inform the primary care provider that you are having these feelings."
>
> **B. "It is normal to have feelings of ambivalence during the first trimester."**
>
> C. "You should be happy that you are going to bring new life into the world."
>
> D. "I am going to make an appointment with the psychiatrist for you to discuss these thoughts."

Ambivalence during the first trimester is a psychological adaptation defined by Reva Rubin. Rubin states that a client who is pregnant usually overcomes ambivalence before the second trimester.

4. "Birth without fear" refers to which of the following birthing methods?

> A. Leboyer
>
> B. Lamaze
>
> **C. Dick-Read**
>
> D. Bradley

The Dick-Read method refers to "childbirth without fear." The Lamaze method focuses on partner-coached breathing techniques and relaxation with the woman panting and using outside focal points during labor. The Leboyer method is not a method of childbirth preparation, but an approach to birth that centers on the responses and needs of the infant through environmental variables. The Leboyer method is referred to as "birth without violence." The Bradley method stresses the partner's involvement as a birthing coach and uses abdominal breathing techniques and focuses on the laboring woman's body promoting general relaxation with an emphasis on natural childbirth.

5. Which of the following birthing methods places emphasis on natural childbirth?

     A. Leboyer

     B. Lamaze

     C. Dick-Read

     D. Bradley

The Bradley method stresses the partner's involvement as the birthing coach and uses abdominal breathing techniques and focuses on the laboring woman's body promoting general relaxation with an emphasis on natural childbirth. The Dick-Read method refers to childbirth "without fear." The Lamaze method focuses on partner-coached breathing techniques and relaxation with the woman panting and using outside focal points during labor. The Leboyer method is not a method of childbirth preparation, but an approach to birth that centers on the responses and needs of the infant through environmental variables that is referred to as "birth without violence."

6. A client who is pregnant should promptly report which of the following symptoms to the primary care provider?

     A. Vaginal bleeding

     B. Swelling of the ankles

     C. Heartburn after eating

     D. Faintness when lying on back

Vaginal bleeding during pregnancy is always a dangerous sign and the client should notify her primary care provider. Swelling of the ankles is a normal occurrence that can be relieved by the client elevating her lower extremities and not sitting or standing for prolonged periods of time. Heartburn frequently occurs because of the slowed gastrointestinal motility and compression of the stomach by the enlarging uterus. Supine hypotension, which can be experienced by the client as a faintness felt when lying on the back, occurs because of the gravid uterus compressing the ascending vena cava. This compression can be detrimental to the fetus. Supine hypotension is easily rectified by instructing the client to lie on her side or in a semi-sitting position.

7. A client who is pregnant reports heartburn occurring frequently after her evening meal. What is the most appropriate recommendation for the nurse to make to this client?

> A. "Lie on your right side for half an hour after eating your evening meal."
>
> B. "Eat most of your day's intake at your midday meal rather than evening."
>
> **C. "Sit up for approximately half an hour after eating your meal."**
>
> D. "Eat larger meals less frequently rather than frequent small meals."

Heartburn is possible during the second and third trimesters due to the client's stomach being displaced by her enlarging uterus and the slowing of gastrointestinal tract motility and digestion brought about by increased progesterone levels. The client should eat small frequent meals not allowing the stomach to get too empty or too full. The client should also sit up for 30 min after meals and check with her primary care provider prior to using over-the-counter antacids.

8. A client who is 7 weeks pregnant is experiencing nausea and vomiting in the morning. The nurse in the prenatal clinic provides teaching that should include which of the following?

> **A. Eat crackers or plain toast before getting out of bed.**
>
> B. Eat a piece of buttered toast before getting out of bed.
>
> C. Skip breakfast and eat lunch after nausea has subsided.
>
> D. Eat a large supper to prevent an empty stomach in the morning.

Nausea and vomiting may occur during the first trimester. The client should eat crackers or dry toast ½ to 1 hr before rising in the morning to relieve discomfort. Instruct the client to avoid an empty stomach, spicy, greasy, or gas-forming foods. Encourage the client to drink fluids between meals.

9. A nurse in the prenatal clinic is providing instruction to a client with lower extremity edema who reports leg cramps. Which of the following should be included in the instruction?

    A. Eliminate calcium and phosphorus from the diet.

    B. Extend the affected leg straight and point the toes.

    C. Lean forward holding onto back of chair with one leg in front and one leg behind.

    D. Bend the leg at the knee while massaging the calf muscle.

Leg cramps are a possible symptom during the third trimester due to the compression of lower extremity nerves and blood vessels by the enlarging uterus which results in poor peripheral circulation as well as an imbalance in the calcium/phosphorus ratio. Leg cramps can be relieved by leaning forward onto the back of a chair with one leg in front or one leg behind. The client's diet and calcium intake should be evaluated. The client should notify her primary care provider if frequent cramping occurs. Other ways to relieve cramps include extending the affected leg and pointing the toes towards the head and massaging the calf muscle while the leg is extended.

Unit 1   Antepartum

Chapter 7:   Antepartum: Diagnostic Interventions
Contributor: Brenda French, MSN, RN

 NCLEX-RN® Connections:

Learning Objective: Review and apply knowledge within "**Antepartum: Diagnostic Interventions**" in readiness for performance of the following nursing activities as outlined by the NCLEX-RN® test plan:

Δ   Assess the client during routine prenatal visits (e.g., weight, blood pressure, fundal height).

Δ   Monitor the client's maternal and fetal diagnostic test results.

Δ   Assist the client undergoing antepartum diagnostic tests.

Δ   Monitor the fetal heart rate during routine prenatal visits.

Diagnostic Procedure and Nursing Management: Prenatal Care

Key Points

Δ   **Prenatal care** dramatically reduces infant and maternal morbidity and mortality rates by the early detection of potential problems. A majority of birth defects occur between 2 and 8 weeks gestation. Prenatal care provides an opportunity to:

•   Ensure adequate daily folic acid.

•   Update immunization status.

•   Encourage smoking cessation.

•   Treat current infections.

•   Obtain genetic testing and provide counseling.

•   Ascertain maternal exposure to hazardous materials.

Key Factors

Δ   In an uneventful pregnancy, **prenatal visits** are **scheduled** every month for 7 months, every 2 weeks during the eighth month, and every week during the last month.

Nursing Management

Δ   Prenatal care begins with an initial assessment and then continues throughout pregnancy.

- At the initial prenatal visit:

  ◊   Determine estimated date of delivery.

  ◊   Obtain medical and nursing history to include: past medical health, family history, social supports, and review of systems (to determine risk factors).

  ◊   Perform a physical assessment to include the client's baseline weight blood pressure, and pelvic examination. Have the client empty her bladder prior to the exam.

- Ongoing prenatal visits include:

  ◊   Monitoring weight, blood pressure, and urine for glucose and protein.

  ◊   Noting presence of edema, urine dipstick for glucose and protein.

  ◊   Monitoring fetal development.

  °   Fetal heart rate can be heard by Doppler at 10 to 12 weeks or heard with an ultrasound stethoscope at 16 to 20 weeks. Listen at the midline, right above the symphysis pubis, by holding the stethoscope firmly on the abdomen.

  °   Start measuring fundal height at 18 weeks. Between 18 and 30 weeks gestation, the fundal height measured in centimeters should equal the week of gestation. Have the client empty her bladder and measure from the level of the symphysis pubis to the upper border of the fundus.

  °   Begin assessing for fetal movement between 16 and 20 weeks.

  ◊   Providing education for self care to include ways to manage common reports and concerns of pregnancy (e.g., nausea and vomiting, fatigue, back ache, varicosities, heartburn, activity, sexuality).

- Perform or assist with **Leopold's maneuvers** to palpate presentation and position of the fetus. *(For information, refer to chapter 13, Therapeutic Procedures to Assist with Labor and Birth).*

- Assist the primary care provider with the **pelvic examination.** This examination is performed to determine the status of the client's reproductive organs and birth canal. Pelvic measurements determine whether the pelvis will allow for the passage of the fetus at delivery.

  ◊   The nurse should encourage the client to **empty her bladder** and **take deep breaths** during the examination to decrease discomfort.

- Assess for **costovertebral angle tenderness** indicative of renal infection.

Routine Laboratory Tests in Prenatal Care

Laboratory Test	Purpose
Blood type, Rh factor, and presence of irregular antibodies	Determines the risk for maternal-fetal blood incompatibility (erythroblastosis fetalis) or neonatal hyperbilirubinemia
CBC with differential, hemoglobin, and hematocrit	Detects anemia and infection
Hemoglobin electrophoresis	Identifies hemoglobinopathies (sickle cell anemia and thalassemia)
Urinalysis with microscopic examination of pH, sediment, specific gravity, color, glucose, albumin, protein, RBCs, WBCs, casts, acetone, and hCG	Identifies diabetes mellitus, gestational hypertension, renal disease, infection, and occult hematuria
One hour glucose tolerance (Oral ingestion or IV administration of concentrated glucose with venous sample taken 1 hr later [fasting not necessary])	Identifies gestational diabetes; done at initial visit for at risk clients, and at 24 to 28 weeks for all pregnant women (> 135 mg/dL requires follow-up)
Three hour glucose tolerance (Fasting overnight prior to oral ingestion or IV administration of concentrated glucose with a venous sample taken 1, 2, and 3 hr later)	Screens for diabetes in clients with elevated 1-hr glucose test; requires two elevated readings for diagnosis
Papanicolaou (PAP) test	Screens for cervical cancer, herpes simplex type 2, and/or human papillomavirus
Vaginal/cervical culture	Detects group B streptococci (routinely obtained at 35 to 37 weeks), bacterial vaginosis, or sexually transmitted infections (e.g., gonorrhea and chlamydia)
Rubella titer	Determines immunity to rubella
PPD (tuberculosis screening), chest screening after 20 wk gestation with positive PPD	Identifies exposure to tuberculosis
Hepatitis B screen	Identifies carriers of hepatitis B
Venereal disease research laboratory	Syphilis screening mandated by law
Human immunodeficiency virus (HIV)	Detects HIV infection (requires consent)
TORCH (acronym for toxoplasmosis, other infections, rubella, cytomegalovirus, and herpes virus) screening when indicated	Screening for a group of infections capable of crossing the placenta and adversely affecting fetal development

Diagnostic Procedure and Nursing Management: Ultrasound

Key Points

Δ   **Ultrasound** – a procedure lasting approximately 20 min that consists of high frequency sound waves used to visualize internal organs and tissues by producing a real time three dimensional pictorial image of the developing fetus and maternal structures (e.g., fetal heartbeat, pelvic anatomy). An ultrasound allows for an early diagnosis of complications, permitting earlier interventions, and thereby decreasing the infant's and mother's morbidity and mortality.

Δ   Two types of ultrasound used in pregnancy:

- **External abdominal ultrasound** – a noninvasive, painless, and safe procedure. An abdominal ultrasound is more useful after the first trimester when the gravid uterus is larger. The ultrasound transducer is moved over the client's abdomen to obtain an image.

- **Internal transvaginal ultrasound** – an invasive procedure in which a probe is inserted vaginally and allows for a more accurate evaluation. An advantage of this procedure is that it does not require a full bladder.

    ◊   It is **especially useful** in **obese clients** and during the **first trimester** to detect an **ectopic pregnancy**, identify abnormalities, and help to establish gestational age.

    ◊   A transvaginal ultrasound may also be used in the **third trimester** in conjunction with abdominal scanning to evaluate for preterm labor.

Δ   **Doppler ultrasound blood flow analysis** – an external ultrasound method of noninvasively studying the **maternal-fetal blood flow** by measuring the velocity at which RBCs are traveling in the uterine and fetal vessels using a handheld ultrasound device that reflects sound waves from a moving target. It is especially useful in fetal intrauterine growth restriction (IUGR), identifying poor placental perfusion, and as an adjunct in pregnancies at risk because of hypertension, diabetes mellitus, multiple fetuses, or preterm labor.

Key Factors

Δ   **Indications** for the use of an **ultrasound** during pregnancy include:

- **Pregnancy confirmation.**

- **Gestational age** confirmation by biparietal diameter (side-to-side) measurement.

- **Multifetal pregnancy** identification.

- Site of **fetal implantation** (uterine or **ectopic**).

- Fetal growth and development assessment.

- Maternal structure assessment.

- **Fetal viability** or death confirmation.

- Fetal abnormalities ruled out or verified.

- Vaginal bleeding evaluation.

- **Placental attachment site** location.

- **Amniotic fluid volume** determination.

- Fetal movement observation (fetal heartbeat, breathing, and activity).

- Placental grading (evaluating placental maturation).

- **Adjunct** for other procedures (e.g., amniocentesis, biophysical profile).

Nursing Management

Δ   For an **abdominal ultrasound**, the nurse should:

- Explain the procedure to the client and that it presents no known risk to her or her fetus.

- Advise the client to **drink 1 to 2 quarts** of **fluid** prior to the ultrasound to **fill** the **bladder** in order to lift and stabilize the uterus, displace the bowels away, and act as an echo-lucent to better reflect sound waves and to get a better image of the fetus.

- Assist the client into a **supine position** with a **wedge** placed **under** her **right hip** to displace the uterus (prevent supine hypotension).

- Apply an ultrasonic/transducer gel to the abdomen before the transducer is moved over the skin to obtain a better fetal image, assuring the gel is at room temperature or warmer to prevent uterine cramping.

- Allow the client to empty her bladder at the termination of the procedure.

Δ   For a **transvaginal ultrasound**, the nurse should:

- Assist the client into a **lithotomy position**. The vaginal probe is covered with a protective device, lubricated with a water soluble gel, and the client or examiner may insert the probe.

- During the procedure, the position of the probe or tilt of the table may be changed to facilitate the complete view of the pelvis.

- Inform the client that some pressure may be felt as the probe is moved.

Δ   Fetal and maternal structures may be pointed out to the client as the ultrasound procedure is performed.

Diagnostic Procedure and Nursing Management: Nonstress Test (NST)

Key Points

Δ **Nonstress test (NST)** – most widely used technique for antepartum evaluation of fetal well-being performed during the third trimester. It is a noninvasive procedure that monitors response of the fetal heart rate to fetal movement. A Doppler transducer, used to monitor the FHR, and a tocotransducer, used to monitor uterine contractions, is attached externally to the client's abdomen to obtain paper tracing strips. The client pushes a button attached to the monitor whenever she feels a fetal movement that is noted on the paper tracing. This allows a nurse to assess the FHR in relationship to the fetal movement.

- The NST is interpreted as reactive if the **FHR accelerates** to **15 beats/min for at least 15 sec** and occurs **two or more times** during a **20-min period**. This assures that the placenta is adequately perfused and the fetus is well-oxygenated.

- **Nonreactive** NST indicates that the **fetal heartbeat does not accelerate** adequately with fetal movement **or no fetal movements** occur in 40 min. If this is so, a further assessment such as a contraction stress test (CST) or biophysical profile (BPP) is indicated.

Δ Disadvantages of a NST include a high rate of false nonreactive results with the fetal movement response blunted by fetal sleep cycles, chronic tobacco smoking, medications, and fetal immaturity.

Key Factors

Δ Indications for the use of a nonstress test during pregnancy include:

- Pregnancies in the third trimester to assess for an intact fetal central nervous system.

- Twice weekly use (after 28 weeks gestation) for clients who have diabetes or are at risk for fetal death.

Nursing Management

Δ For a **NST**, the nurse should:

- Seat the client in a reclining chair or place in a semi-Fowler's or left-lateral position.

- Apply conduction gel to the client's abdomen.

- Apply two belts to the client's abdomen and attach the FHR and uterine contraction monitors.

- Instruct the client to press the button on the handheld event marker each time she feels the fetus move.

- If there are no fetal movements (fetus sleeping), **vibroacoustic stimulation** (sound source, usually laryngeal stimulator) may be activated for 3 sec on the maternal abdomen over the fetal head to **awaken** a **sleeping fetus**.

- If NST is still nonreactive, anticipate a CST and/or BPP.

Diagnostic Procedure and Nursing Management: Contraction Stress Test (CST)

 Key Points

Δ   **Contraction stress test (CST)** – an assessment performed to stimulate contractions (which decrease placental blood flow) and analyze the FHR in conjunction with the contractions to **determine how** the **fetus will tolerate** the **stress of labor**. A pattern of at least three contractions within a 10-min time period with duration of 40 to 60 sec each must be obtained to use for assessment data.

- **Nipple stimulated CST** consists of the woman lightly brushing her palm across the nipple for 2 or 3 min, which causes the pituitary gland to release endogenous oxytocin, and then stopping the nipple stimulation when a contraction begins. The same process is repeated after a 5 min rest period.

    ◊ **Hyperstimulation** of the uterus (uterine contraction longer than 90 sec or more frequent than every 2 min) should be avoided by stimulating the nipple intermittently with rest periods in between and avoiding bimanual stimulation of both nipples unless stimulation of one nipple is unsuccessful.

- **Oxytocin administration CST** is used if nipple stimulation fails and consists of the intravenous administration of oxytocin to induce uterine contractions.

    ◊ Contractions started with oxytocin may be difficult to stop and can lead to preterm labor

Δ   A **negative CST** (normal finding) is indicated if within a 10-min period, with three uterine contractions, there are no late decelerations of the FHR.

Δ   A **positive CST** (abnormal finding) is indicated with persistent and consistent late decelerations on more than half of the contractions. This is suggestive of uteroplacental insufficiency. Variable deceleration may indicate cord compression, and early decelerations may indicate fetal head compression. *(For information, refer to chapter 11, Fetal Assessment During Labor).*

Key Factors

Δ   Indications for the use of a **CST** during pregnancy include:

- High risk pregnancies (e.g., gestational diabetes, postterm pregnancy).
- Nonreactive stress test.

Nursing Management

Δ   For a **CST**, the nurse should:

- Obtain a **baseline** of the **fetal heart rate**, **fetal movement**, and **contractions** for **10 to 20 min** and document.
- Complete an assessment without artificial stimulation if contractions are occurring spontaneously.
- Initiate **nipple stimulation** if there are no contractions. Instruct the client to roll a nipple between her thumb and fingers or brush her palm across her nipple. The client should stop when a uterine contraction begins.
- Monitor and provide adequate rest periods for the client to avoid **hyperstimulation** of the uterus.
- Initiate intravenous **oxytocin** administration if nipple stimulation fails to elicit a sufficient uterine contraction pattern.

Complications and Nursing Management

Δ   Contraction stress testing presents risks that include:

- Hyperstimulation of the uterus.
- Preterm labor.

Δ   Monitor for **contractions** lasting **longer than 90 sec** and/or occurring **more frequently** than **every 2 min**.

Δ   Provide administration of tocolytics as prescribed and encourage bedrest.

Diagnostic Procedure and Nursing Management: Biophysical Profile

Key Points

Δ   **Biophysical profile (BPP)** – uses a real-time ultrasound to visualize physical and physiological characteristics of the fetus and observe for fetal biophysical responses to stimuli.

Δ   **BPP** assesses the fetal well-being by measuring the following **five variables** with a score of 2 for each normal finding, and 0 for each abnormal finding for each variable with a total score of 8 to 10 being normal, 6 equivocal, and < 4 abnormal.

- **Reactive fetal heart rate** (reactive nonstress test) = 2; nonreactive = 0.

- **Fetal breathing movements** (at least 1 episode of 30 sec in 30 min) = 2; absent or less than 30 sec duration = 0.

- **Gross body movements** (at least 3 body or limb extensions with return to flexion in 30 min) = 2; less than 3 episodes = 0.

- **Fetal tone** (at least 1 episode of extension with return to flexion) = 2; slow extension and flexion, lack of flexion, or absent of movement = 0

- **Amniotic fluid volume** (at least 1 pocket of fluid that measures at least 1 cm in 2 perpendicular planes) = 2; pockets absent or less than 1 cm = 0

Key Factors

Δ   Indications for use of a **BPP** during pregnancy include:

- Nonreactive stress test.

- Suspected oligohydramnios or polyhydramnios.

- Suspected fetal hypoxemia and/or hypoxia.

- Premature rupture of membranes.

- Maternal infection.

Nursing Management

Δ   For a **BPP,** the nurse should:

- Follow the same nursing management techniques as those used for an ultrasound.

Diagnostic Procedure and Nursing Management: Amniocentesis

 Key Points

Δ   **Amniocentesis** – the aspiration of amniotic fluid for analysis by insertion of a needle transabdominally into the uterus and amniotic sac under direct ultrasound guidance locating the placenta and determining the position of the fetus. It may be performed after 14 weeks gestation.

Δ   **Alpha-fetoprotein (AFP)** can be measured from the amniotic fluid between 16 and 18 weeks gestation and may be used to assess for neural tube defects in the fetus or chromosomal disorders. May be evaluated to follow up a high level of AFP in maternal serum.

- **High levels** of alpha fetoprotein are associated with neural tube defects such as spina bifida (open spine), anencephaly (incomplete development of fetal skull and brain), or omphalocele (abdominal wall defect). High AFP levels may also be present with normal multifetal pregnancies.

- **Low levels** of alpha fetoprotein are associated with chromosomal disorders (Down syndrome) or gestational trophoblastic disease (hydatidiform mole).

Δ   **Tests for fetal lung maturity** may be performed if gestation is less than 37 weeks, in the event of a rupture of membranes, for preterm labor, or for a complication indicating a cesarean birth. Amniotic fluid is tested to determine if the fetal lungs are mature enough to adapt to extrauterine life or if the fetus will likely have respiratory distress. Determination is made whether the fetus should be removed immediately or if the fetus requires more time in utero with the administration of glucocorticoids to promote fetal lung maturity.

- **Fetal lung tests include:**

  ◊   **Lecithin/sphingomyelin (L/S) ratio** – a 2:1 indicating fetal lung maturity (3:1 for a diabetic client).

  ◊   **Presence of phosphatidylglycerol (PG)** – absence of PG is associated with respiratory distress.

Key Factors

Δ   Indications for the use of an **amniocentesis** during pregnancy include:

- Maternal **age greater** than **35 years.**

- Previous birth with a **chromosomal anomaly**.

- A **parent** who is a **carrier** of a **chromosomal anomaly**.

- A family history of neural tube defects.

- Prenatal diagnosis of a genetic disorder or congenital anomaly of the fetus.

- **Alpha fetoprotein level** for fetal abnormalities.

- **Pulmonary maturity assessment.**

- Fetal hemolytic disease diagnosis.

- Meconium in the amniotic fluid.

- Fetal fibronectin levels elevated indicative of preterm labor.

Nursing Management

Δ   For an **amniocentesis**, the nurse should:

- Explain the procedure to the client and obtain an **informed consent** form from the client.

- Instruct the client to **empty** her **bladder** prior to the procedure to reduce its size and reduce the risk of inadvertent puncture.

- Assist the client into a **supine position** and place a wedge or rolled towel under her right hip to displace the uterus off the vena cava and place a drape over the client exposing only her abdomen.

- Prepare the client for an ultrasound to locate the placenta.

- Obtain the client's **baseline vital signs** and **fetal heart rate** (FHR) and document prior to the procedure.

- Cleanse the abdomen with an antiseptic solution prior to the administration of a local anesthetic given by the primary care provider.

- Advise the client that she will feel slight pressure as the needle is inserted for aspiration. However, she should continue breathing because holding her breath will lower the diaphragm against the uterus and shift the intrauterine contents.

- Monitor the client's vital signs, FHR, and uterine contractions throughout and 30 min following the procedure.

- Have the client rest for 30 min.

- Administer Rh immune globulin (RhoGAM) to the client if Rh-negative (standard practice after an amniocentesis for all Rh-negative women to protect against Rh isoimmunization).

- Advise the client to report to her primary care provider if she experiences fever, chills, leakage of fluid, or bleeding from the insertion site, decreased fetal movement, vaginal bleeding, or uterine contractions after the procedure.

- Encourage the client to drink plenty of liquids and rest for the next 24 hr post-procedure.

Complications and Nursing Management

Δ   Amniocentesis is invasive and presents risks including:

- **Amniotic fluid emboli.**

- Maternal or fetal hemorrhage.

- Fetomaternal hemorrhage with **Rh isoimmunization.**

- Maternal or fetal **infection.**

- Inadvertent **fetal damage** or **anomalies involving limbs.**

- Fetal death.

- Inadvertent maternal intestinal or bladder damage.

- Miscarriage or preterm labor.

- Premature rupture of membranes.

- Leakage of amniotic fluid.

Δ Monitor the client's vital signs, temperature, respiratory status, FHR, uterine contractions, and vaginal discharge for amniotic fluid or bleeding.

Δ Provide medication administration as prescribed, client education, and support.

Diagnostic Procedure and Nursing Management: Percutaneous Umbilical Cord Blood Sampling (PUBS) or Cordocentesis

 Key Points

Δ **Percutaneous umbilical blood sampling (PUBS)** – the obtaining of a fetal blood sampling from the umbilical cord by passing a fine-gauge fiber optic scope (fetoscope) into the amniotic sac using the amniocentesis technique. The needle is advanced into the umbilical cord under ultrasound guidance and blood is aspirated from the umbilical vein. Blood studies from the cordocentesis may consist of:

- **Kleihauer-Betke test** that ensures blood obtained is from the fetus.

- Complete blood count with differential.

- Indirect Coombs' test for Rh antibodies.

- Blood gases.

- Karyotyping (visualization of chromosomes).

Δ A **fetoscope** is also used to **visualize** the **fetus** to assess its well-being by confirming the intactness of the spinal column, obtaining biopsy samples of fetal tissue, and performing elemental surgery (e.g., shunt insertion into the fetal ventricles to relieve hydrocephalus, shunt insertion into fetal bladder to relieve a stenosed urethra).

Δ **PUBS** is the most common method used for fetal blood sampling and transfusion.

Key Factors

Δ Indications for the use of **PUBS** include:

- Diagnosing prenatal blood and chromosomal disorders.

- **Evaluating** for **isoimmune fetal hemolytic anemia** and assessing the need for a **fetal blood transfusion**.

- Karyotyping of malformed fetuses.

- Detecting of fetal infection.

- Determining the acid-base balance status of fetuses with IUGR.

Nursing Management

Δ   For **percutaneous umbilical blood sampling**, the nurse should:

- Follow the same nursing **management techniques** as those used for an **amniocentesis**.

- Perform **continuous FHR monitoring** for **up to 1 hr** following the procedure. Repeat the ultrasound 1 hr following the procedure to detect bleeding and/or hematoma.

Complications

Δ   **PUBS** presents risks that include:

- Those similar to amniocentesis.

- **Cord laceration.**

Δ   Monitor the client's vital signs, temperature, respiratory status, FHR, uterine contractions, and vaginal discharge for amniotic fluid or bleeding.

Δ   Provide medication administration as prescribed, client education, and support.

Diagnostic Procedure and Nursing Management: Chorionic Villus Sampling (CVS)

Key Points

Δ   **Chorionic villus sampling (CVS)** – assessment of a portion of the developing placenta (chorionic villi) is aspirated through a thin sterile catheter or syringe through the abdomen or intravaginally through the cervix under ultrasound guidance and analyzed.

Δ   CVS is a first-trimester alternative to amniocentesis with one of its advantages being an earlier diagnosis of any abnormalities. CVS can be performed at 10 to 12 weeks gestation and rapid results with chromosome studies are available in 24 to 48 hr following aspiration.

Δ   The advantage of an earlier diagnosis should be weighed against the increased risk of fetal anomalies and death.

Key Factors

Δ   Indications for use of **CVS** during pregnancy include:

- Women at risk for giving birth to an infant with a genetic chromosomal abnormality (cannot determine spina bifida or anencephaly).

- Indications similar to those of amniocentesis.

Nursing Management

Δ   For a **CVS**, the nurse should:

- Follow the same nursing management techniques as indicated for amniocentesis with the following exceptions.

    ◊   Instruct the client to drink plenty of fluid to **fill the bladder** prior to the procedure to assist in positioning the uterus for catheter insertion.

    ◊   Assist the client to the lithotomy position for the transvaginal procedure.

Complications

Δ   **CVS** presents risks that include:

- Those similar to amniocentesis.

- **Spontaneous abortion (higher risk with CVS** than with amniocentesis).

Δ   Monitor the client's vital signs, temperature, respiratory status, FHR, uterine contractions, and vaginal discharge for amniotic fluid or bleeding.

Δ   Provide medication administration as prescribed, client education, and support.

Primary Reference:

Lowdermilk, D. L. & Perry, S. E. (2004). *Maternity & women's health care* (8th ed.). St. Louis, MO: Mosby.

Additional Resources:

Hogan, M., & Glazebrook, R. (2003). *Maternal-newborn nursing.* Upper Saddle River, NJ: Pearson Education, Inc.

Ladewig, P., London, M., & Davidson, M., (2006). *Contemporary maternal-newborn nursing care* (6th ed.). Upper Saddle River, NJ: Pearson Education, Inc.

NANDA International (2004). *NANDA nursing diagnoses: Definitions and classification 2005-2006.* Philadelphia: NANDA.

Pillitteri, A. (2003). *Maternal & child health nursing* (4th ed.). Philadelphia: Lippincott Williams & Wilkins.

Potter & Perry (2005). *Fundamentals of nursing* (6th ed.). St. Louis, MO: Mosby.

Chapter 7: Antepartum: Diagnostic Interventions

Application Exercises

1. During a client's first prenatal visit, she asks the nurse how often she will have to come in for prenatal care if all goes well with her pregnancy. Which of the following responses should the nurse give the client?

   A. "Monthly for the first 5 months, then every 2 weeks for the sixth and seventh months, and then weekly until your delivery."

   B. "Monthly for the first 7 months, every 2 weeks for the eighth month, and then every week until you deliver."

   C. "Monthly for the entire pregnancy until you deliver, unless there are complications requiring weekly visits until you deliver."

   D. "Monthly for the first 6 months, every 2 weeks for the seventh and eighth month, and then weekly until you deliver."

2. What explanation should a nurse give to a client who asks why it is important for her to stay off of her back when the fetus is being monitored with electronic fetal monitoring?

   A. The monitor is applied to the maternal back and this would limit access.

   B. It is an uncomfortable position for how long the procedure takes.

   C. It causes a drop in blood pressure decreasing fetal oxygenation.

   D. The fetus is more likely to fall asleep in this position, impairing results.

3. A client who is in preterm labor is scheduled to undergo an amniocentesis. She is also scheduled for a fetal lung maturity test to determine if her fetus can adapt to extrauterine life or will develop respiratory distress. Which of the following is a test for fetal lung maturity?

   A. Alpha fetoprotein

   B. Lecithin/sphingomyelin ratio

   C. Kleihauer-Betke test

   D. Indirect Coombs' test

4. A client who is undergoing a nonstress test asks the nurse to explain why she is using an acoustic vibration device. The nurse states that the device is used to

   A. stimulate uterine contractions.

   B. relax uterine contractions.

   C. sooth the fetus to sleep.

   D. awaken the sleeping fetus.

5. A nurse determines that a client who is pregnant needs further instructions about an amniocentesis when the client states,

        A. "I must report cramping or signs of infection to the physician."

        B. "I should drink lots of fluids and rest for the next 24 hr."

        C. "I need to have a full bladder for the procedure to be done."

        D. "The amniotic fluid can be used to detect genetic abnormalities."

6. A client is scheduled for a nonstress test. The purpose of this test is to evaluate the ability of fetal

        A. activity to increase in response to stress.

        B. heart rate to remain stable with activity.

        C. ability to remain nonreactive with uterine activity.

        D. heart rate to accelerate with fetal movement.

Chapter 7: Antepartum: Diagnostic Interventions

Application Exercises Answer Key

1. During a client's first prenatal visit, she asks the nurse how often she will have to come in for prenatal care if all goes well with her pregnancy. Which of the following responses should the nurse give the client?

   A. "Monthly for the first 5 months, then every 2 weeks for the sixth and seventh months, and then weekly until your delivery."

   B. "Monthly for the first 7 months, every 2 weeks for the eighth month, and then every week until you deliver."

   C. "Monthly for the entire pregnancy until you deliver, unless there are complications requiring weekly visits until you deliver."

   D. "Monthly for the first 6 months, every 2 weeks for the seventh and eighth month, and then weekly until you deliver."

   In an uneventful pregnancy, prenatal visits are scheduled every month for 7 months, every 2 weeks during the eighth month, and every week during the last month until delivery.

2. What explanation should a nurse give to a client who asks why it is important for her to stay off of her back when the fetus is being monitored with electronic fetal monitoring?

   A. The monitor is applied to the maternal back and this would limit access.

   B. It is an uncomfortable position for how long the procedure takes.

   C. It causes a drop in blood pressure decreasing fetal oxygenation.

   D. The fetus is more likely to fall asleep in this position, impairing results.

   The pressure of the gravid abdomen places additional pressure on the mother's vena cava, which can decrease the amount of blood supply and oxygen to the fetus. Having the client lie on her side or sitting up will provide for the greatest amount of blood flow to the fetus. The fetal monitor is applied to the mother's abdomen at the point of maximal impulse. Although lying on the back may be uncomfortable for the mother, this is not the reason why it is contraindicated. Maternal position has no effect on fetal activity or sleep.

3. A client who is in preterm labor is scheduled to undergo an amniocentesis. She is also scheduled for a fetal lung maturity test to determine if her fetus can adapt to extrauterine life or will develop respiratory distress. Which of the following is a test for fetal lung maturity?

> A. Alpha fetoprotein
> **B. Lecithin/sphingomyelin ratio**
> C. Kleihauer-Betke test
> D. Indirect Coombs' test

Lecithin/sphingomyelin (L/S) ratio of 2:1 indicates fetal lung maturity (3:1 for a diabetic client).Alpha-fetoprotein (AFP) can be measured from the maternal serum between 16 and 18 weeks gestation and may be used to assess for neural tube defects in the fetus or chromosomal disorders. Kleihauer-Betke test is used to ensure blood is obtained from the fetus durings PUBS. Indirect Coombs' test is used to detect Rh antibodies in the mother's blood.

4. A client who is undergoing a nonstress test asks the nurse to explain why she is using an acoustic vibration device. The nurse states that the device is used to

> A. stimulate uterine contractions.
> B. relax uterine contractions.
> C. sooth the fetus to sleep.
> **D. awaken the sleeping fetus.**

If there is no fetal movement (fetus sleeping), vibroacoustic stimulation (sound source, usually laryngeal stimulator) is activated for 3 sec on the maternal abdomen over the fetal head to awaken a sleeping fetus. Vibroacoustic stimulation has no effect on uterine contractions.

5. A nurse determines that a client who is pregnant needs further instructions about an amniocentesis when the client states,

> A. "I must report cramping or signs of infection to the physician."
> B. "I should drink lots of fluids and rest for the next 24 hr."
> **C. "I need to have a full bladder for the procedure to be done."**
> D. "The amniotic fluid can be used to detect genetic abnormalities."

A full bladder may be necessary for an abdominal ultrasound and chorionic villus sampling. Amniocentesis requires an empty bladder to prevent an inadvertent puncture from occurring. The client should report any signs of infection to the primary care provider and should drink plenty of fluids and rest for 24 hr following the procedure. The amniocentesis is used to detect genetic abnormalities.

6. A client is scheduled for a nonstress test. The purpose of this test is to evaluate the ability of fetal

> A. activity to develop in response to stress.
> B. heart rate to remain stable with activity.
> C. ability to remain nonreactive with uterine activity.
> **D. heart rate to accelerate with fetal movement.**

A nonstress test is performed on all pregnancies in the third trimester to assess for an intact central nervous system of the fetus by monitoring for fetal heart rate accelerations in response to fetal movement. These accelerations are a reassuring reactive sign of fetal well-being.

Unit 1   Antepartum

Chapter 8:   Complications of Pregnancy
Contributor: Brenda French, MSN, RN

 NCLEX-RN® Connections:

Learning Objective: Review and apply knowledge within "**Complications of Pregnancy**" in readiness for performance of the following nursing activities as outlined by the NCLEX-RN® test plan:

Δ   Recognize possible signs of prenatal complications in the client.

Δ   Monitor maternal and fetal diagnostic test results.

Δ   Plan and provide care to the client who is experiencing complications of pregnancy.

Complication of Pregnancy: Bleeding During Pregnancy

Key Points

Δ   Vaginal bleeding during pregnancy is always abnormal and must be carefully investigated in order to determine the cause.

Δ   Vaginal bleeding can impair both the outcome of the pregnancy and the mother's life.

Key Factors

Δ   The primary causes of bleeding are summarized in the following table according to common causes during each trimester of pregnancy.

Summary of Causes of Bleeding During Pregnancy		
Time	**Complication**	**Signs and symptoms**
First trimester	Spontaneous abortion	Vaginal bleeding, uterine cramping, and partial or complete expulsion of products of conception
	Ectopic pregnancy	Abrupt unilateral lower quadrant abdominal pain with or without vaginal bleeding
Second trimester	Gestational trophoblastic disease	Uterine size increasing abnormally fast, abnormally high levels of hCG, nausea and increased emesis, no fetus present on ultrasound, and scant or profuse dark brown or red vaginal bleeding
	Incompetent cervix	Painless bleeding with cervical dilation leading to fetal expulsion
Third trimester	Placenta previa	Painless bleeding as the cervix dilates
	Abruptio placenta	Vaginal bleeding, sharp abdominal pain, and tender rigid uterus
	Preterm labor	Pink-stained vaginal discharge, uterine contractions becoming regular, cervical dilation and effacement *(For information, refer to chapter 14, Complications of Labor and Birth)*

Complication of Pregnancy: Spontaneous Abortion

Key Points

Δ   **Spontaneous abortion** is when a pregnancy is terminated before 20 weeks gestation (the point of fetal viability) or a fetal weight less than 500 g.

Δ   **Types of abortion** are clinically classified according to symptom and whether the products of conception are partially or completely retained or expulsed. Types of abortions include threatened, inevitable, incomplete, complete, and missed.

Key Factors

Δ   Risk factors for spontaneous abortion include:

•   **Chromosomal abnormalities** (account for 50%).

- Maternal illness, such as insulin dependent diabetes mellitus.

- Advancing maternal age.

- Chronic maternal infections.

- Maternal malnutrition.

- Trauma or injury.

- **Anomalies in the fetus or placenta.**

- Substance abuse.

Diagnostic and Therapeutic Procedures

Δ **Hemoglobin** and **hematocrit,** if considerable blood loss

Δ **Clotting factors** monitored for **disseminated intravascular coagulopathy (DIC)** – a complication with retained products of conception

Δ **WBC** for suspected infection

Δ Serum **human chorionic gonadotropin (hCG)** levels to confirm pregnancy

Δ An **ultrasound** is used to determine the presence of a viable or dead fetus, or partial or complete products of conception within the uterine cavity.

Δ Examination of the **cervix** to observe if opened or closed

Δ **Dilation and curettage** (D&C) to dilate and scrape the uterine walls to remove uterine contents for inevitable and incomplete abortions

Δ **Dilation and evacuation** (D&E) to dilate and evacuate uterine contents after 16 weeks gestation

Δ **Prostaglandin** is administered into the amniotic sac or by a vaginal suppository to augment or induce labor to expulse the products of conception for a late term, incomplete, inevitable, or missed abortion.

Nursing Assessments

Δ Monitor for **signs and symptoms** of a spontaneous abortion, which include:

- **Vaginal spotting** or **moderate to heavy bleeding** with or without pain **in early pregnancy.**

- Passage of tissue (products of conception).

- Mild to severe uterine cramping.

- Backache.

- Rupture of membranes.
- **Dilation** of the **cervix.**
- Fever.
- Abdominal tenderness.
- Signs and symptoms of hemorrhage such as hypotension.

Spontaneous Abortion (Miscarriage) Assessment				
Type	Cramps	Bleeding	Tissue Passed	Cervical Opening
Threatened	With or without slight cramps	Spotting to moderate	None	Closed
Inevitable	Moderate	Mild to severe	None	Dilated with membranes or tissues bulging at cervix
Incomplete	Severe	Continuous and severe	Partial fetal tissue or placenta	Dilated with tissue in cervical canal or passage of tissue
Complete	None	Minimal	Complete expulsion of uterine contents	Closed with no tissue in cervical canal
Missed	None	Brownish discharge	None, prolonged retention of tissue	Closed
Septic	Malodorous	Malodorous discharge	Varies	Usually dilated
Recurrent	Varies	Varies	Yes	Usually dilated

Δ **Nursing assessments** for **spontaneous abortion** include:

- Observing bleeding amount and color (e.g., counting pads).
- Assessing cervix for dilation.
- Subjective findings of client pain for location, type, and quality.
- Assessing amniotic membranes.
- Checking vital signs and temperature.

NANDA Nursing Diagnoses

Δ   Risk for infection related to retained products of conception

Δ   Anticipatory grieving related to the loss of pregnancy and fetus

Nursing Interventions

Δ   **Nursing interventions** for the client with a spontaneous abortion include:

- • Performing a pregnancy test.

- • Using the lay term **miscarriage** with clients because abortion will likely sound insensitive.

- • Placing the client on **bed rest** with the administration of **sedation** for threatened, inevitable, and incomplete abortions.

- • Advising the client to **avoid coitus** with threatened abortion.

- • Avoiding a vaginal exam.

- • Assisting with an ultrasound.

- • Administering analgesics and blood products as prescribed.

- • Determining how much tissue has passed and **saving all passed tissue** for examination.

- • Administering intravenous **oxytocin** (Pitocin) as prescribed to expulse products of conception in **late, incomplete, inevitable, or missed abortions**.

- • Administering **broad spectrum antibiotics** as prescribed for treatment of septic abortion.

- • Assisting with termination of pregnancy (**D&C, D&E**) as indicated based on duration of pregnancy.

- • Administering **RhoGAM** as indicated to Rh negative women.

- • Providing client education and support.

Complication of Pregnancy: Ectopic Pregnancy

 Key Points

Δ   **Ectopic pregnancy** is the abnormal implantation of the fertilized ovum outside of the uterine cavity. The implantation is usually in the fallopian tube, which can result in a tubal rupture causing a fatal hemorrhage.

Key Factors

Δ **Risk factors** for an **ectopic pregnancy** include any factor that **compromises tubal patency** (e.g., pelvic inflammatory disease, contraceptive **intrauterine device [IUD]**).

Diagnostic and Therapeutic Procedures and Nursing Interventions

Δ **Transvaginal ultrasound** showing an empty uterus

Δ Hormone levels of progesterone and **hCG** elevated

Δ WBC count elevated to 15,000/mm³

Δ **Methotrexate** used to inhibit cell division and enlargement of the embryo. Also prevents rupture of the fallopian tube in order to preserve it.

- Instruct the client to **avoid alcohol** consumption and vitamins containing **folic acid** to prevent a **toxic response** to the medication.

- Advise the client to protect herself from sun exposure (photosensitivity).

Δ Rapid surgical treatment

- Linear **salpingostomy** is done to salvage the fallopian tube if not ruptured.

- Laparoscopic **salpingostomy** (removal of the tube) is performed when the tube has ruptured.

Nursing Assessments

Δ Monitor for **signs** and **symptoms** of **ectopic pregnancy** which include:

- One or two missed menses.

- **Unilateral stabbing pain** and tenderness in the lower abdominal quadrant.

- Scant, dark red, or brown vaginal spotting if tube ruptures (bleeding may be into intraperitoneal area).

- **Referred shoulder pain** from blood irritation of the diaphragm or phrenic nerve (common symptom).

- Nausea and vomiting frequently after tube rupture.

- Symptoms of hemorrhage and shock (e.g., hypotension, tachycardia, pallor).

Δ **Nursing assessments** for **ectopic pregnancy** include:

- Abdomen for **unilateral pain.**

- **Vaginal bleeding.**

- Vital signs and temperature.

- Skin color.

- Respirations.

- Urine output.

Nursing Interventions

Δ **Nursing interventions** for a client with an **ectopic pregnancy** include:

- Replacement of fluid loss and maintenance of electrolyte balance.

- Provide client education and psychological support.

- Prepare the client for surgery and postoperative nursing care.

Complication of Pregnancy: Gestational Trophoblastic Disease (Hydatidiform Mole, Choriocarcinoma, and Molar Pregnancy)

 Key Points

Δ **Gestational trophoblastic disease** is the **proliferation** and **degeneration** of **trophoblastic villi** in the **placenta** which becomes swollen, fluid-filled, and takes on the appearance of **grape-like clusters**. The embryo fails to develop beyond a primitive start and these structures are associated with choriocarcinoma, which is a rapidly metastasizing malignancy. **Two types** of **molar growths** are identified by chromosomal analysis.

Δ In the **complete mole**, all **genetic** material is **paternally derived**.

- The ovum has no genetic material or the material is inactive.

- The complete mole contains **no fetus**, placenta, amniotic membranes, or fluid.

- There is no placenta to receive maternal blood; therefore, hemorrhage into the uterine cavity and vaginal bleeding occurs.

- Approximately 20% of complete moles progress toward a choriocarcinoma.

Δ In the **partial mole**, **genetic** material is **derived** both **maternally** and **paternally**.

- A normal ovum is fertilized by two sperm or one sperm in which meiosis or chromosome reduction and division did not occur.

- A partial mole often contains **abnormal embryonic** or **fetal parts**, an amniotic sac, and fetal blood, but congenital anomalies are present.

- Approximately 6% of partial moles progress toward a choriocarcinoma.

Key Factors

Δ   **Risk factors** for **gestational trophoblastic disease** include:

- Low protein intake.

- Under 18 years of age.

- Older than 35 years of age.

Diagnostic and Therapeutic Procedures and Nursing Management

Δ   Serial **hCG** immunoassays for pregnancy are **strongly positive** (1 to 2 million IU compared with a normal pregnancy level of 400,000 IU) and secondary hCG is produced by the overgrowing trophoblastic cells.

Δ   An **ultrasound** will reveal a dense growth with characteristic vesicles, but no fetus in utero.

Δ   **Urinalysis** for proteinuria

Δ   **Suction curettage** to aspirate and evacuate the mole

Δ   **Following mole evacuation**, the client should undergo a **baseline pelvic exam** and **ultrasound** scan of the abdomen in addition to frequent follow-up pelvic exams.

- **Analysis** of **serum hCG** every **1 to 2 weeks until** levels are **normal**, every **2 to 4 weeks** for **6 months**, and every **2 months** for **1 year.** These analyses should be performed in this manner because levels that plateau or increase suggest a malignant transformation.

- **Chemotherapy** for choriocarcinoma in the event of an abnormal rising hCG titer, an enlarging uterus, and findings of malignant cells.

Nursing Assessments

Δ   **Monitor** for **signs** and **symptoms** of **gestational trophoblastic disease** which include:

- **Rapid uterine growth** larger than expected for the duration of the pregnancy due to the overproliferation of trophoblastic cells.

- **Vaginal bleeding** at approximately **16 weeks gestation**. Bleeding is often **dark brown** resembling **prune juice,** or bright red that is either scant or profuse and continues for a few days or intermittently for a few weeks.

- Bleeding accompanied by **discharge** from the **clear fluid-filled vesicles**.

- Excessive vomiting **(hyperemesis gravidarum)** due to **elevated hCG levels.**

- Symptoms of pregnancy-induced hypertension (PIH), including **hypertension**, **edema**, and **proteinuria**, that occur prior to 20 weeks gestation (PIH usually does not occur until after 20 weeks gestation).

Δ **Nursing assessments** for **gestational trophoblastic disease** include:

- Measuring **fundal height.**

- Assessing **vaginal bleeding** and discharge.

- Assessing **gastrointestinal status** and appetite.

- Checking vital signs.

- Assessing the client's extremities and face for edema.

NANDA Nursing Diagnoses

Δ Risk for dysfunctional grieving related to being informed of molar pregnancy

Δ Ineffective health maintenance related to failure to adhere to scheduled follow-up

Nursing Interventions

Δ **Nursing interventions** for **gestational trophoblastic disease** include:

- Advising the client to bring any **clots** or **tissue** passed to the primary care provider **for examination**.

- Administering **immune globulin** (RhoGAM) to Rh negative women.

- Providing client education about the disease procedure and emotional support regarding the loss of an anticipated pregnancy.

- Instructing the client to use reliable **contraception** for **6 months** because a pregnancy would make it impossible to monitor the decline in hCG levels, which is a significant component of follow-up care.

- Instructing the client about the **critical** importance of **follow-up** because of the increased **risk** of **choriocarcinoma.**

Complication of Pregnancy: Incompetent Cervix

 Key Points

Δ **Incompetent cervix** is the painless **passive dilation** of the **cervix** in the absence of uterine contractions. The cervix is incapable of supporting the weight and pressure of the growing fetus and results in expulsion of the products of conception during the second trimester of pregnancy. This usually occurs around week 20 of gestation.

Key Factors

Δ   **Risk factors** for an **incompetent cervix** include:

- History of **cervical trauma** (previous lacerations, excessive dilations, and curettage for biopsy).

- **In utero** exposure to **diethylstilbestrol** (ingested by the client's mother during pregnancy).

- **Congenital structural defects.**

- **Increased maternal age.**

Diagnostic and Therapeutic Procedures and Nursing Management

Δ   An **ultrasound** showing a **short cervix** (less than 20 mm in length) indicates a **reduced cervical competence**.

Δ   Prophylactic **cervical cerclage** is the surgical reinforcement of the cervix with heavy ligature placed submucosally around the cervix to strengthen it and prevent premature cervical dilation. The cerclage is removed at 37 weeks gestation.

Nursing Assessments

Δ   Monitor for **signs** and **symptoms** of an **incompetent cervix, which include:**

- Pink-stained vaginal discharge or **bleeding.**

- Increase in **pelvic pressure.**

- Possible gush of fluid (rupture of membranes).

- Uterine contractions with the expulsion of the fetus.

- Postoperative (cerclage) monitoring for uterine contractions, rupture of membranes, and signs of infection.

Δ   Nursing assessments for an incompetent cervix include:

- Evaluating the client's support systems and availability of assistance if activity restrictions and/or bedrest are prescribed.

- Assessing vaginal discharge.

- Client reports of pressure and contractions.

- Checking the client's vital signs and temperature.

NANDA Nursing Diagnoses

Δ   Impaired physical mobility related to prescribed activity restriction/bed rest

Δ   Anticipatory grieving related to possible loss of fetus

Δ   Sexual dysfunction related to being advised to refrain from intercourse

Nursing Interventions

Δ   **Nursing interventions** for an **incompetent cervix** include:

- Placing the client on **activity restriction/bed rest.**

- Encouraging **hydration** to promote a relaxed uterus (dehydration stimulates uterine contractions).

- Administering **tocolytic** prophylactically to inhibit uterine contractions.

- Advising the client to **refrain from**:

  ◊   **Intercourse.**

  ◊   **Prolonged standing** for more than 90 min.

  ◊   **Heavy lifting.**

- Providing client education about **signs** and **symptoms** to report to the primary care provider for **preterm labor**, rupture of membranes, infection, strong **contractions less than 5 min apart**, severe perineal pressure, and an urge to push.

- Instructing the client about using **the home uterine activity monitor (HUAM)** to monitor for uterine contractions.

- Arranging for the client to follow-up with a home health agency for close observation and supervision.

Complication of Pregnancy: Placenta Previa

 Key Points

Δ   **Placenta previa** occurs when the placenta **abnormally implants** in the **lower segment** of the **uterus near or over** the **cervical os** instead of attaching to the fundus. The abnormal implantation results in bleeding during the third trimester of pregnancy as the cervix begins to dilate and efface.

Δ   **Placenta previa** is classified into **three types** dependent on the degree to which the cervical os is covered by the placenta.

- **Complete** or **total** – when the cervical os is completely covered by the placental attachment.

- **Incomplete** or **partial** – when the cervical os is only partially covered by the placental attachment.

- **Marginal** or **low-lying** – when the placenta is attached in the lower uterine segment but does not reach the cervical os.

Δ The **major complications** associated with placenta previa are **maternal hemorrhage** and **fetal prematurity** or **death**.

Key Factors

Δ **Risk factors** for **placenta previa** include:

- Previous placenta previa.
- **Uterine scarring** (e.g., previous cesarean, curettage, endometritis).
- Maternal age greater than 35 years.
- **Multifetal gestation.**
- Multiple gestations or closely spaced pregnancies.

Diagnostic and Therapeutic Procedures

Δ **Transabdominal** or **transvaginal ultrasound** for **placement** of the **placenta**

Δ **Fetal monitoring** for fetal well-being assessment

Δ Hemoglobin and hematocrit for blood loss assessment

Δ Complete blood count

Δ ABO blood typing and Rh factor

Δ Coagulation profile

Δ Emergency cesarean birth

Nursing Assessments

Δ Monitor for **signs** and **symptoms** of **placenta previa,** which include:

- **Painless, bright red vaginal bleeding** that increases as the cervix dilates.
- A soft, **relaxed, nontender uterus** with **normal tone.**
- A fundal height greater than usually expected for gestational age.
- A fetus in a breech, oblique, or transverse position.
- A palpable placenta.
- Vital signs that are usual and within normal limits.

- A decreasing urinary output.

Δ **Nursing assessments** for **placenta previa** include:

- Assessing **bleeding**, leakage, or contractions.

- **Counting pads** for bleeding amount.

- An abdominal examination.

- Assessing fundal height.

- Leopold's maneuvers (fetal position and presentation).

- Checking the client's vital signs.

- Assessing fluid intake and output.

NANDA Nursing Diagnoses

Δ Decreased cardiac output related to blood loss

Δ Fear related to loss of the fetus

Δ Risk for injury to the fetus related to placenta previa

Nursing Interventions

Δ **Nursing interventions** for **placenta previa** include:

- Bed rest.

- **Nothing inserted vaginally.**

- Intravenous fluids should be administered as prescribed.

- **Corticosteroids** given for **fetal lung maturation** if delivery of the fetus is anticipated (cesarean).

- Blood replacement as prescribed.

Complication of Pregnancy: Abruptio Placenta

📖 Key Points

Δ **Abruptio placenta** is the **premature separation** of the **placenta from the uterus,** which can be a partial or complete detachment. This separation occurs after 20 weeks gestation, which is usually in the **third trimester**. It has significant maternal and fetal morbidity and mortality and is a leading cause of maternal death.

Δ Coagulation defect such as disseminated intravascular coagulopathy is often associated with moderate to severe abruption.

Key Factors

Δ **Maternal hypertension**

Δ Blunt external **abdominal trauma** (motor vehicle crash, maternal battering)

Δ **Cocaine abuse** resulting in vasoconstriction

Δ **Previous** incidents of abruptio placenta

Δ Cigarette smoking

Δ Premature rupture of membranes

Δ Short umbilical cord

Δ **Multifetal pregnancy**

Diagnostic and Therapeutic Procedures and Nursing Management

Δ **Ultrasound** for fetal well-being and **placental assessment**

Δ Hemoglobin and hematocrit decreased

Δ Coagulation factors decreased

Δ Clotting defects (DIC)

Δ Cross and type match for possible blood transfusions

Δ **Biophysical profile** to ascertain fetal well-being

Nursing Assessments

Δ Monitor for **signs** and **symptoms** of **abruptio placenta,** which include:

- **Sudden onset** of **intense localized uterine pain.**
- **Vaginal bleeding** that is bright red or dark.
- A board-like abdomen that is tender.
- A firm **rigid uterus** with contractions (**uterine hypertonicity**).
- Fetal distress.
- Symptoms of hypovolemic shock.

Δ **Nursing assessments** for **abruptio placenta** include:

- Palpating the **uterus** for **tenderness** and **tone.**
- Assessing **bleeding rate**, **amount**, and **color.**

- Assessing **fetal heart rate pattern.**
- Checking the client's vital signs.
- Assessing respiratory and cardiac sounds.
- Assessing the client's skin color and turgor.
- Capillary refill.
- Level of consciousness.
- Urinary output.

Nursing Interventions

Δ   **Nursing interventions** for **abruptio placenta** include:

- Placing the client on **bed rest.**
- **Refraining** from **vaginal exams** (may exacerbate bleeding).
- Administering **blood products** and **fluid volume replacements** to maintain the client's **urine output** at **30 mL/hr** or more and **hematocrit** at **30%** or greater.
- Administering **corticosteroids** to promote fetal lung maturity.
- Administering **immune globulin** in women who are Rh negative.
- Providing emotional support for the client and family.
- Delivering the fetus. This is the treatment of choice. If the fetus is at term, vaginal delivery is preferred. A cesarean delivery should be performed if there are indications of fetal distress or obstetrical complications (cesarean contraindicated with DIC).

Complication of Pregnancy: Hyperemesis Gravidarum (HEG)

 Key Points

Δ   **Hyperemesis gravidarum** is excessive nausea and vomiting (related to elevated hCG levels) that is prolonged past 12 weeks gestation and results in a 5% weight loss from prepregnancy weight, dehydration, electrolyte imbalance, ketosis, and acetonuria.

Δ   **Hyperemesis gravidarum** may be accompanied by liver dysfunction.

Δ   There is a **risk to** the **fetus** for **intrauterine growth restriction (IUGR)** or **preterm birth** if the condition persists.

Risk Factors

- Δ Maternal age younger than 20 years

- Δ Obesity

- Δ First pregnancy

- Δ **Multifetal gestation**

- Δ **Gestational trophoblastic disease**

- Δ Women with a history of psychiatric disorders

- Δ Transient hyperthyroidism

- Δ Vitamin B deficiencies

- Δ High stress levels

Diagnostic and Therapeutic Procedures

- Δ Urinalysis for **ketones** and acetones (breakdown of **protein** and fat) is the most important initial laboratory test.

- Δ Specific gravity elevated

- Δ Chemistry profile revealing electrolyte imbalances such as:

  - • Sodium, potassium, and chloride reduced from low intake.

  - • Acidosis resulting from excessive vomiting.

- Δ Liver enzymes elevated

- Δ Thyroid test indicating hyperthyroidism

- Δ **Hematocrit** concentration is elevated because inability to retain fluid results in hemoconcentration.

Nursing Assessments

- Δ Monitor for **signs** and **symptoms** of **hyperemesis gravidarum,** which include:

  - • **Excessive vomiting** for prolonged periods.

  - • **Dehydration** with possible electrolyte imbalance.

  - • **Weight loss.**

- Decreased blood pressure.

- Increased pulse rate.

- Poor skin turgor.

Δ **Nursing assessments** for **hyperemesis gravidarum** include:

- Intake and output.

- Skin turgor and mucus membranes.

- Vital signs.

- Weight.

NANDA Nursing Diagnoses

Δ Risk for deficient fluid volume related to excessive vomiting

Δ Imbalanced nutrition, less than body requirements, related to inability to keep down food

Nursing Interventions

Δ **Nursing interventions** for **hyperemesis gravidarum** include:

- **Nothing by mouth** (NPO) status for 24 to 48 hr.

- **Intravenous fluids** of lactated Ringer's solution for hydration.

- **Vitamin B$_6$** and other vitamin **supplements** as tolerated.

- Cautious use of **antiemetic** medications for uncontrollable nausea and vomiting (e.g., promethazine, metoclopramide).

- Use of corticosteroids to treat refractory hyperemesis gravidarum.

- Advancing to clear liquids after 24 hr if no vomiting.

- **Advancing diet as** tolerated with frequent, small meals. Start with dry toast, crackers, or cereal, then move to a soft diet, and finally to a normal diet as tolerated.

- In **severe cases,** or if vomiting returns, enteral nutrition per feeding tube or **total parental nutrition (TPN)** may be considered.

Complications of Pregnancy: Gestational Hypertension (GH)/Pregnancy-Induced Hypertension (PIH)

📖 Key Points

Δ   **Hypertensive disease** in **pregnancy** is divided into **clinical subsets** of the disease based on **end-organ effects** and **progresses along** a **continuum** from mild gestational hypertension, mild and severe preeclampsia, eclampsia, and hemolysis, elevated liver enzymes, and low platelets (HELLP) syndrome.

Δ   **Gestational hypertension**, which begins after the 20th week of pregnancy, describes hypertensive disorders of pregnancy whereby the woman has an elevated blood pressure at **140/90 mm Hg** or greater, or a **systolic increase** of **30 mm Hg** or a **diastolic increase** of **15 mm Hg** from the prepregnancy baseline. There is **no proteinuria** or **edema**. The client's blood pressure returns to baseline by 6 weeks postpartum.

Δ   **Mild preeclampsia** is GH with the addition of **proteinuria** of **1 to 2+** and a **weight gain** of more than 2 kg (4.4 lb) per week in the second and third trimesters. Mild edema will also begin to appear in the upper extremities or face.

Δ   **Severe preeclampsia** consists of **blood pressure** that is **160/100 mm Hg** or greater, **proteinuria 3 to 4+**, oliguria, elevated serum creatinine greater than 1.2 mg/dL, **cerebral** or **visual disturbances** (headache and blurred vision), **hyperreflexia** with possible ankle clonus, pulmonary or cardiac involvement, extensive **peripheral edema**, **hepatic dysfunction**, **epigastric** and **right upper quadrant pain**, and thrombocytopenia.

Δ   **Eclampsia** is **severe preeclampsia** symptoms along with the onset of **seizure** activity or **coma**. Eclampsia is usually **preceded by** headache, severe **epigastric pain**, **hyperreflexia**, and hemoconcentrations, which are **warning signs** of **probable convulsions**.

Δ   **HELLP syndrome** is a **variant of GH** in which **hematologic conditions** coexist with severe preeclampsia involving **hepatic dysfunction**. HELLP syndrome is diagnosed by laboratory tests, not clinically.

   •   **H – hemolysis** resulting in anemia and jaundice.

   •   **EL – elevated liver enzymes** resulting in elevated alanine aminotransferase (ALT) or aspartate transaminase (AST), epigastric pain, and nausea and vomiting.

   •   **LP – low platelets** (<100,000/mm^3), resulting in thrombocytopenia, abnormal bleeding and clotting time, bleeding gums, petechiae, and possibly DIC.

Δ   **Gestational hypertensive disease** and **chronic hypertension** may occur **simultaneously**.

Δ **Gestational hypertensive diseases** are associated with placental abruption, acute renal failure, hepatic rupture, **preterm birth**, and **fetal** and **maternal death**.

Key Factors

Δ **No single profile identifies risks** for **gestational hypertensive disorders,** but some high risks include:

- Maternal age younger than 19 or older than 40.
- **First pregnancy.**
- **Morbid obesity.**
- **Multifetal gestation.**
- Chronic renal disease.
- Chronic hypertension.
- Diabetes.
- Rh incompatibility.
- **Molar pregnancy.**
- **Previous history** of **GH.**

Diagnostic and Therapeutic Procedures and Management

Δ Dipstick testing of urine for **proteinuria**

Δ **Twenty-four hr urine collection** for protein and creatinine clearance

Δ Liver enzymes

Δ Serum creatinine, BUN, uric acid, and magnesium increase as renal function decreases

Δ Complete blood count

Δ Clotting studies

Δ Chemistry profile

Δ **Nonstress test**, contraction stress test, biophysical profile, and serial ultrasounds to assess fetal status

Δ **Doppler blood flow analysis** to assess maternal and fetal well-being

Nursing Assessments

Δ   Monitor for **signs** and **symptoms** of **gestational hypertensive disorders,** which include:

- Signs of **progression of hypertensive disease** with indications of worsening liver involvement, renal failure, worsening hypertension, cerebral involvement, and developing coagulopathies.

- **Rapid weight gain** (2 kg [4.4 lb]) per week in the second and third trimesters.

- **Fetal distress.**

Δ   **Vasospasm** contributing to **poor tissue perfusion** is the **underlying mechanism** for the **signs and symptoms** of **pregnancy hypertensive disorders**

Signs and Symptoms of Hypertensive Disorders of Pregnancy	
Condition:	**Results:**
Generalized vasoconstriction	Hypertension
Uteroplacental insufficiency	Intrauterine growth restriction Abruptio placenta Increased uterine contractility
Glomerular damage	Proteinuria Increased plasma uric acid and increased creatinine Oliguria Increased sodium retention
Generalized edema	Periorbital, facial, hand, and abdominal edema Pitting edema after 12 hr of bed rest
Cortical brain spasms	Severe continuous headache Hyperreflexia of deep tendons Seizure activity
Pulmonary edema	Dyspnea and crackles Diminished breath sounds
Retinal arteriolar spasms	Dimming or blurring of vision Flashes of lights or dots before the eyes Scotoma (area of lost/diminished vision)
Hemolysis of RBCs	Decreased hemoglobin Maternal hyperbilirubinemia, jaundice
Hepatic microemboli Liver damage	Elevated liver enzymes (AST, LDH) Nausea and vomiting Epigastric pain Right upper quadrant pain Decreased blood glucose Liver rupture
Platelet aggregation and fibrin deposits	Thrombocytopenia (low platelets) DIC

Δ Nursing assessments for gestational hypertensive disorders include:

- Measuring blood pressure in a standardized manner.

- Observing for edema.

- Checking deep tendon reflexes, bicep and ankle reflexes, and for ankle clonus.

- Assessing fetal heart rate for variability and late or variable decelerations.

- Monitoring respirations.

- Level of consciousness.

- Pulse oximetry.

- Urine output monitoring and clean catch urine sample to assess for proteinuria.

- Daily weights.

- Vital signs.

NANDA Nursing Diagnoses

Δ   Ineffective tissue perfusion related to vasospasm of pregnancy-induced hypertensive disorder

Δ   Risk for injury to the fetus related to gestational hypertensive disorder

Δ   Risk for injury to the mother related to gestational hypertensive disorder

Nursing Interventions

Δ   **Nursing interventions** for **gestational hypertensive disorders** include:

- Maintaining bed rest and encouraging side-lying position.

- Promoting diversional activities.

- Avoiding foods high in sodium.

- Avoiding alcohol and limiting caffeine.

- Increasing fluid intake to 8 glasses/day.

- Putting up side rails for safety and seizure precautions.

- Maintaining a dark quiet environment to avoid stimuli that may precipitate a seizure.

- Maintaining patent airway in the event of a seizure.

- Administering antihypertensive medications as prescribed.

Δ   Administer intravenous **magnesium sulfate,** the medication of choice as an **anticonvulsant** agent for prophylaxis or treatment. It will lower blood pressure and depress the central nervous system.

- Signs of **magnesium sulfate toxicity** include:

  ◊   **Absence** of **patellar** deep tendon **reflexes.**

  ◊   **Urine output less than 30 mL/hr.**

  ◊   **Respirations less than 12/min.**

  ◊   **Decreased level of consciousness.**

- If **magnesium toxicity** is suspected:

  ◊ Immediately **discontinue infusion.**

  ◊ Administer **calcium gluconate**, the **magnesium sulfate antidote**.

  ◊ Prepare for actions to prevent respiratory or cardiac arrest.

Δ **Nursing interventions** for a client receiving **magnesium sulfate** include:

- Informing the client of initially feeling flushed, hot, and sedated with the magnesium sulfate bolus.

- Monitoring the client's blood pressure, pulse, respiratory rate, DTRs, level of consciousness, urinary output (indwelling Foley for accuracy), presence of headache, visual disturbances, epigastric pain, uterine contractions, and fetal heart rate and activity.

- Placing the client on fluid restriction of 100 to 125 mL/hr and maintaining urinary output at 30 mL/hr or greater.

Complication of Pregnancy: Gestational Diabetes

Key Points

Δ Gestational diabetes is an impaired tolerance to glucose with the first onset or recognition during pregnancy. The ideal blood glucose level should fall between 60 mg/dL and 120 mg/dL

Δ Symptoms of diabetes may disappear a few weeks following delivery. However, approximately 50% of women will develop diabetes mellitus within 5 years.

Δ Gestational diabetes causes increased risks to the fetus including:

- **Spontaneous abortion,** which is related to poor glycemic control.

- **Infections** (urinary and vaginal), which are related to increased glucose in the urine and decreased resistance because of altered carbohydrate metabolism.

- **Hydramnios,** which can cause overdistention of the uterus, premature rupture of membranes, preterm labor, and hemorrhage.

- **Ketoacidosis** from diabetogenic effect of pregnancy (increased insulin resistance), untreated hyperglycemia, or inappropriate insulin dosing.

- **Hypoglycemia,** which is caused by overdosing in insulin, skipped or late meals, or increased exercise.

- **Hyperglycemia,** which can cause excessive fetal growth (macrosomia).

Key Factors

Δ **Risk factors** for **gestational diabetes** during pregnancy include:

- Maternal age older than 30 years.

- Obesity.

- Family history of diabetes.

- Previous delivery of a large or stillborn infant.

Diagnostic and Therapeutic Procedures and Management

Δ Routine urinalysis with **glycosuria**

Δ Glucola screening test/1 hr glucose tolerance test (50 g oral glucose load, followed by plasma glucose analysis 1 hr later performed at 24 to 28 weeks gestation) – fasting not necessary

Δ Three hr glucose tolerance test (following overnight fasting, avoidance of caffeine, and abstinence from smoking for 12 hr prior to testing, a fasting glucose is obtained, a 100 g glucose load is given, and serum glucose levels are determined at 1, 2, and 3 hr following glucose ingestion)

Δ Ketones are tested to assess the severity of ketoacidosis

Δ **Biophysical profile** to ascertain fetal well-being

Δ **Amniocentesis with alpha fetoprotein**

Δ **Nonstress test** to assess fetal well-being

Nursing Assessments

Δ Monitor for **signs** and **symptoms** of **gestational diabetes,** which include:

- Hunger and thirst.

- Frequent urination.

- Blurred vision.

- Excess weight gain during pregnancy.

Δ Nursing assessments for **gestational diabetes** include:

- **Monitoring blood glucose.**

- Monitoring fetus.

NANDA Nursing Diagnoses

Δ   Risk for noncompliance with diabetic diet and management related to lack of understanding

Δ   Risk for injury to mother related to macrosomic fetus or birth trauma

Δ   Risk for injury to fetus related to shoulder dystocia or uteroplacental insufficiency

Nursing Interventions

Δ   **Nursing interventions** for **gestational diabetes** include:

- **Client teaching** regarding **signs** and **symptoms** of:
  - ◊   **Hypoglycemia** (e.g., nervousness, headache, **shaking**, weakness, irritability, hunger, blurred vision, **clammy pale skin**, shallow respirations, rapid pulse, tingling of mouth or extremities, personality change).
  - ◊   **Hyperglycemia** (e.g., thirst, nausea and vomiting, abdominal pain, increased urination, **flushed dry skin**, **acetone [fruity breath]**).
- Client education about diet and exercise.
- Administration of **insulin as prescribed.**
- Client instruction on self-administration of insulin.
- **Oral hypoglycemic** medication **contraindicated** (causes **birth defects**).
- Instruct the client to perform **daily kick counts** to assure fetal well-being.

Complication of Pregnancy: TORCH Infection

Key Points, Factors, Nursing Assessments, and Management

Δ **TORCH** is an acronym for a group of infections that can negatively affect a woman who is pregnant. These infections can cross the placenta and have teratogenic affects on the fetus. TORCH does not include all the major infections that present risks to the mother and fetus.

Infection	Risk Factors	Maternal Signs and Symptoms	Management
T – toxoplasmosis	Consumption of raw or undercooked meat or handling cat feces	Influenza symptoms or lymphadenopathy	Spiramycin, sulfadine, combination of pyrimethamine, (potentially harmful to fetus, but parasitic treatment essential) and sulfadiazine
O – other infections	Varies	Dependent on infection	Dependent on infection
R – rubella (German measles)	Contact with children who have rashes or infants born to mothers who had rubella during pregnancy	Rash, muscle aches, joint pain, mild lymphedema, fetal consequences including miscarriage, congenital anomalies, and death	Vaccination of pregnant women is contraindicated because rubella infection may develop. Pregnant women should avoid crowds of young children. Immunize women with low titers prior to pregnancy.
C – cytomegalovirus (member of herpes virus family)	Transmitted by droplet infection from person to person, virus found in semen, cervical, and vaginal secretions, breast milk, placental tissue, urine, feces, and blood. Latent virus may be reactivated and cause disease to the fetus in utero or during passage through birth canal.	Asymptomatic or mononucleosis-like symptoms	No treatment for infection exists. Prevent exposure by frequent handwashing before eating and avoiding crowds of young children.
H – herpes simplex virus (HSV)	Direct contact with oral or genital lesions. Transmission to the fetus is greatest during vaginal birth if the woman has active lesions.	Lesions Initial outbreak	Obtain cultures on women with HSV at or near term. Cesarean delivery is recommended only for mothers with active lesions.

Diagnostic and Therapeutic Procedures and Management

Δ   TORCH screen is an immunologic survey to identify existence of these infections in the mother (to identify fetal risks) or in the newborn (detection of antibodies against infections)

Δ   Prenatal screenings and educating the public is important

Nursing interventions

Δ   Monitor fetal well-being.

Δ   Emphasize to the client the importance of compliance with prescribed treatment.

Δ   Provide client education and emotional support.

Δ   Administer antibiotics as prescribed.

Primary Reference:

Lowdermilk, D. L. & Perry, S. E. (2004). *Maternity & women's health care* (8th ed.). St. Louis, MO: Mosby.

Additional Resources:

Hogan, M., & Glazebrook, R. (2003). *Maternal-newborn nursing*. Upper Saddle River, NJ: Pearson Education, Inc.

Ladewig, P., London, M., & Davidson, M. (2006). *Contemporary maternal-newborn nursing care* (6th ed.). Upper Saddle River, NJ: Pearson Education, Inc.

NANDA International (2004). *NANDA nursing diagnoses: Definitions and classification 2005-2006*. Philadelphia: NANDA.

Chapter 8: Complications of Pregnancy

Application Exercises

1. A nurse is caring for a 16-year-old client who is gravida 1 para 0. The client is admitted to the labor unit having no prenatal care. The client is showing signs of early labor and ruptured membranes. She has a blood pressure of 168/102 mm Hg. She has 3+ protein in her urine, and her face and hands are swollen. What initial medication should the nurse expect to be prescribed for this client?

      A. Calcium gluconate

      B. Oxytocin

      C. Magnesium sulfate

      D. Prostaglandin

2. A woman arrives in the emergency department with abrupt, sharp right-sided lower quadrant abdominal pain, and bright red vaginal spotting. She has missed one menstrual cycle. She tells the nurse that she cannot be pregnant because she has been using an intrauterine device. The nurse should suspect which of the following?

      A. Missed abortion

      B. Ectopic pregnancy

      C. Severe preeclampsia

      D. Hydatidiform mole

3. A client who is pregnant presents with gestational hypertension. Which of the following is the primary adverse effect of this disorder that results in risk to the fetus?

      A. Enlargement of the liver

      B. Increased urinary output

      C. Uteroplacental insufficiency

      D. Pulmonary edema

4. Women with gestational diabetes are at a higher risk for urinary tract infections because they

      A. spill more glucose into the urine.

      B. develop insulin resistance.

      C. have a daily fluid restriction.

      D. have higher ketones in the urine.

5. A client with gestational hypertension reports to the nurse a worsening "stomach pain." The nurse assesses the client's deep tendon reflexes and notes them to be 4+ with positive ankle clonus. Based on this assessment, the nurse should

    A. obtain a urine specimen to assess for proteinuria.

    B. explain that this is normal because of fetal growth.

    C. anticipate the administration of calcium gluconate.

    D. raise padded side rails and darken the room.

6. Magnesium sulfate is being administered intravenously to a client who has severe preeclampsia for seizure prophylaxis. Which of the following indicate magnesium sulfate toxicity? (Select all that apply.)

    _____ Respirations less than 12/min

    _____ Urinary output less than 50 mL/min

    _____ Hyperreflexic deep tendon reflexes

    _____ Decreased level of consciousness

    _____ Flushing and sweating

7. A group of infections that can negatively affect a pregnant woman and are teratogenic to the fetus are referred to as

    A. PIH/GH.

    B. TORCH.

    C. HUAM.

    D. PROM.

8. A client at 4 months gestation comes for a prenatal visit. The client reports continued nausea and vomiting and scant, prune-colored discharge. She has experienced no weight loss and has a fundal height larger than expected for the duration of pregnancy. Which of the following complications should the nurse suspect?

    A. Hyperemesis gravidarum

    B. Threatened abortion

    C. Hydatidiform mole

    D. Preterm labor

Chapter 8: Complications of Pregnancy

Application Exercises Answer Key

1. A nurse is caring for a 16-year-old client who is gravida 1 para 0. The client is admitted to the labor unit having no prenatal care. The client is showing signs of early labor and ruptured membranes. She has a blood pressure of 168/102 mm Hg. She has 3+ protein in her urine, and her face and hands are swollen. What initial medication should the nurse expect to be prescribed for this client?

> A. Calcium gluconate
>
> B. Oxytocin
>
> **C. Magnesium sulfate**
>
> D. Prostaglandin

Magnesium sulfate is an anticonvulsant that would be prescribed for this client who is exhibiting signs and symptoms of severe preeclampsia as evidenced by the elevated blood pressure and 3+ proteinuria. Depending on her gestational age, the primary care provider may want to augment her labor and order a Pitocin (oxytocin) drip. Calcium gluconate is the antidote for magnesium sulfate and will be a standing order to be administered in the event of magnesium sulfate toxicity. Prostaglandin is administered into the amniotic sac or by a vaginal suppository to augment or induce labor.

2. A woman arrives in the emergency department with abrupt, sharp right-sided lower quadrant abdominal pain, and bright red vaginal spotting. She has missed one menstrual cycle. She tells the nurse that she cannot be pregnant because she has been using an intrauterine device. The nurse should suspect which of the following?

> A. Missed abortion
>
> **B. Ectopic pregnancy**
>
> C. Severe preeclampsia
>
> D. Hydatidiform mole

Signs and symptoms of an ectopic pregnancy include unilateral lower quadrant abdominal pain with or without bleeding. A missed abortion occurs when products of conception are retained and there is a brownish discharge. Severe preeclampsia does not have vaginal bleeding unless initiated by worsening complications and presents with an epigastric, right upper quadrant pain. Hydatidiform mole causes dark brown bleeding in the second trimester and is not generally accompanied by abdominal pain.

3. A client who is pregnant presents with gestational hypertension. Which of the following is the primary adverse effect of this disorder that results in risk to the fetus?

      A. Enlargement of the liver

      B. Increased urinary output

      C. Uteroplacental insufficiency

      D. Pulmonary edema

Vasospasm of the vessels supplying the placenta results in uteroplacental insufficiency. Urinary output decreases as the renal glomeruli are damaged. The liver is at risk for rupture from venous congestion caused by microemboli. The fetus is at risk for intrauterine growth restriction from the poor perfusion of the placenta, not macrosomia (large for gestational age).

4. Women with gestational diabetes are at a higher risk for urinary tract infections because they

      A. spill more glucose into the urine.

      B. develop insulin resistance.

      C. have a daily fluid restriction.

      D. have higher ketones in the urine.

Diabetic mothers are at an increased risk for urinary tract infections related to increased glucose in the urine. Ketoacidosis can result from the diabetogenic effect of pregnancy as insulin resistance increases, commonly resulting from untreated hyperglycemia or inappropriate insulin dosing. There is no fluid restriction for gestational diabetes. Ketones are tested to assess the severity of acidosis.

5. A client with gestational hypertension reports to the nurse a worsening "stomach pain." The nurse assesses the client's deep tendon reflexes and notes them to be 4+ with positive ankle clonus. Based on this assessment, the nurse should

      A. obtain a urine specimen to assess for proteinuria.

      B. explain that this is normal because of fetal growth.

      C. anticipate the administration of calcium gluconate.

      D. raise padded side rails and darken the room.

Hyperreflexia and epigastric pain are premonitory signs of a seizure. The nurse should institute seizure precautions and provide for safety by raising the padded bedrails and darkening the room to decrease stimulation. Proteinuria is an indication of preeclampsia, but a urine specimen should not be obtained at this time when the client has indications of imminent convulsions. Calcium gluconate is the antidote for magnesium sulfate, the anticonvulsant of choice.

6. Magnesium sulfate is being administered intravenously to a client who has severe preeclampsia for seizure prophylaxis. Which of the following indicate magnesium sulfate toxicity? (Select all that apply.)

__X__	**Respirations less than 12/min**
_____	Urinary output less than 50 mL/min
_____	Hyperreflexic deep tendon reflexes
__X__	**Decreased level of consciousness**
_____	Flushing and sweating

Signs of magnesium sulfate toxicity include the absence of patellar deep tendon reflexes, urine output less than 30 mL/hr, respirations less than 12/min, and a decreased level of consciousness. Flushing and sweating are side effects of magnesium sulfate but are not signs of toxicity.

7. A group of infections that can negatively affect a pregnant woman and are teratogenic to the fetus are referred to as

A. PIH/GH.

B. TORCH.

C. HUAM.

D. PROM.

TORCH is a group of infectious diseases that are harmful to the pregnant woman and teratogenic to the fetus. TORCH refers to toxoplasmosis, other infections, rubella, cytomegalovirus, and herpes. PIH/GH refers to pregnancy induced hypertension and gestational hypertension. HUAM refers to the home uterine activity monitoring device. PROM refers to premature rupture of membranes.

8. A client at 4 months gestation comes for a prenatal visit. The client reports continued nausea and vomiting and scant, prune-colored discharge. She has experienced no weight loss and has a fundal height larger than expected for the duration of pregnancy. Which of the following complications should the nurse suspect?

        A. Hyperemesis gravidarum

        B. Threatened abortion

        C. Hydatidiform mole

        D. Preterm labor

Hydatidiform mole (gestational trophoblastic disease) exhibits a uterine size that increases abnormally fast. The trophoblastic tissue causes abnormally high levels of hCG that result in excessive nausea and emesis. There is no fetus present on the ultrasound. There may be scant or profuse dark brown or red vaginal bleeding that first occurs in the second trimester, usually around the 16th week of gestation. Hyperemesis gravidarum is accompanied by weight loss and dehydration. Threatened abortion occurs in the first trimester and is indicated by spotting to moderate bleeding, but the uterus is not abnormally enlarged. Preterm labor presents prior to 37 weeks gestation and is accompanied by pink-stained vaginal discharge and uterine contractions that become more regular.

Unit 2   Intrapartum

Chapter 9:   Labor and Birth Processes
Contributor: Sandra Mesics, MSN, RN, CNM

NCLEX-RN® Connections:

Learning Objective: Review and apply knowledge within "**Labor and Birth Processes**" in readiness for performance of the following nursing activities as outlined by the NCLEX-RN® test plan:

Δ   Monitor the mother and fetus during labor and birth.

Δ   Identify the factors that affect the labor and birth process.

Δ   Identify the onset of true labor and intervene as indicated.

Δ   Recognize the different stages of labor and the client's reponses to each.

Key Points

Δ   The intrapartum nurse cares for three clients during each labor and birth:

• Fetus

• Mother

• Family unit

Δ   There are physiological changes that precede the onset of labor.

Δ   The intrapartum nurse collects assessment data on maternal and fetal well-being during labor, the progress of labor, and psychosocial and cultural factors that affect labor.

Key Factors

Five factors affecting the labor and birth process (the five "Ps")

Δ   **Passenger** – consists of the fetus and the placenta. The size of the fetal head, fetal presentation, lie, position, and attitude affect the ability of the fetus to navigate the birth canal. The placenta can be considered a passenger because it must also pass through the canal.

• **Lie** – the relationship of the maternal longitudinal axis (spine) to the fetal longitudinal axis (spine).

132

◊ **Transverse** – fetal long axis is horizontal and forms a right angle to maternal axis and will not accommodate vaginal birth. The shoulder is the presenting part and may require delivery by cesarean birth if the fetus does not spontaneously rotate.

◊ **Parallel or longitudinal** – fetal long axis is parallel to maternal long axis, either a cephalic or breech presentation. Breech presentation may require a cesarean birth.

- **Attitude** – relationship of fetal body parts to one another.

  ◊ **Fetal flexion** – chin flexed to chest, extremities flexed into torso.

  ◊ **Fetal extension** – chin extended away from chest, extremities extended.

- **Presentation** – the part of the fetus that is entering the pelvic inlet first. It can be the back of the head (occiput), chin (mentum), shoulder (scapula), or breech (sacrum).

- **Fetopelvic or fetal position** – the relationship of the presenting part of the fetus (sacrum, mentum, or occiput) preferably the occiput, in reference to its directional position as it relates to one of the four maternal pelvic quadrants. It is labeled with three letters.

  ◊ The first letter references either the right (R) or left (L) side of the maternal pelvis.

  ◊ The second letter references the presenting part of the fetus, either occiput (O), sacrum (S), mentum (M), or scapula (Sc).

  ◊ The third letter references either the anterior (A), posterior (P), or transverse (T) part of the maternal pelvis.

- **Station** – measurement of fetal descent in centimeters with station 0 being at the level of an imaginary line at the level of the ischial spines, minus stations superior to the ischial spines, and plus stations inferior to the ischial spines.

Δ **Passageway** – the birth canal, which is composed of the bony pelvis, cervix, pelvic floor, vagina, and introitus (vaginal opening). The size and shape of the bony pelvis must be adequate to allow the fetus to pass through it. The cervix must dilate and efface in response to contractions and fetal descent.

Δ **Powers** – uterine contractions cause effacement and dilation of the cervix and descent of the fetus. Involuntary urge to push and voluntary bearing down in the second stage helps in the expulsion of the fetus.

Δ **Position of laboring woman** – the client should engage in frequent position changes during labor to increase comfort, relieve fatigue, and promote circulation. Position during second stage is determined by maternal preference, primary care provider preference, the condition of the mother and the fetus.

- Gravity can aid in the fetal descent in upright, sitting, kneeling, and squatting positions.

Δ **Psychological response** – maternal stress, tension, and anxiety can produce physiological changes that impair the progress of labor.

Therapeutic and Diagnostic Procedures and Nursing Interventions:

Δ **Leopold's maneuvers** – abdominal palpation of the number of fetuses, the fetal presenting part, lie, attitude, descent, and the probable location where fetal heart tones may be best auscultated on the woman's abdomen.

Δ **External electronic monitoring (tocotransducer)** – separate transducer applied to maternal abdomen over the fundus that measures uterine activity.

- Displays uterine contraction patterns.

- Easily applied by the nurse, but must be repositioned with maternal movement to assure proper placement.

Δ **Intrauterine pressure catheter (IUPC)** – solid, sterile water-filled catheter inserted inside uterus that measures intrauterine pressure.

- Displays uterine contraction patterns on monitor.

- Requires ruptured membranes and sufficiently dilated cervix to be utilized.

Δ **Laboratory analysis**

- **Urinalysis** – clean catch urine samples obtained to ascertain maternal:

◊ Hydration status via specific gravity.

◊ Nutritional status via ketones.

◊ Proteinuria indicative of pregnancy-induced hypertension.

◊ Urinary tract infection via bacterial count.

- **Blood tests**

◊ Hematocrit level

◊ ABO typing and Rh factor if not previously done.

Assessment and Nursing Diagnoses

Δ   **Assessment of uterine labor contraction** characteristics may be performed by palpation (placing hand over the fundus and describing the contraction intensity as well as manually counting contraction frequency and duration) or by the use of the external or internal monitoring.

- **Frequency** – established from the beginning of one contraction to the beginning of the next.

- **Duration** – the time between the beginning of a contraction to the end of that same contraction.

- **Intensity** – strength of the contraction at its peak described as mild, moderate, or strong.

- **Resting tone of uterine contractions** – tone of the uterine muscle in between contractions.

    ◊   A prolonged contraction duration or too frequent contractions without sufficient time for uterine relaxation in between can reduce blood flow to the placenta. This can result in fetal hypoxia which, decreases the fetal heart rate.

Δ   **Vaginal examination** – performed digitally by the primary care provider or qualified nurse to assess for:

- Cervical dilation (stretching of cervical os adequate to allow fetal passage) and effacement (cervical thinning and shortening).

- Descent of the fetus through the birth canal as measured by fetal station in centimeters.

- Fetal position, presenting part, and lie.

- Membranes – intact or ruptured.

Characteristics of True vs. False Labor (Braxton Hicks contractions) True labor leads to cervical dilation and effacement	
True Labor	**False Labor**
Contractions • Regular frequency • Stronger, last longer, and are more frequent • Felt in lower back, radiating to abdomen • Walking can increase contraction intensity • Continue despite comfort measures	**Contractions** • Painless, irregular frequency, and intermittent • Decrease in frequency, duration, and intensity with walking or position changes • Felt in lower back or abdomen above umbilicus • Often stop with comfort measures such as oral hydration
Cervix (assessed by vaginal exam) • Progressive change in dilation and effacement • Moves to anterior portion • Bloody show	**Cervix (assessed by vaginal exam)** • No significant change in dilation or effacement • Often remains in posterior position • No significant bloody show
Fetus • Presenting part engages in pelvis	**Fetus** • Presenting part is not engaged in pelvis

Δ **Physiologic changes preceding labor (premonitory signs)** include:

- **Lightening** – fetal head descends into true pelvis about 14 days before labor. Feeling that the fetus has "dropped." Easier breathing, but more pressure on bladder, resulting in urinary frequency. More pronounced in primigravidas.

- **Backache** – a constant low, dull backache, caused by pelvic muscle relaxation.

- **Contractions** – beginning with irregular uterine contractions (Braxton Hicks) that eventually progress in strength and regularity.

- **Bloody show** – brownish or blood-tinged mucus discharge caused by expulsion of the cervical mucus plug resulting from the onset of cervical dilation and effacement.

- **Weight loss** – a 0.5 to 1 kg (1 to 3 lb) weight loss.

- **Energy burst** – sometimes called "nesting" response.

- **Gastrointestinal changes** – less common, include nausea, vomiting, and indigestion.

- **Rupture of membranes** – spontaneous rupture of membranes can initiate labor or can occur anytime during labor, most commonly during the transition phase.

  ◊ Labor usually occurs within 24 hr of rupture of membranes.

  ◊ Prolonged rupture of membranes greater than 24 hr before delivery of fetus may lead to an infection.

  ◊ Immediately following the rupture of membranes, the nurse should assess the fetal heart rate for abrupt decelerations indicative of fetal distress to rule out umbilical cord prolapse.

Δ **Assessment of amniotic fluid** – completed once the membranes rupture.

- **Color** should be pale to straw yellow

- **Odor** should not be foul

- **Clarity** should appear watery and clear

- **Volume** is between 500 to 1,200 mL

- **Nitrazine paper** should be utilized by the nurse to test any fluid to confirm that it is amniotic fluid.

  ◊ Nitrazine tests the pH of the fluid and will turn deep blue indicating the **alkalinity** of amniotic fluid and will remain yellow indicating slight acidity if the fluid is urine.

Δ **Mechanism of labor** – the adaptations the fetus makes as it progresses through the birth canal during the birthing process.

- **Engagement** – occurs when the presenting part, usually biparietal (largest) diameter of the fetal head passes the pelvic inlet at the level of the ischial spines. Referred to as station 0.

- **Descent** – the progress of the presenting part (preferably the occiput) through the pelvis. Measured by station during a vaginal examination, as either negative (#) station measured in centimeters if superior to station 0 and not yet engaged or positive (#) station measured in centimeters if inferior to station 0.

- **Flexion** – when the fetal head meets resistance of the cervix, pelvic wall, or pelvic floor. The head flexes bringing the chin close to the chest, presenting a smaller diameter to pass through the pelvis.

- **Internal rotation** – the fetal occiput ideally rotates to a lateral anterior position as it progresses from the ischial spines to the lower pelvis in a corkscrew motion to pass through the pelvis.

- **Extension** – the fetal occiput passes under the symphysis pubis and then the head is deflected anteriorly and is born by extension of the chin away from the fetal chest.

- **Restitution and external rotation** – after the head is born it rotates to the position it occupied as it entered the pelvic inlet (restitution) in alignment with the fetal body and completes a quarter turn to face transverse as the anterior shoulder passes under the symphysis.

- **Expulsion** – after birth of the head and shoulders the trunk of the infant is born by flexing it toward the symphysis pubis.

Stages of Labor			
Stage	Begins with:	Ends with:	Maternal Characteristics:
First stage <u>Duration Primigravida:</u> On average, 8 to 10 hr after reaching active phase <u>Duration Multigravida:</u> On average, 2 to 10 hr after reaching active phase	• Onset of labor	• Complete dilation	• Cervical dilation 1 cm/hr for primigravidas and 1.5 cm/hr for multigravida, on average.
Latent Phase	• Cervix 0 cm • Irregular, mild to moderate contractions • Frequency 5 to 30 min • Duration 30 to 45 sec	• Cervix 3 cm	• Some dilation and effacement • Talkative and eager
Active Phase	• Cervix 4 cm • More regular, moderate to strong contractions • Frequency 3 to 5 min • Duration 40 to 70 sec	• Cervix 7 cm dilated	• Rapid dilation and effacement • Some fetal descent • Feelings of helplessness • Anxiety and restlessness increase as contractions become stronger

Stage	Begins with:	Ends with:	Maternal Characteristics:
Transition	• Cervix 8 to 10 cm • Strong to very strong contractions • Frequency 2 to 3 min • Duration 45 to 90 sec	• Complete dilation at 10 cm	• Tired, restless, and irritable • Feeling out of control, client often states, "cannot continue" • May have nausea and vomiting • Urge to push • Increased rectal pressure and feelings of needing to have bowel movement • Increased bloody show • Most difficult part of labor
Second Stage Duration Primigravida: 30 min to 3 hr Duration Multigravida: 5 to 30 min	• Full dilation • Intense contractions every 1 to 2 min	• Birth	• Pushing results in birth of fetus
Third Stage Duration Primigravida and Multigravida: 5 to 30 min	• Delivery of infant	• Delivery of placenta	• Placental separation and expulsion • Schultze presentation: Shiny fetal surface of placenta emerges first • Duncan presentation: Dull maternal surface of placenta emerges first
Fourth Stage Duration Primigravida and Multigravida: 1 to 4 hr	• Delivery of placenta	• Maternal stabilization of vital signs	• Achievement of vital sign homeostasis • Lochia scant to moderate rubra

NANDA Nursing Diagnoses:

    Δ   Risk for infection related to rupture of membranes

    Δ   Risk for injury related to onset of labor

Primary Reference:

Lowdermilk, D. L. & Perry, S. E. (2004). *Maternity & women's health care* (8th ed.). St. Louis, MO: Mosby.

Additional Resources:

Murray, S. S., & McKinney, E. S., (2006). *Foundations of maternal-newborn nursing* (4th ed.). Philadelphia: Elsevier.

NANDA International (2004). *NANDA Nursing diagnoses: Definitions and classification 2005-2006*. Philadelphia: NANDA.

Chapter 9: Labor and Birth Processes

Application Exercises

1. A client at 38 weeks gestation tells the nurse that it feels like her baby is sitting on her bladder causing her to urinate more frequently. However, the client states it has made it easier for her to breathe. The nurse recognizes that this is a sign of

 A. lightening.

 B. quickening.

 C. contractions.

 D. flexion.

2. A client reports that her contractions started about 2 hr ago, did not go away when she had two glasses of water and rested, and became stronger since she started walking. She thinks the contractions occur every 10 min and last about half a minute. She hasn't had any fluid leak from her vagina, however, she did think she saw some blood when she wiped after voiding. The nurse should recognize that the client is experiencing

 A. Braxton Hicks contractions.

 B. rupture of membranes.

 C. fetal descent.

 D. true contractions.

3. A nurse applies an external fetal monitor and tocotransducer to monitor the fetal heart rate (FHR) and contractions of a client in labor. The FHR is in the 140s. Contractions are every 8 min and 30 to 40 sec in duration. The nurse performs a vaginal exam and finds the cervix is 2 cm dilated, 50% effaced, and the fetus is at a -2 station. One hour later, contractions are every 5 min and 30 to 45 sec in duration, the dilation is still 2 cm, but now the effacement is 80%. Which of the following stages and phases of labor is this client experiencing?

 A. The first stage, latent phase

 B. The first stage, active phase

 C. The first stage, transition phase

 D. The second stage of labor

4. A nurse is admitting a client to the birthing unit. The client suddenly states, "I think I urinated on myself. It's all wet down there, I'm so embarrassed." Which of the following actions should the nurse take at this time?

      A. Test the fluid with Nitrazine paper, which will confirm urine by turning it blue.

      B. Test the fluid with Nitrazine paper, which will confirm urine by turning it pink.

      C. Test the fluid with Nitrazine paper, which will confirm amniotic fluid by turning it blue.

      D. Test the fluid with Nitrazine paper, which will confirm amniotic fluid by turning it yellow.

5. A client experiences a large gush of fluid from her vagina while walking in the hallway of the birthing unit. The nurse's first nursing action after establishing the fluid is amniotic fluid should be to

      A. test the amniotic fluid for meconium.

      B. monitor fetal heart rate for distress.

      C. dry the client and make her comfortable.

      D. monitor the client's maternal contractions.

6. While conducting an admission history for a client at 39 weeks gestation, the client tells the nurse that she has been leaking water from her vagina for 2 days. The nurse knows that this client is at risk for

      A. cord prolapse.

      B. infection.

      C. malpresentation.

      D. hydramnios.

7. A client in active labor becomes nauseous with emesis, is very irritable, and feels she needs to have a bowel movement. She states, "I've had enough. I can't do this anymore. I want to go home right now." The nurse knows that these signs indicate the client is in the

      A. second stage of labor.

      B. fourth stage of labor.

      C. transition phase of labor.

      D. latent phase of labor.

Chapter 9: Labor and Birth Processes

Application Exercises Answer Key

1. A client at 38 weeks gestation tells the nurse that it feels like her baby is sitting on her bladder causing her to urinate more frequently. However, the client states it has made it easier for her to breathe. The nurse recognizes that this is a sign of

>   **A. lightening.**
>   B. quickening.
>   C. contractions.
>   D. flexion.

The client has experienced lightening, whereby the fetus drops down as it prepares to engage. This puts more pressure on the bladder but can alleviate difficulty breathing and indigestion problems. Quickening is the early fetal movements felt by the mother. Contractions occur in the uterine muscle. Flexion pertains to fetal attitude.

2. A client reports that her contractions started about 2 hr ago, did not go away when she had two glasses of water and rested, and became stronger since she started walking. She thinks the contractions occur every 10 min and last about half a minute. She hasn't had any fluid leak from her vagina, however, she did think she saw some blood when she wiped after voiding. The nurse should recognize that the client is experiencing

>   A. Braxton Hicks contractions.
>   B. rupture of membranes.
>   C. fetal descent.
>   **D. true contractions.**

True contractions do not go away with hydration or walking. Instead, they are regular in frequency, duration, and intensity, and become stronger with walking. Braxton Hicks contractions decrease with hydration and walking. Fetal descent is the downward movement of the fetus in the birth canal. Rupture of membranes is when the amniotic membranes rupture and allow the amniotic fluid to escape.

3. A nurse applies an external fetal monitor and tocotransducer to monitor the fetal heart rate (FHR) and contractions of a client in labor. The FHR is in the 140s. Contractions are every 8 min and 30 to 40 sec in duration. The nurse performs a vaginal exam and finds the cervix is 2 cm dilated, 50% effaced, and the fetus is at a -2 station. One hour later, contractions are every 5 min and 30 to 45 sec in duration, the dilation is still 2 cm, but now the effacement is 80%. Which of the following stages and phases of labor is this client experiencing?

    A. The first stage, latent phase

    B. The first stage, active phase

    C. The first stage, transition phase

    D. The second stage of labor

In stage 1, latent phase, the cervix dilates from 0 to 3 cm, and contraction duration ranges from 30 to 45 sec. In stage 1, active phase, the cervix dilates from 4 to 7 cm, and contraction duration ranges from 40 to 70 sec. In stage 1, transition phase, the cervix dilates from 8 to 10 cm, and contraction duration ranges from 45 to 90 sec. The second stage of labor consists of the expulsion of the fetus.

4. A nurse is admitting a client to the birthing unit. The client suddenly states, "I think I urinated on myself. It's all wet down there, I'm so embarrassed." Which of the following actions should the nurse take at this time?

    A. Test the fluid with Nitrazine paper, which will confirm urine by turning it blue.

    B. Test the fluid with Nitrazine paper, which will confirm urine by turning it pink.

    C. Test the fluid with Nitrazine paper, which will confirm amniotic fluid by turning it blue.

    D. Test the fluid with Nitrazine paper, which will confirm amniotic fluid by turning it yellow.

Nitrazine paper will confirm the alkalinity of amniotic fluid by turning it blue. If the fluid is urine, which is acidic, the Nitrazine paper will remain yellow.

5. A client experiences a large gush of fluid from her vagina while walking in the hallway of the birthing unit. The nurse's first nursing action after establishing the fluid is amniotic fluid should be to

      A. test the amniotic fluid for meconium.

      B. monitor fetal heart rate for distress.

      C. dry the client and make her comfortable.

      D. monitor the client's maternal contractions.

Fetal heart rate (FHR) must be monitored for distress. There is a high risk of umbilical cord prolapse with the rupture of membranes, and therefore, FHR is the first thing the nurse should assess once rupture of membranes has been established.

6. While conducting an admission history for a client at 39 weeks gestation, the client tells the nurse that she has been leaking water from her vagina for 2 days. The nurse knows that this client is at risk for

      A. cord prolapse.

      B. infection.

      C. malpresentation.

      D. hydramnios.

Rupture of membranes exceeding 24 hr before delivery increases the risk of infectious organisms entering vaginally into the uterus. While cord prolapse is a risk with rupture of membranes it occurs when the fluid rushes out rather than trickling or leaking out. Malpresentation has nothing to do with the amniotic fluid. Hydramnios means excess amniotic fluid. The client is more likely to have oligohydramnios or insufficient amniotic fluid.

7. A client in active labor becomes nauseous with emesis, is very irritable, and feels she needs to have a bowel movement. She states, "I've had enough. I can't do this anymore. I want to go home right now." The nurse knows that these signs indicate the client is in the

> A. second stage of labor.
>
> B. fourth stage of labor.
>
> **C. transition phase of labor.**
>
> D. latent phase of labor.

The transition phase of labor is the phase where the client becomes irritable, feels rectal pressure that can feel similar to the need to have a bowel movement, and can become nauseous with emesis. The second stage of labor is when the fetus is expulsed. The fourth stage is the recovery period. The latent phase of stage 1 is the beginning of labor and the client is more relaxed, talkative, and eager for labor to progress.

Unit 2　　　　　**Intrapartum**

Chapter 10:　　　**Pain Management: Pharmacologic and Nonpharmacologic**
Contributors: Patricia S. Kupina, EdD, MSN, BSN, RN
　　　　　　　　Lora McGuire, MSN, BSN

NCLEX-RN® Connections:

Δ　**Learning Objective:** Review and apply knowledge within **"Pain Management: Pharmacologic and Nonpharmacologic"** in readiness for performance of the following nursing activities as outlined by the NCLEX-RN® test plan:

- Reinforce and/or teach the client relaxation techniques to assist with the pain of labor.

- Assess and respect the client's rating of pain and level of discomfort throughout labor.

- Assess the client's reaction to nonpharmacologic interventions.

- Plan and provide pharmacologic and nonpharmacologic comfort interventions as appropriate.

- Observe cultural differences in how the client responds and perceives labor pain.

Key Points

Δ　**Gate-control theory of pain** is based on the concept that the sensory nerve pathways that pain sensations use to travel to the brain will only allow a limited number of sensations to travel at any given time. By sending alternate signals through these pathways, the pain signals can be blocked from ascending the neurological pathway and inhibit the brain's perception and sensation of pain.

Δ　The gate-control theory of pain assists in the understanding of how nonpharmacologic pain techniques can work to relieve pain.

Δ **Expressions of pain** and **coping behaviors vary** by individual and **cultural influences**. A nurse should incorporate knowledge about beliefs and behaviors among varying cultural groups in relation to the expression of pain into the nursing plan of care.

- In some cultures, **outward expression** of pain by the client will bring shame on the family.

- In other cultures, outward expression of pain is accepted or expected. The client will be vocally expressive, cry out, and moan during labor.

Δ **Nonpharmacologic pain measures** seek to reduce anxiety, fear, and tension, which are major contributing factors of pain in labor.

Δ **Pharmacologic analgesia** alleviates pain sensations or raises the threshold for pain perception.

Δ **Pharmacologic anesthesia** eliminates pain perceptions by interrupting the nerve impulses to the brain.

Δ **Safety** for the mother and fetus must be the first consideration of the nurse when planning pain management measures.

Key Factors

Δ **Pain** is a **subjective** and **individual** experience, and each client's response to the pain of labor is unique and can be influenced by:

- Cultural background.

- Anxiety.

- Fear.

- Fatigue.

- Full bladder.

- Individual pain tolerance.

- Previous experiences with pain.

- Fetal malposition.

- Cephalopelvic disproportion.

- Childbirth preparation.

- Level of support during labor.

Δ   **Anxiety** and **fear** are associated with pain. As fear and anxiety increase, muscle tension increases, and thus the experience of pain increases. This can become an increasing cycle of pain. The fear, tension, and pain cycle is illustrated below.

Δ   **Pain level** cannot always be assessed by monitoring the outward expressions of the client's pain. Client pain assessment may require persistent questioning and astute observation by the nurse. Cultural **beliefs** and **behaviors** of women during labor and delivery can affect the client's pain management.

- Cultural beliefs and behaviors include:

  ◊   **Native American** and **Cambodian** clients may be **stoic** during labor and birth with reduced outward expressions of pain.

  ◊   **Ethiopian** clients may be **stoic,** but take an **active** role in labor.

  ◊   **Hmong** clients are usually **quiet** and **passive**.

  ◊   **Cuban** clients may be **vocal** but **passive** during labor and delivery.

  ◊   **Arabic** clients may be **passive** but very **expressive** and may have a **low pain tolerance.**

  ◊   **Filipino** clients may assume an **active** role during labor.

  ◊   **African American**, **Puerto Rican**, and **Central American** (Guatemala, Nicaragua, and Salvador) clients may **participate actively** and be **very vocal** in labor.

  ◊   **Chinese** clients may be **vocal** during labor but consider it impolite to accept something the first time it is offered. Therefore, pain medications must be offered more than once. Chinese clients will not pause in a doorway while in labor if ambulating, believing this causes prolonged labor. Chinese clients may request the doors and windows to be unlocked**,** as this is thought to ease the passage of the infant.

  ◊   **Hindu, Sikh, Muslim, Nepalese, Fijian, Pakistani**, and **West Indian** (Trinidad, Jamaica, and Barbados) clients may assume a **passive role** and follow the primary care provider's instructions.

  ◊   **Korean** clients may **participate actively** in labor and be **compliant** with the primary care provider.

  ◊   **Japanese** clients may be **assertive** during labor but may not ask for pain medication.

  ◊   **Vietnamese** clients may believe in an **expectation** to **"suffer in silence."**

◊ **Mexican-American** clients may believe the **supine position** is optimal for the fetus, **accept pain,** and be **active** in labor.

◊ **Brazilian** clients may not participate in **coping techniques** during delivery and should be offered pain relief options.

Δ **Sources of pain** during the stages of labor include:

- **First stage** – labor pain is an internal visceral pain that may be felt as back and leg pain. Pain is caused by:

  ◊ Dilation, effacement, and stretching of the cervix.

  ◊ Distention of the lower uterine segment.

  ◊ Contractions of the uterus with resultant uterine ischemia.

- **Second stage** – labor pain with the event of fetal descent and expulsion is a localized somatic pain. Pain is caused by:

  ◊ Pressure and distention of the vagina and the perineum, described by the client as "burning, splitting, and tearing."

  ◊ Pressure and pulling on the pelvic structures (ligaments, fallopian tubes, ovaries, bladder, and peritoneum).

  ◊ Lacerations of soft tissues (cervix, vagina, and perineum).

- **Third stage** – labor pain with the expelling of the placenta is similar to the pain experienced during the first stage. Pain is caused by:

  ◊ Uterine contractions.

  ◊ Pressure and pulling of pelvic structures.

- **Fourth stage** – pain is caused by:

  ◊ Distention and stretching of the vagina and perineum incurred during the second stage with a splitting, burning, and tearing sensation.

Therapeutic Procedures, Complications, and Nursing Implications

Nonpharmacologic Pain Management

Δ Nonpharmacologic pain management includes **childbirth preparation education, sensory and cutaneous strategies, and frequent maternal position changes**.

- Childbirth preparation methods such as **Lamaze**, **Bradley**, or **Dick-Read** methods and pattern breathing methods are used to promote relaxation and pain relief. *(For information, refer to chapter 6, Prenatal and Childbirth Education).*

- **Nursing implications** for **breathing techniques** include assessing for signs of **hyperventilation** (caused by low blood levels of PCO_2 from blowing off too much CO_2) such as light-headedness and tingling of the fingers.

- If **hyperventilation** occurs, have the client breath into a paper bag or cupped hands.

- Sensory stimulation strategies (based on the gate-control theory) to promote relaxation and pain relief include:

  ◊ Aroma therapy.

  ◊ Breathing techniques.

  ◊ Imagery.

  ◊ Music.

  ◊ Use of focal points.

- **Cutaneous strategies** (based on the gate-control theory) to promote relaxation and pain relief include:

  ◊ Back rubs and massage.

  ◊ **Effleurage.**

    ° Light, gentle circular stroking of the client's abdomen with the fingertips in rhythm with breathing during contractions.

  ◊ **Sacral counterpressure.**

    ° Steady pressure is applied by the support person using the heel of the hand or fist against the client's sacral area to counteract pain in the lower back.

    ° Especially helpful when the source of the back pain is persistent occiput posterior presentation of the fetus resulting in pressure on the spinal nerves.

  ◊ Heat or cold therapy.

  ◊ **Hydrotherapy** (whirlpool or shower) increases maternal endorphin levels.

  ◊ Intradermal water block.

  ◊ Acupressure.

  ◊ **Transcutaneous electrical nerve stimulation** (TENS) unit.

- Frequent maternal position changes to promote relaxation and pain relief include:

  ◊ Semi-sitting.

  ◊ Squatting.

  ◊ Kneeling.

◊ Kneeling and rocking back and forth.

◊ Supine position only with the placement of a wedge under one of the client's hips to tilt the uterus and avoid supine hypotension syndrome.

Pharmacologic Methods of Pain Relief

Δ Pharmacologic methods of pain relief include **analgesia** (sedatives, opioids, and ataractics) and **local/regional anesthetics** (the "caine" medications).

- To avoid slowing the progress of labor, prior to administering analgesic or anesthetic pain relief, the nurse should verify that labor is well established by performing a vaginal exam showing cervical dilation to be at least 4 cm with the fetus engaged.

Δ Analgesia includes the following:

- **Sedatives (Barbiturates)** such as secobarbital (Seconal), pentobarbital (Nembutal), and Phenobarbital (Luminal) are not typically used during labor and birth, but can only be used during the early or latent phase of labor to relieve anxiety and induce sleep.

  ◊ **Adverse effects** of **sedatives** include:

    ° Neonate respiratory depression secondary to the medication crossing the placenta and affecting the fetus.

    ° Unsteady ambulation of the client.

    ° Inhibition of the mother's ability to cope with the pain of labor. Sedatives should not be given if the client is experiencing pain because apprehension can increase and cause the client to become hyperactive and disoriented.

  ◊ **Nursing implications** for **sedative** administration include:

    ° Explaining to the client that the medication will cause drowsiness.

    ° Dimming the lights and providing a quiet atmosphere.

    ° Providing safety for the client by lowering the position of the bed and elevating the side rails of the bed.

    ° Instructing the client to request assistance with ambulation.

    ° Assisting the mother to cope with labor.

    ° Assessing the **neonate** for **respiratory depression.**

- **Opioid analgesics** such as meperidine hydrochloride (Demerol), fentanyl (Sublimaze), butorphanol (Stadol), and nalbuphine (Nubain) act in the central nervous system to decrease the perception of pain without the loss of consciousness. The client may be given opioid analgesics intramuscularly (IM) or intravenously (IV), but the intravenous route is recommended during labor because of its quicker action.

- **Butorphanol (Stadol) and nalbuphine (Nubain)** provide pain relief without causing significant respiratory depression in the mother or fetus. Both IM and IV routes are utilized.
  - ◊ **Adverse effects** of **opioid analgesics** include:
    - ° Crossing the placental barrier. If given to the mother too close to the time of delivery, opioid analgesics can cause respiratory depression in the neonate.
    - ° Reducing gastric emptying, increasing the risk for nausea and emesis.
    - ° Increasing the risk for aspiration of food or fluids in the stomach.
    - ° Sedations.
    - ° Tachycardia.
    - ° Hypotension.
    - ° Decreased FHR variability.
    - ° Allergic reaction.
  - ◊ **Nursing implications** for **opioid analgesics** include:
    - ° **Naloxone (Narcan)** should be available to counteract the effects of respiratory depression in the newborn.
    - ° Administering ataractics or antiemetics as prescribed.
    - ° Monitoring maternal vital signs and continuous FHR monitoring.
- **Ataractics** including phenothiazine medications such as promethazine (Phenergan) or hydroxyzine (Vistaril) can **control nausea** and **anxiety** and potentiate the affects of **opioid analgesia**, reducing opioid requirements. Ataractics do not relive pain and are used as an adjunct with opioids.
  - ◊ **Adverse effects** of ataractics include dry mouth and sedation.
  - ◊ **Nursing implications** for ataractics include providing ice chips or mouth swabs and providing safety.
- **Epidural and spinal regional analgesia** consists of using analgesics such as fentanyl (Sublimaze) and sufentanil (Sufenta), which are short-acting opioids that are administered as a motor block into the epidural or intrathecal space without anesthesia. These opioids produce regional analgesia providing rapid pain relief while still allowing the client to sense contractions and maintain the ability to bear down.
  - ◊ **Adverse effects** of **epidural** and **spinal analgesia** include:
    - ° Decreased gastric emptying resulting in nausea and vomiting.
    - ° Inhibition of bowel and bladder elimination sensations.
    - ° Bradycardia or tachycardia.
    - ° Hypotension.

° Respiratory depression.

° Allergic reaction and pruritus.

◊ **Nursing implications** for **epidural and spinal analgesia** include:

° Instituting safety precautions such as putting side rails up on the client's bed. The client may experience dizziness and sedation, increasing maternal risk for injury.

° Assessing the client for nausea and emesis and administering ataractics or antiemetics as prescribed.

° Monitoring maternal vital signs.

° Monitoring for allergic reaction.

° Continuous FHR pattern monitoring.

Δ **Anesthesia** used in childbirth includes **two types**: regional blocks and general anesthesia. **Regional blocks** are most commonly used and consist of pudendal block, epidural block, spinal block, and paracervical nerve block. **General anesthesia** is rarely used except in emergency situations.

Δ **Regional blocks** include the following:

• **Pudendal block** consists of a **local anesthetic** such as lidocaine (Xylocaine) or bupivacaine (Marcaine) being administered transvaginally into the space in front of the pudendal nerve. This type of block has no maternal or fetal systemic effects but does provide **local anesthesia** to the **perineum, vulva**, and **rectal areas** during **delivery, episiotomy**, and **episiotomy repair**. It is **administered** during the **second stage** of labor 10 to 20 min before delivery providing analgesia prior to spontaneous expulsion of the fetus or forceps-assisted or vacuum-assisted birth.

◊ **Adverse effects** of **pudendal block** include:

° Broad ligament hematoma.

° Compromise of maternal bearing down reflex.

◊ **Nursing interventions** pertaining to a **pudendal block** include:

° Instructing the client about the method.

° Coaching the client about when to bear down.

° Assessing the perineal and vulvar area postpartum for hematoma.

• **Epidural block** consists of a **local anesthetic** bupivacaine (Marcaine) along with an analgesic morphine (Duramorph) or fentanyl (Sublimaze) injected into the **epidural space** at the level of the fourth or fifth vertebrae. This **eliminates** all **sensation** from the level of the umbilicus to the thighs, relieving the discomfort of uterine contractions, fetal descent, and pressure and stretching of the perineum. It is **administered** when the client is in **active labor** and **dilated** to at least **4 cm**.

- **Continuous infusion** or **intermittent injections** may be administered through an indwelling epidural catheter. **Patient-controlled epidural analgesia** (PCEA) is a new technique for labor analgesia and is becoming a favored method of acute pain relief management for labor and birth.

  ◊ **Adverse effects** of an **epidural block** include:

    ° Maternal hypotension.

    ° Fetal bradycardia.

    ° Inability to feel the urge to void.

    ° Loss of the bearing down reflex.

  ◊ **Nursing interventions** of an **epidural block** include:

    ° Administering a bolus of IV fluids to help offset maternal hypotension as prescribed.

    ° The nurse helping to position and steady the client into either a sitting or side-lying modified Sims' position with the back curved to widen the intervertebral space for insertion of the epidural catheter.

    ° Encouraging the client to remain in the side-lying position after insertion of the epidural catheter to avoid supine hypotension syndrome with compression of the vena cava.

    ° Coaching the client in pushing efforts and requesting an evaluation of epidural pain management by anesthesia if pushing efforts are ineffective.

    ° Monitoring maternal blood pressure and pulse, observing for hypotension, respiratory depression, and sometimes oxygen saturations if necessitated.

    ° Continuously assessing FHR patterns.

    ° Maintaining the IV line as well as having oxygen and suction ready.

    ° Assessing for orthostatic hypotension. If present, be prepared to administer an IV vasopressor such as ephedrine, position the client laterally, increase IV fluids, and initiate oxygen.

    ° Providing client safety such as raising bed rails and not allowing the client to ambulate unassisted until all motor control has returned.

    ° Assessing the maternal bladder for distention at frequent intervals and catheterizing if necessary to assist with voiding.

    ° Monitoring for the return of sensation in the client's legs postdelivery prior to standing. Assisting the client with standing and walking for the first time postdelivery after receiving an epidural anesthesia.

- **Spinal block** consists of a **local anesthetic** injected into the **subarachnoid space** into the **spinal fluid** at the third, fourth, or fifth lumbar interspace, alone or in combination with an analgesic such as fentanyl (Sublimaze). The **spinal block eliminates** all sensations from the level of the **nipples to the feet**. It is commonly used for **cesarean births**. A low spinal block may be used for a vaginal birth, but is not used for labor. A spinal block is **administered** in the **late second stage** or **before cesarean birth**.

◊ **Adverse effects** of a spinal block include:

  ° Maternal hypotension.

  ° Fetal bradycardia.

  ° Loss of the bearing down reflex in the mother with a higher incidence of operative births.

  ° Potential headache from leakage of cerebrospinal fluid at the puncture site.

  ° Higher incidence of maternal bladder and uterine atony following birth.

◊ **Nursing interventions** for a **spinal block** include:

  ° Instructing the client about the method.

  ° Assessing maternal vital signs every 10 min.

  ° Assessing the client's uterine contractions.

  ° Assessing level of anesthesia.

  ° Assessing FHR patterns.

  ° Providing client safety to prevent injury by raising bed rails, assisting client with repositioning, and ambulating.

  ° Recognizing signs of impending birth including sitting on one buttock, making grunting sounds, and bulging of the perineum.

  ° Assessing for maternal hypotension and being prepared to administer an IV vasopressor, positioning the mother laterally, increasing IV fluids, and initiating oxygen.

  ° Encouraging interventions to relieve a postpartum headache resulting from a **cerebrospinal fluid leak.** Interventions include placing the client in a supine position, promoting bed rest in a dark room, administering oral analgesics, caffeine, and fluids. An autologous blood patch is the most beneficial and reliable relief measure for cerebrospinal fluid leaks.

  ° Instructing the client to bear down for expulsion of the fetus because during a vaginal birth, the mother will not feel her contractions.

- **Paracervical block** consists of lidocaine (Xylocaine) being injected into the cervical mucosa early in labor **during** the **first stage** to block the pain of uterine contractions.

  ◊ **Adverse effects** include fetal bradycardia. Improper technique can result in serious toxicity. Therefore, it is **rarely used today.**

  ◊ **Nursing interventions** include monitoring the labor progress because the client does not feel sensations or contractions.

Δ **General anesthesia** is rarely used for vaginal or cesarean births when there are no complications present. It is used only in the event of a delivery complication or emergency when there is a contraindication to nerve block analgesia or anesthesia. General anesthesia produces unconsciousness.

- **Nursing assessments** for **general anesthesia** include:

  ◊ Monitoring maternal vital signs.

  ◊ Monitoring FHR patterns.

- **Nursing interventions** for **general anesthesia** include:

  ◊ Ensuring the client has had nothing by mouth.

  ◊ Ensuring IV infusion is in place.

  ◊ Premedicating the client with clear oral antacid to neutralize acidic stomach contents.

  ◊ Administering a histamine H_2-receptor blocker such as ranitidine (Zantac) to decrease gastric acid production as prescribed.

  ◊ Administering metoclopramide (Reglan) to increase gastric emptying as prescribed.

  ◊ Administering a short-acting barbiturate such as thiopental to render the client unconscious as prescribed.

  ◊ Administering succinylcholine, a muscle relaxant to facilitate passage of an endotracheal tube as prescribed.

  ◊ Placing a wedge under one of the client's hips to displace the uterus.

  ◊ Assisting with applying cricoid pressure before intubation.

  ◊ Maintaining an open airway and cardiopulmonary function.

  ◊ Assessing the client postpartum for maternal signs of decreased uterine tone, which can lead to hemorrhage and fetal narcosis, both of which can be produced by pharmacologic agents used in general anesthesia.

  ◊ Facilitating parent-newborn attachment as soon as possible.

Nursing Assessments

Δ   Assess the laboring client's beliefs and expectations related to discomfort, pain relief, and birth plans regarding pain relief methods.

Δ   Assess the client's level, quality, frequency, duration, intensity, and location of pain through verbal and nonverbal cues. Use an analogue scale allowing the client to indicate on a scale from 0 to 10 the severity of her pain with 10 representing the most severe pain.

•   **Signs and symptoms of pain** include:

◊   Behavioral manifestations such as crying, moaning, screaming, gesturing, writhing, avoidance or withdrawal, and inability to follow instructions.

◊   Increasing blood pressure, tachycardia, and hyperventilation.

◊   Client verbalizations of pain.

Δ   Assess maternal vital signs for an increase in blood pressure, heart rate, and respiratory rate, which may indicate an increase in pain.

Δ   Evaluate the client's response to pain relief methods used (verbal report that pain is relieved or being relieved, appears relaxed between contractions).

Δ   Assess the well-being of the mother and fetus. This is the primary responsibility of the nurse when any pharmacologic pain relief method is used.

•   Monitor maternal response to the medication including respiratory rate, blood pressure, and pulse (particularly during epidural administration).

•   Assess the fetal heart rate continuously during administration of maternal analgesia and anesthesia.

NANDA Nursing Diagnoses

Δ   Acute pain related to the processes of labor and birth

Δ   Fear related to deficient knowledge pertaining to analgesic and anesthetic administration procedures

Δ   Risk for maternal injury related to the effects of analgesia and anesthesia on sensation and motor control

Δ   Impaired fetal gas exchange related to the administration of analgesia and anesthesia

Nursing Interventions

Δ Teach the laboring client techniques to relieve labor pain such as patterned breathing and progressive relaxation exercises.

Δ As guided by the client, employ the following:

- Focal points, music, and guided imagery.

- Touch, effleurage, or counterpressure as needed.

- Hydrotherapy (shower, whirlpool bath) if not contraindicated.

- TENS device if trained to do so, as well as acupressure, hypnosis, biofeedback, or aromatherapy.

- Warm or cold compresses as needed.

Δ A nurse is responsible for administering the prescribed pain medications at the proper time.

Timing and Effectiveness of Pain Relief Measures During Labor

First Stage (Latent Phase)	First Stage (Active Phase)	Transition	Second Stage	Third Stage
Nonpharmacologic methods ──→				
Sedatives ───────→			Spinal Block ──────────────────→	
	Opioids ──────→			
	Epidural ───→			
			Pudendal ──────────→	
			Local infiltration ──────→	

Δ A nurse is responsible for helping the client maintain the proper position during administration of pharmacological interventions and assisting the client with positioning for comfort after administration during labor and birth.

Δ A nurse provides for client safety after the administration of any pharmacologic intervention by putting the bed in a low position, maintaining side rails in the up position, placing the call light within the client's reach, and advising the client and her partner to call for assistance if the client needs to leave the bed or ambulate.

Δ Monitoring of maternal vital signs and temperature.

Δ Monitoring of FHR patterns.

Primary Reference:

Lowdermilk, D. L. & Perry, S. E. (2004). *Maternity & women's health care* (8th ed.). St. Louis, MO: Mosby.

Additional Resources:

Leifer, G. (2005). *Maternity nursing: An introductory text* (9th ed.). St. Louis, MO: Saunders.

NANDA International (2004). *NANDA nursing diagnoses: Definitions and classification 2005-2006*. Philadelphia: NANDA.

Chapter 10: Pain Management: Pharmacologic and Nonpharmacologic

Application Exercises

1. A client at 39 weeks gestation comes to the birthing unit for evaluation of labor. The client states that she has not been able to rest for 2 days and is exhausted. The FHR is within normal limits and contractions are mild at every 7 to 8 min. The cervical exam is 2 cm, 50% effaced, and -2 station. The primary care provider has admitted the client and prescribed a sedative. What are the nursing implications?

   A. The nurse explains that the medication will provide pain relief.

   B. The nurse should dim the lights and provide a quiet environment.

   C. The nurse should inform the client that the cervix must first be dilated to 4 cm.

   D. The nurse should inform the client of impending labor and neonate respiratory depression risks.

Scenario: A client is sleeping well and wakes up 2 hr later. Her contractions are every 3 to 5 min and stronger. Her cervix is 3 cm dilated, 80% effaced, and -1 station. The client states that she wants pain medication at this time.

2. What are some interventions the nurse can suggest at this time? (Select all that apply.)

   _____ Patterned breathing techniques

   _____ Frequent emptying of the bladder

   _____ Butorphanol (Stadol) 2 mg IV as prescribed

   _____ Application of heat or cold

   _____ Distraction or a focal point

3. The client is 5 cm dilated and displays restlessness, moaning, and is beginning to hyperventilate. She says the breathing and other techniques aren't working, and asks the nurse to give her something for pain. The nurse obtains a prescription for butorphanol, 2 mg IV. What are the nursing implications for this medication? (Select all that apply.)

   _____ The nurse informs the client that this medication will abolish all sensation of pain.

   _____ The nurse monitors the client for signs of allergic or adverse reactions.

   _____ The nurse has naloxone available to administer for respiratory depression of the neonate.

   _____ The nurse has an emesis basin available in the event of nausea and vomiting.

   _____ The nurse observes the newborn for respiratory depression if birth occurs within 6 to 8 hr of dose.

4. The client rests and sleeps between contractions for the next 2 hr. She begins to report lower back pain. The likely cause of this pain is persistent occiput posterior presentation. Which of the following nonpharmacologic nursing interventions should best alleviate this pain?

      A. Abdominal effleurage

      B. Sacral counterpressure

      C. Hydrotherapy if not contraindicated

      D. Back rub and massage

5. The client is 8 cm dilated, 100% effaced, the fetus is at -1 station, and the membranes have ruptured. She states the pain is worse than ever and wants more of the intravenous pain medication, butorphanol, which she received 3 hr earlier. What is the best nursing action?

      A. Administer the IV butorphanol for pain relief as requested by the client because enough time has elapsed since the last dose.

      B. Advise the client that she may have another dose of the IV butorphanol in 1 hr.

      C. Advise the client that delivery is too near and provide and encourage nonpharmacologic comfort measures.

      D. Notify the primary care provider and obtain a prescription for an epidural placement.

6. A nurse anesthetist explains the epidural procedure to the client, who agrees that this is the best way to help suppress her pain. What is the role of the nurse before, during, and after epidural administration? (Select all that apply.)

      _____   Administer a bolus of IV fluids per anesthesia protocol prior to epidural insertion.

      _____   Position the client in the lithotomy position for epidural catheter insertion.

      _____   Monitor maternal vital signs for tachypnea and hypertension.

      _____   Have oxygen and suction ready in the event of respiratory depression.

      _____   Palpate the client's bladder for distention and insert an indwelling Foley catheter if necessary.

      _____   Encourage the client to ambulate to the bathroom every 1 to 2 hr to void.

7. A disadvantage of using an epidural block for pain management during labor is that it can cause

      A. postspinal headache.

      B. maternal hypotension.

      C. neonate respiratory distress.

      D. fetal tachycardia.

8. A primipara in active labor for 10 hr required two administrations of meperidine (Demerol) for pain control. The last dose was administered 30 min prior to an unexpected precipitous delivery. Which of the following medications should the nurse be prepared to administer?

       A. Naloxone (Narcan) to the mother

       B. Promethazine (Phenergan) to the mother

       C. Naloxone (Narcan) to the neonate

       D. Promethazine (Phenergan) to the neonate

9. The most important nursing intervention for a client in labor who has just received epidural anesthesia would be to monitor the

       A. fetus for tachycardia.

       B. mother for hypotension.

       C. mother for facial edema.

       D. fetus for irregular heartbeats.

10. A client in the transition phase of labor is breathing with rapid shallow respirations when she reports dizziness. The nurse should

       A. administer oxygen via a face mask.

       B. place the client in a side-lying position.

       C. have the client breathe into her cupped hands.

       D. administer a bolus of intravenous fluids.

11. A client in the labor and delivery unit is in the second stage of labor. Labor has been progressing well without complications and the client is expected to deliver vaginally in approximately 20 min. The primary care provider is preparing to administer lidocaine (Xylocaine) for pain relief and perform an episiotomy. The nurse knows that the type of regional anesthetic block that will most likely be used will be which of the following?

       A. Pudendal block

       B. Epidural block

       C. Spinal block

       D. Paracervical block

Chapter 10: Pain Management: Pharmacologic and Nonpharmacologic

Application Exercises Answer Key

1. A client at 39 weeks gestation comes to the birthing unit for evaluation of labor. The client states that she has not been able to rest for 2 days and is exhausted. The FHR is within normal limits and contractions are mild at every 7 to 8 min. The cervical exam is 2 cm, 50% effaced, and -2 station. The primary care provider has admitted the client and prescribed a sedative. What are the nursing implications?

    A. The nurse explains that the medication will provide pain relief.

    B. The nurse should dim the lights and provide a quiet environment.

    C. The nurse should inform the client that the cervix must first be dilated to 4 cm.

    D. The nurse should inform the client of impending labor and neonate respiratory depression risks.

The nurse should dim the lights and provide a quiet environment. Sedatives can only be given in the latent phase of labor to relieve anxiety and induce sleep because these medications cross the placental barrier and cause respiratory depression if given later in labor. Therefore, cervical dilation must be less than 4 cm. This client is only 2 cm dilated, so labor is not impending at this time. The client is in the latent phase so it is safe to administer sedatives.

Scenario: A client is sleeping well and wakes up 2 hr later. Her contractions are every 3 to 5 min and stronger. Her cervix is 3 cm dilated, 80% effaced, and -1 station. The client states that she wants pain medication at this time.

---

2. What are some interventions the nurse can suggest at this time? (Select all that apply.)

    __X__   **Patterned breathing techniques**

    __X__   **Frequent emptying of the bladder**

    __X__   **Butorphanol (Stadol) 2 mg IV as prescribed**

    __X__   **Application of heat or cold**

    __X__   **Distraction or a focal point**

Nonpharmacologic comfort measures can be safely used at this time while the client is in the latent phase of labor. In addition, she may have the opioid analgesic.

3. The client is 5 cm dilated and displays restlessness, moaning, and is beginning to hyperventilate. She says the breathing and other techniques aren't working, and asks the nurse to give her something for pain. The nurse obtains a prescription for butorphanol, 2 mg IV. What are the nursing implications for this medication? (Select all that apply.)

    _____   The nurse informs the client that this medication will abolish all sensation of pain.

    X   **The nurse monitors the client for signs of allergic or adverse reactions.**

    X   **The nurse has naloxone available to administer for respiratory depression of the neonate.**

    X   **The nurse has an emesis basin available in the event of nausea and vomiting.**

    _____   The nurse observes the newborn for respiratory depression if birth occurs within 6 to 8 hr of dose.

Opioid analgesics reduce the perception of pain or raise the pain threshold, but do not abolish all pain sensation. There is a risk of an allergic reaction and a high incidence of pruritus with opioid medications. Opioid medications can also increase nausea and vomiting, so an emesis basin should be available to the client. Naloxone should be available to administer for respiratory depression of the neonate. The newborn should be observed for respiratory depression if birth occurs within 1 to 4 hr of dosing the mother with butorphanol.

4. The client rests and sleeps between contractions for the next 2 hr. She begins to report lower back pain. The likely cause of this pain is persistent occiput posterior presentation. Which of the following nonpharmacologic nursing interventions should best alleviate this pain?

    A. Abdominal effleurage

    B. Sacral counterpressure

    C. Hydrotherapy if not contraindicated

    D. Back rub and massage

Sacral counterpressure is the application of steady pressure to the lower back to counteract the pressure exerted on the spinal nerves by the fetus, which especially occurs with an occiput posterior presentation. Abdominal effleurage is a gentle stroking of the abdomen in rhythm with breathing during contractions. Hydrotherapy, a back rub, and massage may be helpful, but counterpressure is most effective in relieving back discomfort.

5. The client is 8 cm dilated, 100% effaced, the fetus is at -1 station, and the membranes have ruptured. She states the pain is worse than ever and wants more of the intravenous pain medication, butorphanol, which she received 3 hr earlier. What is the best nursing action?

A. Administer the IV butorphanol for pain relief as requested by the client because enough time has elapsed since the last dose.

B. Advise the client that she may have another dose of the IV butorphanol in 1 hr.

C. Advise the client that delivery is too near and provide and encourage nonpharmacologic comfort measures.

D. Notify the primary care provider and obtain a prescription for an epidural placement.

Notify the primary care provider and obtain a prescription for epidural anesthesia if the client is requesting pharmacologic pain relief. It is too close to delivery for IV opioid administration. It is possible that the client might deliver while the opioid is at its peak level causing respiratory depression in the neonate. It does not make a difference how frequently the butorphanol is prescribed to be given if it is too near delivery time to administer a opioid.

6. A nurse anesthetist explains the epidural procedure to the client, who agrees that this is the best way to help suppress her pain. What is the role of the nurse before, during, and after epidural administration? (Select all that apply.)

   X   **Administer a bolus of IV fluids per anesthesia protocol prior to epidural insertion.**

               Position the client in the lithotomy position for epidural catheter insertion.

               Monitor maternal vital signs for tachypnea and hypertension.

   X   **Have oxygen and suction ready in the event of respiratory depression.**

   X   **Palpate the client's bladder for distention and insert indwelling Foley catheter if necessary.**

               Encourage the client to ambulate to the bathroom every 1 to 2 hr to void.

An IV bolus of fluids may be administered prior to epidural anesthesia to compensate for hypotension. The client is either in a sitting position or modified Sims' position to widen the intervertebral space for catheter insertion. Maternal vital signs are monitored for hypotension and respiratory depression. Oxygen and suction should be available for respiratory depression or aspiration. Epidural anesthesia diminishes the client's ability to recognize the urge to void. Therefore, bladder palpation for distention with possible catheterization is necessary. The client should not ambulate to the bathroom without assistance while receiving epidural anesthesia.

7. A disadvantage of using an epidural block for pain management during labor is that it can cause

    A. postspinal headache.

    B. maternal hypotension.

    C. neonate respiratory distress.

    D. fetal tachycardia.

Maternal hypotension is an adverse effect of an epidural block. Postspinal headache is an adverse effect of a spinal block resulting from the leakage of cerebrospinal fluid at the puncture site. Neonate respiratory distress occurs with analgesic pain medications administered too near the time of delivery. Fetal bradycardia is an adverse effect of epidural blocks.

---

8. A primipara in active labor for 10 hr required two administrations of meperidine (Demerol) for pain control. The last dose was administered 30 min prior to an unexpected precipitous delivery. Which of the following medications should the nurse be prepared to administer?

    A. Naloxone (Narcan) to the mother

    B. Promethazine (Phenergan) to the mother

    C. Naloxone (Narcan) to the neonate

    D. Promethazine (Phenergan) to the neonate

Naloxone (Narcan) (a opioid antagonist) should be administered to the neonate for respiratory depression. Ataractics are administered as adjuncts to opioid medications to reduce the amount of opioid medication required or to counteract nausea.

9. The most important nursing intervention for a client in labor who has just received epidural anesthesia would be to monitor the

    A. fetus for tachycardia.

    B. mother for hypotension.

    C. mother for facial edema.

    D. fetus for irregular heartbeats.

Monitor the mother for hypotension, because hypotension is an adverse effect of epidural analgesia. Epidural analgesia also causes fetal bradycardia, not irregular heartbeats. Epidurals have no effect on maternal edema.

10. A client in the transition phase of labor is breathing with rapid shallow respirations when she reports dizziness. The nurse should

       A. administer oxygen via a face mask.
       B. place the client in a side-lying position.
       C. have the client breathe into her cupped hands.
       D. administer a bolus of intravenous fluids.

Have the client breathe into her cupped hands. This client is hyperventilating resulting from low CO_2 levels in her blood, which is causing her to feel dizzy. Oxygen via a face mask would be indicated for low oxygenation. IV fluid bolus would be indicated for hypotension. A side-lying position provides optimal uteroplacental perfusion and fetal oxygenation, but has no effect on hyperventilation.

11. A client in the labor and delivery unit is in the second stage of labor. Labor has been progressing well without complications and the client is expected to deliver vaginally in approximately 20 min. The primary care provider is preparing to administer lidocaine (Xylocaine) for pain relief and perform an episiotomy. The nurse knows that the type of regional anesthetic block that will most likely be used will be which of the following?

       A. Pudendal block

       B. Epidural block

       C. Spinal block

       D. Paracervical block

A pudendal block is the transvaginal injection of a local anesthetic into the area in front of the pudendal nerve anesthetizing the perineum, vulva, and rectal areas for episiotomy, expulsion of the fetus, and episiotomy repair. Epidural blocks can be administered in the first stage of labor after the cervix is dilated to 4 cm or greater. Spinal blocks are administered late in the second stage, but most commonly preceding a cesarean delivery. Paracervical blocks are used early in labor to block pain of uterine contractions and are rarely used today because of serious adverse effects.

Unit 2   Intrapartum

Chapter 11:   Fetal Assessment During Labor
Contributor: Sandra Mesics, MSN, RN, CNM

⟳ NCLEX-RN® Connections:

Learning Objective: Review and apply knowledge within **"Fetal Assessment During Labor"** in readiness for performance of the following nursing activities as outlined by the NCLEX-RN® test plan:

Δ   Continually check the heart rate of the fetus.

Δ   Monitor the fetus throughout labor.

Δ   Recognize reassuring and nonreassuring fetal heart rate patterns and intervene as indicated.

▌Diagnostic Procedures: FHR Pattern and Uterine Contraction Monitoring

✎ Key Points

Δ   During labor, uterine contractions compress the **uteroplacental arteries**, temporarily stopping maternal blood flow into the uterus and intervillous spaces of the placenta, decreasing fetal circulation and oxygenation. Circulation to the uterus and placenta resumes during uterine relaxation between contractions.

Δ   Evaluation of fetal well-being during labor is accomplished by monitoring the fetal heart rate (FHR) pattern in relationship to the contraction pattern.

Δ   The FHR and uterine contractions can be monitored manually or electronically as well as externally or internally.

Δ   A **normal, reassuring** fetal heart rate is **110 to 160 beats/min** with good variability consisting of FHR accelerations above the baseline of at least 15 beats/min, lasting 15 sec or more with a return to baseline in less than 2 min.

   •   Absent variability (considered nonreassuring)

   •   Minimal variability (< 5 beats/min)

   •   Moderate variability (6 to 25 beats/min)

   •   Marked variability (> 25 beats/min)

Δ It is the responsibility of the nurse to assess FHR patterns, implement nursing interventions, and report nonreassuring patterns to the primary care provider.

Δ The emotional, informational, and comfort needs of the mother and the family must be incorporated into the plan of care while continuing to assess the FHR pattern's response to the labor process.

Key Factors

Δ The method and frequency of fetal surveillance during labor will vary and depend on maternal-fetal risk factors as well as the preference of the facility, primary care provider, and client.

Δ **Guidelines** for **intermittent auscultation** or **continuous electronic fetal monitoring** include:

- **Low-risk women**

  ◊ During latent phase, every 60 min.

  ◊ During active phase, every 30 min.

  ◊ During second stage, every 15 min.

- **High-risk women**

  ◊ During latent phase, every 30 min.

  ◊ During active phase, every 15 min.

  ◊ During second stage, every 5 min.

- **Routine**

  ◊ Upon **rupture of membranes**, either spontaneously or artificially.

  ◊ Preceding and subsequent to ambulation.

  ◊ Prior to and following administration of or a change in medication anesthesia.

  ◊ At peak action of anesthesia.

  ◊ Following vaginal examination.

  ◊ Following expulsion of an enema.

  ◊ After urinary catheterization.

  ◊ In the event of abnormal or excessive uterine contractions.

Δ **Indications** for the use of **intermittent auscultation** and **uterine contraction palpation** include:

- Low risk labor and delivery

  ◊ Frequently done in home births and birthing centers.

  ◊ Allows for greater maternal freedom of movement.

Δ   **Indications** for the use of **continuous fetal monitoring** include:

- Multiple gestations.

- Placenta previa.

- Oxytocin (Pitocin) infusion (augmentation or induction of labor).

- Fetal bradycardia.

- Maternal complications (e.g., diabetes, pregnancy-induced hypertension, renal disease).

- Intrauterine growth restriction.

- Post dates.

- Meconium-stained amniotic fluid.

- Abruption placenta – suspected or actual.

- Abnormal nonstress test or contraction stress test.

- Abnormal uterine contractions.

- Fetal distress.

- Facility and primary care provider preference.

Types of FHR Pattern and Contraction Monitoring

Intermittent Auscultation and Uterine Contraction Palpation

Δ   **Intermittent auscultation** of the FHR and **uterine contraction palpation** is a low technology method that can be performed using a hand-held Doppler ultrasound device, an ultrasound stethoscope, or fetoscope in conjunction with palpation of contractions at the fundus for frequency, duration, and intensity.

Δ   To perform **intermittent auscultation** of FHR and **palpation** of **uterine contractions:**

- Perform Leopold's maneuvers to determine point of maximum impulse (PMI).

- Auscultate at PMI using listening device.

- Palpate abdomen at uterine fundus to assess uterine activity.

- Count FHR for 30 to 60 sec to determine baseline rate.

- Auscultate FHR during a contraction and for 30 sec following the completion of the contraction.

- Identify any nonreassuring FHR patterns and notify the primary care provider.

Continuous Electronic Fetal Monitoring

Δ **Continuous external fetal monitoring** is accomplished by securing an ultrasound transducer over the client's abdomen to determine PMI, which records the FHR pattern, and a tocotransducer on the fundus that records the uterine contractions.

- **Advantages** of external fetal monitoring include:
  - ◊ **Noninvasive** and reduces risk for infection.
  - ◊ Membranes do not have to be ruptured.
  - ◊ Cervix does not have to be dilated.
  - ◊ Placement of transducers can be performed by the nurse.
  - ◊ Records permanent record of FHR tracing.

- **Disadvantages** of external fetal monitoring include:
  - ◊ Contraction intensity is not measurable.
  - ◊ Movement of the client requires frequent repositioning of transducers.
  - ◊ Quality of recording is affected by client obesity and fetal position.

Δ For **proper placement** of external **monitoring equipment:**

- Use **Leopold's maneuvers** to locate the fetal presenting part and the optimal location for placement of the ultrasound transducer for the best possible auscultation of FHR.

- Palpate uterine activity at the fundus to identify proper placement location for the tocotransducer to monitor uterine contractions.

- Provide education regarding the procedure to the client and the client's partner during placement and adjustments of the fetal monitor equipment.

- Encourage frequent maternal position changes. Explain to the client that adjustments of the monitor may be necessary with position changes.

- If the client needs to void and can ambulate, and it is not contraindicated. The nurse can disconnect the external monitor for the client to use the bathroom.

- If disconnecting of FHR monitor is contraindicated or internal FHR monitor is being used, the nurse can bring the client a bedpan.

- Assess and document findings and interventions.

- Keep client and family informed.

Δ   **Continuous internal fetal monitoring with a scalp electrode** is performed by attaching a small spiral electrode to the presenting part of the fetus to monitor the FHR. The electrode wires are then attached to a leg plate that is placed on the client's thigh and then attached to the fetal monitor.

- May be utilized in conjunction with an **intrauterine pressure catheter (IUPC),** which is a solid or fluid filled transducer placed inside the uterine cavity to monitor the frequency, duration, and intensity of contractions. The average pressure is usually 50 to 85 mm Hg.

- **Advantages** of internal fetal monitoring include:

    ◊   **Early detection** of **abnormal FHR patterns** suggestive of fetal distress.

    ◊   **Accurate** recording of **uterine contraction intensity.**

    ◊   Recording not affected by maternal obesity or maternal and fetal movement.

    ◊   **Accurate** assessment of **FHR variability**.

    ◊   Allows greater maternal freedom of movement without compromising tracing.

- **Disadvantages** of internal fetal monitoring include:

    ◊   The **membranes must have ruptured** to utilize internal monitoring.

    ◊   The **cervix** must be adequately **dilated** to a minimum of **2 to 3 cm**.

    ◊   **Presenting part** must have **descended** enough to place electrode.

    ◊   Potential risk of injury to fetus if electrode is not properly applied.

    ◊   Contraindicated with vaginal bleeding.

    ◊   Potential risk of infection to the client and the fetus.

    ◊   A primary care provider, nurse practitioner/midwife, or specially trained registered nurse must perform this procedure.

Nursing Assessments and Interventions

Δ   **Reassuring fetal heart rate patterns** consist of a heart rate of 110 to 160 beats/min with **beat-to-beat variability of 15 beats/min**, lasting at least 15 sec, with a **return to baseline in less than 2 min** with **no decelerations.**

Δ   Each uterine contraction is comprised of the following:

- **Increment** – the beginning of the contraction as intensity is increasing.

- **Acme** – the peak intensity of the contraction.

- **Decrement** – the decline of the contraction intensity as the contraction is ending.

Δ   **Nonreassuring fetal heart rate patterns** are associated with fetal hypoxia and include:

- Fetal bradycardia.

- Fetal tachycardia.

- Absence of FHR variability.

- Late decelerations.

- Variable decelerations.

Fetal Heart Rate Patterns	Causes/Complications	Nursing Interventions
Accelerations (variable transitory increase in the FHR above baseline)	• Healthy fetal/placental exchange • Intact fetal central nervous system (CNS) response to fetal movement • Vaginal exam • Fundal pressure	• Reassuring • No interventions required • Indicate reactive nonstress test
Fetal bradycardia (FHR <110 beats/min for 10 min or more)	• Uteroplacental insufficiency • Umbilical cord prolapse • Maternal hypotension • Prolonged umbilical cord compression • Fetal congenital heart block • Anesthetic medications	• Notify the primary care provider. • Discontinue oxytocin if it is being infused. • Help the client into a side-lying position. • Administer oxygen (8 to 10 L/min by mask). • Start an IV line if one is not in place. • Administer tocolytic medication as prescribed. • Stimulate the fetal scalp.
Fetal tachycardia (FHR >160 beats/min for 10 min or more)	• Maternal infection, chorioamnionitis • Fetal anemia • Fetal heart failure • Fetal cardiac dysrhythmias • Maternal use of cocaine or methamphetamines • Maternal dehydration	• If maternal fever exists, administer antipyretics as prescribed. • Administer oxygen (8 to 10 L/min by mask). • Bolus of IV fluids.

Fetal Heart Rate Patterns	Causes/Complications	Nursing Interventions
Decrease or loss of FHR variability (decrease or loss of irregular fluctuations in the baseline of the FHR)	• Medications that depress the CNS such as narcotics, barbiturates, tranquilizers, or general anesthetics • Fetal hypoxemia with resulting acidosis • Fetal sleep cycle • Congenital abnormalities	• Stimulate the fetal scalp. • Assist primary care provider with application of scalp electrode or fetal blood pH sampling. • Position the client into a left lateral position.
Early deceleration of FHR (slowing of FHR with start of contraction with return of FHR to baseline at end of contraction)	• Compression of the fetal head resulting from uterine contraction • Vaginal exam • Fundal pressure	• No intervention required.
Late deceleration of FHR (slowing of FHR after contraction has started with return of FHR to baseline well after contraction has ended)	• Uteroplacental insufficiency causing inadequate fetal oxygenation • Maternal hypertension	• Notify the primary care provider. • Discontinue oxytocin if being infused. • Change the client to a side-lying position. • Administer oxygen 8 to 10 L/min per mask. • Start an IV line if not in place or increase the IV rate. • Prepare for an assisted vaginal birth or cesarean birth.
Variable deceleration of FHR (transitory, abrupt slowing of FHR <110 beats/min, variable in duration, intensity, and timing in relation to uterine contraction)	• Umbilical cord compression • Short cord • Prolapsed cord • Nuchal cord (around fetal neck) • Oligohydramnios	• Change the client's position. • Discontinue oxytocin if it is being infused. • Administer oxygen at 8 to 10 L/min per mask. • Perform or assist with a vaginal examination. • Assist with amnioinfusion if ordered.

NANDA Nursing Diagnoses

Δ   Risk for fetal injury related to improper application of monitoring device or misinterpretation of FHR patterns

Δ   Impaired physical mobility related to restricted movement with continuous external electronic fetal monitoring

Δ   Anxiety related to lack of knowledge about monitoring procedures

Complications and Nursing Interventions

△ Complications that can occur as a result of fetal monitoring include:

- **Misinterpretation** of FHR patterns.

- **Maternal or fetal infection** if electrode equipment is not correctly applied on internal monitoring.

- **Fetal trauma** if fetal monitoring electrode or IUPC are inserted into the vagina improperly.

- **Supine hypotension** secondary to maternal position during continuous electronic monitoring.

△ Nursing interventions include:

- Ensuring electronic fetal monitoring equipment is functioning properly.

- Continuing to monitor FHR patterns.

- Monitoring maternal vital signs and obtaining maternal temperature every 1 to 2 hr.

- Using aseptic techniques if assisting with procedures.

- Encouraging frequent repositioning of the client. If the client is lying supine, place a wedge under one of the client's hips to tilt the uterus.

Therapeutic and Diagnostic Procedure: Leopold's Maneuvers

 Key Points

△ **Leopold's maneuvers** consist of performing external palpations of the maternal uterus through the abdominal wall to determine the:

- Number of fetuses.

- Presenting part.

- Fetal lie.

- Fetal attitude.

- Degree of fetal descent into the pelvis.

- Expected location of the **point of maximal impulse (PMI).**

△ **PMI** is the optimal location where the fetal heart tones are auscultated the loudest on the woman's abdomen. These tones are best heard directly over the fetal back.

- In **vertex presentation, PMI** is either in the right or left lower quadrant of below the maternal umbilicus.

- In **breech presentation, PMI** is either in the right or left upper quadrant above the maternal umbilicus.

Nursing Assessments and Interventions

Δ   **Preceding Leopold's maneuvers**:

- Ask the client to empty her bladder before beginning the assessment.

- Position the client in the supine position with a pillow under her head and with her knees slightly flexed.

- Place a rolled towel under her right hip to displace the uterus to the left and prevent supine hypotension/vena cava syndrome.

Δ   To **perform Leopold's maneuvers:**

- **Identify the fetal part occupying the fundus**. The head should feel round, firm, and freely movable. The breech should feel irregular and softer.

  ◊   Identify fetal lie and presenting part.

- **Locate and palpate the smooth contour** of the **fetal back** using the palm of one hand and the irregular small parts of the feet, hands, and elbows using the palm of the other hand.

  ◊   Identify fetal presentation.

- **Determine the fetal presenting part** over the true pelvis inlet by gently grasping the lower segment of the uterus between the thumb and fingers. If the head is presenting and not engaged, determine whether the head is flexed or extended.

  ◊   Identify fetal attitude.

- Face the client's feet and **outline the fetal head** using the palmar surface of the fingertips on both hands to palpate the **cephalic prominence**. If the cephalic prominence is on the same side as the small parts, the head is flexed with vertex presentation. If the cephalic prominence is on the same side as the back, the head is extended with a face presentation.

  ◊   Identify the attitude of the head.

Δ   **Upon completion** of the **Leopold's maneuvers:**

- If using an external ultrasound transducer, place the tocotransducer based on the findings obtained from the maneuvers for optimal auscultation of the FHR.

- Auscultate the FHR post maneuvers to assess the fetal tolerance to the procedure.

- Document the findings from the maneuvers.

Therapeutic and Diagnostic Procedure: Ultrasound Imaging

 Key Points

- Δ **Ultrasound imaging** uses high-frequency waves to visualize the fetus, placenta, and the beating of the fetal heart using a transducer applied to the abdomen at the PMI.

  - The procedure is **painless and a safe method** to assess the fetus and placenta. It is **noninvasive** and does not require rupture of the membranes.

- Δ **Ultrasound imaging** provides assessment, confirmation, or determination of the following during labor and delivery:

  - Gestational age.

  - Placental and fetal position.

  - Fetal movements such as heartbeat, breathing, and body movement activity.

  - Amniotic fluid volume.

  - Vaginal bleeding.

  - Fetal and placental abnormalities.

Nursing Assessments and Interventions

- Δ Provide the client and the client's partner with education regarding the procedure.

- Δ Assist the primary care provider as necessary.

- Δ A full bladder is only necessary if pregnancy is not full-term.

Therapeutic and Diagnostic Procedure: Doppler Ultrasound Blood Flow

Key Points

- Δ **Doppler ultrasound** utilizes **sound wave reflection** on a moving target. It is a noninvasive method of studying blood flow in the maternal-fetal blood circulation using a handheld ultrasound device. The Doppler effect gives information about **blood flow** and any resistance to blood flow in a particular area.

Δ   **Doppler ultrasound** is an adjunct in management of high risk pregnancies and is especially utilized in labor and delivery for:

- Multiple fetuses.

- Preterm labor.

- Poorly perfused placenta.

- Maternal hypertension.

- Maternal diabetes.

- Fetal intrauterine growth restriction.

 Nursing Assessments and Interventions

Δ   Use Doppler earpieces or connect the transducer to a speaker.

Δ   Apply water-soluble gel to the head of the Doppler hand-held transducer and place the transducer head over the PMI and count fetal heart rate.

Δ   Auscultate the FHR pattern as it coincides with the uterine contractions.

Δ   Promptly report FHR that is less than 110 beats/min or greater than 160 beats/min, loss or decrease in variability, or any FHR decelerations to the primary care provider.

Therapeutic and Diagnostic Procedure: Fetal Scalp Blood Sampling

Key Points

Δ   **Fetal scalp blood sampling** is performed by obtaining a sample of blood from the fetal scalp through the cervical opening once the cervix has sufficiently dilated and the membranes have ruptured.

- This sampling is obtained to assess the fetal blood gases consisting of the pH, PO_2 and PCO_2.

Nursing Assessments and Interventions

Δ   Continue to monitor FHR pattern.

Δ   Communicate nonreassuring FHR to primary care provider so that a decision can be made whether to perform a fetal scalp blood sampling.

Δ   Assist with swabbing the fetal scalp with disinfectant prior to the primary care provider performing the scalp puncture.

Therapeutic and Diagnostic Procedure: Fetal Oxygen Saturation Monitoring

Key Points

Δ   **Fetal oxygen saturation monitoring/fetal pulse oximetry** is performed by inserting a specially designed sensor next to the fetal cheek or temple area to assess fetal oxygen saturation ($FSpO_2$).

- Normal $FSpO_2$ is 30 to 70%

- Criteria for use of fetal oxygen saturation includes:

    ◊   Used in single fetus gestation.

    ◊   At least 36 weeks gestation.

    ◊   Vertex presentation.

    ◊   Nonreassuring FHR.

    ◊   Ruptured membranes.

    ◊   Cervix dilated to at least 2 cm.

    ◊   Fetal station at least -2.

- The value of fetal oxygen saturation is that it gives further information to support the decision of whether to allow labor to continue or to intervene with augmentation of labor to expedite delivery or to perform an emergency cesarean delivery.

Nursing Assessments and Interventions

Δ   Assist in interpreting data obtained from fetal blood gas.

Δ   Identify potential candidates for fetal oxygen saturation monitoring.

Δ   Communicate findings to primary care provider.

Δ   Assist the primary care provider during procedure as needed.

Δ   Document findings and interventions.

Primary Reference:

Lowdermilk D. L. & Perry, S. E. (2004). *Maternity & women's health care* (8ᵗʰ ed.). St. Louis, MO: Mosby.

Additional Resource:

Murray, S. S. & McKinney, E. S. (2006). *Foundations of maternal-newborn nursing* (4ᵗʰ ed.). Philadelphia: Elsevier.

NANDA International (2004). *NANDA nursing diagnoses: Definitions and classification 2005-2006.* Philadelphia: NANDA.

Chapter 11: Fetal Assessment During Labor

Application Exercises

Scenario: A client is in active labor. Her cervix is dilated to 5 cm and her membranes are intact. The FHR and uterine contractions are being monitored by an external electronic fetal monitor. The nurse notes a fetal heart rate of 115 to 120 beats/min with occasional increases up to 158 beats/min that last for 25 sec, and beat-to-beat variability of 20 beats/min. There is no slowing of FHR from baseline noted.

1. This client is exhibiting signs of which of the following? (Select all that apply.)

   _____ Reassuring FHR patterns
   _____ Nonreassuring FHR patterns
   _____ Moderate variability
   _____ Decrease or loss of variability
   _____ FHR accelerations
   _____ FHR decelerations
   _____ No FHR decelerations
   _____ Normal baseline FHR
   _____ Fetal bradycardia
   _____ Fetal tachycardia

2. One hour later during assessment, the client is still at 5 cm dilation with intact membranes. The nurse notes that the FHR variability is decreased and resembles a straight line. The mother has not had any pain medication. Variability is difficult to assess accurately on external monitoring. What first must occur for an internal scalp electrode to be applied?

   A. Dilation and effacement of the cervix

   B. Rupturing of the membranes

   C. Administration of analgesics

   D. Antiseptic swabbing of presenting part

3. The nurse auscultates the fetal heart rate (FHR) and determines a rate of 150 to 155 beats/min. Which of the following nursing interventions is most appropriate?

   A. Inform the client that the FHR is normal and document the findings.

   B. Document and reassess the FHR in 5 min because the rate is too high.

   C. Report the FHR to the primary care provider immediately and then document.

   D. Document and tell the mother she is having a boy because the heart rate is fast.

4. Which of the following is the best rationale for utilizing internal fetal heart rate monitoring?

    A. Internal monitoring can be used through the entire birth process.

    B. External monitoring is more subject to extraneous artifacts.

    C. Internal monitoring is more accurate than external monitoring.

    D. External monitoring increases risk of maternal and fetal infection.

5. A nurse places an external fetal monitor on a client who is in labor. Which of the following instructions is most appropriate for the nurse to give to the client?

    A. "Lie supine so the tracing shows up the best on the paper."

    B. "Keep your legs flat so your abdomen is not tense."

    C. "Lie on your side if that makes you feel comfortable."

    D. "Avoid moving so there will not be any interference on the monitor."

6. The nurse knows that a fetus is best oxygenated during which of the following?

    A. Peak of the uterine contraction

    B. Increment of the uterine contraction

    C. Decrement of the uterine contraction

    D. Relaxation between uterine contractions

7. A client delivering in a birthing center is in the second stage of labor and is having no complications. Intermittent auscultation of FHR and uterine palpation of contractions is being performed to monitor FHR patterns. How frequently should the nurse assess the FHR?

    A. Every 60 min

    B. Every 30 min

    C. Every 15 min

    D. Every 5 min

8. What is the appropriate initial nursing intervention for late decelerations on the fetal monitor?

    A. Reposition the client to left lateral position.

    B. Take no action because this is a normal pattern.

    C. Increase the intravenous fluid rate.

    D. Decrease the intravenous fluid rate.

9. Transitional accelerations of the FHR from baseline should be interpreted by the nurse as indicative of

        A. intact CNS response to fetal movement.

        B. fetal response to maternal fever.

        C. fetal distress requiring intervention.

        D. fetal hypoxia requiring maternal oxygen.

Chapter 11: Fetal Assessment During Labor

Application Exercises Answer Key

Scenario: A client is in active labor. Her cervix is dilated to 5 cm and her membranes are intact. The FHR and uterine contractions are being monitored by an external electronic fetal monitor. The nurse notes a fetal heart rate of 115 to 120 beats/min with occasional increases up to 158 beats/min that last for 25 sec, and beat-to-beat variability of 20 beats/min. There is no slowing of FHR from baseline noted.

1. This client is exhibiting signs of which of the following? (Select all that apply.)

__X__	**Reassuring FHR patterns**
_____	Nonreassuring FHR patterns
__X__	**Moderate variability**
_____	Decrease or loss of variability
__X__	**FHR accelerations**
_____	FHR decelerations
__X__	**No FHR decelerations**
__X__	**Normal baseline FHR**
_____	Fetal bradycardia
_____	Fetal tachycardia

There is a normal FHR baseline of 115 to 120 beats/min (110 to 160 beats/min is normal). Therefore, there is no evidence of fetal bradycardia or tachycardia. There is a moderate variability (6 to 25 beat/min) with FHR accelerations increasing to 158 beats/min, lasting for 25 sec. There are no FHR decelerations because the FHR does not slow down. These are all reassuring FHR patterns.

2. One hour later during assessment, the client is still at 5 cm dilation with intact membranes. The nurse notes that the FHR variability is decreased and resembles a straight line. The mother has not had any pain medication. Variability is difficult to assess accurately on external monitoring. What first must occur for an internal scalp electrode to be applied?

> A. Dilation and effacement of the cervix
>
> **B. Rupturing of the membranes**
>
> C. Administration of analgesics
>
> D. Antiseptic swabbing of presenting part

Prior to the insertion of an internal fetal monitor and IUPC, the membranes must have ruptured. The cervix is already adequately dilated at 5 cm. Internal monitoring requires 2 to 3 cm dilation. Analgesics can cause a decrease or loss of FHR variability, so administration does not improve loss of variability. Antiseptic swabbing should be done to the presenting part prior to application of the electrode, but only after the amniotic membranes have ruptured.

3. The nurse auscultates the fetal heart rate (FHR) and determines a rate of 150 to 155 beats/min. Which of the following nursing interventions is most appropriate?

> **A. Inform the client that the FHR is normal and document the findings.**
>
> B. Document and reassess the FHR in 5 min because the rate is too high.
>
> C. Report the FHR to the primary care provider immediately and then document.
>
> D. Document and tell the mother she is having a boy because the heart rate is fast.

Normal fetal heart rate is between 110 and 160 beats/min. Therefore, this finding does not need to be reported to the primary care provider. FHR is not associated with the gender of the fetus.

4. Which of the following is the best rationale for utilizing internal fetal heart rate monitoring?

> A. Internal monitoring can be used through the entire birth process.
>
> B. External monitoring is more subject to extraneous artifacts.
>
> **C. Internal monitoring is more accurate than external monitoring.**
>
> D. External monitoring increases risk of maternal and fetal infection.

Internal monitoring of the FHR is more accurate than external monitoring. External monitoring can be used throughout the birth process. The membranes must have ruptured and the cervix dilated to at least 2 to 3 cm before an internal monitor can be placed. Internal monitoring, not external monitoring, increases fetal and maternal risk for infection.

5. A nurse places an external fetal monitor on a client who is in labor. Which of the following instructions is most appropriate for the nurse to give to the client?

> A. "Lie supine so the tracing shows up the best on the paper."
> B. "Keep your legs flat so your abdomen is not tense."
> **C. "Lie on your side if that makes you feel comfortable."**
> D. "Avoid moving so there will not be any interference on the monitor."

It is optimal for the client to lie on her side to increase uteroplacental perfusion and fetal oxygenation. Supine positioning is contraindicated to avoid vena cava syndrome. Keeping the legs flat does not decrease abdominal tension. The client is encouraged to reposition herself frequently to promote fetal oxygenation and assist in the progress of labor. The ultrasound transducer and tocotransducer simply need to be readjusted by the nurse with client repositioning to maintain a good signal on the monitor.

6. The nurse knows that a fetus is best oxygenated during which of the following?

> A. Peak of the uterine contraction
> B. Increment of the uterine contraction
> C. Decrement of the uterine contraction
> **D. Relaxation between uterine contractions**

A fetus is most oxygenated during the relaxation period between contractions. During contractions, the arteries to the uteroplacental intervillous spaces are compressed resulting in a decrease in fetal circulation and oxygenation. The constriction is most acute during the contraction acme (peak of the uterine contraction intensity), but is also present on the increment and decrement (incline and decline of the contraction).

7. A client delivering in a birthing center is in the second stage of labor and is having no complications. Intermittent auscultation of FHR and uterine palpation of contractions is being performed to monitor FHR patterns. How frequently should the nurse assess the FHR?

      A. Every 60 min

      B. Every 30 min

      C. Every 15 min

      D. Every 5 min

With low-risk women, the FHR should be assessed every 15 min in the second stage of labor. In high-risk women, FHR should be assessed every 5 min in the second stage of labor. Every 60 min, FHR assessments are done during the latent phase for low risk-women. Every 30 min, assessments are done in the active phase for low-risk women and in the latent phase for high-risk women.

8. What is the appropriate initial nursing intervention for late decelerations on the fetal monitor?

      A. Reposition the client to left lateral position.

      B. Take no action because this is a normal pattern.

      C. Increase the intravenous fluid rate.

      D. Decrease the intravenous fluid rate.

Late decelerations are an abnormal FHR pattern caused by uteroplacental insufficiency. The initial nursing action should be to reposition the client to the left lateral position to increase uteroplacental perfusion. Increasing IV fluid rate is an intervention for late decelerations but is not the initial nursing intervention that should be taken.

9. Transitional accelerations of the FHR from baseline should be interpreted by the nurse as indicative of

      A. intact CNS response to fetal movement.

      B. fetal response to maternal fever.

      C. fetal distress requiring intervention.

      D. fetal hypoxia requiring maternal oxygen.

Occasional accelerations indicate the fetal CNS is intact and responding to fetal movement. This is referred to as baseline variability. Lack of variable accelerations would indicate fetal distress requiring intervention and oxygen via a face mask for the mother. Maternal fever causes tachycardia and prolonged, rather than transient, FHR accelerations.

Unit 2   Intrapartum

Chapter 12:   Nursing Care During the Stages of Labor
Contributor: Sandra Mesics, MSN, RN, CNM

⟳ NCLEX-RN® Connections:

Learning Objective: Review and apply knowledge within "**Nursing Care During the Stages of Labor**" in readiness for performance of the following nursing activities as outlined by the NCLEX-RN® test plan:

Δ   Monitor the client and fetus throughout labor.

Δ   Perform ongoing assessment of the client's labor progress.

Δ   Plan and provide care for the client during labor.

Δ   Reinforce and/or teach relaxation techniques during labor.

Δ   Assist with delivery of newborns.

📖 Key Points

Δ   Assessment begins when first contacting the client. This can be by telephone or in person.

Δ   During admission, the nurse orients the client and her partner to the unit.

Δ   During admission to the birthing facility, assessment includes:

   •   An admission history, review of antepartum care, and review of the birth plan.

   •   Laboratory results.

   •   A **20 to 30 min baseline monitoring** of fetal heart tones and uterine contraction patterns.

   •   Maternal vital signs.

   •   Status of amniotic membranes.

Δ   Maternal and fetal assessments are performed continuously throughout the labor process.

   •   Normal **uterine activity** pattern consists of contractions with a frequency of every **2 to 5 min** and a duration of less than **90 sec**, with an intensity that is **moderate** to **strong**

   •   Normal **fetal heart rate** is **110 to 160** beats/min

Δ   In the presence of vaginal bleeding, vaginal examinations should be avoided until placenta previa or placenta abruptio is ruled out. If necessary, vaginal examinations should be done by the primary care provider.

Δ   Cervical dilation is the single most important indicator of the progress of labor.

Δ   Nursing care during the labor process involves supporting and informing the partner.

Δ   The priority nursing care at the moment of birth is to assess and stabilize the neonate.

Key Factors

Δ   Cultural values and religious beliefs can influence a client's relationship with her family and her primary care provider during labor.

Δ   Fetal lie, presentation, and attitude can affect the progress of labor.

Δ   Fetal size in relationship to the mother's pelvis can affect the progress of labor.

Δ   The frequency, duration, and strength (intensity) of the uterine contractions cause fetal descent and cervical dilation.

Δ   The fetal heart rate is an indicator of fetal well-being and fetal tolerance to labor and should be monitored throughout labor and immediately after birth.

Therapeutic and Diagnostic Procedures:
   (Refer to chapter 9, Labor and Birth Processes for this section)

Assessments, Nursing Diagnoses, and Nursing Interventions

First Stage

Δ   **Nursing Assessments** during first stage of labor include:

   •   **Leopold's maneuvers** to determine:

      ◊   Number of fetuses.

      ◊   Presenting part.

      ◊   Fetal lie.

- **Vaginal examination** as indicated (only when signs indicate that progress has occurred or not contraindicated) to allow examiner to assess if client is in true labor and if membranes have ruptured.

  ◊ Encourage the client to take slow, deep breaths prior to the vaginal exam.

  ◊ Monitor the cervical dilation and effacement.

  ◊ Monitor the fetal station and presentation.

  ◊ Prepare for an impending delivery as the presenting part moves into positive stations and begins to push against the pelvic floor (**crowning**).

- Assessments related to possible **rupture of membranes**:

  ◊ When suspected rupture of membranes occurs, the nurse should first assess the fetal heart rate to assure there is no fetal distress from possible umbilical cord prolapse with the possibility of the cord wrapping around the fetal neck, which can occur with the gush of amniotic fluid.

  ◊ **Nitrazine paper,** which will turn blue in the presence of alkaline amniotic fluid (pH 6.5 to 7.4).

  ◊ **Ferning test** exhibits a frond-like ferning pattern when a small amount of amniotic fluid is viewed on a slide under a microscope.

  ◊ The amniotic fluid should be assessed for odor. The fluid should be free of foul odor and be a normal, clear straw color. Abnormal findings include the presence of meconium, a foul odor, or an abnormal color (yellow or port-wine). (*Refer to Chapter 14, Complications of Labor and Birth*)

- **Bladder palpation** performed on a regular basis to prevent bladder distention, which can impede fetal descent through the birth canal and cause trauma to the bladder.

  ◊ Clients may experience the inability to feel the urge to void secondary to the labor process or anesthesia.

  ◊ Encourage the client to engage in frequent voiding.

- **Blood pressure, pulse, and respiration measurements**

  ◊ Latent phase every 30 to 60 min

  ◊ Active phase every 30 min

  ◊ Transition phase every 15 to 30 min

- **Temperature** assessment every 4 hr (every 1 to 2 hr if membranes have ruptured).

- **Contraction monitoring**
  - ◊ Latent phase every 30 to 60 min
  - ◊ Active phase every 15 to 30 min
  - ◊ Transition phase every 10 to 15 min
- **Fetal heart rate monitoring (normal range 110 to 160 beats/min)**
  - ◊ Latent phase every 30 to 60 min
  - ◊ Active phase every 15 to 30 min
  - ◊ Transitional phase every 15 to 30 min

Δ **NANDA Nursing Diagnoses** during the first stage of labor include:

- Deficient knowledge related to the birthing process
- Risk for injury to mother and fetus related to bearing down efforts prior to complete dilation
- Acute pain related to increased contraction frequency and intensity
- Risk for impaired urinary elimination related to sensory impairment secondary to labor or anesthesia
- Impaired fetal gas exchange related to uteroplacental insufficiency
- Risk for ineffective coping related to the birthing process

Δ **Nursing Interventions** during the first stage of labor include:

- During the **first stage, latent phase** of labor, the nurse:
  - ◊ Provides the client and coach education about what to expect during labor and on implementing relaxation measures: breathing (deep cleansing breaths help divert focus away from contractions), effleurage (gentle circular stroking of the abdomen in rhythm with breathing during contractions), diversional activities (distraction, concentration on a focal point, or imagery).
  - ◊ Encourages upright positions, application of warm/cold packs, ambulation, or hydrotherapy if not contraindicated to promote comfort.
  - ◊ Encourages voiding every 2 hr.
- During **first stage, active phase** of labor, the nurse:
  - ◊ Provides client/fetal monitoring.
  - ◊ Encourages frequent position changes.
  - ◊ Encourages voiding at least every 2 hr.
  - ◊ Encourages deep cleansing breaths.
  - ◊ Encourages relaxation.

◊   Provides nonpharmacologic comfort measures.

◊   Provides pharmacologic pain relief as prescribed.

- During **first stage, transition phase** of labor, the nurse:

◊   Continues to encourage voiding every 2 hr.

◊   Continues to monitor and support the client and fetus.

◊   Encourages a rapid pant-pant-blow breathing pattern if the client has not learned a particular breathing pattern prenatally.

◊   Discourages pushing efforts until the cervix is fully dilated.

◊   Listens for client statements expressing the need to have a bowel movement. This sensation is a sign of complete dilation and fetal descent.

◊   Prepares the client for the birth.

◊   Observes for perineal bulging or crowning (appearance of the fetal head at the perineum).

◊   Encourages the client to begin bearing down with contractions once the cervix is fully dilated.

Second Stage

Δ   **Nursing Assessments** during the second stage of labor (begins with complete dilation and effacement) include:

- Blood pressure, pulse, and respiration measurements every 5 to 30 min.

- Assessment of every contraction.

- Assessment of each pushing effort made by client.

- Assessment for an increase in bloody show.

- Assessment of cervical dilation status.

- Assessment of the fetal heart rate continuously every 15 min and immediately following birth.

- Assessment for perineal lacerations, which usually occur as the fetal head is expulsed. Perineal lacerations are defined in terms of depth.

◊   **First degree** – laceration extends through the skin and structures superficial to the muscles.

◊   **Second degree** – laceration extends through the skin and muscles into the perineum.

◊   **Third degree** – laceration extends through the skin, muscles, perineum, and anal sphincter muscle.

◊   **Fourth degree** – laceration extends through skin, muscles, anal sphincter, and the anterior rectal wall.

Δ **NANDA Nursing Diagnoses** during the second stage of labor include:

- Acute pain related to pushing efforts and stretching of the perineum

- Anxiety related to inability to control stools during pushing efforts

- Risk for infection related to prolonged rupture of membranes over 24-hr period

Δ **Nursing Interventions** during second stage include:

- Continuous client/fetal monitoring.

- Assisting in positioning client for effective pushing

- Assisting in coaching pushing efforts and in encouraging bearing down efforts during contractions.

- Promoting rest between contractions.

- Providing comfort measures such as cold compresses.

- Cleansing the client's perineum as needed if fecal material is expelled during pushing.

- Providing feedback on labor progress to the client.

Third Stage

Δ **Nursing Assessments** during third stage of labor include:

- Blood pressure, pulse, and respiration measurements every 15 min.

- Assessment for signs of placental separation from the uterus as indicated by:

  ◊ Fundus firmly contracting.

  ◊ Swift gush from introitus of dark blood.

  ◊ Umbilical cord appears to lengthen as placenta descends.

  ◊ Vaginal fullness on exam.

- Assignment of 1 and 5 min Apgar scores to the newborn.

Δ **NANDA Nursing Diagnoses** during the third stage of labor include:

- Risk for infection related to perineal laceration

- Risk for infection related to retained placental fragments

Δ **Nursing Interventions** during the third stage of labor include:

- Instructing the client to push once signs of placental separation are indicated.

- Promoting family-infant bonding, which facilitates the release of endogenous oxytocics.

- Administering analgesics as prescribed.

- Administering oxytocics as prescribed once the placenta is expulsed to stimulate the uterus to contract and thus prevent hemorrhage.

- Gently cleansing vulvar area with warm water or normal saline and applying perineal pad or ice pack to perineum.

Fourth Stage

Δ   **Nursing Assessments** during fourth stage of labor include: (*For information, refer to chapter 15, Postpartum Physiological Changes and Nursing Care*)

- Maternal vital signs

- Uterine tone

- Lochia

- Urinary output

- Maternal newborn bonding activities

Δ   **NANDA Nursing Diagnoses** during the fourth stage of labor include:

- Risk for deficient fluid volume related to uterine atony and hemorrhage

- Acute pain related to hemorrhoids or episiotomy

Δ   **Nursing interventions** during the fourth stage of labor include:

- Massaging the uterine fundus and/or administering oxytocics as prescribed to maintain uterine tone to prevent hemorrhage.

- Encouraging voiding to prevent bladder distention.

Complications and Nursing Interventions

(*Refer to chapter 14, Complications of Labor and Birth for this section*)

Primary Reference:

Lowdermilk, D. L. & Perry, S. E. (2004). *Maternity & women's health care* (8th ed.). St. Louis, MO: Mosby.

Additional Resources:

NANDA International (2004). *NANDA nursing diagnoses: Definitions and classification 2005-2006*. Philadelphia: NANDA.

Chapter 12: Nursing Care During the Stages of Labor

Application Exercises

1. An adolescent client who is primigravida and 39 weeks gestation comes to the birthing unit with her partner because she has been having regular contractions. She states that her "bag of water" may have ruptured. Which of the following is the priority assessment the nurse should perform at this time?

> A. Fetal heart rate monitoring
>
> B. Vaginal exam
>
> C. Nitrazine paper test
>
> D. Leopold's maneuvers

2. To verify that a client's amniotic membranes have ruptured, the nurse should perform which of the following assessments?

> A. Ultrasound examination
>
> B. Amniocentesis
>
> C. Nitrazine paper test
>
> D. Ballottement test

3. A client and her partner have not taken prepared childbirth classes prior to labor. When is the best time for the nurse to provide the client and coaching partner education during the labor process?

> A. The first stage, latent phase
>
> B. The first stage, active phase
>
> C. The first stage, transition phase
>
> D. The second stage of labor

4. A client is in the transition phase of labor and feels that she needs to have a bowel movement with the peak of contractions. Which of the following is the most appropriate nursing intervention?

> A. Assist the client to the bathroom.
>
> B. Prepare for impending delivery.
>
> C. Prepare to remove a fecal impaction.
>
> D. Encourage the client to take deep, cleansing breaths.

5. A client fully dilated is bearing down with every contraction. After 2 hr, she delivers a female infant. As soon as the infant is delivered, the primary care provider clamps the cord and allows the client's partner to cut the umbilical cord. The infant is then placed on the client's abdomen. What should be the nurse's primary responsibility at this point?

    A. Assess the uterine fundus for tone.

    B. Assess for placental separation.

    C. Assess the client for signs of hemorrhage.

    D. Assess Apgar scores at 1 and 5 min.

6. A nurse is caring for a client in active labor. Her vaginal exam 1 hr ago was 3 cm dilation, 50 percent effacement, and - 3 station. Her membranes ruptured spontaneously. The nurse should assess for which of the following signs?

    A. Prolapsed cord

    B. Premature rupture of membranes

    C. Infection

    D. Fetal tachycardia

7. Visibility of the fetal head in the birth canal prior to delivery is called

    A. rotation.

    B. bulging.

    C. crowning.

    D. engagement.

8. A client is in the transition phase of labor. Which of the following maternal behaviors should the nurse most expect to observe?

    A. Cheerful, talkative, and seeking information

    B. Significantly restless and irritable

    C. Feelings of elation that labor is almost over

    D. A little apprehensive and uncertain

9. A nurse frequently palpates the client's bladder and encourages frequent voiding every 1 to 2 hr during labor predominantly because a

    A. full bladder increases the risk for fetal trauma.

    B. full bladder increases the risk for bladder infections.

    C. distended bladder will be traumatized by frequent pelvic exams.

    D. distended bladder reduces pelvic space needed for birth.

Chapter 12: Nursing Care During the Stages of Labor

Application Exercises Answer Key

1. An adolescent client who is primigravida and 39 weeks gestation comes to the birthing unit with her partner because she has been having regular contractions. She states that her "bag of water" may have ruptured. Which of the following is the priority assessment the nurse should perform at this time?

> **A. Fetal heart rate monitoring**
>
> B. Vaginal exam
>
> C. Nitrazine paper test
>
> D. Leopold's maneuvers

The most important initial assessment with suspected rupture of membranes is assessing the fetal heart rate (FHR) to ensure there is no fetal distress as a result of possible prolapse of the umbilical cord during the escape of the amniotic fluid. A prolapsed cord could result in either compression of the cord or the cord wrapping around the fetus's neck. The nurse should perform Leopold's maneuvers to determine fetal lie, presentation, and attitude, and monitor contraction pattern in conjunction with FHR monitoring. However, these assessments would not be of initial concern. If the FHR rate was within normal limits, the nurse should then perform a Nitrazine and/or ferning test to assess for the rupture of membranes. The nurse would then perform a vaginal exam to assess cervical dilation, effacement, and fetal station after labor progress has been firmly established.

2. To verify that a client's amniotic membranes have ruptured, the nurse should perform which of the following assessments?

> A. Ultrasound examination
>
> B. Amniocentesis
>
> **C. Nitrazine paper test**
>
> D. Ballottement test

The Nitrazine paper test confirms the presence of amniotic fluid by turning blue to indicate alkalinity between a pH of 6.5 to 7.4. An ultrasound examination utilizes high-frequency sound waves directed at the maternal abdomen to perform a fetal assessment. Amniocentesis is performed to remove amniotic fluid from the uterus for fetal testing. Ballottement is the rebounding of an unengaged fetus against an examiner's finger on palpation when the cervix is tapped.

3. A client and her partner have not taken prepared childbirth classes prior to labor. When is the best time for the nurse to provide the client and coaching partner education during the labor process?

      A. The first stage, latent phase

      B. The first stage, active phase

      C. The first stage, transition phase

      D. The second stage of labor

During the latent phase of the first stage the client is talkative and eager for the labor to progress and is not yet in a lot of pain. At this time, the client and her coaching partner will be most receptive to any educational information. As the labor progresses through the active and transition phases of the first stage and into the second stage of delivery, the client will be in too much pain from contractions to focus on educational information.

4. A client is in the transition phase of labor and feels that she needs to have a bowel movement with the peak of contractions. Which of the following is the most appropriate nursing intervention?

      A. Assist the client to the bathroom.

      B. Prepare for impending delivery.

      C. Prepare to remove a fecal impaction.

      D. Encourage the client to take deep, cleansing breaths.

The urge to have a bowel movement is a sign of complete dilation and fetal descent. If there is fecal material present at the rectum, the nurse cleanses the perineum rather than escorting the client to the bathroom. The nurse should not remove a fecal impaction. Although encouraging deep cleansing breaths is indicated, this has nothing to do with the client's sensation of needing to have a bowel movement.

5. A client fully dilated is bearing down with every contraction. After 2 hr, she delivers a female infant. As soon as the infant is delivered, the primary care provider clamps the cord and allows the client's partner to cut the umbilical cord. The infant is then placed on the client's abdomen. What should be the nurse's primary responsibility at this point?

<blockquote>

A. Assess the uterine fundus for tone.

B. Assess for placental separation.

C. Assess the client for signs of hemorrhage.

D. Assess Apgar scores at 1 and 5 min.

</blockquote>

The nurse's primary responsibility is to stabilize and assess the neonate. The nurse assesses the neonate for any signs of distress, and assigns 1 and 5 min Apgar scores. The nurse also prepares for expulsion of the placenta, monitors the client for signs of hemorrhage, and ascertains that the uterine fundus has a good tone. However, these responsibilities are not the first priority immediately following birth of the neonate.

6. A nurse is caring for a client in active labor. Her vaginal exam 1 hr ago was 3 cm dilation, 50 percent effacement, and - 3 station. Her membranes ruptured spontaneously. The nurse should assess for which of the following signs?

<blockquote>

A. Prolapsed cord

B. Premature rupture of membranes

C. Infection

D. Fetal tachycardia

</blockquote>

The nurse should always assess for signs of a prolapsed cord when membranes rupture. The client is in labor so the rupture of membranes is not premature. Labor has not continued for 24 hr past rupture of membranes, so infection is not a concern at this point. Abrupt fetal heart rate is indicative of prolapsed cord decelerations, not tachycardia.

7. Visibility of the fetal head in the birth canal prior to delivery is called

<blockquote>

A. rotation.

B. bulging.

C. crowning.

D. engagement.

</blockquote>

Crowning is the appearance of the fetal head in the birth canal at the perineum. Bulging is the bulging of the perineum, but without the visibility of the fetal head. Engagement pertains to fetal station 0 at the level of the maternal ischial spines. Rotation is a mechanism of labor when the fetal head rotates to align with the maternal pelvis to allow for passage.

8. A client is in the transition phase of labor. Which of the following maternal behaviors should the nurse most expect to observe?

      A. Cheerful, talkative, and seeking information

      B. Significantly restless and irritable

      C. Feelings of elation that labor is almost over

      D. A little apprehensive and uncertain

During the transition phase, the client experiences significant restlessness and irritability. The client is cheerful, talkative, and seeks information during the latent phase and becomes more apprehensive and uncertain as labor progresses into the active phase. Feelings of elation may occur during the latent phase but then would not occur again most likely until immediately following delivery in the second stage.

9. A nurse frequently palpates the client's bladder and encourages frequent voiding every 1 to 2 hr during labor predominantly because a

      A. full bladder increases the risk for fetal trauma.

      B. full bladder increases the risk for bladder infections.

      C. distended bladder will be traumatized by frequent pelvic exams.

      D. distended bladder reduces pelvic space needed for birth.

A distended bladder reduces pelvic space, impedes the fetal descent necessary for delivery, and places the bladder at risk for trauma during the labor process. Urinary stasis, which can occur with prolonged bladder distention due to a full bladder, does increase bladder infection risk. However, this is not the primary concern at this time. A full bladder does not place the fetus at risk for trauma.

Unit 2   Intrapartum

Chapter 13:   Therapeutic Procedures to Assist with Labor and Birth

Contributor: Sandra Mesics, MSN, RN, CNM

 NCLEX-RN® Connections:

Learning Objective: Review and apply knowledge within **"Therapeutic Procedures to Assist with Labor and Birth"** in readiness for performance of the following nursing activities as outlined by the NCLEX-RN® test plan:

Δ   Provide the client education regarding purpose and preparation for diagnostic tests and therapeutic procedures.

Δ   Assess the client's status during and after diagnostic tests and therapeutic procedures.

Δ   Assist in the performance of diagnostic tests and therapeutic procedures as appropriate.

Δ   Monitor the results of the client's diagnostic tests and therapeutic procedures.

Therapeutic Procedure and Nursing Management: Amnioinfusion

Key Points

Δ   **Amnioinfusion** of normal saline or lactated Ringer's solution as prescribed is instilled into the amniotic cavity through a transcervical catheter introduced into the uterus to supplement the amount of amniotic fluid. The instillation will reduce severity of variable decelerations caused by cord compression or dilute meconium-stained amniotic fluid.

Key Factors

Δ   Indications for **amnioinfusion** include:

•   **Oligohydramnios** (scant amount or absence of amniotic fluid) caused by any of the following:

◊   Uteroplacental insufficiency.

◊ Premature rupture of membranes.

◊ Postmaturity of the fetus.

- **Fetal cord compression** secondary to:

◊ Postmaturity of fetus (macrosomic, large body), which places the fetus at risk for variable deceleration from cord compression.

- **Meconium-stained amniotic fluid** secondary to either:

◊ Fetal distress.

◊ Postmaturity of fetus.

Nursing Assessments

Δ Nursing assessment for **amnioinfusion** requires continuous monitoring to prevent uterine overdistention and increased uterine tone which can initiate, accelerate, or intensify uterine contractions and cause nonreassuring fetal heart rate (FHR) changes.

Δ Continually assess intensity and frequency of the client's uterine contractions.

Δ Continually monitor FHR.

Nursing Interventions

Δ Assist with amniotomy or stripping of membranes if membranes have not already ruptured. Membranes must have ruptured to perform amnioinfusion

Δ Warm fluid utilizing a blood warmer prior to infusion.

Δ Perform nursing measures to maintain comfort and dryness because the infused fluid will continuously leak out.

Therapeutic Procedure and Nursing Management: Amniotomy

Key Points

Δ **Amniotomy** is the artificial rupture of the amniotic membranes (AROM) by the primary care provider using an **Amnihook** or other sharp instrument.

- Labor usually begins within 12 hr after the membranes rupture.

- The client is at an increased risk for cord prolapse or infection.

Key Factors

Δ   Labor progression is too slow and augmentation or induction of labor is indicated.

Δ   Amnioinfusion is indicated for cord compression or meconium-stained amniotic fluid necessitating AROM.

Nursing Assessments

Δ   Assure presenting part of the fetus is engaged prior to amniotomy to prevent cord prolapse.

Δ   Monitor FHR prior to and following AROM to assess for cord prolapse evidenced by variable or late decelerations.

Δ   Assess characteristics of amniotic fluid including color, odor, and consistency.

- Meconium-stained fluid may be associated with fetal distress.
- Presence of blood in the amniotic fluid may be indicative of abruptio placentae or fetal trauma.
- Amniotic fluid emitting a foul smell may indicate infection.

Nursing Interventions

Δ   Record the time of rupture.

Δ   Limit maternal activity following AROM to reduce risk of infection or malposition of the fetus.

Therapeutic Procedure and Nursing Management: External Cephalic Version

Key Points

Δ   **External cephalic version (ECV)** is the attempt to manipulate the abdominal wall to direct a malpositioned fetus into a normal vertex cephalic presentation after 37 weeks gestation.

Δ   There is a high risk of prolapse of the umbilical cord surrounding this procedure.

Key Factors

Δ   Indication for ECV is a malpositioned fetus in a breech or transverse position after 37 weeks gestation.

Δ   Contraindications for external cephalic version include:

- Uterine anomalies.

- Previous cesarean birth.

- Cephalopelvic disproportion.

- Placenta previa.

- Multifetal gestation.

- Oligohydramnios

Diagnostic Procedure

Δ   **Ultrasound scanning** is performed prior to the procedure to:

- Evaluate fetal position.

- Locate the umbilical cord.

- Assess placental placement to rule out placenta previa.

- Determine the amount of amniotic fluid.

- Determine fetal age.

- Assess for the presence of anomalies.

- Evaluate pelvic adequacy for delivery.

- Guide the direction of the fetus during the procedure.

Nursing Assessments

Δ   During and after the procedure:

- Perform a nonstress test to evaluate fetal well-being.

- Continuously monitor FHR and patterns to assess for bradycardia and variable decelerations.

- Monitor maternal vital signs.

- Assess maternal comfort due to the discomfort the procedure may cause.

Δ   Postprocedure, monitor for:

- Uterine activity, contraction frequency, duration, and intensity.

- Rupture of membranes.

- Bleeding until maternal condition is stable.

- Decrease in fetal activity.

Nursing Interventions

Δ   Obtain an informed consent from the client.

Δ   Ensure **RH immune globulin (RhoGAM)** was administered at 28 weeks gestation if mother is Rh-negative prior to external version.

Δ   Administer intravenous fluid and tocolytics to relax uterus to permit easier manipulation prior to external version.

Δ   Monitor the client's blood pressure to detect if vena cava compression with resulting hypotension is occurring.

Δ   Monitor for maternal pain.

Δ   Rh-negative clients require assistance with the performance of a **Kleihauer-Betke test.** The test detects the presence and amount of fetal blood in the maternal circulation because manipulation can cause fetomaternal bleeding.

•   If more than 15 mL of fetal blood is present, the dosage of Rh immune globulin must be increased to suppress the maternal immune response to fetal Rh-positive blood.

Therapeutic Procedure and Nursing Management: Bishop Score

Key Points and Nursing Assessments

Δ   **Bishop score** is used to determine the maternal readiness for labor by evaluating if the cervix is favorable by rating the following.

•   Cervical dilation

•   Cervical effacement

•   Cervical consistency (firm, medium, or soft)

•   Cervical position (posterior, midposition, or anterior)

•   Presenting part station

Δ   The five factors are assigned a numerical value of 0 to 3, the total score is calculated, and a score of 9 or more for nulliparas and 5 or more for multiparas indicates readiness for labor induction.

Key Factors

Δ   Any condition in which augmentation or induction of labor is indicated.

Nursing Interventions

Δ   Assist with cervical ripening and labor augmentation and induction procedures as indicated.

Therapeutic Procedure and Nursing Management: Cervical Ripening

Key Points

Δ **Cervical ripening** increases cervical readiness for labor by either a chemical or mechanical method to promote cervical softening, dilation, and effacement.

- Cervical ripening makes labor induction more successful.

- Cervical ripening lowers the dosage of oxytocin (Pitocin) needed for induction.

  ◊ For certain clients, cervical ripening is adequate to induce labor and eliminates the need for oxytocin administration.

- **Chemical agents** consist of prostaglandin gel (Cytotec, Cervidil, Prepidil) which is applied to the cervix to "ripen" it (soften and thin) and to increase cervical readiness prior to the induction of labor.

- **Mechanical methods** ripen the cervix by utilizing:

  ◊ **Balloon catheters** inserted into the intracervical canal to dilate the cervix.

  ◊ **Hydroscopic dilators** and **sponges** to absorb fluid from the surrounding tissues and then enlarge.

  ◊ **Laminaria tents** made from desiccated seaweed.

  ◊ **Synthetic dilators** and **sponges** containing magnesium sulfate (Lamicel) are inserted into the endocervix without rupture of the membranes. The dilators and sponges absorb fluid and expand causing cervical dilation.

- Insertion of fresh dilators may be necessary for further dilation as required.

- Membrane stripping and amniotomy may also be used to ripen the cervix.

Key Factors

Δ Failure of the cervix to dilate and efface.

Δ Failure of labor to progress.

Nursing Assessments

Δ   During **cervical ripening**, the nurse should assess for:

- Urinary retention.

- Rupture of membranes.

- Uterine tenderness or pain.

- Contractions.

- Vaginal bleeding.

- Fetal distress.

Nursing Interventions

Δ   Document the number of dilators and/or sponges inserted during the procedure.

Δ   Assist with augmentation or induction of labor as prescribed.

Therapeutic Procedure and Nursing Management: Induction of Labor

Key Points

Δ   **Induction of labor** is the deliberate initiation of uterine contractions to stimulate labor before spontaneous onset to bring about the birth either by chemical or mechanical means.

Δ   Methods include:

- Prostaglandins applied cervically.

- Administration of intravenous oxytocin (Pitocin).

- Amniotomy or stripping of membranes.

- Nipple stimulation to trigger the release of endogenous oxytocin.

Key Factors

Δ   Indications for induction of labor include:

- Postterm pregnancy (beyond 42 weeks).

- Dystocia (prolonged, difficult labor).

  ◊   Inadequate uterine contractions

- Prolonged rupture of membranes.

  ◊ Predisposes the mother and fetus to risk of infection.

- Maternal medical complications.

  ◊ Rh isoimmunization

  ◊ Diabetes

  ◊ Pulmonary disease

  ◊ Pregnancy-induced hypertension

- Fetal demise.

- Chorioamnionitis.

Nursing Assessments

Δ Nursing assessments for a client with induction of labor include:

- Cervical ripening

  ◊ If **cervical ripening agents** (Cytotec, Cervidil, and Prepidil) are used, baseline data on fetal and maternal well being are obtained.

  ◊ The nurse should monitor FHR and uterine activity after administration of cervical ripening agents.

  ◊ The nurse should notify the primary care provider if uterine hyperstimulation or FHR distress is noted.

- Amniotomy or amniotic membrane stripping

  ◊ When amniotomy is performed, the nurse should record a baseline assessment of the FHR prior to the procedure and continuously during and after the procedure.

  ◊ The nurse should assess the amount, color, consistency, and odor of the amniotic fluid.

  ◊ The nurse should document the time of amniotomy and the findings.

- Oxytocin

  ◊ Prior to the administration of oxytocin, it is essential that the nurse confirm that the fetus is engaged in the birth canal at a minimum of station 0.

◊ **Intrauterine pressure catheter (IUPC)** may be used to monitor frequency, duration, and intensity of contractions.

◊ When oxytocin is administered, assessments include maternal blood pressure, pulse, and respirations every 30 min and with every change in dose.

◊ Monitor FHR and contraction pattern every 15 min and with every change in dose.

◊ Assess fluid intake and urinary output.

Δ A **Bishop score** rating should be obtained prior to starting any labor induction protocol.

NANDA Nursing Diagnoses

Δ Deficient knowledge related to labor induction methods

Δ Risk of injury to the mother and fetus related to cervical ripening, amniotomy, or oxytocin administration

Nursing Interventions

Δ Assist with or perform administration of labor induction agents as prescribed.

Δ Increase oxytocin as prescribed until desired contraction pattern is obtained and then maintain the dose if:

• Contraction frequency of 2 to 3 min.

• Contraction duration of 60 to 90 sec.

• Contraction intensity of 40 to 90 mm Hg on IUPC.

• Uterine resting tone of 10 to 15 mm Hg.

• Cervical dilation of 1 cm/hr.

• Reassuring FHR between 110 to 160 beats/min.

Δ Discontinue oxytocin if uterine hyperstimulation occurs. Symptoms of uterine hyperstimulation include:

• Contraction frequency more often than every 2 min.

• Contraction duration longer than 90 sec.

• Contraction intensity results in pressures greater than 90 mm Hg as shown by IUPC.

• Uterine resting tone greater than 20 mm Hg between contractions.

• No relaxation of uterus between contractions

- A nonreassuring fetal heart rate is noted.

  ◊ Abnormal baseline less than 110 or greater than 160 beats/min

  ◊ Loss of variability

  ◊ Late or prolonged decelerations

Δ Interventions for oxytocin uterine hyperstimulation include:

- Notifying the primary care provider.

- Positioning the client in a side-lying position to increase uteroplacental perfusion.

- Keeping the intravenous line open and increasing fluid rate up to 200 mL/hr unless contraindicated.

- Administering oxygen by a face mask at 8 to 10 L/min as prescribed.

- Administering the tocolytic, terbutaline (Brethine) 0.25 mg subcutaneously as prescribed to diminish uterine activity.

- Monitoring of FHR and patterns in conjunction with uterine activity.

- Documenting responses to interventions.

Therapeutic Procedure and Nursing Management: Augmentation of Labor

 Key Points

Δ **Augmentation of labor** is the stimulation of hypotonic contractions once labor has spontaneously begun, but progress is inadequate.

Δ Certain primary care providers favor active management of labor to establish effective labor with the aggressive use of amniotomy, oxytocin, or rupture of membranes. This ensures that the client delivers within 12 hr of admission to the labor unit so that the risk of cesarean birth will be decreased.

Key Factors, Nursing Assessment, and Nursing Interventions

Δ Risk factors requiring augmentation of labor, administration procedures, nursing assessments and interventions, and possible procedure complications are the same for labor induction. *(Refer to previous section, Induction of labor).*

Therapeutic Procedure and Nursing Management: Episiotomy

📖 Key Points

Δ   An **episiotomy** is an incision made into the perineum to enlarge the vaginal opening to more easily facilitate delivery and minimize soft tissue damage.

- This procedure is controversial, has an increasing decline in favorability, and is not believed to be effective in minimizing perineal trauma.

- Indications for an episiotomy

  ◊   Shorten the second stage of labor

  ◊   Facilitate forceps-assisted or vacuum-assisted delivery

  ◊   Prevent cerebral hemorrhage in a fragile preterm fetus

  ◊   Facilitate birth of a macrosomic (large) infant

Δ   The site and direction of the incision designates the type of episiotomy.

- **Median (midline) episiotomy** extends from the vaginal outlet toward the rectum, and is the most commonly used.

  ◊   More effective

  ◊   Much easier to repair

  ◊   Associated with higher incidence of third- and fourth-degree lacerations

- **Mediolateral episiotomy** extends from the vaginal outlet posterolateral, either to the left or right of the midline, and is used when posterior extension is likely.

  ◊   Third-degree laceration may occur

  ◊   Blood loss is greater and the repair is more difficult

- Local anesthetic is administered to the perineum prior to the incision.

Key Factors

Δ   Prolonged second stage of labor

Δ   Macrosomic fetus

Δ   Forceps-assisted or vacuum-assisted birth

Nursing Assessments

(For information regarding nursing assessments and interventions, refer to chapter 15, Postpartum Physiological Changes and Nursing Care).

Nursing Interventions

Δ   Encourage alternate labor positions to reduce pressure on the perineum and promote perineal stretching in order to reduce the necessity for an episiotomy.

Therapeutic Procedure and Nursing Management: Vacuum-Assisted Birth

Key Points

Δ   **Vacuum-assisted birth** involves the use of a cuplike suction device that is attached to the fetal head. Traction is applied during contractions to assist in the descent and birth of the head, after which, the vacuum cup is released and removed preceding delivery of the fetal body.

Δ   The suction device should not be left in place for more than 25 min.

Δ   Conditions for use consist of a vacuum-assisted birth include:

• Vertex presentation.

• Ruptured membranes.

• Absence of cephalopelvic disproportion.

Δ   When operative vaginal birth is necessary, vacuum assistance is preferred over forceps assistance.

Δ   Risks associated with vacuum-assisted births include:

• Cephalohematoma.

• Scalp lacerations.

• Subdural hematoma of the neonate.

• Maternal lacerations to the cervix, vagina, or perineum.

Key Factors

Δ   Indications for vacuum-assisted birth include:

• Maternal exhaustion and ineffective pushing efforts.

• Fetal distress during second stage of labor.

Nursing Assessments

Δ   Nursing assessments for a client who is undergoing a vacuum-assisted delivery include:

- • Assessing and recording FHR before and during vacuum assistance.

- • Assessing for bladder distention and catheterizing if necessary.

- • Observing the infant for cephalohematoma, subdural hematoma, or lacerations after delivery.

- • Checking for caput succedaneum. Caput succedaneum is a normal occurrence and should resolve within 24 hr.

NANDA Nursing Diagnoses

Δ   Deficient knowledge related to vacuum-assisted delivery

Δ   Risk of injury to the fetus from vacuum administration

Nursing Interventions

Δ   Provide support and education regarding the procedure to the client and partner.

Δ   Assist the client into the lithotomy position to allow for sufficient traction of the vacuum cup when it is applied to the fetal head.

Δ   Alert newborn and postpartum care providers that vacuum assistance was utilized.

Δ   Prepare for forceps-assisted birth if vacuum-assisted birth is not successful.

Therapeutic Procedure and Nursing Management: Forceps-Assisted Birth

Key Points

Δ   **Forceps-assisted birth** consists of using an instrument with two curved spoon-like blades to assist in the delivery of the fetal head. Traction is applied during contractions.

Δ   Risks associated with forceps-assisted births include:

- • Lacerations of the cervix.

- • Lacerations of the vagina and perineum.

- • Injury to the bladder.

- • Facial bruising on the neonate.

- • Facial nerve palsy of the neonate.

Key Factors

Δ   Indications for forceps-assisted birth include:

• Fetal distress during labor.

• Abnormal presentations or a breech position requiring delivery of the head.

• Arrest of rotation.

Nursing Assessments

Δ   Nursing assessments for a client with forceps-assisted delivery include:

• Assessing and recording FHR before, during, and after forceps assistance.

◊ Compression of the cord between the fetal head and forceps will cause a decrease in the FHR.

◊ If FHR decrease occurs, the forceps are removed and reapplied.

• Assessing to assure the client's bladder is empty and catheterizing if necessary.

• Assessing to ensure that the fetus is engaged and that membranes have ruptured.

• Observing the infant for bruising and abrasions at the site of forceps application after delivery.

• Checking the mother for any possible injuries after birth.

◊ Vaginal or cervical lacerations indicated by bleeding in spite of contracted uterus

◊ Urine retention resulting from bladder or urethral injuries

◊ Hematoma formation in the pelvic soft tissues resulting from blood vessel damage

NANDA Nursing Diagnoses

Δ   Deficient knowledge related to forceps-assisted delivery

Δ   Risk of injury to the mother and fetus from forceps administration

Nursing Interventions

Δ   Nursing interventions for a client who is to undergo a forceps or vacuum-assisted delivery include:

- Explaining the procedure to the client and the client's support person.

- Assisting the client into the lithotomy position.

- Assisting with the procedure as necessary.

- Reporting to newborn and postpartum nursing caregivers that forceps or vacuum-assisted delivery methods were used.

Therapeutic Procedure and Nursing Management: Cesarean Birth

 Key Points

Δ   **Cesarean birth** is the delivery of the fetus through a transabdominal incision of the uterus to preserve the life or health of the mother and fetus when there is evidence of complications.

- Incisions are currently made horizontally into the lower segment of the uterus.

- Previously made as a classical vertical incision into the muscular body of the uterus.

Δ   Possible complications of a cesarean birth include:

- Maternal

  ◊   Aspiration.

  ◊   Amniotic fluid pulmonary embolism.

  ◊   Wound infection.

  ◊   Wound dehiscence.

  ◊   Thrombophlebitis.

  ◊   Hemorrhage.

  ◊   Urinary tract infection.

  ◊   Injuries to the bladder or bowel.

  ◊   Anesthesia associated complications.

- Fetal

  ◊   Premature birth of fetus if gestational age is inaccurate.

  ◊   Fetal injuries during surgery.

Key Factors

Δ   Indications and risk factors for cesarean birth include:

- Cephalopelvic disproportion.

- Malpresentation, particularly breech presentation.

- Placental abnormalities.

  ◊   Placenta previa

  ◊   Abruptio placenta

- Fetal distress.

- High risk pregnancy.

  ◊   Hypertensive disorders such as preeclampsia and eclampsia

  ◊   Active genital herpes outbreak

  ◊   Positive HIV status

  ◊   Maternal diabetes

- Previous cesarean birth.

- Dystocia.

- Multiple gestations.

- Umbilical cord prolapse.

Nursing Assessments

Δ   Preoperative nursing assessments for a client with a cesarean birth include:

- Assessing and recording FHR, maternal vital signs, and blood pressure.

- Assisting with obtaining abdominal ultrasound to assess if a cesarean birth is indicated.

Δ   Postoperative nursing assessments for a client with a cesarean birth include:

- Monitoring for signs of infection and excessive bleeding at the incision site.

- Assessing the client for symptoms of burning and pain on urination, which could be suggestive of a urinary tract infection.

- Assessing the uterine fundus for firmness or tenderness.

- Assessing the lochia for amount and characteristics.

  ◊   A tender uterus and foul smelling lochia may indicate endometritis.

- Assessing for productive cough or chills, which could be symptoms of pneumonia.

- Assessing for a positive Homans' sign.

  ◊ Pain in the posterior and lateral aspects of the lower extremity when the foot is dorsiflexed. This symptom suggests the presence of a thrombus.

- Monitoring intake and output.

NANDA Nursing Diagnoses

Δ Deficient knowledge related to cesarean birth

Δ Risk of injury to the mother and fetus from surgical procedure

Δ Risk of infection from surgical procedure

Δ Impaired mobility related to bed rest following the procedure

Nursing Interventions

Δ Preoperative nursing interventions for a client who is to undergo a cesarean birth include:

- Preparing the client and the client's support person and explaining the procedure to them.

- Obtaining an informed consent form from the client.

- Determining if the client has had nothing by mouth since midnight before the procedure. If the client has, notify the anesthesiologist.

- Positioning the client in a supine position with a wedge under one hip to laterally tilt her and keep her off of her vena cava and descending aorta. This will help maintain optimal perfusion of oxygenated blood to the fetus during the procedure.

- Inserting an indwelling urinary catheter.

- Administering any preoperative medications.

- Preparing the surgical site.

- Inserting an intravenous line.

- Assuring preoperative diagnostic tests are complete including an Rh factor test.

- Providing emotional support.

Δ Intraoperative nursing interventions for a client who is to undergo a cesarean birth include:

- Assisting in positioning the client on the operating table.

- Continuing to monitor FHR.

- Continuing to monitor vital signs, IV fluids, and urinary output.

Δ Postoperative nursing care for a client who is to undergo a cesarean delivery include:

- Monitoring vital signs per protocol.

- Providing pain relief and antiemetics as prescribed.

- Encouraging turning, coughing, and deep breathing to prevent pulmonary complications.

- Encouraging splinting of the incision with pillows.

- Encouraging ambulation to prevent thrombus formation.

Therapeutic Procedure and Nursing Management: Vaginal Birth after Cesarean Birth (VBAC)

Key Points

Δ **Vaginal birth after cesarean birth (VBAC)** is when the client delivers vaginally after having had a previous cesarean birth.

Key Factors

Δ Indications for vaginal birth after cesarean birth include:

- Previous documented low segment transverse incision.

- No current contraindications.

  ◊ Large for gestational age infant

  ◊ Malpresentation

  ◊ Cephalopelvic disproportion

  ◊ Previous classical vertical uterine incision

Nursing Assessments

Δ Nursing assessments for a client attempting a VBAC include:

- Reviewing medical records for evidence of a previous low segment transverse cesarean incision.

- Assessing and recording FHR during the labor.

- Assessing and recording contraction patterns for strength, duration, and frequency of contractions.

- Assessing for signs of uterine rupture.

NANDA Nursing Diagnoses

Δ   Deficient knowledge related to VBAC process

Δ   Anxiety related to fear of ruptured uterus, repeat cesarean birth, or ability to deliver vaginally

Δ   Risk of injury to the mother and fetus from possible rupture of uterus

Nursing Interventions

Δ   Nursing interventions for a client attempting a VBAC include:

- Explaining the procedure to the client and the client's support person.

- Promoting relaxation and breathing techniques during labor.

- Providing analgesia as prescribed and requested.

Primary Reference:

Lowdermilk, D. L. & Perry, S. E. (2004). *Maternity & women's health care* (8th ed.). St. Louis, MO: Mosby.

Additional Resources:

Murray S. S. & McKinney, E. S. (2006). *Foundations of maternal-newborn nursing* (4th ed.). Philadelphia: Elsevier.

NANDA International (2004). *NANDA nursing diagnoses: Definitions and classification 2005-2006*. Philadelphia: NANDA.

Chapter 13: Therapeutic Procedures to Assist with Labor and Birth

Application Exercises

1. Which of the following positions should a nurse place a client in prior to a cesarean birth?

      A. Trendelenburg position with the lower extremities elevated

      B. Left lateral side-lying position with head elevated

      C. Prone position with a wedge under the right hip

      D. Supine position with a wedge under the right hip

2. A client at 42 weeks gestation is admitted to the labor and delivery unit. During an ultrasound, it is noted that the fetus is large for gestational age. The nurse reviews the prescription from the primary care provider to begin an amnioinfusion. The nurse knows that amnioinfusion is indicated for which of the following reasons? (Select all that apply.)

      _____   Oligohydramnios

      _____   Hydramnios

      _____   Fetal cord compression

      _____   Hydration

      _____   Meconium in amniotic fluid

3. A nurse is providing continuous monitoring throughout a client's amnioinfusion for complications of overdistention of the uterus. For which of the following contraction patterns should the nurse observe?

      A. Hypotonic

      B. Hypertonic

      C. Irregular

      D. Absent

4. A client in the labor and delivery unit has been in labor for 12 hr. Her membranes are still intact. The primary care provider has decided to perform an amniotomy in an effort to facilitate the progress of labor. The nurse performs a pelvic examination to ensure which of the following prior to the performance of the amniotomy?

      A. Fetal engagement

      B. Fetal lie

      C. Fetal attitude

      D. Fetal position

5. A primary care provider is going to attempt to perform an external cephalic version and manipulate the maternal abdominal wall to direct a malpositioned fetus into a normal vertex cephalic presentation. The nurse reviews the client's chart to ensure that there are no contraindications to the performance of this procedure. Select all of the following that would prohibit the primary care provider from performing this manipulation.

_____ Previous cesarean birth

_____ Small for gestational age fetus

_____ Hydramnios

_____ Placenta previa

_____ Cephalopelvic disproportion

6. Which of the following medications should the nurse anticipate will be necessary to administer preceding an external version for a client with Rh-negative blood who did not receive adequate prenatal care?

A. Prostaglandin

B. Magnesium sulfate

C. RhoGAM

D. Oxytocin

7. A client is admitted to the labor and delivery unit at 42 weeks gestation and is started on intravenous oxytocin for an induction of labor. For which of the following contraction patterns should the nurse discontinue the infusion of oxytocin?

A. Frequency of 2 to 3 min, duration of 60 to 90 sec, intensity with 40 to 90 mm Hg, and resting tone 10 to 15 mm Hg

B. Frequency 2 to 3 min, duration 90 to 120 sec, intensity with 90 to 120 mm Hg, and uterine resting tone 20 to 40 mm Hg

C. Frequency of 1 to 2 min, duration 15 to 30 sec, intensity 15 to 40 mm Hg, and uterine resting tone 0 to 10 mm Hg

D. Frequency of 1 to 2 min, duration 45 to 60 sec, intensity with 40 to 90 mm Hg, and resting tone 10 to 15 mm Hg

8. In addition to oxytocin administration, other methods of augmenting or inducing labor include which of the following?

A. Cervical ripening

B. Amnioinfusion

C. Cesarean birth

D. Episiotomy

9. A client at 39 weeks gestation in the latent phase of labor is admitted to the labor and delivery unit. The client is attempting a vaginal birth after a cesarean birth. In reviewing the client's medical record, the nurse should recognize which of the following as a contraindication to a VBAC?

    A. A low transverse incision

    B. A horizontal incision

    C. A classical vertical incision

    D. A full-thickness incision

10. A client at 37 weeks gestation is admitted to the labor and delivery unit, but labor is not progressing well. Which of the following is an indication for induction of labor?

    A. Placenta previa

    B. Cephalopelvic disproportion

    C. Chorioamnionitis

    D. Maternal herpes infection

11. Which of the following is true of clients who have previously experienced a cesarean birth?

    A. Vaginal birth after cesarean (VBAC) is recommended.

    B. Labor may be safe if the uterine incision was low transverse.

    C. Type of abdominal incision is indicative of the type of uterine incision.

    D. Labor is more risky if there were vaginal deliveries prior to a cesarean birth.

Chapter 13: Therapeutic Procedures to Assist with Labor and Birth

Application Exercises Answer Key

1. Which of the following positions should a nurse place a client in prior to a cesarean birth?

   A. Trendelenburg position with the lower extremities elevated

   B. Left lateral side-lying position with head elevated

   C. Prone position with a wedge under the right hip

   D. Supine position with a wedge under the right hip

   The client will need to be positioned supine, on her back, for the cesarean surgery. Placing a wedge under one of the client's hips, preferably the right, will tilt the client so she will not experience pressure of her gravid uterus compressing the descending aorta or inferior vena cava. This could possibly compromise circulation to the fetus. Trendelenburg position, on the back with legs elevated, still places pressure on the maternal descending aorta and vena cava, compromising uteroplacental circulation. Prone position on the mother's stomach would be contraindicated along with the side-lying position, both of which would make surgical approach inaccessible.

2. A client at 42 weeks gestation is admitted to the labor and delivery unit. During an ultrasound, it is noted that the fetus is large for gestational age. The nurse reviews the prescription from the primary care provider to begin an amnioinfusion. The nurse knows that amnioinfusion is indicated for which of the following reasons? (Select all that apply.)

__X__	**Oligohydramnios**
_____	Hydramnios
__X__	**Fetal cord compression**
_____	Hydration
__X__	**Meconium in amniotic fluid**

   Oligohydramnios is an inadequate amount of amniotic fluid, less than 300 mL, which can contribute to intrauterine growth restriction of the fetus, restrict fetal movement, and cause fetal distress during labor. Oligohydramnios can also lead to fetal cord compression, which decreases fetal oxygenation. Meconium staining of the amniotic fluid with thick fresh meconium places the fetus at risk for meconium aspiration syndrome. Hydramnios is excessive amniotic fluid. Amnioinfusion does not increase hydration. Intravenous fluids or oral intake would provide this.

3. A nurse is providing continuous monitoring throughout a client's amnioinfusion for complications of overdistention of the uterus. For which of the following contraction patterns should the nurse observe?

> A. Hypotonic
>
> **B. Hypertonic**
>
> C. Irregular
>
> D. Absent

Overdistention of the uterus can increase uterine tone which can initiate, accelerate, or intensify uterine contractions. Hypotonic is a decrease in contraction intensity, duration, and frequency with the contractions possibly even stopping and becoming absent. Irregular contractions are more likely to occur with hypotonic contractions.

4. A client in the labor and delivery unit has been in labor for 12 hr. Her membranes are still intact. The primary care provider has decided to perform an amniotomy in an effort to facilitate the progress of labor. The nurse performs a pelvic examination to ensure which of the following prior to the performance of the amniotomy?

> **A. Fetal engagement**
>
> B. Fetal lie
>
> C. Fetal attitude
>
> D. Fetal position

Prior to the performance of an amniotomy, the amniotic membranes should have ruptured. It is also imperative that the fetus is engaged at a level 0 station and at the level of the maternal ischial spines to prevent prolapse of the umbilical cord. Fetal lie pertains to the axis of the maternal spine in relation to the axis of the fetal spine. Fetal attitude is the relationship of the fetal extremities and chin to the fetal torso. Fetal position refers to the direction of a reference point in the fetal presenting part to the maternal pelvis.

5. A primary care provider is going to attempt to perform an external cephalic version and manipulate the maternal abdominal wall to direct a malpositioned fetus into a normal vertex cephalic presentation. The nurse reviews the client's chart to ensure that there are no contraindications to the performance of this procedure. Select all of the following that would prohibit the primary care provider from performing this manipulation.

__X__	**Previous cesarean birth**
_____	Small for gestational age fetus
_____	Hydramnios
__X__	**Placenta previa**
__X__	**Cephalopelvic disproportion**

A previous cesarean birth places the mother at risk for uterine rupture. Placenta previa is when the placenta is attached to the lower portion of the cervix partially or completely over the cervical os. This can place the mother at risk for hemorrhage. Cephalopelvic disproportion is when the fetal head is larger than the maternal pelvis. This would most likely require a cesarean birth, in which case external version would be unnecessary and could possibly cause uterine rupture. A small for gestational age fetus does not present a risk for external version. Oligohydramnios, not hydramnios is a contraindication for this procedure.

6. Which of the following medications should the nurse anticipate will be necessary to administer preceding an external version for a client with Rh-negative blood who did not receive adequate prenatal care?

   A. Prostaglandin

   B. Magnesium sulfate

   C. RhoGAM

   D. Oxytocin

RhoGAM or RH immune globulin is given to Rh-negative mothers at 28 weeks gestation to prevent isoimmunization in which maternal antibodies attack the RBCs of an Rh-positive fetus. During the external version, there is a risk of fetal blood entering the maternal circulation. Prostaglandin is a cervical ripening agent. Magnesium sulfate is a tocolytic medication used to decrease contractions or for seizure prevention in eclampsia, which is a severe form of pregnancy-induced hypertension. Magnesium sulfate or another tocolytic medication would be administered prior to external version to relax the uterus for easier manipulation, but these have nothing to do with the lack of prenatal care for a client with Rh-negative blood. Oxytocin is administered to increase contraction frequency, intensity, and duration in labor augmentation and induction.

7. A client is admitted to the labor and delivery unit at 42 weeks gestation and is started on intravenous oxytocin for an induction of labor. For which of the following contraction patterns should the nurse discontinue the infusion of oxytocin?

    A. Frequency of 2 to 3 min, duration of 60 to 90 sec, intensity with 40 to 90 mm Hg, and resting tone 10 to 15 mm Hg

    B. Frequency 2 to 3 min, duration 90 to 120 sec, intensity with 90 to 120 mm Hg, and uterine resting tone 20 to 40 mm Hg

    C. Frequency of 1 to 2 min, duration 15 to 30 sec, intensity 15 to 40 mm Hg, and uterine resting tone 0 to 10 mm Hg

    D. Frequency of 1 to 2 min, duration 45 to 60 sec, intensity with 40 to 90 mm Hg, and resting tone 10 to 15 mm Hg

Discontinue oxytocin if uterine hyperstimulation occurs with contraction frequency more often than every 2 min; contraction duration longer than 90 sec; contraction intensity results with pressures greater than 90 mm Hg as shown by IUPC; and a uterine resting tone greater than 20 mm Hg between contractions showing no relaxation of uterus between contractions.

8. In addition to oxytocin administration, other methods of augmenting or inducing labor include which of the following?

    A. Cervical ripening

    B. Amnioinfusion

    C. Cesarean birth

    D. Episiotomy

Cervical ripening increases cervical readiness for labor by either chemical or mechanical means to promote the softening, dilation, and effacement of the cervix. In some instances, cervical ripening alone is enough to induce labor. Amnioinfusion instills fluid into the uterine cavity but is not intended to initiate labor. However, overdistention of the uterus can increase uterine activity. Cesarean birth is a method of delivery, not an induction method. Episiotomy extends the vaginal outlet, but does not induce labor.

9. A client at 39 weeks gestation in the latent phase of labor is admitted to the labor and delivery unit. The client is attempting a vaginal birth after a cesarean birth. In reviewing the client's medical record, the nurse should recognize which of the following as a contraindication to a VBAC?

      A. A low transverse incision

      B. A horizontal incision

      C. A classical vertical incision

      D. A full-thickness incision

A classical vertical incision places the client at a high risk for uterine rupture. The nurse reviews the medical record for evidence that the previous cesarean incision was a low transverse incision, which is an incision made in a horizontal line. A full-thickness incision is an incision made through the skin, fat, nerves, blood vessels, and muscle. A cesarean delivery requires a full-thickness incision, but it is the location and placement of the incision to avoid uterine rupture that is of importance in this question. Therefore, a full-thickness incision is too general to identify if there is risk.

10. A client at 37 weeks gestation is admitted to the labor and delivery unit, but labor is not progressing well. Which of the following is an indication for induction of labor?

      A. Placenta previa

      B. Cephalopelvic disproportion

      C. Chorioamnionitis

      D. Maternal herpes infection

Chorioamnionitis is an infection of the amniotic membrane and is an indication for inducing labor. Placenta previa, cephalopelvic disproportion, and maternal herpes infection are all contraindications for induction of labor.

11. Which of the following is true of clients who have previously experienced a cesarean birth?

      A. Vaginal birth after cesarean (VBAC) is recommended.

      B. Labor may be safe if the uterine incision was low transverse.

      C. Type of abdominal incision is indicative of the type of uterine incision.

      D. Labor is more risky if there were vaginal deliveries prior to a cesarean birth.

Labor may be safe if the uterine incision was low transverse. VBAC is not always recommended. The type of abdominal incision does not indicate which type of uterine incision was used. Prior vaginal deliveries before a cesarean birth have no bearing on the safety or risk of a cesarean birth.

Unit 2   Intrapartum

Chapter 14:   Complications of Labor and Birth
                Contributor: Sandra Mesics, MSN, RN, CNM

⟳ NCLEX-RN® Connections:

Learning Objective: Review and apply knowledge within **"Complications of Labor and Birth"** in readiness for performance of the following nursing activities as outlined by the NCLEX-RN® test plan:

Δ   Recognize the signs and symptoms of complications of labor.

Δ   Plan and provide care to clients experiencing complications of labor.

Complication of Labor and Birth: Preterm Labor

📖 Key Points

Δ   **Preterm labor** is defined as uterine contractions and cervical changes that occur between 20 and 37 weeks gestation.

Key Factors

Δ   Risk factors for preterm labor include:

•   Infections of the urinary tract, vagina, or chorioamnionitis (infection of the amniotic sac).

•   Previous preterm birth.

•   Multifetal pregnancy.

•   Hydramnios (excessive amniotic fluid).

•   Age below 17 or above 35.

•   Low socioeconomic status.

•   Smoking.

•   Substance abuse.

- Domestic violence.

- History of multiple miscarriages or abortions.

- Diabetes or hypertension.

- Lack of prenatal care.

- Incompetent cervix.

  ◊ Cervix unable to remain closed to sustain pregnancy

- Placenta previa or abruptio placentae *(For information, refer to chapter 8, Complications of Pregnancy).*

- Preterm premature rupture of membranes.

- Short interval between pregnancies.

- Uterine abnormalities.

- Diethylstilbestrol (DES) exposure in utero.

  ◊ Agent widely used from 1948 to 1971 to diminish miscarriages

  ◊ DES is no longer used. DES exposure is now known to cause increased incidents of vaginal clear cell carcinoma in women who were exposed to DES while in utero.

Diagnostic Procedures

Δ **External monitoring** of the fetal heart rate during preterm labor to assess the fetal well-being.

Δ Testing for **fetal fibronectin**, a protein in the amniotic fluid that appears between 24 and 34 weeks of gestation. This protein can be found in the vaginal secretions when the fetal membrane integrity is lost.

Δ An **ultrasound measurement** of **endocervical length** that assesses for a shortened cervix, which is suggested in certain studies to precede preterm labor.

Δ **Home uterine activity monitoring (HUAM)** is a uterine contraction monitoring device that can be used by the client at home.

- HUAM is not considered to be effective in preventing preterm labor.

Δ **Cervical cultures** detect if there is a presence of infectious organisms. Culture and sensitivity results guide prescription of an appropriate antibiotic, if indicated.

Δ **Biophysical profile** and a **nonstress test** may be performed to provide information about the fetal well-being. *(For information, refer to chapter 11, Fetal Assessment During Labor.)*

Nursing Assessments

Δ   Nursing assessment for preterm labor begins with prenatal care. A nurse should assess for risk factors for preterm labor when interviewing a client.

Δ   Clients experiencing preterm labor may exhibit the following signs:

- Low backache.
- Pressure in the pelvis and cramping.
- Increase, change, or blood in vaginal discharge.
- Regular uterine contractions with a frequency of every 10 min or greater, lasting for 1 hr or longer.
- Gastrointestinal cramping, sometimes with diarrhea.
- Premature rupture of membranes.
- Urinary frequency.

Δ   Assessment of a client with preterm labor includes:

- Monitoring fetal heart rate (FHR) and contractions.
- Obtaining a vaginal swab for fetal fibronectin testing.
- Assisting with the collection of cervical cultures.

NANDA Nursing Diagnoses

Δ   Deficient knowledge related to symptoms and treatment of preterm labor

Δ   Risk for maternal/fetal injury related to preterm birth

Δ   Fear/anxiety related to possible preterm birth

Nursing Interventions

Δ   Management of a client who is in preterm labor includes focusing on stopping uterine contractions by restricting activity, ensuring hydration, identifying and treating any infection, administering tocolytic medications, and assuring fetal well-being by accelerating fetal lung maturity with glucocorticoids.

Δ   **Activity Restriction**

- Modified bed rest with bathroom privileges
- Encourage the client to rest in the left lateral position to increase blood flow to the uterus and decrease uterine activity.
- Avoidance of sexual intercourse

Δ   **Ensuring hydration**

- Dehydration stimulates the pituitary gland to secrete an antidiuretic hormone and oxytocin. Preventing dehydration will prevent the release of oxytocin, which stimulates uterine contractions.

Δ   **Identifying and treating any infection**

- Have the client report any vaginal discharge, noting color, consistency, and odor.

- Monitor maternal vital signs and temperature.

  ◊ Amniotic fluid infection should be suspected with the occurrence of elevated maternal temperature and tachycardia.

- Monitor fetal heart rate.

  ◊ Fetal tachycardia, a prolonged increase in the fetal heart rate greater than 160 beats/min may indicate infection which is frequently associated with preterm labor.

Tocolytics: Medications to Relax Uterine Contractions

- Tocolytic medications inhibit uterine activity by suppressing contractions.

- Contraindications to tocolytic medication administration include:

  ◊ Greater than 34 weeks gestation (the maternal and fetal risks from the tocolytics outweigh the benefits to the fetus of prolonging the pregnancy).

  ◊ Acute fetal distress.

  ◊ Severe pregnancy-induced hypertension or eclampsia.

  ◊ Vaginal bleeding.

  ◊ Cervical dilation greater than 6 cm.

- Due to serious potential adverse side effects to the mother and fetus, it is critical that the nurse provide close monitoring of the client.

  ◊ Monitor pulmonary function.

  ◊ Monitor daily weights.

  ◊ Restrict the client's oral and intravenous fluid restriction to 1,500 to 2,400 mL/24 hr to reduce the risk of pulmonary edema.

- **Tocolytic therapy** should be discontinued immediately if the client exhibits signs and symptoms of **pulmonary edema,** which include:
    ◊ Chest pain.
    ◊ Shortness of breath.
    ◊ Respiratory distress.
    ◊ Audible wheezing and crackles.
    ◊ Productive cough containing blood-tinged sputum.

Ritodrine (Yutopar) – a tocolytic that is administered intravenously.

- A beta-adrenergic agonist that relaxes uterine smooth muscle by stimulation of beta$_2$ receptors in the smooth muscle fibers.

Adverse Effects	Nursing Interventions
<ul><li>Maternal and fetal tachycardia</li><li>Hypotension</li><li>Shortness of breath, tachypnea, chest pain, and pulmonary edema</li><li>Nausea, vomiting, diarrhea, and ileus</li><li>Tremors, restlessness, and apprehensive feeling</li></ul>	<ul><li>Discontinue infusion and notify the primary care provider for any of the following adverse reactions:<ul><li>Maternal pulse greater than 120 to 140/min.</li><li>Blood pressure less than 90/60 mm Hg.</li><li>Signs of pulmonary edema such as dyspnea and crackles.</li><li>Fetal heart rate greater than 180 beats/min.</li></ul></li><li>Have propranolol (Inderal) available to reverse adverse cardiovascular effects.</li></ul>

Terbutaline (Brethine) – a tocolytic that can be administered subcutaneously or orally.

- A beta-adrenergic agonist that relaxes uterine smooth muscle by stimulation of beta$_2$ receptors in the smooth muscle fibers.
- Oral medication is frequently prescribed for the client to take while at home.

Adverse Effects	Nursing Interventions
<ul><li>Tachycardia (normal side effect that should decrease over time)</li><li>Shortness of breath</li><li>Infection at the injection site</li></ul>	<ul><li>The nurse should educate the client and family about adverse effects to observe for and to notify the primary care provider if necessary.</li><li>Nurse should assess:<ul><li>Vital signs.</li><li>Respiratory effort.</li><li>Injection site for infection if administered subcutaneously.</li></ul></li></ul>

Magnesium sulfate – a tocolytic that is administered intravenously.

- A uterine tocolytic that relaxes the smooth muscle of the uterus
- Magnesium sulfate is the most commonly used tocolytic.
  - o Causes fewer maternal and fetal side effects than other tocolytics.

Adverse Effects	Nursing Interventions
<ul><li>Lethargy and weakness</li><li>Visual blurring and headache</li><li>Nausea and vomiting</li><li>Depression of deep tendon reflexes</li><li>Decrease in respiratory rate</li><li>Decrease in urinary output</li><li>Cardiac arrest</li></ul>	<ul><li>Monitor for magnesium sulfate toxicity and discontinue for any of the following adverse effects.<ul><li>o Loss of deep tendon reflexes</li><li>o Urinary output less than 25 to 30 mL/hr</li><li>o Respiratory depression less than 12/min</li><li>o Pulmonary edema</li><li>o Chest pain</li></ul></li><li>Calcium gluconate should be available to administer as an antidote for magnesium sulfate toxicity.</li></ul>

Nifedipine (Procardia) – a tocolytic that is administered orally.

- A calcium channel blocker, nifedipine inhibits calcium from entering the smooth muscle cells and thereby reduces uterine contractions.

Adverse Effects	Nursing Interventions
<ul><li>Maternal transient tachycardia</li><li>Hypotension</li><li>Headache and dizziness</li><li>Maternal flushing</li><li>Peripheral edema</li><li>Fetal uteroplacental insufficiency related to maternal hypotension</li></ul>	<ul><li>Do not combine nifedipine with magnesium sulfate.<ul><li>o Concurrent use can cause severe hypotension.</li></ul></li><li>Monitor for adverse reactions.</li></ul>

Indomethacin (Indocin) – can be administered orally or rectally.

- A nonsteroidal anti-inflammatory drug (NSAID) that suppresses preterm labor by blocking the production of prostaglandins. This inhibition of prostaglandins suppresses uterine contractions.
- Indomethacin can cause severe fetal side effects. Treatment should only be used if other methods fail.

Adverse Effects	Nursing Interventions
<ul><li>Gastrointestinal distress, nausea, and vomiting<ul><li>Exacerbates peptic ulcer disease</li></ul></li><li>Oligohydramnios (insufficient amniotic fluid)</li><li>Reduced platelet aggregation<ul><li>Increases risk of bleeding and hemorrhage</li></ul></li><li>Neonate intracranial hemorrhage</li><li>Constriction of fetal ductus arteriosus leading to premature closure</li></ul>	<ul><li>Indomethacin treatment should not exceed 48 hr.</li><li>Should only be used if gestational age is greater than 32 weeks.</li><li>Monitor for postpartum hemorrhage.</li><li>Administer indomethacin with food or administer rectally to decrease gastrointestinal distress.</li></ul>

Glucocorticoids: Medications to Promote Fetal Lung Maturity

Δ **Antenatal glucocorticoids** administered as prescribed to promote fetal lung maturity to reduce or prevent respiratory distress in preterm labor between 24 and 34 weeks gestation.

Betamethasone or dexamethasone – glucocorticoids that are administered intramuscularly.

- Require a 24-hr period of administration to be effective.

Adverse Effects	Nursing Interventions
<ul><li>Maternal infection</li><li>Pulmonary edema if administered with beta-adrenergic medications</li><li>May worsen conditions of diabetes and hypertension</li></ul>	<ul><li>Administer medication deep intramuscularly in gluteal muscle of client 24 to 48 hr prior to birth of preterm neonate.</li><li>Monitor mother and neonate for pulmonary edema by assessing lung sounds.</li><li>Educate the client regarding signs of pulmonary edema (chest pain, shortness of breath, and crackles).</li><li>Monitor for maternal and neonate hyperglycemia.</li><li>Monitor neonate for heart rate changes</li></ul>

Complication of Labor and Birth: Preterm Birth

Key Point

- △ **Preterm birth** occurs after 20 weeks gestation and before 37 weeks of gestation.

- △ Once the cervix has dilated to 4 cm, preterm birth is probable.

Key Factors

- △ Risk factors for premature birth include:

  - Premature labor.

  - Premature rupture of membranes (PROM).

  - Preterm premature rupture of membranes (PPROM).

  - At least 50% of women who experience a preterm birth have no identifiable risk factors.

Nursing Assessments

- △ Assess preterm neonate for **respiratory distress syndrome (RDS).**

  - Retractions of the chest wall during inspiration

  - Nasal flaring on inspiration

  - Expiratory grunting

  - Changes in the respiratory and heart rates

NANDA Nursing Diagnoses

- △ Impaired gas exchange of the neonate related to preterm birth

- △ Interrupted family process related to preterm birth

- △ Risk for sudden infant death syndrome related to premature neonate

Nursing Interventions

- △ Administer glucocorticoids for a 24-hr period prior to delivery to promote fetal lung development in an attempt to prevent respiratory distress syndrome.

(For information on neonate care at preterm birth, refer to chapter 23, Assessment and Management of Newborn Complications).

Complication of Labor and Birth: Premature Rupture of Membranes (PROM) and Preterm Premature Rupture of Membranes (PPROM)

Key Points

Δ   **PROM** is the spontaneous rupture of the amniotic membranes 1 hr or more prior to the onset of true labor.

Δ   **PPROM** is the spontaneous rupture of membranes after 20 weeks gestation and prior to 37 weeks gestation.

Key Factors

Δ   Infection is the major risk of PROM and PPROM for both the client and the fetus. Once the amniotic membranes have ruptured, micro-organisms can ascend from the vagina into the amniotic sac. PPROM is often preceded by infection.

Δ   **Chorioamnionitis** is the infection of the amniotic membranes.

•   There is an increased risk of infection if there is a lag period over the 24-hr period from when the membranes rupture to delivery.

Nursing Assessments

Δ   Nursing assessments for PPROM include:

•   The client reporting a gush or leakage of fluid from the vagina.

•   Assessing the client for a prolapsed umbilical cord.

◊   Abrupt FHR variable deceleration

◊   Visible or palpable cord at the introitus

•   A positive Nitrazine paper test (blue, pH 6.5 to 7.5) or positive ferning test is conducted on amniotic fluid to verify rupture of membranes.

- Assess cervical dilation, effacement, and station. A strict sterile technique is used on all vaginal exams to avoid introduction of micro-organisms that may cause infection.

- Monitor vital signs, temperature, fetal heart rate (FHR), and uterine contractions.
    - ◊ Observe for signs of infection.
    - ◊ Assess for signs of fetal compromise.

NANDA Nursing Diagnoses

Δ Risk for infection due to ruptured membranes

Δ Risk for injury related to possible preterm birth

Δ Deficient knowledge related to self-care activities

Δ Anxiety related to pregnancy outcome

Nursing Interventions

Δ For most women, **PROM** signifies the onset of true labor if gestational duration is at term.

- Prepare for birth if indicated.

Δ Nursing management for **PROM** and **PPROM** is dependent on gestational duration, if there is evidence of infection, or an indication of fetal or maternal compromise.

Δ Expect management at home if dilation is less than 3 cm, no signs of infection, no contractions, and no malpresentation.

- Advise the client to adhere to bed rest with bathroom privileges.

- Encourage hydration.

- Administer medications as prescribed.
    - ◊ Antibiotics to treat infections
    - ◊ Sedatives to reduce anxiety
    - ◊ Glucocorticoids to promote fetal lung maturity

- Provide reassurance to reduce maternal anxiety.

Δ Provide client education on self-care with **PROM** and **PPROM**

- The client should conduct a self assessment for uterine contractions.

- The client should record daily kick counts for fetal movement.

- The client should monitor for foul-smelling vaginal discharge.

  ◊ Refrain from inserting anything vaginally.

- The client should abstain from intercourse.

- The client should avoid tub baths.

- The client should wipe perineal area from front to back after voiding and fecal elimination.

- The client should take her temperature every 4 hr when awake and report a temperature that is anything greater than 38° C (100° F).

Complication of Labor and Birth: Prolapsed Umbilical Cord

Key Points

Δ A **prolapsed umbilical cord** occurs when the umbilical cord is displaced, preceding the presenting part of the fetus, or protruding through the cervix.

- This results in cord compression and compromised fetal circulation.

Key Factors

Δ Risk factors for prolapsed umbilical cord include:

- Rupture of amniotic membranes (ROM)

  ◊ It is necessary to check FHR immediately following rupture of membranes.

- Abnormal fetal presentation.

  ◊ Any presentation other than vertex (occiput is the presenting part)

  ◊ Transverse lie

- Presenting part is high in the pelvis and not yet engaged when the membranes rupture. This leaves room for the cord to descend and precede the presenting part.

- Small for gestational age infant.

- Unusually long umbilical cord.

- Multifetal pregnancy.

- Cephalopelvic disproportion.

  ◊ Can result in a loose fit between fetal presenting part and maternal pelvis, leaving room for the cord to slip down.

- Placenta previa.

- Hydramnios or polyhydramnios.
  ◊ Excessive amniotic fluid, more than 2,000 mL
- Oligohydramnios.
  ◊ Decreased amount of amniotic fluid, less than 300 mL

 ## Nursing Assessments

Δ Nursing assessments for a client with a prolapsed **umbilical cord** include:

- Client stating that she can feel something coming through the vagina.
- Visualization or palpation of the umbilical cord protruding from the introitus.
- Assessment that shows FHR to have variable decelerations.
- Extreme increase in fetal activity that occurs and then ceases. This may be suggestive of severe fetal hypoxia.

NANDA Nursing Diagnoses

Δ Risk for injury to fetus from asphyxia

Δ Risk for injury to the mother from emergency cesarean birth

Δ Anxiety related to concern about fetal well-being

Nursing Interventions

Δ Nursing interventions for a client with **umbilical cord prolapse** include relieving the cord compression immediately and increasing fetal oxygenation.

- Call for assistance immediately.
- Notify the primary care provider of the prolapsed cord.
- Position the client's hips higher than her head.
  ◊ Reposition the client in a knee-chest position, Trendelenburg position, or a side-lying position with a rolled towel under the client's right or left hip to relieve pressure on the cord.
  ◊ Using a sterile gloved hand, insert two fingers into the vagina and apply finger pressure on either side of the cord to the fetal presenting part to elevate it off of the cord.
  ◊ Apply a sterile saline-soaked towel to the cord to prevent drying and to maintain blood flow if it is protruding from the vaginal introitus.

◊ Closely monitor the FHR with an electronic fetal monitor for variable decelerations indicative of fetal asphyxia and hypoxia from cord compression.

◊ Administer oxygen at 8 to 10 L via a face mask. This will improve fetal oxygenation.

◊ **Amnioinfusion** of normal saline or Lactated ringer's solution as prescribed should be instilled into the amniotic cavity through a transcervical catheter introduced into the uterus to alleviate cord compression if it is caused by oligohydramnios.

◊ Prepare the client for a cesarean birth if other measures fail.

◊ Inform and educate the client and her support person about the interventions.

Complication of Labor and Birth: Precipitate Labor

Key Points

Precipitate labor is defined as labor that lasts 3 hr or less from the onset of contractions to the time of birth.

Key Factors

Δ Risk factors for **precipitate labor** include:

• **Hypertonic uterine dysfunction**

◊ Nonproductive, uncoordinated, painful, uterine contractions during labor that are too frequent and too long in duration and do not allow for relaxation of the uterine muscle between contractions (uterine tetany).

◊ Hypertonic contractions do not contribute to the progression of labor (cervical effacement, dilation, and fetal descent).

◊ Hypertonic contractions can result in uteroplacental insufficiency leading to fetal hypoxia.

• **Oxytocin stimulation** may be administered to augment or induce labor by increasing intensity and duration of contractions.

◊ Oxytocin stimulation can lead to hypertonic uterine contractions

• Multiparous client.

◊ May move through the stages of labor more rapidly

📋 **Nursing Assessments**

Δ   Nursing assessments **during labor** include:

- Increased or bloody vaginal discharge.
- Palpable uterine contractions.
- Progress of cervical dilation and effacement.
- Low backache.
- Abdominal pressure and cramping.
- Diarrhea.
- Fetal presentation, station, and position.
- Status of amniotic membranes. Membranes can be intact or ruptured.

Δ   Nursing assessments **during status postbirth** include:

- Assessing maternal perineal area for signs of trauma or lacerations.
- Assessing neonate color for signs of hypoxia.
- Assessing for signs of trauma to presenting part of neonate, especially on cephalic presentation.

NANDA Nursing Diagnosis

Δ   Risk for trauma to mother and/or fetus related to precipitate labor

Nursing Interventions

Δ   Mother should not be left unattended.

- Provide reassurance and emotional support to help the mother remain calm.
- Prepare for emergency delivery of the newborn.

Δ   Encourage the mother to pant with an open mouth between contractions to control the urge to push.

Δ   Encourage the client to maintain a side-lying position to optimize uteroplacental perfusion and fetal oxygenation.

Δ   Prepare for the rupturing of membranes upon crowning (fetal head visible at perineum) if not already ruptured.

Δ   Do not attempt to stop delivery.

Δ   Control the rapid delivery by applying light pressure to the perineal area and fetal head, gently pressing upward toward the vagina. This will ease the rapid expulsion of the fetus and help to prevent cerebral damage to the newborn and perineal lacerations to the mother.

- Deliver the fetus between contractions assuring the cord is not around the fetal neck.

- If the cord is around the fetal neck, attempt to gently slip it over the head. If not possible, clamp the cord with two clamps and cut between the clamps.

Δ   Suction mucus from the neonate's mouth and nose with a bulb syringe when the head appears.

Δ   Next, deliver the anterior shoulder located under the maternal symphysis pubis: next, the posterior shoulder; and then allow the rest of the fetal body to slip out.

Δ   Assess for complications of precipitate labor:

- **Maternal**

  ◊   **Cervical, vaginal,** and/or **perineal lacerations**

  ◊   Resultant tissue trauma secondary to rapid birth

  ◊   Uterine rupture

  ◊   Amniotic fluid embolism

  ◊   Postpartum hemorrhage

- **Fetal/Neonate**

  ◊   Fetal hypoxia

       °   Fetal hypoxia can be caused by uteroplacental insufficiency resulting from hypertonic uterus.

       °   An umbilical cord around the fetal neck can result in asphyxia and cause a decrease in fetal oxygenation.

  ◊   **Fetal intracranial hemorrhage**

       °   Resulting from cephalic trauma during rapid birth.

Complication of Labor and Birth: Meconium-Stained Amniotic Fluid

Key Points

Δ   Meconium passage in the amniotic fluid during the antepartum period prior to the start of labor is typically not associated with an unfavorable fetal outcome.

- May be the result of corrected acute or chronic fetal stress

- The physiologic passage of meconium

Δ   There is an association between meconium in third trimester and the presence of hypertensive disorders and/or fetal postmaturity.

Key Factors

Δ   Causes of meconium-stained amniotic fluid include:

- A normal physiologic function occurring with fetal maturity with an increased incidence after 38 weeks gestation.

- Umbilical cord compression results in fetal hypoxia that stimulates the vagal nerve in mature fetuses.

  ◊   The vagus nerve is responsible for heart rate and gastrointestinal peristalsis.

- Hypoxia stimulates the vagal nerve, which induces peristalsis of the fetal gastrointestinal tract and relaxation of the anal sphincter, resulting in release of meconium (the first stool of the fetus or neonate) as well as fetal bradycardia.

Diagnostics

Δ   Intrapartal meconium requires further careful evaluation if birth is not imminent to determine necessary interventions.

- Electronic fetal monitoring
- Fetal scalp blood sampling

Nursing Assessments

Δ   The presence of meconium in the amniotic fluid can be determined by visual inspection of the amniotic fluid.

- The fluid will have a greenish black color and a thick fresh consistency.

Δ   Criteria for evaluation of meconium-stained amniotic fluid

- **Consistency** – thick, fresh consistency indicative of fetal stress.

- **Timing** – thick, fresh meconium first passed in late labor with variable or late FHR decelerations (ominous sign).

- Presence of other indicators. The existence of meconium alone in the amniotic fluid is not a sign of fetal distress. It must be accompanied by variable or late FHR decelerations with or without acidosis, which is confirmed by scalp blood sampling to be considered ominous.

Nursing Interventions

Δ   At the time of birth, the nurse should be prepared to suction the nasopharynx of the neonate.

- Suctioning reduces the incidence and severity of meconium aspiration syndrome in the neonate.

Complication of Labor and Birth: Postterm Pregnancy

 Key Points

Δ   **Postterm pregnancy** is one that extends beyond the end of the 42nd week of gestation.

Δ   **Postterm pregnancy** places the mother at risk for:

- Postpartum hemorrhage.

- Birth canal trauma from advanced fetal bone maturation with hardening of the fetal skull. This can cause:

    ◊   Infection.

    ◊   Labor augmentation or induction with tocolytics.

    ◊   Forceps-assisted or vacuum-assisted birth.

    ◊   Cesarean birth delivery.

Δ   **Postterm pregnancy** places the fetus at risk for:

- Fetal distress.

- Prolonged labor.

- Dystocia or shoulder dystocia.

- Meconium-stained amniotic fluid.

- Asphyxia.

- Macrosomia (large for gestational age), which occurs when the placenta continues to provide sufficient nutrients to support continued fetal growth after 40 weeks of gestation. A macrosomic infant can result in:

    ◊   Labor dystocia.

    ◊   Perineal lacerations and extension of episiotomy.

- A decrease in amniotic fluid, oligohydramnios, leading to fetal hypoxia as a result of cord compression without the cushioning of sufficient amniotic fluid.

Δ **Postterm pregnancy** places the neonate at risk for:

- Asphyxia.

- Meconium aspiration syndrome.

- Dysmaturity syndrome.

- Hypoglycemia.

- Polycythemia (hyperviscous blood secondary to overproduction of red blood cells).

- Respiratory distress.

Key Factors

Δ Risks factors for **postterm pregnancy** include:

- Placental estrogen deficiency, which results in reduction in prostaglandin precursors and decreased formation of oxytocin receptors in the uterine myometrium.

  ◊ Since oxytocin stimulates uterine contractions, a decrease in myometrium oxytocin receptors results in a decrease in uterine contractibility.

- A previous postterm pregnancy increases a client's risk of having another postterm pregnancy by 30 to 40%.

Δ Misdiagnosis of postterm pregnancy can result from the inaccurate dating of pregnancy secondary to:

- Irregular menstrual cycle pattern.

- Inaccurate date of last menstrual pregnancy.

- Delayed or no prenatal care.

Therapeutics and Nursing Interventions

Δ **Amnioinfusion** of normal saline or lactated Ringer's solution as instilled into the amniotic cavity through a transcervical catheter introduced into the uterus.

Nursing Assessments

Δ   Nursing assessments for a client with postterm pregnancy include:

- Observing for maternal weight loss greater than 1.4 kg (3 lb)/week and a decrease in the size of the uterus related to diminishing amniotic fluid and resultant oligohydramnios.
- Antepartum assessment and management of postterm pregnancy include:
  ◊   Taking daily fetal movement counts.
  ◊   Nonstress and contraction stress tests.
  ◊   Biophysical profiles.
  ◊   Measuring Doppler flow.
  ◊   Amniotic fluid index.
  ◊   Checking cervix to determine if it is favorable for induction of labor.
  ◊   Assessing vaginal secretions for the amount of fibronectin. Low levels indicate an increased risk for prolonged pregnancy.
- Monitoring FHR during labor for signs of distress.
- Monitoring contractions and progression of labor.
- Assessing for meconium-stained amniotic fluid, which occurs more commonly in postterm infants upon rupture of membranes.

NANDA Nursing Diagnoses

Δ   Deficient knowledge of risks of postterm pregnancy and required fetal surveillance during postterm pregnancy

Δ   Risk for fetal injury due to possible cephalopelvic disproportion or meconium aspiration syndrome

Nursing Interventions

Δ   Nursing interventions for a client with postterm pregnancy include:

- Explaining procedures such as fetal kick counts, nonstress tests, and biophysical profiles to the client and the client's support person.
- Assisting with **amnioinfusion** if prescribed to:
  ◊   **Alleviate oligohydramnios** (low amniotic fluid volume), which can lead to compression of the fetal cord resulting in fetal hypoxia as evidenced by variable or prolonged FHR decelerations and the passage of meconium by increasing the fluid volume within the amniotic sac and relieving the cord compression.

◊ Dilute the meconium present in the amniotic fluid by infusing the amniotic cavity with more fluid.

Δ **Determining if acidosis is occurring. Fetal scalp pH sampling** or **fetal oxygen saturation** is used to determine this. Acidosis can also be an indication of fetal hypoxia.

- Inducing labor with oxytocin at 41 to 42 weeks gestation if the cervix is ripe (soft and favorable for induction).

- Administering a **prostaglandin insert** or **gel** if the cervix is not ripe enough for induction. The insert or gel will soften the cervix for the induction of labor.

- Continue monitoring the fetus.

Complication of Labor and Birth: Dystocia (Dysfunctional Labor)

 Key Points

Δ **Dystocia or dysfunctional labor** is a difficult or abnormal labor related to the **five powers of labor (powers, passenger, passageway, psyche, and position).**

Δ Atypical uterine contraction patterns prevent the normal process of labor. These contractions can be **hypotonic** (weak, inefficient, or completely absent) or **hypertonic** (excessively frequent, uncoordinated, and of strong intensity with inadequate uterine relaxation) with failure to efface and dilate the cervix for the progression of labor.

Key Factors

Δ Risk factors for dysfunctional labor include:

- Short stature, overweight status.

- Age greater than 40 years.

- Uterine abnormalities (congenital malformations, overdistention from multiple gestation or hydramnios).

- Pelvic soft tissue obstructions or pelvic contracture.

- Cephalopelvic disproportion (fetal head is larger than maternal pelvis).

- Fetal macrosomia.

- Fetal malpresentation, malposition.

- Multifetal pregnancy.

- Hypertonic or hypotonic uterus.

- Maternal fatigue, fear, or dehydration.
- Inappropriate timing of anesthesia or analgesics.

Therapeutics and Diagnostics

Δ   Ultrasound used to rule out cephalopelvic disproportion and malposition

Δ   Amniotomy or stripping of membranes if not ruptured

Δ   Oxytocin infusion

Δ   Vacuum-assisted birth

Δ   Cesarean birth

Nursing Assessments

Δ   Nursing assessments of a client with dysfunctional labor

- Note a lack of progress in dilatation, effacement, or fetal descent during labor.

- Assess contractions for duration, frequency, and intensity.

- Assess ability to indent uterus at contraction peaks and between contractions.

  ◊   Hypotonic uterus is easily indentable, even at peak of contractions.

  ◊   Hypertonic uterus cannot be indented, even between contractions.

- Observe the client as having ineffective pushing with no voluntary urge to bear down.

- Assess fetal size, lie, presentation, and attitude by using Leopold's maneuvers.

- **Persistent occiput posterior position** is when the fetal occiput is directed toward the posterior maternal pelvis rather than the anterior pelvis.

  ◊   Persistent occiput posterior position prolongs labor and the client has a great deal of back pain as the fetus presses against the maternal sacrum.

  ◊   The client should be positioned on her hands and knees to help the fetus to rotate from a posterior to anterior position.

  ◊   **Counterpressure** should be applied with the fist or heel of the hand to the sacral area. This technique can help to alleviate discomfort.

- Continue assessing FHR in response to labor.

NANDA Nursing Diagnoses

Δ   Fatigue related to long labor

Δ   Pain related to labor and interventions to strengthen labor

Δ   Anxiety related to slow progress of labor

Δ   Risk for injury to fetus/mother from birth trauma

Nursing Interventions

Δ   Nursing interventions for a client with **dysfunctional labor** include:

- Assisting with the application of a fetal scalp electrode and/or intrauterine pressure catheter.

- Assisting with amniotomy (artificial rupture of membranes).

- Encouraging the client to engage in regular voiding to empty her bladder.

- Encouraging position changes to aid in fetal descent or open up pelvic outlet.

- Encourage ambulation to enhance the progression of labor

- Encourage hydrotherapy and other relaxation techniques to aid in the progression of labor

- Assisting mother into a beneficial position for pushing and coaching mother in bearing down with contractions.

- Preparing for a possible forceps-assisted, vacuum-assisted, or cesarean birth.

Δ   **Nursing interventions for a client with hypotonic contractions include:**

- Ruling out cephalopelvic disproportion

- Administering oxytocin if prescribed to augment labor. Oxytocin is not administered for hypertonic contractions

Δ   **Nursing interventions for a client with hypertonic contractions include:**

- Administering analgesics if prescribed (for rest from hypertonic contractions).

- Maintaining hydration.

- Promoting rest and relaxation and provide comfort measures between contractions.

- Placing the client in lateral position and providing oxygen by mask.

Complication of Labor and Birth: Large for Gestational Age (LGA)

Key Points

Δ   Risks for complications associated with large for gestational age fetuses (LGA) weighing 4,000 g or more (macrosomic) include:

•   Shoulder dystocia, resulting in fetal injury to clavicles, or asphyxia.

•   Erb-Duchenne paralysis due to birth trauma.

•   Neonatal hypoglycemia.

Δ   **Shoulder dystocia** occurs when a fetus's anterior shoulder cannot pass under the maternal symphysis pubis after delivery of the fetal head.

Key Factors

Δ   Postterm pregnancy

Δ   Maternal diabetes

Nursing Assessments

Δ   Nursing assessments for a client with an LGA fetus include:

•   Assessing for fetal size while doing Leopold's maneuvers.

•   Monitoring progression of labor for signs of labor dystocia.

•   Assessing FHR for tolerance of labor.

•   Monitoring contractions for duration, strength, and frequency.

NANDA Nursing Diagnoses

Δ   Risk for injury to mother from birth trauma

Δ   Risk for injury to the fetus from birth trauma

Nursing Interventions

Δ   Nursing interventions for a LGA infant include:

•   Preparing for a possible vacuum-assisted or forceps-assisted birth.

- Preparing to place the client in McRobert's position (lithotomy position with legs flexed to chest to maximize pelvic outlet).

- Preparing to apply suprapubic pressure to aid in the delivery of the anterior shoulder located inferior to the maternal symphysis pubis.

- Assessing the neonate for birth trauma such as broken clavicle or Erb-Duchenne paralysis.

(For information about nursing interventions for an LGA neonate, refer to chapter 23, Assessment and Management of Newborn Complications.)

Complication of Labor and Birth: Rupture of the Uterus

Key Points

Δ   **Rupture of the uterus**

- Extension through the entire uterine wall muscle into the peritoneal cavity or broad ligament is a complete rupture of the uterus.

- Extension into the peritoneum, but not into the peritoneal cavity or broad ligament, is an incomplete rupture of the uterus.

  ◊   Partial separation can occur at an old cesarean scar

- Bleeding uterine rupture is usually internal

Key Factors

Δ   Risk factors for rupture of the uterus include:

- Separation of the scar from a previous classic vertical cesarean incision through the uterus.

- Uterine trauma from an accident or surgery.

- Congenital uterine abnormality.

- Overdistention of the uterus from an LGA infant, multifetal gestation, or polyhydramnios.

- Hyperstimulation of the uterus, either spontaneous or from oxytocin administration.

- External or internal fetal version done to correct malposition of the fetus.

- Forceps-assisted birth.

Δ   Rupture of the uterus occurs more often in multigravida clients.

📋 **Nursing Assessments**

Δ   Nursing assessments for a client with a ruptured uterus include:

- Assessing the FHR for signs of distress, bradycardia, late decelerations, tachycardia, and absent variability.

- Client reporting of something tearing inside.

- Contractions stopping and relief of pain.

- Palpating fetal parts though the abdomen.

- Assessing for symptoms of shock: hypotension, tachypnea, pallor, and cool clammy skin.

NANDA Nursing Diagnoses

Δ   Risk for injury to fetus from asphyxia

Δ   Risk for injury to the mother from hypovolemic shock or emergency cesarean birth

Δ   Anxiety related to fetal and maternal well-being

Nursing Interventions

Δ   Nursing interventions for uterine rupture include:

- Administering intravenous fluids.

- Administering blood product transfusions if prescribed.

- Assisting with a laparotomy and blood transfusions for an incomplete uterine rupture.

- Assisting with a hysterectomy and blood transfusion for a complete uterine rupture.

- Preparing the client for an immediate cesarean birth.

- Informing the client and her support system about the treatment.

Complication of Labor and Birth: Amniotic Fluid Embolism

Key Points

Δ   **Amniotic fluid embolism** is caused by a rupture in the amniotic sac or
    maternal uterine veins accompanied by a high intrauterine pressure that causes
    infiltration of the amniotic fluid and its contents into the maternal circulation.
    This infiltrated amniotic fluid then travels to and obstructs pulmonary vessels and
    causes respiratory distress and circulatory collapse.

Δ   Meconium-stained amniotic fluid or fluid containing other particulate matter can
    cause more maternal damage because it more readily clogs the pulmonary veins
    completely.

Δ   Serious coagulation problems such as disseminated intravascular coagulopathy can
    occur.

Key Factors

Δ   Risk factors for amniotic fluid embolism include:

   • Multiparity.

   • Tumultuous labor.

   • Abruptio placentae.

   • Oxytocin administration.

   • Fetal macrosomia.

   • Fetal demise.

   • Meconium-stained amniotic fluid.

Nursing Assessments

Δ   Nursing assessments for a client with amniotic fluid embolism

   • Client is exhibiting signs of respiratory distress, which include:

      ◊   Restlessness.

      ◊   Dyspnea.

      ◊   Cyanosis.

      ◊   Pulmonary edema.

      ◊   Respiratory arrest.

- Client is exhibiting signs of circulatory collapse, which include:
  - ◊ Tachycardia.
  - ◊ Hypotension.
  - ◊ Shock.
  - ◊ Cardiac arrest.
- Client is exhibiting signs of coagulation failure, which include:
  - ◊ Bleeding from incisions and venipuncture sites.
  - ◊ Petechiae and ecchymosis.
  - ◊ Uterine atony.

NANDA Nursing Diagnoses

Δ   Ineffective tissue perfusion related to amniotic fluid embolism

Δ   Anxiety related to respiratory distress

Nursing Interventions

Δ   Nursing interventions for amniotic fluid embolism include:

- Administering oxygen via a mask at 8 to 10 L.
- Assisting with intubation and mechanical ventilation as indicated.
- Performing cardiopulmonary resuscitation if necessary.
- Positioning the client on her side with her pelvis tilted at a 30 degree angle to displace the uterus.
- Administering intravenous fluids.
- Administering blood products as prescribed to correct coagulation failure.
- Inserting an indwelling urinary catheter and measuring hourly urine output.
- Monitoring maternal and fetal status.
- Preparing the client for an emergency cesarean birth if fetus is not yet delivered.

Complication of Labor and Birth: Fetal Distress

 Key Points

Δ   **Fetal distress** is present when:

- The fetal heart rate is below 110 beats/min or above 160 beats/min.

- The fetal heart rate shows decreased or no variability.

- There is fetal hyperactivity or no fetal activity.

- The fetal blood pH is less than 7.2.

Key Factors

Δ Complications of pregnancy

Δ Fetal anomalies

Δ Uterine anomalies

Δ Complications of labor and birth

Nursing Assessments

Δ Monitor uterine contractions.

Δ Monitor FHR.

Δ Monitor findings of ultrasound and any other prescribed diagnostics.

NANDA Nursing Diagnoses

Δ Anxiety related to possible fetal demise

Δ Risk for injury to fetus related to complications of labor and birth

Nursing Interventions

Δ Position the client in a left side-lying reclining position with legs elevated.

Δ Administer oxygen via a face mask as prescribed.

Δ Discontinue oxytocin if being administered.

Δ Increase intravenous fluid rate to treat hypotension if indicated.

Δ Monitor maternal vital signs and FHR.

Δ Prepare the client for an emergency cesarean birth.

Primary Reference:

Lowdermilk, D. L. & Perry, S. E. (2004). *Maternity & women's health care* (8th ed.). St. Louis, MO: Mosby.

Additional Resources:

Murray, S. S. & McKinney, E. S. (2006). *Foundations of maternal-newborn nursing* (4th ed.). Philadelphia: Elsevier.

NANDA International (2004). *NANDA nursing diagnoses: Definitions and classification 2005-2006*. Philadelphia: NANDA.

Chapter 14: Complications of Labor and Birth

Application Exercises

1. If contractions are of too long a duration or do not have complete relaxation or uterine tone in between contractions, the most likely adverse effect will be

    A. prolonged labor.

    B. reduced fetal oxygen supply.

    C. impairment of cervical dilation.

    D. increased maternal stress.

2. A client is admitted to the labor and delivery unit at 28 weeks gestation. A catheterized urine specimen is ordered. Which of the following is the most likely reason for this order?

    A. Preterm labor frequently causes urinary tract infections.

    B. This is a standard order for all clients who are admitted to the labor and delivery unit.

    C. To prevent bladder distention because labor reduces the sensation to urinate.

    D. Infections are strongly associated with the occurrence of preterm labor.

3. A client is admitted to the labor and delivery unit. With the use of Leopold's maneuvers, it is noted that the fetus is in a breech presentation. For which of the following possible complications should the nurse observe?

    A. Precipitate labor

    B. Premature rupture of membranes

    C. Postmaturity syndrome

    D. Prolapsed umbilical cord

4. Which of the following therapeutic interventions should the nurse anticipate for a client with a breech presentation?

        A. Amniotomy

        B. Amnioinfusion

        C. External version

        D. Cesarean birth

5. A client in labor is reporting severe back pain. During assessment, the fetus is noted to be in the occiput posterior position. Which of the following maternal positions might the nurse suggest to help facilitate normal labor progress?

        A. Hands and knees position

        B. Lithotomy position

        C. Trendelenburg position

        D. Supine position with a rolled towel under one hip

6. A client at 32 weeks gestation is admitted to the unit because she is having contractions. Her vaginal exam indicates she is 3 cm dilated and experiencing contractions every 5 to 10 min. She states that she feels pelvic pressure but the contractions are not painful. Which of the following tests should the nurse expect to be ordered?

        A. Testing for meconium in the amniotic fluid

        B. Testing for fetal fibronectin in the amniotic fluid

        C. Amniotic fluid volume index

        D. Biophysical profile testing

7. A client at 32 weeks gestation is admitted and determined to be in preterm labor. Based on the nurse's knowledge regarding risk factors contributing to the onset of preterm labor, what other tests might the nurse anticipate will be ordered?

        A. Complete blood count

        B. Ultrasound

        C. Biophysical profile

        D. Vaginal culture

8. A primary care provider prescribes modified bed rest and tocolytic terbutaline (Brethine) given subcutaneously to stop contractions for a client in preterm labor. Ten minutes after the terbutaline is administered, the client calls the nurse, saying that her heart is racing and pounding. The nurse's most appropriate intervention should be to

    A. notify the primary care provider immediately and anticipate the prescription of an antidote to counteract the adverse side effects.

    B. provide reassurance that this is a normal side effect of the medication and should lessen with time.

    C. administer nifedipine (Procardia) as prescribed to relieve the client's hypertension.

    D. reposition the client in a side-lying position to increase uteroplacental perfusion.

9. A primary care provider prescribes two doses of betamethasone intramuscularly 24 hr apart for a client with hypertension in preterm labor to promote fetal lung maturity. The nurse knows that which of the following is the priority for monitoring while the client is on this medication?

    A. Blood glucose level

    B. Complete blood count

    C. Blood pressure

    D. Oxygen saturation

10. A client receiving oxytocin to stimulate labor is having contractions every 2 min lasting 90 sec, with incomplete relaxation of the uterus between contractions and an increase in fetal activity. The nurse recognizes that the client is

    A. experiencing hypotonic labor.

    B. entering the second stage of labor.

    C. responding appropriately to the oxytocin.

    D. experiencing hyperstimulation of the uterus.

11. Indicate the rationale for a nonstress test with a postterm client.

    A. To evaluate uterine relaxation response

    B. To assess the well-being of the fetus

    C. To assess fetal response to uterine stimulation

    D. To evaluate fetal response to acoustic stimulation

Scenario: A nurse is caring for a client in active labor. When last examined 2 hr ago, the client's cervix was 3 cm dilated, 100% effaced, membranes intact, and the fetus was at a -2 station. The client suddenly states she is "wet down there." The nurse notices that the FHR is 80 beats/min. The nurse performs a sterile glove examination and notices clear fluid and a pulsing loop of umbilical cord in the client's vagina.

12. Which of the following actions should the nurse perform first?

> A. Place the client in Trendelenburg position.
>
> B. Apply pressure to the presenting part with the fingers.
>
> C. Give the client oxygen at 10 L via a face mask.
>
> D. Call for assistance.

13. When completing an admission history for an 18-year-old client at 39 weeks gestation, the client states that she has been leaking water from her vagina for 2 days. The nurse knows that this client is at risk for

> A. cord prolapse.
>
> B. infection.
>
> C. malpresentation.
>
> D. placental abruption.

14. A nurse is caring for a client at 42 weeks gestation in active labor. This fetus is at risk for which of the following?

> A. Intrauterine growth restriction
>
> B. Hyperglycemia
>
> C. Meconium aspiration
>
> D. Polyhydramnios

Chapter 14: Complications of Labor and Birth

Application Exercises Answer Key

1. If contractions are of too long a duration or do not have complete relaxation or uterine tone in between contractions, the most likely adverse effect will be

   A. prolonged labor.
   B. reduced fetal oxygen supply.
   C. impairment of cervical dilation.
   D. increased maternal stress.

   When the uterus contracts, there is a constriction of the blood vessels that provide oxygenation and nutrients to the fetus. If there is inadequate relaxation between contractions, there is a reduction of oxygenation to the fetus. These contractions are referred to as hypertonic contractions, can produce maternal stress, but are not the most adverse effect. Hypertonic contractions usually cause precipitate labor, not prolonged labor. Hypertonic contractions do not usually impede cervical dilation.

2. A client is admitted to the labor and delivery unit at 28 weeks gestation. A catheterized urine specimen is ordered. Which of the following is the most likely reason for this order?

   A. Preterm labor frequently causes urinary tract infections.
   B. This is a standard order for all clients who are admitted to the labor and delivery unit.
   C. To prevent bladder distention because labor reduces the sensation to urinate.
   D. Infections are strongly associated with the occurrence of preterm labor.

   Infections of the urinary tract, vagina, or amniotic sac (chorioamnionitis) are often associated with preterm labor. A urinary catheter is not the standard procedure during admission to a labor and delivery unit. While labor and/or administered anesthetics can reduce the sensation to urinate, this is managed by the nurse by encouraging frequent voiding every 1 to 2 hr and palpating the bladder for distention. Preterm labor does not cause urinary tract infections.

3. A client is admitted to the labor and delivery unit. With the use of Leopold's maneuvers, it is noted that the fetus is in a breech presentation. For which of the following possible complications should the nurse observe?

        A. Precipitate labor

        B. Premature rupture of membranes

        C. Postmaturity syndrome

        D. Prolapsed umbilical cord

Breech presentation would most likely cause dystocia (prolonged, difficult labor) rather than a precipitate labor. It has no effect on the rupture of membranes and is not associated with postmaturity syndrome.

4. Which of the following therapeutic interventions should the nurse anticipate for a client with a breech presentation?

        A. Amniotomy

        B. Amnioinfusion

        C. External version

        D. Cesarean birth

External version would initially be attempted. If this fails, a cesarean birth would be indicated. Amniotomy is the artificial rupture of membranes and amnioinfusion is the infusion of normal saline or Lactated ringer's solution, neither of which has any affect on a breech presentation.

5. A client in labor is reporting severe back pain. During assessment, the fetus is noted to be in the occiput posterior position. Which of the following maternal positions might the nurse suggest to help facilitate normal labor progress?

    A. Hands and knees position

    B. Lithotomy position

    C. Trendelenburg position

    D. Supine position with a rolled towel under one hip

Having the client assume a position on her hands and knees may help the fetus rotate from a posterior to an anterior position. The lithotomy position is when the client lies on her back with her knees elevated. The Trendelenburg and supine positions both require the client to lie on her back. None of these positions put the client in a position that would assist in the rotation of the fetus.

6. A client at 32 weeks gestation is admitted to the unit because she is having contractions. Her vaginal exam indicates she is 3 cm dilated and experiencing contractions every 5 to 10 min. She states that she feels pelvic pressure but the contractions are not painful. Which of the following tests should the nurse expect to be ordered?

    A. Testing for meconium in the amniotic fluid

    B. Testing for fibronectin in the amniotic fluid

    C. Amniotic fluid volume index

    D. Biophysical profile testing

Fibronectin present in the amniotic fluid is a predictor of preterm labor. Fibronectin is also a sign that would coincide with the other signs the client is exhibiting. Meconium is the presence of the first fetal stool, and would not likely occur at 32 weeks. An amniotic fluid volume index determines the amount of amniotic fluid present in the amniotic cavity. Biophysical profile testing assesses five characteristics to determine fetal well-being.

7. A client at 32 weeks gestation is admitted and determined to be in preterm labor. Based on the nurse's knowledge regarding risk factors contributing to the onset of preterm labor, what other tests might the nurse anticipate will be ordered?

    A. Complete blood count

    B. Ultrasound

    C. Biophysical profile

    D. Vaginal culture

A vaginal culture would be performed as well as a urinalysis to rule out infection, which can trigger preterm labor. A complete blood count, ultrasound, and biophysical profile would not reveal any pertinent information regarding preterm labor.

8. A primary care provider prescribes modified bed rest and tocolytic terbutaline (Brethine) given subcutaneously to stop contractions for a client in preterm labor. Ten minutes after the terbutaline is administered, the client calls the nurse, saying that her heart is racing and pounding. The nurse's most appropriate intervention should be to

> A. notify the primary care provider immediately and anticipate the prescription of an antidote to counteract the adverse side effects.
>
> **B. provide reassurance that this is a normal side effect of the medication and should lessen with time.**
>
> C. administer Nifedipine (Procardia) as prescribed to relieve the client's hypertension.
>
> D. reposition the client in a side-lying position to increase uteroplacental perfusion.

Tachycardia is what the client is describing. A racing and pounding heart is a normal side effect of Terbutaline, which should subside with time. The primary care provider does not need to be notified at this time unless the condition persists or exacerbates. Procardia is also a tocolytic and would not be prescribed at this time since Terbutaline has already been administered. Repositioning the client in a side-lying position, which does help uteroplacental perfusion and fetal oxygenation, does not address the client's complaints.

9. A primary care provider prescribes two doses of betamethasone intramuscularly 24 hr apart for a client with hypertension in preterm labor to promote fetal lung maturity. The nurse knows that which of the following is the priority for monitoring while the client is on this medication?

> A. Blood glucose level
>
> B. Complete blood count
>
> **C. Blood pressure**
>
> D. Oxygen saturation

Betamethasone can worsen conditions of hypertension. Therefore, the client's blood pressure should be closely monitored while the client is on this medication. Betamethasone can also worsen diabetes. If the client had diabetes the nurse should closely monitor blood glucose levels. This medication will not have an adverse effect on CBC or oxygen saturation.

10. A client receiving oxytocin to stimulate labor is having contractions every 2 min lasting 90 sec, with incomplete relaxation of the uterus between contractions and an increase in fetal activity. The nurse recognizes that the client is

        A. experiencing hypotonic labor.

        B. entering the second stage of labor.

        C. responding appropriately to the oxytocin.

        D. experiencing hyperstimulation of the uterus.

The client is experiencing hyperstimulation of the uterus, also referred to as hypertonic contractions. The second stage of labor is the expulsion of the fetus. The client is responding to the oxytocin, but excessively and contraction pattern parameters are being exceeded. The oxytocin should be discontinued.

11. Indicate the rationale for a nonstress test with a postterm client.

        A. To evaluate uterine relaxation response

        B. To assess the well-being of the fetus

        C. To assess fetal response to uterine stimulation

        D. To evaluate fetal response to acoustic stimulation

A nonstress test assesses the well-being of a fetus. Nonstress testing has no relationship to uterine relaxation. Contraction stress tests assess the fetal response to uterine contractions and fetal ability to withstand the stress of labor. Acoustic stimulation is a form of nonstress testing used to awaken the fetus if there appears to be minimal response.

Scenario: A nurse is caring for a client in active labor. When last examined 2 hr ago, the client's cervix was 3 cm dilated, 100% effaced, membranes intact, and the fetus was at a -2 station. The client suddenly states she is "wet down there." The nurse notices that the FHR is 80 beats/min. The nurse performs a sterile glove examination and notices clear fluid and a pulsing loop of umbilical cord in the client's vagina.

12. Which of the following actions should the nurse perform first?

   A. Place the client in Trendelenburg position.

   B. Apply pressure to the presenting part with the fingers.

   C. Give the client oxygen at 10 L via a face mask.

   D. Call for assistance.

   Calling for assistance would be the first nursing action. All of the other interventions would be done after calling for assistance.

13. When completing an admission history for an 18-year-old client at 39 weeks gestation, the client states that she has been leaking water from her vagina for 2 days. The nurse knows that this client is at risk for

   A. cord prolapse.

   B. infection.

   C. malpresentation.

   D. placental abruption.

   If the membranes have been ruptured for more than 24 hr before the completion of birth, there is a high risk of infection. Micro-organisms can migrate from the vagina into the amniotic cavity. Cord prolapse is a risk upon the rupture of membranes but is more likely to occur with a gush rather than a trickle of fluid. Malpresentation and placental abruption are not associated with rupture of membranes.

14. A nurse is caring for a client at 42 weeks gestation in active labor. This fetus is at risk for which of the following?

      A. Intrauterine growth restriction

      B. Hyperglycemia

      C. Meconium aspiration

      D. Polyhydramnios

Postterm neonates are at risk for aspiration of meconium. Postterm pregnancies result in oligohydramnios, not polyhydramnios. A postterm neonate is at risk for hypoglycemia, not hyperglycemia. Intrauterine growth restriction would occur earlier in the pregnancy, not at this point.

Unit 3   Postpartum

Chapter 15:   Postpartum Physiological Changes and Nursing Care
Contributor: Pat S. Kupina, EdD, MSN, RN

⟳ NCLEX-RN® Connections:

> **Learning Objective:** Review and apply knowledge within **"Postpartum Physiological Changes and Nursing Care"** in readiness for performance of the following nursing activities as outlined by the NCLEX-RN® test plan:
>
> Δ   Assess the postpartum client.
>
> Δ   Provide appropriate postpartum nursing care.

📖 Key Points

Δ   The **fourth stage of labor** is the maternal recovery period. This stage lasts from 1 to 4 hr during which the postpartum client experiences psychological and physiological changes as body systems begin to stabilize with internal organs returning to the nonpregnant state. Also during this stage, parent-infant bonding should begin to occur.

Δ   The **postpartum period** begins after the delivery of the placenta and ends when the body returns to the prepregnant state. It takes approximately 6 weeks for a woman's body to return to the prepregnant state.

Δ   Many **physiological** and **psychological adjustments** occur during the postpartum period (also known as the **puerperium**).

Δ   **Physiological maternal changes** consist of uterine involution, lochia flow, cervical involution, decrease in vaginal distention, changes in ovarian function and menstruation, breast changes, urinary tract changes, gastrointestinal tract changes, and cardiovascular changes.

Δ   The **initial dangers** of the **postpartum** period are **hemorrhage** and **shock** followed by the danger of **infection**.

Δ   The **main goals** during the **immediate postpartum** period are to assist the client's recovery and return to a prepregnant state, identify any deviations from the norm, provide comfort measures and pharmacologic pain relief as prescribed, promote safety measures to prevent injury, prevent infection, provide client education about self-care and newborn care, and promote family-infant bonding.

Key Factors

Δ **Oxytocin**, a hormone released from the **pituitary gland,** coordinates and strengthens uterine contractions.

- **Breastfeeding** stimulates the release of endogenous oxytocin from the pituitary gland.

- **Pitocin (exogenous oxytocin)** may be administered postpartum to improve the quality of the uterine contractions.

Δ **Uterine contractions** compress the intramyometrial blood vessels as the uterine muscle contracts, resulting in constriction of the blood vessels, thereby achieving and maintaining **hemostasis** (termination of blood flow).

- A **firm** and contracted **uterus prevents excessive bleeding** and **hemorrhage**.

- Uncomfortable uterine cramping is referred to as **afterpains.**

Δ **Placental hormones** (estrogen, progesterone, and placental enzyme insulinase) markedly **decrease** with the **expulsion** of the **placenta,** lowering blood glucose levels and dramatically reducing estrogen and progesterone levels.

- **Decreased estrogen** is associated with **breast engorgement, diaphoresis** (profuse perspiration), and **diuresis** (increased formation and excretion of urine) of excess extracellular fluid accumulated during pregnancy.

- **Decreased estrogen diminishes vaginal lubrication**. Local dryness and intercourse discomfort may persist until ovarian function returns and menstruation resumes.

- **Decreased progesterone** results in an increase in muscle tone throughout the body.

- **Decreased placental enzyme insulinase** results in reversal of the diabetogenic effects of pregnancy resting in lower blood glucose levels immediately puerperium.

Δ **Lactating and nonlactating women** differ in the timing of the first ovulation and the resumption of menstruation.

- **Prolactin** levels increase throughout pregnancy. In lactating women, prolactin levels remain elevated postpartum. In nonlactating women, prolactin levels decrease postpartum.

- **Increased** levels of **prolactin** in lactating women **suppress ovulation.**

Therapeutic and Diagnostic Procedures and Nursing Implementations

Δ **Negative indirect Coombs' test of mother's blood** indicates that Rh-negative mother has not been sensitized by the Rh-positive fetus (RhoGAM administration to prevent sensitization in future pregnancies).

Δ **Kleihauer Betke test** determines the amount of fetal blood in maternal circulation if a large fetomaternal transfusion is suspected. If 15 mL or more of fetal blood is detected the mother should receive an increased RhoGAM dose.

Δ **Laceration** and/or **episiotomy repair is** performed by the primary care provider. The nurse should assist as necessary during the procedure.

Δ **Complete blood count** monitors hemoglobin and hematocrit, white blood cell count, platelet counts, and antibody screen, and informs the primary care provider of any abnormalities.

Nursing Assessments and Interventions

Δ **Postpartum assessments immediately following delivery** include monitoring the client's vital signs, uterine firmness and its location in relation to the umbilicus, uterine position in relation to the midline of the abdomen, and amount of vaginal bleeding.

- Every **15 min x 4** for first hour, if all factors stable

- Every **30 min x 2** for second hour, if all factors stable

- **Hourly x 2** for at least 2 hr

- Then **every 4 to 8 hr** for remainder of hospitalization

Δ A **focused physical assessment** should include assessing the client's:

- Fundal height, uterine placement, and uterine consistency.

- Lochia color, amount, and consistency.

- Cervical, vaginal, and perineal healing.

- Breasts.

- Vital signs.

- Bowel and gastrointestinal function.

- Bladder function.

- Comfort level.

- Teaching needs.

Thermoregulation

Δ **Postpartum chill**, which occurs in the first 2 hr puerperium, is an uncontrollable shaking chill in the client immediately following birth. Postpartum chill is possibly related to a nervous system response, vasomotor changes, a shift in fluids, and/or the work of labor. Postpartum chill is a normal occurrence of no clinical significance as long as it is not followed by an elevated temperature.

- Provide the client with warm blankets and fluids.

- Assure the client that these chills are a self-limiting common occurrence that will only last a short while.

Fundus

Δ **Physical changes** of the uterus include **involution of the uterus. Involution** occurs with **contractions** of the uterine smooth muscle, whereby the uterus returns to its prepregnant state. The uterus also rapidly decreases in size from approximately 1,000 g (2.2 lb) to 50 to 60 g (< 2 oz) over a period of 6 weeks with the fundal height steadily descending into the pelvis approximately one fingerbreadth (1 cm) per day.

- Immediately after delivery, the fundus should be midline, approximately at the level of the umbilicus, and firm. At 12 hr postpartum the fundus may be palpated at 1 cm above the umbilicus.

- **Every 24 hr**, the **fundus** should **descend** approximately **1 to 2 cm** being located halfway between the symphysis pubis and the umbilicus by the sixth postpartum day.

- By 10 days postpartum, the uterus lies within the true pelvis and should not be abdominally palpable.

Δ The nurse should **assess** the **fundal height**, **uterine placement**, and **uterine consistency.**

- Explain the procedure to the client.

- Apply clean gloves, lower perineal pad, and observe lochia flow as the fundus is palpated.

- Cup one hand just above the symphysis pubis to support the lower segment of the uterus, and with the other hand, palpate the abdomen to locate the fundus.

- Document the fundal height, location, and uterine consistency.

  ◊ Determine the **fundal height** by placing fingers on the abdomen and measuring **how many fingerbreadths** (cm) fit between the fundus and the umbilicus above, below, or at the umbilical level.

  ◊ Determine if the **fundus** is **midline** in the pelvis or displaced laterally (caused by a full bladder).

  ◊ Determine if the fundus is **firm or boggy.** If the fundus is **boggy** (not firm), lightly massage the fundus in a circular motion.

Δ **Nursing interventions** related to **uterine involution** include:

- Administering oxytocics intramuscularly or intravenously as prescribed after the placenta is delivered to promote uterine contractions and to prevent hemorrhage.

  ◊ Oxytocics include oxytocin (Pitocin), methylergonovine maleate (Methergine), and ergonovine maleate (Ergonate).

- Monitoring for adverse affects of the oxytocics.

  ◊ Oxytocin may cause hypotension.

  ◊ Methylergonovine maleate and ergonovine maleate may cause hypertension.

- Encouraging early breastfeeding for the lactating mother. This will stimulate the production of natural oxytocin and will help prevent hemorrhage.

- Encouraging frequent emptying of the bladder every 2 to 3 hr to keep the bladder empty and to prevent possible uterine displacement and atony.

Lochia

Δ **Physical changes** in **vaginal discharge** include **lochia,** which is the blood flow from the uterus during puerperium. Lochia consists of blood from the vessels of the placental attachment site to the uterus and debris from the exfoliation of the **decidua** (thickened lining of uterine endometrium during pregnancy).

- There are three stages of lochia:

  ◊ **Lochia rubra** – bright red color, bloody consistency, fleshy odor, may contain small clots, transient flow increase during breastfeeding and upon rising. Lasts 1 to 3 days after delivery.

  ◊ **Lochia serosa** – pinkish brown color, serosanguineous consistency, contains old blood, serum, leukocytes, and tissue debris. Lasts from approximately day 4 to day 10 after delivery.

  ◊ **Lochia alba** – yellowish, white creamy color, fleshy odor, contains leukocytes, decidua, epithelial cells, mucus, serum, and bacteria. Lasts from approximately day 11 up to and beyond 6 weeks postpartum.

- **Lochia amount** is assessed by the quantity of saturation on the perineal pad as being either:

  ◊ Scant (< 2.5 cm).

  ◊ Light (< 10 cm).

  ◊ Moderate (> 10 cm).

  ◊ Heavy (one pad saturated within 2 hr).

  ◊ Excessive blood loss (one pad saturated in 15 min or less or pooling of blood under buttocks).

Δ   The nurse should **assess** the **lochia** flow for normal **color, amount**, and **consistency.**

- Lochia typically trickles from the vaginal opening but flows more steadily during uterine contractions.

- Massaging the uterus or ambulation may result in a gush of lochia with the expression of clots and dark blood that has pooled in the vagina, but should soon decrease back to a trickle of bright red lochia when in the early puerperium.

Δ   **Nursing interventions** for **abnormal lochia** include notifying the primary care provider and performing prescribed interventions based on the cause of the abnormality.

- **Abnormal lochia** is evidenced by:

  ◊ Excessive spurting of bright red blood from the vagina, possibly indicating a cervical or vaginal tear.

  ◊ Numerous large clots and excessive blood loss (saturation of one pad in 15 min or less) may be indicative of a hemorrhage.

  ◊ Foul odor is suggestive of an infection.

  ◊ Persistent lochia rubra in early postpartum period beyond 3 days is suggestive of retained placental fragments.

  ◊ Continued flow of lochia serosa or alba beyond the normal length of time may indicate endometritis especially if accompanied by a fever, pain, or abdominal tenderness.

Cervix, Vagina, and Perineum

Δ   **Physical changes** of the **cervix, vagina**, and **perineum** are as follows:

- The **cervix** is soft directly after birth and may be edematous, bruised, and have some small lacerations. Within 2 to 3 days postpartum, it shortens and regains its form becoming firm with the os gradually closing.

  ◊ Lacerations can delay the production of estrogen-influenced cervical mucus and are a predisposing factor to infection.

- The **vagina** has a thin mucosa and is absent of rugae (folds in vaginal mucosa) as a result of low estrogen postpartum. The distended vagina gradually returns to its prepregnancy size with the reappearance of rugae and a thickening of the vaginal mucosa. However, muscle tone is never restored completely.

- The soft tissues of the **perineum** may show evidence of an erythematous and edematous **introitus** especially in areas of an episiotomy or lacerations. Possible hematomas may be present as well as hemorrhoids (anal varicosities). The pelvic floor muscles may be overstretched and weak.

Δ   The nurse should **assess** for **cervical**, **vaginal**, and **perineal healing**.

- Observe for perineal erythema, edema, and hematoma.

- Assess episiotomy and lacerations if present for approximation and drainage and quantity and quality.

    ◊   A bright red trickle of blood from the episiotomy site in the early postpartum period is a normal finding.

Δ   **Nursing interventions** for perineal **tenderness**, **laceration**, and **episiotomy** include the following:

- Promote **measures** to **soften stools**.

- Educate the client on **proper cleansing** to **prevent infection.**

    ◊   The client should wash her hands thoroughly before and after voiding.

    ◊   The client should use a squeeze bottle filled with warm water or antiseptic solution after each voiding to cleanse the perineal area.

    ◊   The client should clean her perineal area from front to back (urethra to anus).

    ◊   The client should blot dry, not wipe.

    ◊   Topical application of antiseptic cream or spray should be used sparingly by the client.

    ◊   The client's perineal pad should be changed from front to back after voiding or defecating.

- Promote **comfort measures.**

    ◊   Apply ice packs to the client's perineum for the first 24 to 48 hr to reduce edema and provide anesthetic effect.

    ◊   Encourage sitz baths at a temperature of 38° to 40° C (100° to 104° F) or cooler at least twice a day.

    ◊   Administer analgesia such as non-opioids (acetaminophen), non-steroidal anti-inflammatories (ibuprofen), and opioids (codeine, hydrocodone) as prescribed for pain and discomfort. Opioid analgesia may be administered via a PCA (patient controlled analgesia) pump for cesarean deliveries.

    ◊   Apply topical anesthetics (Americaine spray or Dermoplast) to the client's perineal area as needed or witch hazel compresses (Tuck's) to the rectal area for hemorrhoids.

Breasts

Δ **Physical changes** of the **breasts** include the **secretion of colostrum,** which occurs during pregnancy and **2 to 3 days** immediately after birth. **Milk** is produced in the breasts **2 to 3 days after** the delivery of the infant.

Δ The nurse should **assess** the client's **breasts** as well as the client's ability to assist the infant with latching on if breastfeeding.

- Colostrum secretion in lactating and non-lactating clients

- Engorgement of the breast tissue as a result of lymphatic circulation, milk production, and temporary vein congestion

- Redness and tenderness of the breast

- Cracked nipples and indications of mastitis (infection in a milk duct of the breast with concurrent flu-like symptoms)

- Ascertain that the breastfeeding infant has latched on correctly to prevent sore nipples

- Ineffective infant feeding patterns related to maternal discomfort, infant positioning, or difficulty with infant latching onto the breast

Δ **Nursing interventions** pertaining to the client's **breasts** and **breastfeeding** include:

- Encouraging early demand breastfeeding for the lactating mother, which will also stimulate the production of natural oxytocin and help prevent uterine hemorrhage.

- Assisting the client into a comfortable position and having her try various positions during breastfeeding (cradle hold, side-lying, and football hold) and explaining how varying positions can prevent nipple soreness.

- Teaching the client the importance of proper latch techniques (the infant takes in part of the areola and nipple, not just the tip of the nipple) to prevent nipple soreness from occurring.

- Informing the client that breastfeeding causes the release of oxytocin, which stimulates uterine contractions. This is a normal occurrence and beneficial to uterine tone.

Cardiovascular System and Fluid and Hematologic Status

Δ **Physical changes** in the **cardiovascular system** in the postpartum period include:

- The cardiovascular system undergoes a decrease in blood volume during the postpartum period related to:

  ◊ **Blood loss during childbirth** (average blood loss is 500 mL in an uncomplicated vaginal delivery and 1,000 mL for a cesarean birth).

◊ **Diaphoresis** and **diuresis** of the **excess fluid** accumulated during the last part of the pregnancy. Loss occurs within the first 2 to 3 days postdelivery.

- **Hypovolemic shock** does not usually occur in response to the normal blood loss of labor and birth, because:

  ◊ During pregnancy, there is a 50% increase in circulating blood volume. This pregnancy-induced hypervolemia permits most women to tolerate considerable blood loss during childbirth.

  ◊ **Readjustments** in the **maternal vasculature** occur in response to the following:

    ° Elimination of the placenta diverting 500 to 750 mL of blood into the maternal systemic circulation.

    ° Rapid reduction in the size of the uterus putting more blood into the maternal systemic circulation.

Δ **Physical changes** in **blood values, coagulation factors,** and **fibrinogen levels** during the puerperium include:

- **Increased hematocrit** and **hemoglobin** values are present immediately after delivery for up to 72 hr. This elevation is a consequence of diaphoresis and diuresis of excess fluid from pregnancy. Secondary to a greater loss of plasma volume than number of red blood cells, there is a resultant hemoconcentration of the blood leading to a temporary rise in hematocrit and hemoglobin levels.

- **Leukocytosis** (white blood cell count elevation) up to 20,000 to 25,000/mm^3 for the first 10 to 14 days without the presence of infection and then returns to normal.

- **Coagulation factors** and **fibrinogen levels increase** during pregnancy and remain elevated for 2 to 3 weeks postpartum. This **hypercoagulability** is in conjunction with **vessel damage** incurred during childbirth, **venous stasis** of the lower extremities during the later part of pregnancy, and client **immobility** during recovery. Hypercoagulability predisposes the postpartum woman to **thrombus formation** and **thromboembolism.**

Δ **Vital sign changes** include:

- **Blood pressure** is usually unchanged with an uncomplicated pregnancy but may have an insignificant slight transient increase.

- Possible **orthostatic hypotension** within the first 48 hr postpartum may occur immediately after standing up with feelings of faintness or dizziness resulting from splanchnic (viscera/internal organs) engorgement that can occur after birth.

- Elevation of **pulse, stroke volume,** and **cardiac output** for the first hour postpartum and then gradually decreasing to a prepregnant state baseline by 8 to 10 weeks.

- **Elevation of temperature** to 38° C (100° F) resulting from dehydration after labor during the first 24 hr may occur, but should return to normal after 24 hr postpartum.

Δ   The nurse should **assess** for **cardiovascular** and **vital sign** changes and **monitor blood component** changes.

- **Vital signs** should be assessed per postpartum parameters of every 15 min x 4, every 30 min x 2, and then hourly x 2 for the stable client, followed by monitoring every 4 to 8 hr thereafter for the remainder of the hospitalization.

- A **Homans' sign** assessment is performed by the nurse, which is comprised of having the nurse passively dorsiflex the foot and determining if the client experiences discomfort and pain in the calf (positive Homans' sign). This may be an early sign of venous thrombosis and should be reported to the primary care provider immediately. The nurse should also inspect the client's legs for redness, swelling, and warmth, which are additional signs of **venous thrombosis**.

Δ   **Nursing interventions** for **abnormal cardiovascular, vital sign, or blood component findings** include notifying the primary care provider and performing prescribed interventions based on the cause of the abnormality.

- Encouraging early ambulation to prevent venous stasis and thrombosis.

- Application of TED hose to the client's lower extremities to prevent venous stasis and thrombosis.

- Administering medications as prescribed.

  ◊ For example, intramuscular administration of immune globulin (RhoGAM) within 72 hr after birth to prevent sensitization in Rh-negative mothers with an Rh-positive infant or as indicated by negative indirect Coombs' tests.

Δ   Continuing to monitor the client's vital signs and laboratory data.

Gastrointestinal System and Bowel Function

Δ   **Physical changes** in the **gastrointestinal system** may show evidence of:

- An increased appetite following delivery.

- Constipation with bowel evacuation delayed until 2 to 3 days after birth.

- Hemorrhoids.

Δ   The nurse should **assess** the **gastrointestinal system** including **bowel function**.

- Assess the client for reports of hunger. A good appetite is expected.

- Assess the client for bowel sounds and the return of normal bowel function.

  ◊ Spontaneous bowel movement may not occur for 2 to 3 days after delivery secondary to decreased intestinal muscle tone during labor and puerperium and prelabor diarrhea and dehydration. The client may also anticipate discomfort with defecation because of perineal tenderness, episiotomy, lacerations, or hemorrhoids.

- Assess the client's rectal area for varicosities (hemorrhoids).

- Operative vaginal birth (forceps-assisted and vacuum-assisted) and anal sphincter lacerations increase the risk of temporary postpartum anal incontinence that usually resolves within 6 months.

Δ **Nursing interventions** for **gastrointestinal** and **bowel function** include:

- Encouraging measures to soften stools and promote bowel function such as early ambulation, increased fluids, and high fiber food sources.

- Administering stool softeners (docusate sodium) as prescribed to prevent constipation.

  ◊ Enemas and suppositories are contraindicated.

Urinary System and Bladder Function

Δ The **urinary system** may show evidence of:

- **Urinary retention** secondary to loss of bladder elasticity and tone and/or loss of bladder sensation resulting from trauma, medications, or anesthesia.

  ◊ A **distended bladder** as a result of urinary retention can cause **uterine atony** and **displacement** to one side, usually to the right, and the ability of the uterus to contract is lessened.

- **Postpartal diuresis** with increased urinary output begins within 12 hr of delivery and is caused by a decrease in estrogen levels and the removal of increased venous pressure in lower extremities.

Δ The nurse should **assess** the **urinary system** and **bladder function**.

- Assess the client's ability to void every 2 to 3 hr (perineal/urethral edema may cause pain and difficulty in voiding during the first 24 to 48 hr).

- Assess the client's bladder elimination pattern (should be voiding every 2 to 3 hr). Excessive urine diuresis (1,500 to 3,000 mL/day) is normal within the first 2 to 3 days after delivery.

- Assess for signs of a distended bladder including:

  ◊ Fundal height above the umbilicus or baseline level.

  ◊ Fundus displaced from the midline over to the side.

  ◊ Bladder bulges above the symphysis pubis.

◊ Excessive lochia.

◊ Tenderness over the bladder area.

◊ Frequently voiding less than 150 mL of urine is indicative of urinary retention with overflow.

Δ **Nursing interventions** for the urinary system and bladder function include:

• Encouraging the client to **frequently empty** her bladder every 2 to 3 hr to prevent possible displacement of the uterus.

• Measuring the client's first few voidings after delivery.

• Encouraging the client to increase oral fluid intake to replace fluids lost at delivery and to prevent or correct dehydration.

• Catheterizing if necessary for bladder distention if the client is unable to void and drain the bladder entirely to ensure complete emptying of the bladder and allow uterine involution.

Musculoskeletal System

Δ **Physical changes** of the **musculoskeletal system** involve a reversal of the musculoskeletal adaptations that occurred during pregnancy. By 6 to 8 weeks after birth:

• The joints return to their pregnant state and are completely restabilized. The feet, however, may remain permanently increased in size.

• **Muscle tone** begins to be **restored** throughout the body with the removal of progesterone's effect following delivery of the placenta.

◊ The **rectus abdominis muscles** of the abdomen and the **pubococcygeal muscle** tone are restored following placental expulsion. The abdominal wall muscles (**rectus abdominis**) may **separate** as result of uterine overdistention, and this is referred to as **diastasis recti abdominis**.

Δ The nurse should **assess** the **musculoskeletal system** for changes.

• Assess the client's abdominal wall for **diastasis recti** (a separation of the rectus muscle) anywhere from 2 to 4 cm. It usually resolves within 6 weeks.

Δ **Nursing interventions** pertaining to the **musculoskeletal system** include:

• Teaching the client postpartum strengthening exercises, and advising her to start with simple exercises, gradually progressing to more strenuous ones.

• Instructing clients who have had a cesarean birth to postpone abdominal exercises until about 4 weeks after delivery.

• Advising a client on good body mechanics and proper posture.

Comfort Level

Δ   Nursing assessments and interventions for the client's **comfort level** include:

- Monitoring for reports of pain due to episiotomy, lacerations, incisions, afterpains, and sore nipples.

- Assessing location, type, and quality of the pain to guide nursing interventions and patient education.

- Administering pain medications as prescribed.

Immune System

Δ   **Review rubella status** – a client with a titer of less than 1:8 is administered a subcutaneous injection of rubella vaccine during the postpartum period to protect a subsequent fetus from malformations. The nurse **must obtain an informed consent** and **emphasize** to the client the importance of **not getting pregnant for 3 months following the rubella vaccination** because of its **teratogenic effects** on the **fetus**.

Δ   **Review hepatitis B status** – infants born to infected mothers should receive the hepatitis B vaccine and the hepatitis B immune globulin (HBIG) within 12 hr of birth.

Δ   **Review the Rh status** – all Rh-negative mothers with Rh-positive infants must be given Rh immune globulin (RhoGAM) administered intramuscularly within 72 hr of the infant being born to suppress antibody formation in the mother.

Δ   Test the client who receives both the rubella vaccine and RhoGAM after 3 months to determine if immunity to rubella has been developed.

Primary Reference:

Lowdermilk, D. L. & Perry, S. E. (2004). *Maternity & women's health care* (8th ed.). St. Louis, MO: Mosby.

Additional Resources:

Littleton, L. Y. & Engebretson, J. C. (2005). *Nursing care of the low-risk postpartum family: maternity nursing care*. New York: Thomson – Delmar Learning.

NANDA International (2004). *NANDA nursing diagnoses: Definitions and classification 2005-2006*. Philadelphia: NANDA.

Piotrowski, K. A. (2003). *Study guide to accompany maternity nursing*. Lowdermilk, L. Y. & Perry, S. E. (Eds.). St. Louis, MO: Mosby.

Chapter 15: Postpartum Physiological Changes and Nursing Care

Application Exercises

1. After delivery, the uterus contracts and gradually returns to its prepregnant state. This is referred to as which of the following?

      A. Uterine inversion

      B. Uterine subinvolution

      C. Uterine involution

      D. Uterine exfoliation

2. A nurse is performing a fundal assessment on a client in her second postpartum day and observes the perineal pad for lochia. She notes the pad to be saturated approximately 4 ½ in with lochia that is bright red in color containing small clots and a fleshy odor. The nurse knows that this finding is

      A. moderate lochia rubra, a normal finding.

      B. excessive lochia rubra with abnormal clotting.

      C. light lochia rubra with abnormal clotting.

      D. scant lochia serosa, a normal finding.

3. During ambulation to the bathroom, a postpartum client experiences a gush of dark red blood that soon stops. On assessment, the nurse finds the client's uterus to be firm and midline, at the level of the umbilicus. The nurse interprets this finding as

      A. a sign of a possible postpartum hemorrhage.

      B. an indication of a cervical or perineal laceration.

      C. a normal postural discharge of lochia.

      D. abnormally excessive lochia rubra flow.

4. A nurse is assessing a postpartum client for fundal height, location, and consistency. The fundus is found to be displaced laterally to the right and the uterus is boggy. The nurse understands that the most likely cause of the displacement of the uterus and boggy tone is

      A. poor involution.

      B. urinary retention.

      C. hemorrhage.

      D. infection.

5. A client is in the fourth stage of labor, has just delivered a newborn, and is stable. The nurse knows that during the maternal recovery period vital signs should be assessed at regular intervals. Which of the following are appropriate vital sign intervals for the fourth stage of labor?

    A. Every 15 min x 2, every 30 min x 4, hourly x 4
    B. Every 15 min x 4, every 30 min x 2, hourly x 2
    C. Every 15 min x 8, every 30 min x 4, hourly x 2
    D. Every 15 min x 6, every 30 min x 4, hourly x 8

6. Women are able to tolerate a great deal of blood loss during birth averaging 500 mL for an uncomplicated vaginal delivery and 1,000 mL for a cesarean birth without hypovolemic shock occurring. There are several readjustments to the maternal cardiovascular system and vasculature which make this possible. (Select all that apply.)

    _____ A 50% increase in circulating blood volume during pregnancy
    _____ Diversion of blood into systemic circulation with elimination of placenta
    _____ Rapid reduction in size of uterus putting more blood into systemic circulation
    _____ Diaphoresis eliminating excess fluid volume accumulated during pregnancy
    _____ Diuresis for the first 2 to 3 days, which eliminates excess fluid from pregnancy
    _____ Elevation of pulse, stroke volume, and cardiac output for first hour postpartum

7. Which of the following nursing interventions will promote comfort for a client with a small hematoma of the perineal area? (Select all that apply.)

    _____ Apply ice to the perineal area for the first 24 to 48 hr.
    _____ Apply warm packs to the perineal area for the first 24 to 48 hr.
    _____ Encourage sitz baths at least twice a day.
    _____ Use a topical antiseptic cream or spray on the perineal area.
    _____ Obtain an order for an indwelling urinary catheter.

8. A Homans' sign is performed on all postpartum clients to assess for which of the following possible complications?

    A. Hemorrhage
    B. Subinvolution
    C. Hypovolemia
    D. Thrombosis

Chapter 15: Postpartum Physiological Changes and Nursing Care

Application Exercises Answer Key

1. After delivery, the uterus contracts and gradually returns to its prepregnant state. This is referred to as which of the following?

  A. Uterine inversion

  B. Uterine subinvolution

  C. Uterine involution

  D. Uterine exfoliation

  Uterine involution is the return of the uterus to the prepregnant state, and postpartum contractions aid in this occurring. Uterine inversion is a condition in which the uterus turns inside out and can be caused by the placenta being removed too vigorously prior to its natural detachment process. Uterine subinvolution is the delay of the uterus in returning to the prepregnancy state. Uterine exfoliation is the shedding of the decidua tissue layers.

2. A nurse is performing a fundal assessment on a client in her second postpartum day and observes the perineal pad for lochia. She notes the pad to be saturated approximately 4 ½ in with lochia that is bright red in color containing small clots and a fleshy odor. The nurse knows that this finding is

  A. moderate lochia rubra, a normal finding.

  B. excessive lochia rubra with abnormal clotting.

  C. light lochia rubra with abnormal clotting.

  D. scant lochia serosa, a normal finding.

  The client has moderate lochia rubra containing small clots with a fleshy odor which is a normal finding for the second day postpartum. There are three stages of lochia. Lochia rubra is bright red in color, with a bloody consistency that may have small clots, has a fleshy odor, and lasts 1 to 3 days after birth. Lochia serosa is pinkish brown in color with a serosanguineous consistency, and lasts approximately from day 4 to day 10 after delivery. Lochia alba is yellowish white in color, has a fleshy odor, and lasts from approximately day 11 up to and beyond 6 weeks postpartum. The amount of lochia is assessed by the quantity of saturation on the perineal pad with scant being less than 2.5 cm, light less than 10 cm, moderate more than 10 cm, heavy one pad within 2 hr, and excessive one pad within 15 min.

3. During ambulation to the bathroom, a postpartum client experiences a gush of dark red blood that soon stops. On assessment, the nurse finds the client's uterus to be firm and midline, at the level of the umbilicus. The nurse interprets this finding as

        A. a sign of a possible postpartum hemorrhage.

        B. an indication of a cervical or perineal laceration.

        C. a normal postural discharge of lochia.

        D. abnormally excessive lochia rubra flow.

Lochia typically trickles from the vaginal opening but flows more steadily during uterine contractions. Massaging the uterus or ambulation may result in a gush of lochia with the expression of clots and dark blood that has been pooled in the vagina, but should soon decrease back to a trickle of bright red lochia when in the early puerperium. Excessive blood loss consists of one pad saturated in 15 min or less or the pooling of blood under buttocks and is not affected by the client's postural changes.

4. A nurse is assessing a postpartum client for fundal height, location, and consistency. The fundus is found to be displaced laterally to the right and there is uterine atony. The nurse understands that the most likely cause of the displacement of the uterus and boggy tone is

        A. poor involution.

        B. urinary retention.

        C. hemorrhage.

        D. infection.

Urinary retention can result in a distention of the bladder. A distended bladder can cause uterine atony and lateral displacement from the midline, usually to the right. Poor involution and hemorrhage are results of uterine atony; they do not cause it. Infection does not cause uterine displacement or atony and would be characterized by foul-smelling vaginal discharge and elevated temperature.

5. A client is in the fourth stage of labor, has just delivered a newborn, and is stable. The nurse knows that during the maternal recovery period vital signs should be assessed at regular intervals. Which of the following are appropriate vital sign intervals for the fourth stage of labor?

> A. Every 15 min x 2, every 30 min x 4, hourly x 4
>
> **B. Every 15 min x 4, every 30 min x 2, hourly x 2**
>
> C. Every 15 min x 8, every 30 min x 4, hourly x 2
>
> D. Every 15 min x 6, every 30 min x 4, hourly x 8

The fourth stage of labor is referred to as the maternal recovery period which lasts from 1 to 4 hr. If all factors are stable, postpartum assessments of vital signs as well as uterine firmness, location, and position should be done every 15 min x 4 for the first hour, every 30 min x 2 for the second hour, hourly x 2 for at least 2 hr, and then every 4 to 8 hr for the remainder of the client's hospitalization.

6. Women are able to tolerate a great deal of blood loss during birth averaging 500 mL for an uncomplicated vaginal delivery and 1,000 mL for a cesarean birth without hypovolemic shock occurring. There are several readjustments to the maternal cardiovascular system and vasculature which make this possible. (Select all that apply.)

> __X__ **A 50% increase in circulating blood volume during pregnancy**
>
> __X__ **Diversion of blood into systemic circulation with elimination of placenta**
>
> __X__ **Rapid reduction in size of uterus putting more blood into systemic circulation**
>
> _____ Diaphoresis eliminating excess fluid volume accumulated during pregnancy
>
> _____ Diuresis for the first 2 to 3 days which eliminates excess fluid from pregnancy
>
> _____ Elevation of pulse, stroke volume, and cardiac output for first hour postpartum

The 50% increase in circulating blood volume during pregnancy, diversion of blood into the maternal systemic circulations from the expulsion of the placenta, and reduced uterine size contribute to preventing hypovolemic shock from occurring with the normal blood loss of birth. Diaphoresis, diuresis, and elevated pulse, stroke, and cardiac output do occur but do not counteract the affects of blood loss.

7. Which of the following nursing interventions will promote comfort for a client with a small hematoma of the perineal area? (Select all that apply.)

  __X__ **Apply ice to the perineal area for the first 24 to 48 hr.**

  _____ Apply warm packs to the perineal area for the first 24 to 48 hr.

  __X__ **Encourage sitz baths at least twice a day.**

  __X__ **Use a topical antiseptic cream or spray on the perineal area.**

  _____ Obtain an order for an indwelling urinary catheter.

To promote perineal comfort for a small hematoma, ice should be applied for the first 24 to 48 hr to reduce swelling and provide anesthetic effects. Sitz baths and use of a topical antiseptic cream or spray should be encouraged. Warm packs will increase circulation to the area and increase swelling. Use of indwelling urinary catheters is not indicated and can lead to infection.

8. A Homans' sign is performed on all postpartum clients to assess for which of the following possible complications?

  A. Hemorrhage

  B. Subinvolution

  C. Hypovolemia

  D. Thrombosis

Homans' sign is performed by passively dorsiflexing the client's foot and assessing for the presence of calf pain to assess for thrombosis. Thrombosis is the formation of blood clots. The postpartum client is at increased risk for thrombosis due to venous stasis in the lower extremities, postpartum elevated clotting factors, and hemoconcentration of the blood resulting from diaphoresis and diuresis. Hemorrhage is a risk from uterine atony. Hypovolemia is low blood volume that can occur from hemorrhage. Subinvolution is the delay of the uterus to its prepregnant state.

Unit 3   Postpartum

Chapter 16:   Bonding and Integration of Infant into Family Structure
Contributor: Pat S. Kupina, EdD, MSN, RN

↻ **NCLEX-RN® Connections:**

Learning Objective: Review and apply knowledge within **"Bonding and Integration of Infant into Family Structure"** in readiness for performance of the following nursing activities as outlined by the NCLEX-RN® test plan:

Δ   Assist the client/family with the integration of an infant into the family structure.

📖 Key Points

Δ   Bonding and integration of the infant into the family structure is dependent on successful adaptation of the individual members of the family unit.

Δ   Bonding and attachment are terms used to describe the emotional process where parents come to love and accept their child and the child comes to love and accept the parents.

Δ   Bonding behaviors can be promoted by delaying nursing/medical procedures during the first hour after birth to allow for unlimited parent-infant contact.

Δ   Bonding behaviors can be impaired secondary to maternal or neonatal complications that delay parent-infant contact following birth.

Key Factors

Δ   The mother's **emotional** and **physical condition** (e.g., unwanted pregnancy, teenage pregnancy, history of depression, difficult pregnancy and delivery) and the infant's physical condition (e.g., prematurity, congenital anomalies) after birth **can affect the family's bonding process**.

Δ   **Separation** of the mother and infant after birth due to maternal or neonatal complications can **negatively affect** or **delay the bonding process**.

Δ   **Culture**, **age**, and **socioeconomic level** are factors that can **influence the bonding process**.

Assessments and Nursing Interventions

Δ   Assessment of bonding and integration of the infant into the family structure requires that the nurse understand the normal postpartum psychological changes the mother undergoes in the attainment of the maternal role and the recognition of deviations.

Psychosocial and Maternal Adaptation

Δ   **Psychosocial adaptation** and **maternal adjustment postpartum** consist of three phases.

- **Taking-in phase** – begins immediately following birth lasting a few hours to a couple of days. Characteristics include passive-dependent behavior, and relying on others to meet needs for comfort, rest, closeness, and nourishment. The client focuses on her own needs and is concerned about the overall health of her newborn. She is excited and talkative, repeatedly reviewing the labor and birth experience.

- **Taking-hold phase** – the second maternal phase, which begins the second or third postpartum day and lasts 10 days to several weeks. The woman's focus is on asserting her independence in competently caring for her newborn. She may verbalize anxiety about exhaustion, feelings of incompetence in her new role, and still needs nurturing and acceptance by others. The client may experience postpartum blues at this time. This is an optimal period for nurses to provide client teaching.

- **Letting-go phase** – the stage when the client assumes her position at home and her new maternal role, focusing on the forward movement of the family as a unit. She may reassert the relationship with her partner and resume sexual intimacy at this time. Increased demands of home and newborn care may lead to mild depression.

Δ   **Nursing assessments** include noting the mother's condition after birth, observing the maternal adaptation process, assessing maternal emotional readiness to care for the infant, and assessing how comfortable the mother appears in providing infant care.

- Assess for **behaviors** that **facilitate and indicate mother-infant bonding** as evidenced by:
  - ◊   Views and takes in physical characteristics of the infant.
  - ◊   Holds the infant face to face (en face) maintaining eye contact.
  - ◊   Recognizes the infant as a unique person.
  - ◊   Considers the infant a family member.
  - ◊   Identifies the infant's unique characteristics and relates them to other family members.
  - ◊   Touches the infant and maintains close physical proximity and contact.

◊ Provides physical care for the infant such as feeding and diapering.

◊ Smiles at, talks to, coos, and sings to the infant.

◊ Communicates pride in the infant.

◊ Assigns meaning to the infant's behavior and views positively.

- Assess for **behaviors** that **impair and indicate a lack of mother-infant bonding**:

   ◊ Apathy when the infant cries.

   ◊ Disgust when the infant voids, stools, or spits up.

   ◊ Expresses disappointment in the infant.

   ◊ Turns away from the infant.

   ◊ Does not seek close physical proximity to infant.

   ◊ Does not talk about infant's unique features.

   ◊ Shows no evidence of pride in the infant.

   ◊ Handles the infant roughly.

   ◊ Methodically cares for the newborn without evidence of positive bonding behaviors.

   ◊ Ignores the infant entirely.

   ◊ Views the infant's behavior as being deliberately uncooperative or disruptive.

- Assess for **signs of mood swings, conflict about maternal role,** and/or **personal insecurity** as evidenced by expressions of:

   ◊ Feelings of being "down."

   ◊ Emotional lability with frequent crying.

   ◊ Flat affect and being withdrawn.

   ◊ Feelings of inadequacy.

   ◊ Feelings of anxiety related to ineffective breastfeeding.

   ◊ Feeling unable to care for the newborn.

Δ **Nursing Interventions** to assist with maternal-infant bonding include:

- Facilitating the bonding process by placing the infant skin-to-skin with the mother soon after birth in an en face position.

- Encouraging the parents to bond with the infant through cuddling, feeding, diapering, and inspecting the infant.

- Providing a quiet and private environment that enhances the family bonding process.

- Providing frequent praise, support, and reassurance to the mother during the taking-hold phase, as she moves toward independence in care of the newborn and adjusts to the maternal role.

- Encouraging the mother/parents to discuss their feelings, fears, and anxieties about caring for their newborn.

Paternal Adaptation

Δ **Paternal adaptation** consists of the father becoming engrossed with the infant, transitioning to fatherhood, and developing a parent-infant bond.

- **Engrossment** is the term used to describe the father being absorbed and preoccupied with the infant and is characterized by:

    ◊ Touching, holding, and maintaining eye-to-eye contact with the infant.

    ◊ Observing the infant for features similar to his own to validate his claim on the infant.

    ◊ Communicating with the infant.

    ◊ Expressing pride in the infant.

- **Paternal transition to fatherhood** consists of a predictable three-stage process during the first few weeks of transition.

    ◊ **Expectations** – the first stage in which the father has preconceived ideas about what it will be like when the infant comes home.

    ◊ **Reality** – the second stage in which the father comes to the realization that his expectations might not be based on fact. He may experience feelings of sadness, ambivalence, jealousy of the infant, frustration, a desire to become more involved, and/or surprise at the reward of parenting.

    ◊ **Transition to mastery** – the third stage in which the father makes the determination to become more actively involved with the infant.

- The **development** of the **father-infant bond** consists of three stages.

    ◊ **Making a commitment** – characterized by a sense of duty and willingness to take responsibility for nurturing the parent-infant relationship in spite of any difficulties. The father experiences a sense of reward from interactions with the infant and has a sense of gaining a new perspective.

    ◊ **Becoming connected** – characterized by having feelings of joy and wonderment on first meeting with the infant and bonding. The father begins to perceive the infant as responsive, familiar, and predictable.

    ◊ **Making room for the infant** – characterized by changes in work and personal time so as to be more physically and emotionally available to the infant.

Δ **Nursing assessment** of **father-infant bonding** includes observing for the characteristics of engrossment with the infant.

Δ **Nursing interventions** to assist in the **father-infant bonding** process include:

- Providing education on infant care when the father is present.

- Assisting the father in his transition to fatherhood by providing guidance and involving him as a full partner rather than just a helper.

- Encouraging couples to verbalize their expectations including the negotiation of the division of labor of household and infant care.

Sibling Adaptation

Δ The addition of an infant into the family unit affects everyone in the family including **siblings** who may experience a temporary separation from the mother and changes in the parents' behavior with the newborn requiring much of the parents' time.

Δ **Nursing assessment** of sibling adaptation to the infant includes:

- Assessing for positive responses from the sibling.

  ◊ Interest and concern for the infant

  ◊ Increased independence

- Assessing for adverse responses from the sibling.

  ◊ Signs of sibling rivalry and jealousy

  ◊ Regression in toileting and sleep habits

  ◊ Aggression toward the infant

  ◊ Increased attention-seeking behaviors and whining

Δ **Nursing interventions** to facilitate sibling acceptance of the infant include:

- Taking the sibling on a tour of the hospital room and maternity unit.

- Encouraging the parents to:

  ◊ Have a gift from the infant to give the sibling.

  ◊ Get a T-shirt that says "I'm a big brother" or "sister."

  ◊ Let the sibling be in the first group to see the infant.

  ◊ Arrange for one parent to spend time with the sibling while the other parent is caring for the infant.

  ◊ Give preschool and school-age children a newborn doll as their "baby."

  ◊ Give the sibling a photograph of the new infant to take to school.

  ◊ Let older siblings help in providing care for the infant.

NANDA Nursing Diagnoses

Δ   Readiness for enhanced parenting related to realistic expectations and receptivity to nursing education on infant care

Δ   Risk for impaired parenting related to maladaptive coping strategies

Δ   Risk for impaired parent-infant attachment related to maternal physical or psychological complications

Δ   Fatigue related to multiple role demands placed on the new parent

Δ   Ineffective family coping related to unwanted pregnancy, teenage pregnancy, history of depression, difficult pregnancy and/or delivery, prematurity, or congenital anomalies of the infant

Complications and Nursing Implications

Δ   **Impaired parenting** related to maladaptive coping strategies includes:

 •   Emotional detachment and inability to care for the infant, placing the newborn at risk for neglect and failure to thrive.

 •   Failure to bond, which increases the risk of physical and/or emotional abuse.

Δ   **Nursing interventions** for impaired parenting include:

 •   Emphasizing verbal and nonverbal communication skills between the mother, caregivers, and the infant.

 •   Providing continued assessment of the new mother's parenting abilities as well as any other caregivers for the infant.

 •   Encouraging the continued support of grandparents and other family members.

 •   Providing home visits and group sessions for discussion regarding infant care and parenting problems.

 •   Giving the mother/caregivers information about social networks that provide a support system where the mother and caregivers can seek assistance.

 •   Involving outreach programs concerned with self-care, parent-child interactions, child injuries, and failure to thrive.

 •   Notifying programs that provide prompt and effective community interventions to prevent more serious problems from occurring.

Primary Reference:

Lowdermilk, D. L. & Perry, S. E. (2004). *Maternity & women's health care* (8th ed.). St. Louis, MO: Mosby.

Additional Resources:

NANDA International (2004). *NANDA nursing diagnoses: Definitions and classification 2005-2006.* Philadelphia: NANDA.

Piotrowski, K. A. (2003). *Study guide to accompany maternity nursing.* Lowdermilk, L. Y. & Perry, S. E. (Eds.). St. Louis, MO: Mosby.

Chapter 16: Bonding and Integration of Infant into Family Structure

Application Exercises

1. A nurse concludes that the father of a newborn is not showing positive signs of parent-infant bonding and appears to be very anxious and nervous when the infant's mother asks him to bring her the infant. Which of the following is a good way to promote father-infant bonding?

    A. Hand the father the newborn and insist he change the diaper.

    B. Ask the father why he is so anxious and nervous.

    C. Tell the father that he will get used to the newborn in time.

    D. Provide education about infant care when the father is present.

2. A client in the early postpartum period is very excited and talkative. She is repeatedly telling the nurse every detail of her labor and birth. Because the woman will not stop talking, the nurse is having difficulty completing her postpartum assessments. The appropriate response of the nurse is to

    A. come back later when the client has quieted down and stopped talking.

    B. realize the client is in the taking-in phase of maternal adjustment.

    C. tell the client to be quiet for a moment so she can finish her assessments.

    D. try and redirect the client's focus so that she will become quiet.

3. A nurse is caring for a client who is 1 day postpartum. The nurse is assessing for maternal adaptation and mother-infant bonding. Behaviors that indicate the need for nursing interventions include which of the following? (Select all that apply.)

    _____ Methodically cares for the newborn without evidence of bonding.

    _____ Touches the infant and maintains close physical proximity.

    _____ Views the infant's behavior as uncooperative during diaper changing.

    _____ Identifies and relates infant's characteristics to family members.

    _____ Interprets the infant's behavior as meaningful and a way of expressing needs.

4. A nurse is conducting a home health visit at the home of a couple with a 1-week-old infant. This is their first child. During a conversation with the infant's father, he shares feelings of sadness, ambivalence, frustration, and jealousy of the time his wife spends with the infant. He insists to the nurse that he loves his new baby and does not understand why he feels the way he does. The first nursing intervention that should be implemented at this time is for the nurse to

   A. notify social services to see if some counseling services can be arranged.

   B. explain that this is normal and that he is in the reality stage of paternal adaptation.

   C. suggest to the new mother that she spend some time with her husband.

   D. provide client teaching to the couple about how to share newborn care together.

5. A home health nurse is conducting a visit at the home of a client who has a 2-month-old infant and a 4-year-old son. The mother expresses frustration about the behavior of the 4-year-old who was previously toilet trained and is now frequently wetting himself. The nurse provides client education and explains to the mother that

   A. the 4-year-old was probably not ready for toilet training and should wear pull-ups.

   B. this is an adverse sibling response to the infant with a regression in toileting habits.

   C. this is abnormal and counseling should be sought out for the 4-year-old child.

   D. this can be resolved by sending the 4-year-old child to preschool where it won't be tolerated.

Chapter 16: Bonding and Integration of Infant into Family Structure

Application Exercises Answer Key

1. A nurse concludes that the father of a newborn is not showing positive signs of parent-infant bonding and appears to be very anxious and nervous when the infant's mother asks him to bring her the infant. Which of the following is a good way to promote father-infant bonding?

    A. Hand the father the newborn and insist he change the diaper.

    B. Ask the father why he is so anxious and nervous.

    C. Tell the father that he will get used to the newborn in time.

    D. Provide education about infant care when the father is present.

    Nursing interventions to assist the father in bonding with the infant include providing education about infant care when the father is present. Provide guidance to the father and involve him as a full partner rather than as just a helper. It would not be helpful to push the father into providing care such as changing a diaper without first providing education. Asking the father why he is anxious and nervous does help facilitate the expression of his feelings, but does not assist him with attaining skills to care for the infant.

2. A client in the early postpartum period is very excited and talkative. She is repeatedly telling the nurse every detail of her labor and birth. Because the woman will not stop talking, the nurse is having difficulty completing her postpartum assessments. The appropriate response of the nurse is to

    A. come back later when the client has quieted down and stopped talking.

    B. realize the client is in the taking-in phase of maternal adjustment.

    C. tell the client to be quiet for a moment so she can finish her assessments.

    D. try and redirect the client's focus so that she will become quiet.

    The taking-in phase begins immediately following birth and lasts a few hours to a couple of days. The woman is excited and talkative during this phase and repeatedly reviews the labor and birth experience. The nurse must complete vital sign and focused assessments per the postpartum protocol and cannot delay the assessments. The nurse can continue with her assessments while the client talks.

3. A nurse is caring for a client who is 1 day postpartum. The nurse is assessing for maternal adaptation and mother-infant bonding. Behaviors that indicate the need for nursing interventions include which of the following? (Select all that apply.)

   __X__   **Methodically cares for the newborn without evidence of bonding.**

   _____   Touches the infant and maintains close physical proximity.

   __X__   **Views the infant's behavior as uncooperative during diaper changing.**

   _____   Identifies and relates infant's characteristics to family members.

   _____   Interprets the infant's behavior as meaningful and a way of expressing needs.

Behaviors that facilitate and indicate mother-infant bonding include viewing the characteristics of the infant, face to face (en face) with the infant maintaining eye contact, recognizing the infant as a unique person, considering the infant a family member, identifying the infant's unique characteristics and relating them to other family members, touching the infant and maintaining close physical proximity and contact, providing physical care such as feeding and diapering, smiling, talking, cooing, and singing to the infant, communicating pride in the infant, and assigning a meaning to the infant's behavior and viewing behaviors positively. Behaviors that impair and show lack of mother-infant bonding include apathy when the infant cries, disgust when the infant voids, stools, or spits up, an expression of disappointment in the infant, turning away from the infant, not seeking a close physical proximity with the infant, not talking about the infant's unique features, showing no evidence of pride, handling the infant roughly, methodically caring for the newborn without evidence of positive bonding behaviors, ignoring the infant entirely, and viewing the infant's behaviors as being deliberately uncooperative or disruptive.

4. A nurse is conducting a home health visit at the home of a couple with a 1-week-old infant. This is their first child. During a conversation with the infant's father, he shares feelings of sadness, ambivalence, frustration, and jealousy of the time his wife spends with the infant. He insists to the nurse that he loves his new baby and does not understand why he feels the way he does. The first nursing intervention that should be implemented at this time is for the nurse to

   A. notify social services to see if some counseling services can be arranged.

   B. explain that this is normal and that he is in the reality stage of paternal adaptation.

   C. suggest to the new mother that she spend some time with her husband.

   D. provide client teaching to the couple about how to share newborn care together.

Paternal transition to fatherhood consists of three stages during the first few weeks of transition. The first stage is "expectations" in which the father has preconceived ideas about what it will be like when the infant comes home. The second stage is "reality" in which the father comes to the realization that his expectations might not be based on fact. He may experience feelings of sadness, ambivalence, jealousy of the infant, frustration, a desire to become more involved, and/or surprised at the reward of parenting. The third stage is "transition to mastery," at which point the father makes the determination to become more actively involved with the infant. Providing care together or helping the father to become more involved in providing care can help alleviate his feelings of jealousy and allow for the mother to have more available time to spend with her husband. However, explaining to the father that his feelings are normal should be done first. As this is a normal stage in the transition to fatherhood and the father is sharing his feelings and openly seeking assistance, there is nothing indicative of the need to notify social services at this point.

5. A home health nurse is conducting a visit at the home of a client who has a 2-month-old infant and a 4-year-old son. The mother expresses frustration about the behavior of the 4-year-old who was previously toilet trained and is now frequently wetting himself. The nurse provides client education and explains to the mother that

   A. the 4-year-old was probably not ready for toilet training and should wear pull-ups.

   B. this is an adverse sibling response to the infant with a regression in toileting habits.

   C. this is abnormal and counseling should be sought out for the 4-year-old child.

   D. this can be resolved by sending the 4-year-old child to preschool where it won't be tolerated.

Adverse responses from the sibling to a new infant can include signs of sibling rivalry and jealousy, regression in toileting and sleep habits, aggression toward the infant, increased attention-seeking behaviors, and whining. Some nursing interventions to facilitate sibling acceptance of the infant include encouraging the parents to have a gift from the infant to give the sibling, getting a T-shirt that says "I'm a big brother" or "sister," arranging for one parent to spend time with the sibling while the other parent is caring for the infant, and giving preschool and school-age children a newborn doll as their "baby."

Unit 3   Postpartum

Chapter 17:   Assessment and Management of Postpartum Complications

Contributor: Pat S. Kupina, EdD, MSN, RN

⟳ NCLEX-RN® Connections:

Learning Objective: Review and apply knowledge within **"Assessment and Management of Postpartum Complications"** in readiness for performance of the following nursing activities as outlined by the NCLEX-RN® test plan:

Δ   Assess the client for symptoms of postpartum complications.

Δ   Monitor the client for symptoms indicative of postpartum complications.

Δ   Plan and provide care for the client experiencing a postpartum complication.

Postpartum Complication: Postpartum Hemorrhage

📖 Key Points

Δ   Postpartum hemorrhage is a serious complication of childbirth that can result in hypovolemic shock. It is the leading cause of maternal morbidity and mortality in the United States.

Δ   Postpartum hemorrhage is defined by:

•   Greater than 500 mL of blood loss after a vaginal birth.

•   Greater than 1,000 mL of blood loss after a cesarean birth.

•   A 10% change in hematocrit from the labor admission values to the postpartum values.

Δ   **Anemia** can result from postpartum hemorrhage and the nurse should:

•   Monitor the client's hemoglobin and hematocrit levels.

•   Educate the client about dietary sources of iron and folic acid.

Δ   **Hypovolemic shock** resulting from low fluid volume is a potential complication of postpartum hemorrhage and the nurse should:

•   Monitor the client for signs of hypovolemic shock (e.g., hypotension, tachycardia with a weak and thready pulse, rapid shallow respirations, oliguria).

- Provide interventions to restore circulating blood volume and treat the cause of the hemorrhage.

Key Factors

Δ Several risk factors contribute to the potential for postpartum hemorrhage including:

- **Uterine atony.**
- Complications during pregnancy (e.g., placenta previa, abruptio placenta).
- Precipitous delivery.
- Administration of magnesium sulfate therapy during labor.
- **Lacerations** and **hematomas.**
- Inversion of uterus.
- Subinvolution of the uterus.
- **Retained placental fragments.**
- **Coagulopathies (e.g., disseminated intravascular coagulopathy).**

Diagnostic Procedures

Δ Hemoglobin and hematocrit assess for anemia and blood loss.

Δ Coagulation profile (e.g., prolonged prothrombin time).

Nursing Assessments

Δ Monitor for signs and symptoms of postpartum hemorrhage, which include:

- **Uterine atony.**
- **Blood clots** larger than a quarter.
- Perineal **pad saturation** in **15 min** or less.
- Return of lochia rubra once lochia has progressed to serosa or alba.
- Constant oozing, trickling, or frank flow of bright red blood from the vagina.
- A **rising pulse rate** and **decreasing blood pressure** (often first warning of inadequate blood volume).
- Skin that is pale, cool, and clammy with poor turgor and pale mucous membranes.
- Oliguria.

    Δ   Assess the client for the source of bleeding.

- Fundus for height, firmness, and position
- Lochia for color, quantity, and clots
- Signs of bleeding from lacerations, episiotomy site, or hematomas
- Vital signs for rate, quality, and equality

NANDA Nursing Diagnoses

    Δ   Risk for deficient fluid volume related to excessive blood loss

    Δ   Ineffective tissue perfusion related to hypovolemia

Nursing Interventions

    Δ   Nursing interventions for postpartum hemorrhage include:

- **Stopping** the client's **blood loss**.
- Maintaining or initiating **intravenous fluids** to correct and sustain the fluid balance and circulating volume.
  - ◊ Fluid volume replacement with intravenous infusion of crystalloids (lactated Ringer's solution and normal saline).
  - ◊ Rapid volume expanders with colloids (albumin).
  - ◊ Blood products (packed red blood cells and fresh frozen plasma).
- Providing **oxygen** to the client at 2 to 3 L per nasal cannula as prescribed to increase red blood cell saturation and monitor oxygen saturation with a pulse oximeter.
- Inserting an **indwelling urinary catheter** to assess the client's kidney function and obtain an accurate measurement of urinary output.
- **Elevating** the client's **legs** to a 20 to 30 degree angle to increase venous return.
- Avoiding the Trendelenburg position unless prescribed as it may interfere with cardiac and respiratory function.

    Δ   Provide discharge instructions to a client who has had a postpartum hemorrhage. Instruct the client to limit physical activity to conserve strength and to increase iron and protein intake to promote the rebuilding of RBC volume.

Postpartum Complication: Uterine Atony

📖 Key Points

Δ   **Uterine atony** is a **hypotonic uterus** that is not firm and is described as "**boggy.**" The inability of the uterine myometrium to contract and stay contracted around the open blood vessels of the uteroplacental implantation site is the most common cause of postpartum hemorrhage.

Δ   **Uterine atony** if untreated will result in postpartum hemorrhage and may result in uterine inversion.

Key Factors

Δ   Risk factors for uterine atony include:

- Retained placental fragments.

- Prolonged labor.

- Oxytocin induction or augmentation of labor.

- Overdistention of the uterine muscle (e.g., multiparity, multiple gestations [high parity], polyhydramnios [hydramnios], macrosomic fetus [large for gestational age]).

- Precipitate labor.

- Magnesium sulfate administration as a tocolytic.

- Anesthesia and analgesia administration.

- Trauma during labor and birth from operative delivery (e.g., forceps-assisted or vacuum-assisted birth, cesarean birth).

Therapeutic Procedures

Δ   **Bimanual compression** by the primary care provider consists of:

- Insertion of a fist into the vagina applying pressure with the knuckles against the anterior side of the uterus and then placing the other hand on the abdomen and massaging the posterior uterus.

Δ   **Manual exploration** of the **uterine cavity** for **retained placental fragments** is performed by the primary care provider.

Δ   Surgical management such as a hysterectomy.

Nursing Assessments

Δ   Monitor for signs and symptoms of uterine atony, which include:

- A uterus that is larger than normal and boggy with possible lateral displacement on pelvic examination.

- Prolonged lochial discharge.

- Irregular or excessive bleeding.

Δ   Assessments for uterine atony include:

- Fundal height, consistency, and location.

- Lochia quantity, color, and consistency.

Nursing Interventions

Δ   Nursing interventions for uterine atony:

- Ensure urinary bladder is empty.

- Fundal massage of the boggy uterus until firm.

  ◊   Fundal massage is performed with one hand placed above the symphysis pubis to support the lower uterine segment while the other hand gently but firmly massages the fundus in a circular motion.

- Express clots that may have accumulated in the uterus.

  ◊   It is **critical not to express clots prior to the uterus becoming firmly** contracted because pushing on an uncontracted **uterus can invert** the uterus and result in extensive hemorrhage.

- Administer oxytocics.

  ◊   **Oxytocin** (Pitocin)

    °   Monitor for **adverse reactions** of **water intoxication** (e.g., lightheadedness, nausea, vomiting, headache, malaise). More serious symptoms can progress to cerebral edema with seizures, coma, and death.

  ◊   **Methylergonovine maleate** (Methergine)

    °   Monitor for adverse reactions including **hypertension**, nausea, vomiting, and headache.

  ◊   **Ergonovine maleate** (Ergotrate)

    °   Monitor for adverse reactions including **hypertension**, headache, dizziness, nausea, and vomiting.

◊ **Prostaglandin F** (Hemabate, Prostin 15M)

   ° Monitor for adverse reactions including **fever**, chills, headache, nausea, vomiting, and diarrhea.

• **If** the **uterus** becomes **firm:**

◊ Continue assessing the maternal hemodynamic status.

• **If uterine atony persists:**

◊ Anticipate surgical intervention such as a hysterectomy.

Postpartum Complication: Subinvolution of the Uterus

📖 Key Points

Δ **Subinvolution** is the failure of the uterus to resume its prepregnant state and may result in late postpartum bleeding. The uterus remains enlarged with continued lochial discharge. Subinvolution of the uterus may result in postpartum hemorrhage.

Key Factors

Δ **Risk factors** that can **slow** the **involution** of the uterus include:

• Pelvic infection and **endometritis**.

• Incomplete expulsion of the placenta leaving **retained placental fragments.**

• Excessive vigorous massaging of the uterus.

Diagnostic and Therapeutic Procedures

Δ Blood, intracervical, and intrauterine **bacterial cultures** check for evidence of infection and/or endometritis.

Δ **Dilation and curettage (D&C)** is performed by the primary care provider to remove retained placental fragments if indicated.

Nursing Assessments

Δ Monitor for signs and symptoms of subinvolution of the uterus, which include:

• A uterus that is enlarged and higher than normal in the abdomen relative to the umbilicus,

• A boggy, noncontracted uterus.

• Prolonged lochia discharge with irregular or excessive bleeding.

Δ   Assessments for subinvolution of the uterus include:

- Fundal height by palpation and fingerbreadth measurement from the level of the umbilicus.

- Fundal position and consistency.

- Lochia.

Nursing Interventions

Δ   **Nursing interventions** for the client with **subinvolution** of the **uterus**:

- Encourage the client to utilize factors that can enhance uterine involution

  ◊   Breastfeeding.

  ◊   Early and frequent ambulation.

  ◊   Frequent voiding.

- Administer oxytocics as prescribed to promote uterine contractions and expel the retained fragments of placenta.

  ◊   The **most commonly used** oxytocic medication in the treatment of subinvolution of the uterus is **ergonovine** as prescribed to stimulate uterine contractions. Therapy includes 0.2 mg IM every 4 hr lasting 2 to 3 days.

- Administer **antibiotic therapy** as prescribed to prevent or treat infection.

Postpartum Complication: Inversion of the Uterus

 Key Points

Δ   **Inversion** of the **uterus** is the turning inside out of the uterus and may be partial or complete. Uterine inversion is an emergency situation that can result in postpartum hemorrhage and requires immediate intervention.

Key Factors

Δ   **Risk factors** for **uterine inversion** include:

- Retained placenta.

- Abnormally adherent placental tissue.

    ◊   **Placenta accreta** – a slight penetration of the placenta into the myometrium.

    ◊   **Placenta increta** – a deep penetration by the placenta into the myometrium.

    ◊   **Placenta percreta** – a perforation by the placenta into the uterus.

- Multiparity.

- Fundal implantation of the placenta.

- Vigorous fundal pressure.

- Excessive **traction** applied to the **umbilical cord.**

- Uterine atony.

- Leiomyomas (a benign uterine fibroid tumor).

Δ   **Uterine inversion** occurs **most frequently** in **multiparous women** with placenta accreta or increta.

Therapeutic Procedures

Δ   **Manual replacement** of the uterus into the uterine cavity and repositioning of the uterus by the primary care provider.

Nursing Assessments

Δ   Monitor the client for an inverted uterus.

- **Complete inversion** as evidenced by a large, red, rounded mass that protrudes 20 to 30 cm outside the introitus.

- **Partial inversion** as evidenced by the palpation of a smooth mass through the dilated cervix.

Δ   Assess for an inverted uterus by:

- Visualizing the introitus.

- Performing a pelvic exam.

Nursing Interventions

Δ **Nursing interventions** for an **inversion** of the **uterus** include:

- **Preventing** uterine inversion by the **avoidance** of **strong pulls** on the **umbilical cord** unless the placenta has definitely separated.

- Administering tocolytics or halogenated anesthetics to relax the uterus prior to the primary care provider's attempt at replacement of the uterus into the uterine cavity and uterus repositioning.

- Following replacement of the uterus into the uterine cavity:

  ◊ Closely observe the client's response to treatment and assess for stabilization of hemodynamic status.

  ◊ Avoid aggressive fundal massage.

  ◊ Administer oxytocics as prescribed.

  ◊ Administer broad spectrum antibiotics for infection prophylaxis.

  ◊ Anticipate surgery if nonsurgical interventions and management are unsuccessful.

Postpartum Complication: Retained Placenta

Key Points

Δ **Retained placenta** consists of the placenta in its entirety or fragments of it remaining in the uterus. A retained placenta prevents the uterus from contracting, resulting in uterine atony or subinvolution of the uterus as well as possible uterine inversion, hemorrhage, or endometritis.

Key Factors

Δ **Risk factors** for **retained placental fragments** include:

- Partial separation of a normal placenta.

- Entrapment of a partially or completely separated placenta by a constricting ring of the uterus.

- Mismanagement of the third stage of labor with excessive traction on the umbilical cord prior to complete separation of the placenta.

- Abnormally adherent placental tissue to the uterine wall.

Δ **Placental retention** because of poor separation is **common** in **preterm births** between 20 and 24 weeks gestation.

Therapeutic Procedures

Δ **Manual separation** and **removal** of the **placenta** is done by the primary care provider (there is a risk of instigating hemorrhage with this procedure).

Δ **D&C** if oxytocics are ineffective in expelling the placental fragments.

Nursing Assessments

Δ Monitor for signs and symptoms of retained placental fragments, which include:

- Uterine atony, subinvolution, or inversion.

- Excessive bleeding or **blood clots larger than a quarter.**

- The return of lochia rubra once lochia has progressed to serosa alba.

- Malodorous lochia or vaginal discharge.

- Elevated temperature.

Δ Nursing assessments for retained placental fragments include:

- Assessing the uterus for fundal height, consistency, and position.

- Assessing for lochia color, amount, consistency, and odor.

- Monitoring vital signs and temperature.

Nursing Interventions

Δ **Nursing interventions** for **retained placenta** include:

- Administering oxytocics to expel retained fragments of the placenta.

- Administering tocolytic to relax the uterus prior to D&C if placental expulsion with oxytocics is unsuccessful.

- Anticipating surgical intervention such as a hysterectomy if postpartum bleeding is present and continues.

Postpartum Complication: Lacerations and/or Hematomas

Key Points

Δ **Lacerations** sustained during labor and birth consist of the tearing of soft tissues in the birth canal and adjacent structures including the cervical, vaginal, vulvar, perineal, and/or rectal areas. **Perineal lacerations** are the most frequent, occurring in the lower genital tract.

Δ An **episiotomy** may **extend** and become a third- or fourth-degree laceration.

Δ A **hematoma** is a collection of 250 to 500 mL of clotted blood within tissues that is usually the result of a breakage of blood vessels in the soft tissues of the vagina or perineum. Hematomas typically appear as a bulging bluish mass.

• **Pelvic hematomas** may be vulvar, vaginal, or retroperitoneal in origin with vulvar hematomas being the most common and usually visible.

• A hematoma may form in the upper portion of the vagina or upward into the broad ligament, which can result in extensive hemorrhaging.

Δ **Pain** is the **distinguishable symptom** of **hematomas** rather than noticeable bleeding.

Δ Postpartum lacerations and hematomas can result in **postpartum hemorrhage** or **infection** of the **laceration**.

Key Factors

Δ **Risk factors** for **lacerations** and **hematomas** during labor and birth include:

• Operative vaginal birth (e.g., forceps-assisted, vacuum assisted birth).

• Precipitate birth.

• Cephalopelvic disproportion.

• Size (macrosomic infant) and abnormal presentation or position of the fetus.

• Prolonged pressure of the fetal head on the vaginal mucosa.

• Previous scarring of the maternal birth canal from infection, injury, or operation.

Δ **Damage** is usually **more pronounced** in **nulliparous** than multiparous women because the tissues are firmer, more resistant, and less distensible.

Δ **Light-skinned women**, especially those with reddish hair, have less distensible tissue than darker-skinned women.

Therapeutic Procedures

Δ   **Repair** and **suturing** of episiotomy or lacerations is done by the primary care provider.

Δ   **Ligation** of bleeding vessel or **surgical incision** for **evacuation** of clotted blood from the hematoma is done by the primary care provider.

Nursing Assessments

Δ   Monitor for signs and symptoms of lacerations and hematoma, which include:

- Palpation of a **firm contracted uterus in spite of vaginal bleeding.**

- Constant oozing, slow trickle, or frank blood flow from the vagina that is bright red in comparison to lochia, which is dark red and not profuse or continuous.

- Continuous oozing, trickle, or blood flow from **laceration** or episiotomy.

- Severe perineal or rectal pain or a feeling of pressure in the vagina may indicate the presence of a vulvar, vaginal, or retroperitoneal **hematoma.**

- Inability to void may be secondary to pressure on the urethra from a hematoma.

- Feelings of an urge to defecate because of hematoma pressure on the rectum.

- Signs of fluid volume depletion from excessive blood loss from lacerations/hematomas.

Δ   Nursing assessments for lacerations and hematomas include:

- **Visually** or **manually inspecting** the cervix, vagina, perineum, and rectum for lacerations and/or hematomas.

- Assessing an **episiotomy for extension** into a third- or fourth-degree laceration.

- Evaluating **lochia.**

- Continuing to assess the client's vital signs and hemodynamic status.

Nursing Interventions

Δ **Nursing interventions** for the client with **lacerations** and **hematomas** include:

- Identifying the source of the bleeding.

- Assisting the primary care provider with repair procedures.

- Treating small vulvar hematomas with the application of ice packs.

- Encouraging sitz baths.

- Encouraging cleansing of the perineal area with a water bottle filled with warm tap water after voiding and defecation.

Postpartum Complication: Coagulopathies (Idiopathic Thrombocytopenic Purpura and Disseminated Intravascular Coagulation)

 Key Points

Δ **Idiopathic thrombocytopenic purpura (ITP)** is a coagulopathy that is an autoimmune disorder in which the life span of platelets is decreased by antiplatelet antibodies. This platelet depletion can result in severe hemorrhage following a cesarean birth, lacerations, and as an increased incidence of postpartum uterine bleeding and vaginal hematomas.

Δ **Disseminated intravascular coagulation (DIC)** is a coagulopathy in which clotting and anticlotting mechanisms occur at the same time.

- Extensive clotting consumes and destroys substantial amounts of clotting factors including platelets, fibrinogen, prothrombin, and factors V and VII.

- This exhaustive depletion of clotting factors results in widespread external and/or internal bleeding, which in turn, brings about the formation of small clots in the microcirculation triggering vascular occlusion of small vessels with resultant vital organ ischemia.

- Fibrinolysis first increases and then decreases with the degradation of fibrin, leading to accumulated fibrin split products in the blood having anticoagulant properties, which prolong the prothrombin time.

Δ **Coagulopathies** are suspected when the usual measures to stimulate uterine contractions fail to stop vaginal bleeding.

Δ DIC can result in **hemorrhage**, **renal failure**, and **organ ischemia** with resultant tissue death leading to **major organ failure** throughout the body.

Key Factors

Δ **Risk factors** for **ITP** are genetic factors inherited from parents.

Δ **Risk factors** for **DIC** that occur secondary to other complications include:

- Abruptio placenta.

- Amniotic fluid embolism.

- Missed abortion.

- Fetal death in utero (fetus has died but is retained in the uterus for at least 6 weeks).

- Severe preeclampsia or eclampsia (gestational hypertension).

- Septicemia.

- Cardiopulmonary arrest.

- Hemorrhage.

- Hydatidiform mole.

Diagnostic and Therapeutic Procedures

Δ **Laboratory tests** include:

- CBC with differential.

- Blood typing and crossmatch.

- **Clotting factors.**

    ◊ Platelet levels (thrombocytopenia)

    ◊ Fibrinogen levels (decreased)

    ◊ Prothrombin time (increased)

    ◊ Fibrin split product levels (increased)

Δ **Splenectomy** may be performed by the primary care provider if **ITP** does not respond to medical management.

Δ **Surgical intervention** (hysterectomy) for **DIC** performed by the primary care provider as indicated.

Nursing Assessments

Δ   Monitor for signs and symptoms of **ITP** and **DIC,** which include:

- Unusual spontaneous bleeding from the client's gums and nose (epistaxis).

- Oozing, trickling, or flow of blood from incision, lacerations, or episiotomy.

- Petechiae and ecchymoses.

- Excessive bleeding from venipuncture, injection sites, or slight traumas.

- Tachycardia, hypotension, and diaphoresis.

- Oliguria.

Δ   Nursing assessments for **ITP** and **DIC** include:

- Assessing skin, venipuncture, and injection sites.

- Assessing lacerations, episiotomy, and any traumas for bleeding.

- Assessing vital signs and hemodynamic status.

- Monitoring of urinary output usually by insertion of an indwelling urinary catheter for accuracy.

Nursing Interventions

Δ   Nursing interventions for **ITP** focus on control of platelet stability.

- Transfuse platelets

- Assist in preparing the client for splenectomy if **ITP** does not respond to medical management and provide postsurgical care.

Δ   Nursing interventions for **DIC** focus on assessing for and correcting the underlying cause (removal of dead fetus, treatment of infection, preeclampsia or eclampsia, or removal of placental abruption).

- Administering fluid volume replacement.

- Administering blood component therapy.

- Monitoring for complications from the administration of blood and blood products.

- Administering pharmacologic interventions including antibiotics, vasoactive medications, and uterotonic agents as prescribed.

- Administering supplemental oxygen.

- Providing protection from injury.

Postpartum Complication: Thrombophlebitis

 Key Points

Δ   **Thrombosis** is the formation of a blood clot or clots on the interior of a blood vessel and is usually caused by inflammation.

Δ   **Thrombophlebitis** is the inflammation of a vessel wall caused by the attachment of a blood clot to that wall with consequential partial occlusion of the vessel.

- **Thrombophlebitis of the veins** is classified into **two types:**

  ◊   **Superficial venous thrombosis** involving the saphenous or surface veins.

  ◊   **Deep vein thrombosis (DVT)** involving the deep venous system and can extend from the foot to the iliofemoral region.

Δ   Thrombophlebitis can lead to a pulmonary embolism.

Key Factors

Δ   **Venous stasis** and **hypercoagulation** are the **major causes** of **thromboembolic disease** which presents a risk for all postpartum women secondary to the normal hypercoagulability of the blood during pregnancy and the early puerperium and venous stasis of the lower extremities.

Δ   **Risk factors** leading to postpartum **thromboembolic** disease include:

- Postpartum immobility or inactivity.

- Prolonged standing or sitting.

- Cesarean birth.

- Varicose veins or varicosities.

- Diabetes mellitus.

- Smoking.

- Multiparity.

- History of venous thrombosis.

- Obesity.

- Maternal age over 35 years.

Diagnostic and Therapeutic Procedures and Nursing Interventions

Δ   **Arterial blood gas analysis**

- Apply pressure to the puncture site until bleeding stops. Monitor the site carefully for bleeding due to anticoagulation therapy.

Δ   Daily monitoring of **platelet count** for potential heparin-induced antiplatelet antibodies, **prothrombin time (PT)**, and **partial thromboplastin time** (PTT) while the client is receiving heparin.

- Monitor PT/INR while the client is on warfarin (Coumadin).

Δ   **Venography** is an **invasive** procedure associated with serious complications. It is the most definitive method of **diagnosing DVT** and may be performed by the primary care provider if indicated.

Δ   **Noninvasive methods** more commonly used to **show** the presence of a **thrombus** include:

- Doppler ultrasound scanning.

- Computed tomography (CT).

- Magnetic resonance imaging (MRI).

Nursing Assessments

Δ   Monitor for signs and symptoms of **thrombophlebitis,** which include:

- **Tenderness, pain, and heat** on palpation.

- Positive **Homans' sign** (pain in calf with passive dorsiflexion).

- Localized redness and an enlarged, superficial-hardened vein is an indication of a **superficial vein thrombosis**.

- Unilateral leg pain that extends above the knee, calf tenderness, swelling, extremity coolness, and a pale color indicating signs of **deep vein thrombosis.**

- Increased extremity diameter with edema of an affected extremity and swelling attributable to venous inflammation.

- Low-grade fever and chills.

Δ   Nursing assessments for **thrombophlebitis** include:

- Lower extremities for color and temperature.

- Bilateral lower extremity pulses.

- Pain level.

- Serial calf and thigh **circumference measurements** (compare the size of both lower extremities).

- Vital signs and temperature.

NANDA Nursing Diagnoses

Δ   Acute pain related to thrombosis

Δ   Deficient knowledge related to anticoagulant therapy for thrombophlebitis

Nursing Interventions

Δ   **Nursing interventions** for **thrombophlebitis disease** include:

- Providing **client education** and **encouragement** pertaining to measures for **prevention** of **thrombophlebitis**.

  ◊   Initiating early and frequent ambulation postpartum.

  ◊   Avoiding prolonged periods of standing, sitting, or immobility.

  ◊   Elevating legs when sitting.

  ◊   Avoiding crossing legs, which will reduce the circulation and exacerbate venous stasis.

  ◊   Maintaining fluid intake of 2,500 mL per day to prevent dehydration, which causes circulation to be sluggish.

  ◊   Discontinuing smoking, which is known to be a risk factor.

  ◊   Measuring lower extremities for fitted elastic support hose/TED (thromboembolic disorder) hose to lower extremities.

Δ   **Nursing interventions** for **superficial venous thrombosis** include:

- Administering analgesics (nonsteroidal antiinflammatory agents).

- Encouraging rest with affected extremity elevated.

- Applying local heat as prescribed.

Δ   **Nursing interventions** for **deep venous thrombosis** include:

- Administering **anticoagulants** as prescribed.

  ◊   Initially, **intravenous heparin** is administered by continuous infusion for 5 to 7 days with doses adjusted according to coagulation studies. **Protamine sulfate**, the **heparin antidote**, should be readily available to counteract the development of heparin-induced antiplatelet antibodies.

◊ **Warfarin (Coumadin)** is then administered orally and is continued by the client for approximately 3 months. **Vitamin K,** the **warfarin antidote,** should be readily available for prolonged clotting times.

- Elevating the affected extremity during bedrest.

- Administering analgesia.

- Encouraging TED hose use when the client is being permitted to ambulate.

Δ Provide **client teaching** about monitoring for **signs** of **adverse effects** of **anticoagulants**.

- Bleeding from the gums or nose

- Increased vaginal bleeding

- Blood in the urine

- Bruising easily

Δ Provide **client teaching** about **precautions** to take while on anticoagulants.

- Avoid taking aspirin or ibuprofen (increases bleeding tendencies).

- Use an electric razor for shaving.

- Avoid alcohol use (inhibits warfarin).

- Brush teeth gently.

- Avoid rubbing or massaging legs.

- Avoid periods of prolonged sitting or crossing legs.

Postpartum Complication: Pulmonary Embolus

Key Points

Δ An **embolus** occurs when fragments or the entire clot dislodge and move into circulation.

Δ A **pulmonary embolism** is a **complication** of **DVT** that occurs if the embolus is carried to the pulmonary artery or one of its branches and lodges in a lung occluding the vessel and obstructing blood flow to the lungs.

Key Factors

Risk factors for pulmonary embolism are the same as those for thrombophlebitis *(For information, refer to thrombophlebitis section).*

Diagnostic and Therapeutic Procedures

Δ   **Diagnostic studies** to determine **pulmonary embolism** include:

- Ventilation/perfusion lung scan.

- Chest radiographic study.

- Radioisotope lung scan.

- Pulmonary angiogram.

Δ   **Embolectomy** surgically removes the embolus.

Nursing Assessments

Δ   Monitor for signs and symptoms of **pulmonary embolus,** which include:

- Dyspnea.

- Tachypnea.

- Cough.

- Hemoptysis (coughing up blood-streaked sputum).

- Pleuritic chest pain.

- Heart murmurs and/or right-sided heart failure.

- Peripheral edema.

- Distended neck veins.

- Elevated temperature.

- Chills.

- Hypotension.

- Apprehension.

Δ   Nursing assessments for **pulmonary embolus** include:

- Vital signs and temperature.

- Respiratory status and auscultated lung sounds.

- Heart sounds.

- Client pain level.

- Mental status.

- Neck vein distention.

NANDA Nursing Diagnoses

Δ   Ineffective tissue perfusion related to respiratory distress

Δ   Deficient knowledge related to thromboembolic disease and interventions

Nursing Interventions

Δ   **Nursing interventions** for **pulmonary embolism** include:

- Placing the client in a semi-Fowler's position with the head of the bed elevated to facilitate breathing.

- Administering oxygen to the client by mask as prescribed.

- Administering continuous intravenous heparin.

  ◊   Monitor the client for excessive anticoagulation as indicated by blood in the urine or stool, bleeding from gums, easy bruising, and/or flank pain.

- Administering an analgesic to reduce pain and anxiety as prescribed (reduces oxygen demand and dyspnea).

Postpartum Complication: Puerperal Infections (Endometritis, Mastitis, and Wound Infections)

 Key Points

Δ   **Postpartum** or **puerperal infection** is any infection of the genital birth canal that occurs after miscarriage, abortion, or childbirth with the presence of a fever of 38° C (100° F) or greater for 2 consecutive days or more during the first 10 days of the puerperium not counting the first 24 hr. The major complication of puerperal infection is **septicemia**.

Δ   **Endometritis** is an infection of the endometrial lining, decidua, and adjacent myometrium of the uterus. **Endometritis,** if untreated, can quickly progress to **parametritis**. Parametritis is an infection spread by the lymphatic system through the uterine wall to the broad ligament or the entire pelvis and can continue to spread causing **peritonitis**, an infection of the peritoneum and possibly a **pelvic abscess**.

- It is the most frequently occurring puerperal infection.

- Endometritis usually begins on the second to fifth postpartum day, generally starting as a localized infection at the placental attachment site and spreading to involve the entire uterine endometrium.

Δ   **Sites** of **wound infections** include cesarean **incisions**, **episiotomies**, **lacerations**, and/or any trauma wounds sustained to the birth canal during labor and birth.

Δ **Mastitis** is an infection of the breast involving the interlobular connective tissue and is usually unilateral. Mastitis may progress to an **abscess** if untreated.

- It occurs most commonly in first-time breastfeeding mothers well after the establishment of milk flow, which is usually 2 to 4 weeks after delivery.

- **Staphylococcus** is usually the infecting organism.

Key Factors

Δ The **immediate postpartum period** following birth is a time of **increased risk for all women** for **micro-organisms entering** the **reproductive tract** and migrating into the blood and other parts of the body, which could result in life-threatening septicemia.

- **Factors** that **increase** this **risk** in **all postpartum women** are:
  ◊ An open cervix into the uterus after birth with exposure to the external environment through the vagina.
  ◊ Well-supplied exposed blood vessels.
  ◊ Wounds from lacerations, incisions, and/or hematomas.
  ◊ Alkalinity of amniotic fluid, blood, and lochia during pregnancy and the early postpartum period decreasing the acidity of the vagina.

Δ **Risk factors** for **endometritis** include:

- Cesarean birth.
- Retained placental fragments and manual extraction of the placenta.
- **Prolonged rupture of membranes**.
- Internal fetal/uterine pressure monitoring.
- Multiple vaginal examinations after rupture of membranes.
- Prolonged labor.
- Postpartum hemorrhage.

Δ **Risk factors** for **mastitis** include:

- Milk stasis from a blocked duct.
- Nipple trauma and cracked or fissured nipples.
- Poor breastfeeding technique with improper latching of the infant onto the breast, which can lead to sore and cracked nipples.
- Decrease in breastfeeding frequency due to supplementation with bottle-feeding.
- Poor hygiene with inadequate handwashing between handling perineal pads and the breasts.

Diagnostic and Therapeutic Procedures

Δ   Laboratory studies may include:

- Blood, intracervical, or intrauterine **bacterial cultures** to reveal the offending organism.

- WBC count (leukocytosis).

- RBC sedimentation rate (distinctly increased).

- RBC count (anemia).

Δ   The primary care provider may need to **open** and **drain** the **wound** or perform **wound debridement** if indicated.

Nursing Assessments

Δ   Monitor for signs and symptoms of **all puerperal infections,** which include:

- Elevated temperature of at least 38° C (100° F) for two or more consecutive days.

- Flu-like symptoms such as body aches, chills, fever, and malaise.

- Tachycardia and an increased pulse rate.

- Anorexia and nausea.

Δ   Monitor for signs and symptoms of **endometritis,** which include:

- Pelvic pain.

- Uterine tenderness and enlargement.

- Scant, normal, or profuse lochia (varies depending on causative organism).

- Lochia that is either malodorous or purulent.

Δ   Monitor for signs and symptoms of **wound infection,** which include:

- Wound erythema, edema, warmth, tenderness, pain, seropurulent drainage, and wound dehiscence (separation of wound or incision edges) or evisceration (protrusion of internal contents through the separated wound edges).

Δ   Monitor for signs and symptoms of **mastitis,** which include:

- Painful or tender localized hard mass and reddened area usually on one breast.

- Axillary adenopathy in the affected side (enlarged tender axillary lymph nodes) with an area of inflammation that may be red, swollen, warm, and tender.

    Δ   **Assessments** for **puerperal infections** include:

- Obtaining frequent vital signs and temperature.
- Assessing fundal height, position, and consistency.
- Performing a pelvic exam.
- Observing lochia for color, quantity, and consistency.
- Inspecting incisions, episiotomy, and lacerations.
- Inspecting breasts.

NANDA Nursing Diagnoses

    Δ   Impaired tissue integrity related to the effects of the infection

    Δ   Acute pain related to tissue tenderness

    Δ   Risk for impaired parenting related to maternal pain and discomfort

    Δ   Risk for ineffective breastfeeding related to nipple fissure pain

    Δ   Ineffective infant feeding pattern related to maternal breast pain

Nursing Interventions

    Δ   **Nursing interventions** for **puerperal infections** include:

- Utilizing and providing client education on preventative measures.
  - ◊ Using aseptic techniques with proper handwashing and gloving for labor and birth.
  - ◊ Emphasizing to the client thorough handwashing and good maternal perineal hygiene.
- Maintaining or initiating IV access.
- Administering IV broad-spectrum antibiotic therapy (penicillins or cephalosporins) as prescribed.
- Providing comfort such as warm blankets or cool compresses, depending on the client's symptoms.
- Educating the client about the signs of worsening conditions to report and the importance of adherence to the treatment plan with the completion of a full course of antibiotics.
- Encouraging a diet high in protein to promote tissue healing.

    Δ   **Nursing interventions** for **endometritis** include:

- Administering intravenous **antibiotics** as prescribed.

- Administering **analgesics** as prescribed.

- Encouraging mothers to **maintain interaction** with their **newborns** to **facilitate bonding**.

Δ **Nursing interventions** for **wound infection** include:

- Performing wound care.

- Providing or encouraging comfort measures such as sitz baths, perineal care, and warm or cold compresses.

- Teaching the client good hygiene techniques (e.g. changing perineal pads from front to back, performing thorough handwashing prior to and after perineal care).

Δ **Nursing interventions** for **mastitis** include:

- Providing client education regarding breast hygiene:

    ◊ Thoroughly wash hands prior to breastfeeding.

    ◊ Maintain cleanliness of breasts with frequent changes of breast pads.

    ◊ Air-dry nipples.

Δ Providing client education about correctly positioning the infant and properly latching the infant onto the nipple, including both the nipple and the areola. The mother should release the infant's grasp on the nipple prior to removing the infant from the breast.

Δ Encouraging the use of ice packs or warm packs to the affected breast for discomfort.

Δ Instructing the woman to continue breastfeeding frequently, especially on the affected side, at least every 2 to 4 hr.

Δ Instructing how to completely empty the breasts at each feeding for prevention of milk stasis, which provides a medium for bacterial growth.

Δ Instructing the client to begin breastfeeding from the unaffected breast first to initiate the letdown reflex in the affected breast which is distended or tender.

Δ Encouraging rest, analgesics, and a fluid intake of at least 3,000 mL per day.

Δ Encouraging the client to wear a well-fitting bra for support.

Δ Reporting redness and fever.

Postpartum Complication: Urinary Tract Infection (Considered a Puerperal Infection if Occurs in the First 10 Postpartum Days)

Key Points

Δ   **Urinary tract infections** (UTI) are a common postpartum infection secondary to bladder trauma incurred during the delivery or a break in aseptic technique during bladder catheterization.

Δ   A potential complication of urinary tract infection is the progression to **pyelonephritis** with permanent renal damage leading to **acute** or **chronic renal failure**.

Key Factors

Δ   **Predisposing factors** for **urinary tract infections** include:

- Postpartal hypotonic bladder and/or urethra (urinary stasis and retention).

- Epidural anesthesia.

- Urinary bladder catheterization.

- Frequent pelvic examinations.

- Genital tract injuries.

- History of urinary tract infections.

- Cesarean birth.

Diagnostic Procedures

Δ   Urinalysis to check for white blood cells, red blood cells, protein, and bacteria.

Nursing Assessments

Δ   Monitor for signs and symptoms of **urinary tract infections,** which include:

- Urgency, frequency, and dysuria.

- Urinary retention, hematuria, and pyuria.

- Pain in the suprapubic area.

- Pain at the costovertebral angle (pyelonephritis).

- Elevated temperature and chills.

- Malaise.

- Malodorous cloudy urine that is possibly blood-tinged.

Δ   Assessments for urinary tract infections include:

- Vital signs and temperature.

- Pain or discomfort in the pelvic area and with voiding.

- Urine (cloudy, blood-tinged, malodorous, sediment).

NANDA Nursing Diagnoses

Δ   Impaired urinary elimination related to urinary tract infection

Δ   Urinary retention related to hypotonic bladder and/or urethra

Δ   Urinary incontinence related to urgency and frequency caused by urinary tract infection

Nursing Interventions

Δ   **Nursing interventions** for **urinary tract infections** include:

- Obtaining either a random or clean-catch urine sample.

- Administering antibiotics and teaching the client the importance of completing the entire course of antibiotics as prescribed.

- Teaching the client proper perineal hygiene, wiping from front to back.

- Encouraging an increase in fluids, 3,000 mL/day to dilute the bacteria and flush the bladder.

- Recommending cranberry juice to promote urine acidification, which inhibits bacterial multiplication.

Postpartum Complication: Postpartum "Blues" Depression

 Key Points

Δ   **Postpartum depression** occurs in approximately 50 to 80% of women during the first few days after birth and generally continues for up to 10 days. It is characterized by tearfulness, insomnia, lack of appetite, and feeling of letdown. The mother may experience an intense fear and/or anxiety, anger, and inability to cope with the slightest problems and become despondent.

Δ   Postpartum depression, if unresolved, can progress to a more severe disorder – **postpartum psychosis**. Postpartum psychosis is characterized by delusional thinking and possible hallucinations.

- The nurse should monitor the client for suicidal or delusional thoughts and monitor the infant for failure to thrive secondary to an inability of the mother to provide newborn care.

- The nurse should ensure the safety of the client and infant, which is at risk.

  ◊ Psychiatric supervision is necessary with a likely prescription of antipsychotic medications.

  ◊ Involve outreach programs concerned with self-care, parent-child interactions, child injuries, and failure to thrive.

  ◊ Notify programs that provide prompt and effective community interventions to prevent more serious problems from occurring.

Key Factors

Δ **Contributing factors** of **postpartum depression** include:

- Hormonal changes with a rapid decline in estrogen and progesterone levels.

- Postpartum physical discomfort and/or pain.

- Fatigue from the work of labor and demands of new role.

- Individual socioeconomic factors.

- Decreased social support system.

- Anxiety about assuming new role as a mother.

- History of previous depressive episode.

- Low self-esteem.

- Dissatisfaction with education, economics, or choice of partner.

Nursing Assessments

Δ Monitor for signs and symptoms of **postpartum depression,** which include:

- Tearfulness.

- Insomnia.

- Lack of appetite.

- Weight loss.

- Feeling of letdown.

- Flat affect.

- Ambivalence toward infant and family.

Δ Assessments for postpartum depression include:

- Mood and affect.

- Interactions between mother and infant.

NANDA Nursing Diagnoses

△ Risk for impaired parenting related to depressive symptoms

△ Risk for infant failure to thrive related to maternal ambivalence and neglect of infant

Nursing Interventions

△ **Nursing interventions** for **postpartum "blues" (depression)** include providing appropriate support, client education, and referrals.

- Reinforce that feeling down in the postpartum period is normal and self-limiting. Encourage the mother to notify her primary care provider if the condition persists.

- Advise the client to get plenty of rest and to nap when the infant sleeps.

- Reinforce the importance of the client taking time out for herself.

- Encourage the client to communicate feelings, validate and address personal conflicts, and reinforce personal power and autonomy.

- Schedule a follow-up visit prior to the traditional 6-week postpartum visit for clients who are at risk for postpartum depression.

- Provide information on community resources such as La Leche League or community mental health centers.

- Encourage the client to seek counseling and make referrals to social agencies or couples counseling as indicated.

- Reinforce the importance of compliance with any prescribed antidepressant medication regimen.

Primary Reference:

Lowdermilk, D. L. & Perry, S. E. (2004). *Maternity & women's health care*. (8th ed.). St. Louis, MO: Mosby.

Additional Resources:

NANDA International (2004). *NANDA nursing diagnoses: Definitions and classification 2005-2006*. Philadelphia: NANDA.

Piotrowski, K. A. (2003). *Study guide to accompany maternity nursing*. Lowdermilk, L. Y. & Perry, S. E. (Eds.). St. Louis, MO: Mosby.

Chapter 17: Assessment and Management of Postpartum Complications

Application Exercises

1. A nurse is assessing a client who is postpartum and exhibiting signs of tearfulness, insomnia, lack of appetite, and a feeling of letdown. The nurse knows these signs and symptoms are characteristics of

   A. postpartum fatigue.

   B. a psychiatric disorder.

   C. the letting-go phase.

   D. postpartum depression

2. Postpartum depression occurs in approximately 50 to 80% of women during the first few days after birth and generally lasts up to 10 days. Identify contributing factors of postpartum depression. (Select all that apply.)

   _____   Fatigue from the work of labor and birth

   _____   Disappointment in the characteristics of the infant

   _____   Individual or family socioeconomic factors

   _____   Anxiety about assuming a new role as a mother

   _____   Rapid decline in estrogen and progesterone

   _____   Postpartum physical discomfort and/or pain

3. A client just delivered her fifth infant 4 hr ago after an oxytocin induction. The infant weighed 9 lb 10 oz. The client informs the nurse that she feels "funny" and indicates her perineal pad is saturated. An assessment was completed 15 min ago. Upon reassessment, the nurse notes excessive rubra flow with the pad saturated and the client's skin is cool and clammy. Vital signs show a normal blood pressure, but tachycardia is noted. The nurse recognizes that this client is most likely experiencing which of the following?

   A. Puerperal infection resulting in excessive lochia

   B. Normal postpartum physiological changes

   C. Hypovolemic shock from postpartum hemorrhage

   D. Hematomas from a large for gestational age infant

4. A postpartum client whose uterus does not remain contracted after birth is at high risk for which of the following?

      A. Puerperal infection

      B. Postpartum hemorrhage

      C. Urinary bladder distention

      D. Prolonged lochia discharge

5. A nurse is assessing the vital signs on a postpartum client who delivered vaginally 10 hr earlier. Findings indicate a temperature of 38° C (100° F), pulse 76 beats/min, respirations 18/min, and blood pressure 124/70 mm Hg. The client reports feeling sweaty and having to urinate frequently but is otherwise comfortable. How should the nurse interpret these findings?

      A. The client is demonstrating signs and symptoms of hypovolemic shock indicated by her slow pulse and diaphoresis.

      B. The client's elevated temperature and diaphoresis are an indication of puerperal infection and need to be addressed.

      C. The client is bradycardic and the primary care provider should be notified for further assessment.

      D. The client's vital signs and reports of feeling sweaty are normal and there is no need for intervention at this time.

6. Which of the following is the earliest indication of hypovolemia caused by hemorrhage in a postpartum client?

      A. Increasing pulse and decreasing blood pressure

      B. Increasing pulse and increasing respiratory rate

      C. Pale, cool, clammy skin, and pale mucous membranes

      D. Altered mental status and level of consciousness

7. A client reports pain in the perineal area. During assessment, the nurse observes a small hematoma on the vulva. Which of the following is the best initial treatment for this?

    A. Incision and removal of the clot

    B. Ligation of the bleeding vessel

    C. Ice to the area and analgesics

    D. Oxytocin immediately after birth

8. Which of the following clients is at the greatest risk for postpartum infection?

    A. A client who experienced a precipitate labor less than 3 hr in duration.

    B. A client with premature rupture of membranes and prolonged labor.

    C. A client who delivered a large for gestational age infant.

    D. A client with a boggy uterus that is not well-contracted.

9. A client who is breastfeeding has mastitis. This client should be taught to do which of the following?

    A. Limit the amount of time the infant nurses on each breast.

    B. Nurse the infant only on the unaffected breast until resolved.

    C. Completely empty each breast at each feeding or with a pump.

    D. Wear a tight-fitting bra or breast binder until lactation has ceased.

10. A postpartum client who is being discharged 2 days after delivery has been diagnosed with a urinary tract infection. The nurse reviews discharge instructions with the client. Which of the following statements by the client indicates the need for further teaching by the nurse? (Select all that apply.)

    _____ "I will perform perineal cleansing and apply the perineal pad in a back-to-front direction to maintain good hygiene."

    _____ "I will drink juices such as cranberry, plum, and prune to make my urine more acidic to inhibit bacterial growth."

    _____ "I will drink large amounts of fluids, 3,000 mL per day, to flush the bacteria from my urinary tract."

    _____ "I should delay nursing my baby until I have finished taking the antibiotic in approximately 8 days."

    _____ "I will go to the bathroom as soon as I feel the urge to urinate and not hold it."

Chapter 17: Assessment and Management of Postpartum Complications

Application Exercises Answer Key

1. A nurse is assessing a client who is postpartum and exhibiting signs of tearfulness, insomnia, lack of appetite, and a feeling of letdown. The nurse knows these signs and symptoms are characteristics of

      A. postpartum fatigue.

      B. a psychiatric disorder.

      C. the letting-go phase.

      D. postpartum depression

Postpartum depression in the mother is characterized by tearfulness, insomnia, lack of appetite, and feeling letdown. Postpartum fatigue results from the work of labor. Postpartum depression is not a psychiatric disorder but a normal occurrence most likely resulting from several factors, one of which is a change in hormone levels postpartum. It is normally self-limiting. If postpartum depression is unresolved, it can progress to the psychiatric disorder of postpartum psychosis, characterized by delusional thinking and possible hallucinations. The letting-go phase is the phase in which the mother assumes her position at home and her new maternal role, focusing on the forward movement of the family unit.

2. Postpartum depression occurs in approximately 50 to 80% of women during the first few days after birth and generally lasts up to 10 days. Identify contributing factors of postpartum depression. (Select all that apply.)

    X   **Fatigue from the work of labor and birth**

    _____   Disappointment in the characteristics of the infant

    X   **Individual or family socioeconomic factors**

    X   **Anxiety about assuming a new role as a mother**

    X   **Rapid decline in estrogen and progesterone**

    X   **Postpartum physical discomfort and/or pain**

There are several factors that contribute to postpartum depression including maternal fatigue from the work of labor and birth, socioeconomic factors, maternal anxiety about assuming a new role, the rapid decline in maternal estrogen and progesterone levels with the expulsion of the placenta, and postpartum physical discomfort and/or pain. Disappointment in the characteristics of the infant would be an indication of impaired mother-infant bonding unrelated to postpartum depression but rather other issues.

3. A client just delivered her fifth infant 4 hr ago after an oxytocin induction. The infant weighed 9 lb 10 oz. The client informs the nurse that she feels "funny" and indicates her perineal pad is saturated. An assessment was completed 15 min ago. Upon reassessment, the nurse notes excessive rubra flow with the pad saturated and the client's skin is cool and clammy. Vital signs show a normal blood pressure, but tachycardia is noted. The nurse recognizes that this client is most likely experiencing which of the following?

    A. Puerperal infection resulting in excessive lochia

    B. Normal postpartum physiological changes

    C. Hypovolemic shock from postpartum hemorrhage

    D. Hematomas from a large for gestational age infant

Postpartum hypovolemic shock is a complication of postpartum hemorrhage. The indication of postpartum hemorrhage is excessive blood loss with a pad saturated in 15 min or less. The client was induced with oxytocin, her infant was macrosomic (large for gestational age), and she has a high parity of five births. All of these are predisposing factors for postpartum hemorrhage and resultant hypovolemic shock. The client also exhibits signs of "feeling funny" with altered mental status, cool clammy skin, and tachycardia, which are signs of hypovolemic shock. Therefore, the signs and symptoms this client is experiencing are not normal postpartum physiologic changes. Hematomas may have been acquired from trauma sustained during the prolonged labor of a macrosomic infant and could be the cause of this client's excessive blood loss. However, hematomas in and of themselves are not the complication affecting the decline in this client's hemodynamic status.

4. A postpartum client whose uterus does not remain contracted after birth is at high risk for which of the following?

    A. Puerperal infection

    B. Postpartum hemorrhage

    C. Urinary bladder distention

    D. Prolonged lochia discharge

Postpartum hemorrhage is the major complication of uterine atony, which is the failure of the uterus to remain contracted after birth. Uterine atony is not a risk factor for puerperal infection unless it is caused by retained placental fragments with the retained placenta being the infectious risk factor, not the hypotonic uterus. Distention of the urinary bladder can displace the boggy uterus that is not firm but it does not cause uterine atony. Prolonged lochia discharge is a sign and symptom of uterine atony.

5. A nurse is assessing the vital signs on a postpartum client who delivered vaginally 10 hr earlier. Findings indicate a temperature of 38° C (100° F), pulse 76 beats/min, respirations 18/min, and blood pressure 124/70 mm Hg. The client reports feeling sweaty and having to urinate frequently but is otherwise comfortable. How should the nurse interpret these findings?

   A. The client is demonstrating signs and symptoms of hypovolemic shock indicated by her slow pulse and diaphoresis.

   B. The client's elevated temperature and diaphoresis are an indication of puerperal infection and need to be addressed.

   C. The client is bradycardic and the primary care provider should be notified for further assessment.

   D. The client's vital signs and reports of feeling sweaty are normal and there is no need for intervention at this time.

An elevated temperature in the first 24 hr postpartum is a normal finding. Therefore, an elevated temperature at 10 hr postpartum is a normal finding. The client's heart and respiratory rate are normal. Diaphoresis and diuresis also occur for the first couple of days following birth so that the body can eliminate the excess fluid of pregnancy required to increase blood volume to sustain the fetus. Signs of hypovolemic shock include tachycardia and decreased blood pressure.

6. Which of the following is the earliest indication of hypovolemia caused by hemorrhage in a postpartum client?

   A. Increasing pulse and decreasing blood pressure

   B. Increasing pulse and increasing respiratory rate

   C. Pale, cool, clammy skin, and pale mucous membranes

   D. Altered mental status and level of consciousness

A rising pulse rate and decreasing blood pressure are often the first signs of inadequate blood volume. Skin that is cool, clammy, and pale along with pale mucous membranes are changes that occur in the physical status of a client with decreased blood volume, but they are not the first sign of inadequate blood volume. Altered mental status and changes in level of consciousness are later signs of decreased blood volume which leads to hypoxia and low oxygen saturation.

7. A client reports pain in the perineal area. During assessment, the nurse observes a small hematoma on the vulva. Which of the following is the best initial treatment for this?

      A. Incision and removal of the clot

      B. Ligation of the bleeding vessel

      C. Ice to the area and analgesics

      D. Oxytocin immediately after birth

Ice to the area and analgesics are the best initial treatments. Incision and removal of the clot and ligation of the bleeding vessel would be performed by a primary care provider if there is continuous blood loss. Oxytocin is administered immediately after birth to assist the uterus in contracting.

8. Which of the following clients is at the greatest risk for postpartum infection?

      A. A client who experienced a precipitate labor less than 3 hr in duration.

      B. A client with premature rupture of membranes and prolonged labor.

      C. A client who delivered a large for gestational age infant.

      D. A client with a boggy uterus that is not well-contracted.

All of the choices present a risk for postpartum infection. However, premature rupture of membranes with a prolonged labor poses the greatest risk with an open passage to the uterus for pathogens to enter. Precipitate labor and a large for gestational age infant place the client at risk for trauma and lacerations during delivery. A boggy uterus places the client at risk for hemorrhage and infection. These risks are not as great as the rupture of membranes that exceeds 24 hr prior to delivery, which would be the case in premature rupture of membranes (greater than 24 hr prior to birth) and a prolonged labor.

9. A client who is breastfeeding has mastitis. This client should be taught to do which of the following?

      A. Limit the amount of time the infant nurses on each breast.

      B. Nurse the infant only on the unaffected breast until resolved.

      C. Completely empty each breast at each feeding or with a pump.

      D. Wear a tight-fitting bra or breast binder until lactation has ceased.

Instruct the client to completely empty each breast at each feeding for the prevention of milk stasis, which provides a medium for bacterial growth. Frequent breastfeeding should be encouraged to promote milk flow. The client should be instructed to continue breastfeeding, especially on the affected side. The client should wear a well-fitting bra, not one that is too tight or a binder.

10. A postpartum client who is being discharged 2 days after delivery has been diagnosed with a urinary tract infection. The nurse reviews discharge instructions with the client. Which of the following statements by the client indicates the need for further teaching by the nurse? (Select all that apply.)

   __X__   **"I will perform perineal cleansing and apply the perineal pad in a back-to-front direction to maintain good hygiene."**

   _____   "I will drink juices such as cranberry, plum, and prune to make my urine more acidic to inhibit bacterial growth."

   _____   "I will drink large amounts of fluids, 3,000 mL per day, to flush the bacteria from my urinary tract."

   __X__   **"I should delay nursing my baby until I have finished taking the antibiotic in approximately 8 days."**

   _____   "I will go to the bathroom as soon as I feel the urge to urinate and not hold it."

Acidification of urine inhibits bacterial multiplication. Increased fluids can help to flush the bacteria from the urinary tract. Breastfeeding does not have to be delayed until the course of antibiotics is completed. Perineal cleansing and pad application should be done front-to-back, not back-to-front.

Unit 3   Postpartum

Chapter 18:   Discharge Teaching: Postpartal Care
Contributor: Pat S. Kupina, EdD, MSN, RN

⟳ NCLEX-RN® Connections:

Learning Objective: Review and apply knowledge within **"Discharge Teaching: Postpartal Care"** in readiness for performance of the following nursing activities as outlined by the NCLEX-RN® test plan:

Δ   Provide discharge instructions regarding postpartum care.

📖 Key Points

Δ   Discharge planning is especially important with the current short length of a hospital stay. Discharge planning begins at the time of admission with time spent during the hospitalization on providing client education regarding postpartum self-care.

Δ   It is critical that the client be taught to recognize physical signs and symptoms that might be indicative of postpartum complications and when to notify the primary care provider or seek emergency assistance.

Key Factors

Δ   A contributing factor that enhances learning includes utilizing a variety of teaching methods such as discussion, demonstration, videos, DVDs, magazines, pamphlets, and handouts.

Δ   Health complications related to the mother or infant can affect learning.

Nursing Assessments

Δ   Inquire about the mother's current knowledge regarding self-care.

Δ   Assess the mother's home support system and who will be there to assist her. Include support persons in teaching sessions.

Δ   Determine the mother's readiness for learning and her ability to verbalize or demonstrate what she has been instructed to do by the nurse.

NANDA Nursing Diagnoses

Δ   Deficient knowledge related to postpartum self-care

Δ   Risk for self care deficit related to inadequate knowledge or postpartum fatigue

Δ   Risk for infection related to the client not performing proper hygiene with perineal care and/or breastfeeding

Nursing Interventions

Δ   Provide client education on **danger signs to report to** her **primary care provider**.

  • Chills or fever greater than 38° C (100.4° F) for 2 days or more.

  • Fundus not midline and firm upon self-palpation.

    ◊   Instruct the client on self-massage of fundus if not firm.

  • Change in vaginal discharge with increased amount, large clots, change to a previous lochia color such as bright red bleeding, and a foul odor.

    ◊   Normal lochial flow pattern shows:

      °   Bright red vaginal drainage for 2 to 3 days.

      °   Blood-tinged serous vaginal drainage from days 4 to 10.

      °   White vaginal discharge from day 11 to 6 weeks.

  • Pain or tenderness in the abdominal or pelvic areas that does not resolve with analgesics.

  • Episiotomy, laceration, or incision pain, that does not resolve with analgesics, foul-smelling drainage, redness, and/or edema.

  • Calf with localized pain and tenderness, redness, and swelling. A lower extremity with either areas of redness and warmth or coolness and paleness.

  • Breast(s) with localized area of pain and tenderness with redness and swelling and/or nipples with cracks or fissures.

  • Urination with burning, pain, frequency, urgency. Urine that is cloudy or has blood.

  • Postpartum depression (when the client feels apathy toward the infant, cannot provide self or infant care, or has feelings that she might hurt herself or her infant).

Δ   Instruct the client to have a 6-week **postpartum follow-up** visit with her primary care provider for an uncomplicated vaginal birth and within 2 weeks for a cesarean birth. Date and time of the follow-up appointment should be included in the discharge instructions given to the client in writing upon discharge from the hospital.

Δ   Provide **client teaching on self-care** to include:

- **Perineal care**

  ◊   Cleanse with warm water after each voiding and bowel movement.

  ◊   Wipe perineal area from front to back.

  ◊   Remove and apply perineal pads from front to back.

- **Breast care**

  ◊   Wear a well-fitting bra continuously for the first 72 hr after birth.

  ◊   **Breast care for lactating women.**

  - Breasts will secrete golden-yellow colostrum the first 2 to 3 days during feedings and the milk will come in around the third or fourth day.

  - Void prior to breastfeeding.

  - Emphasize the **importance of handwashing prior to breastfeeding** to prevent infection.

  - Proper latching (the infant's mouth should cover part of the areola and not just the tip of the nipple).

  - Use of various holding positions (cradle hold, football hold, side-lying) to help prevent nipple soreness, and **break suction** by inserting finger into infant's mouth **prior to pulling the infant away from** the **breast**.

  - Initiate nursing with the opposite breast from the last nursing episode and allow for complete emptying of the first breast so that each breast will be completely emptied at least every other feeding to prevent breast engorgement or mastitis from milk stasis.

  - For **breast engorgement**, use **cool compresses** between feedings and use warm compresses or a **warm shower** to the breasts prior to breastfeeding to **increase milk flow** and **letdown reflex**.

  - The best **technique to relieve breast engorgement** is to completely empty the breasts. Allow the infant to nurse every 2 hr. Massaging the breast during feeding can help with emptying. Feed 15 to 20 min per breast until one breast softens per feeding before switching to the other side. If the infant does not soften the second breast, a breast pump may be used to empty the breast.

  - After feeding, the client should apply a small amount of breast milk to her nipple and allow it to **air dry.** This technique will toughen the **nipples** if the nipples are tender and sore.

  - Adequate fluid intake is important to replace fluid lost from breastfeeding and to produce an adequate amount of milk for the infant.

- For flat nipples, which can impede breastfeeding, suggest to the client that she roll the nipples between her fingers just before feeding to help them become more erect to make it easier for the infant to latch on.

- Apply breast creams as prescribed and wear breast shields in the bra to soften the nipples if they are irritated and cracked.

- Advise the client who is breastfeeding that nursing stimulates the release of endogenous oxytocin, which causes the uterus to contract and may cause discomfort or moderate sexual arousal and that these sensations are normal.

◊ Breast care for nonlactating women:

- Suppression of lactation is necessary for women not breastfeeding. **Avoid** breast stimulation and **running warm water** over the breast for prolonged periods until no longer lactating.

- For **breast engorgement,** which may occur on the second or third postpartum day, apply **cold compresses** 15 min on and 45 min off. Fresh **cabbage leaves** can be placed inside the bra. Mild analgesics may be taken for pain and discomfort of breast engorgement.

- **Rest/Sleep**

◊ Plan at least one daily rest period; rest when the infant naps.

- **Activity**

◊ Do not perform housework requiring heavy lifting for at least 3 weeks.

◊ Do not lift anything **heavier than the infant.**

◊ Avoid sitting for prolonged periods of time with legs crossed (to prevent thrombophlebitis).

◊ Limit stair climbing for the first few weeks postpartum.

◊ Clients who have had a cesarean delivery should wait until the 6-week follow-up visit before performing strenuous exercise, heavy lifting, or excessive stair climbing.

- **Nutrition**

◊ Teach the client the importance of eating a nutritious diet including all food groups that are **high in protein**. This will aid in tissue repair. The client should also drink **at least 6 to 8 glasses** of **fluids** per day.

◊ Encourage lactating women to increase fluids to **at least 8 to 10 glasses** per day and add an **additional 500 calories** daily to the prepregnancy diet including calcium-enriched foods.

- **Postpartum exercises**
  - ◊ Teach the client how to perform **Kegel exercises** to regain perineal floor muscles: Tighten the pelvic floor as if stopping the flow of urine, hold this position for 3 to 10 sec, relax for 3 to 10 sec and repeat with tightening. Do a cycle of 10 tightenings 8 times a day for best results.
  - ◊ Teach the client how to perform **pelvic tilt** exercises to strengthen back muscles and relieve strain on the lower back. These exercises involve alternately arching and straightening the back (can be performed sitting, standing, or on hands and knees).

- **Sexual intercourse**
  - ◊ Teach the client to avoid sexual intercourse until the episiotomy/ laceration is healed and vaginal discharge has turned white (lochia alba). This usually takes 2 to 4 weeks or until the client is seen by her primary care provider/midwife.
  - ◊ Physiological reactions to sexual activity may be slower and less intense for the first 3 months following birth.
  - ◊ Recommend water-soluble lubricants with intercourse for discomfort from vaginal dryness which usually disappears when ovulation and menstruation return.

- **Contraception**
  - ◊ Advise clients to begin using contraception upon resumption of sexual activity and that pregnancy can occur while breastfeeding even though menses has not returned.
  - ◊ Menses for nonlactating mothers may not resume until around 4 to 10 weeks.
  - ◊ Menses for lactating mothers may not resume for 3 months or until cessation of breastfeeding.

Complications and Nursing Implications

Δ Deficient knowledge regarding self-care places the client at risk for infection or injury.

- Assess the client's understanding of nursing instruction by having the client verbalize and demonstrate self-care techniques.
- Provide reinforcement of client education as needed.

Primary Reference:

Lowdermilk, D. L. & Perry, S. E. (2004). *Maternity & women's health care* (8th ed.). St. Louis, MO: Mosby.

Additional Resources:

NANDA International (2004). *NANDA nursing diagnoses: Definitions and classification 2005-2006*. Philadelphia: NANDA.

Piotrowski, K. A. (2003). *Study guide to accompany maternity nursing*. Lowdermilk, D. L. & Perry, S. E. (Eds.). St. Louis, MO: Mosby.

Chapter 18: Discharge Teaching: Postpartal Care

Application Exercises

1. A nurse is conducting a home health visit on a client who is 2 weeks postpartum and is breastfeeding. The client reports breast engorgement. Which of the following recommendations should the nurse make?

    A. Apply cold compresses between feedings.

    B. Take a warm shower right after feedings.

    C. Apply breast milk to the nipples and allow them to air dry.

    D. Use the various infant positions for feedings.

2. A client who is 4 weeks postpartum should contact her primary care provider for which of the following client findings?

    A. Scant, non-odorous white vaginal discharge

    B. Uterine cramping during breastfeeding

    C. Sore nipple with cracks and fissures

    D. Decreased response with sexual activity

3. A nurse is conducting a home visit with a client who is 3 months postpartum and breastfeeding her infant. Menses has not yet resumed. The client is discussing contraception with the nurse stating that she does not want to have another child for a couple of years. The nurse understands that this client needs further instruction if the client makes which of the following statements?

    A. "I have already started using oral contraceptives."

    B. "Because of our beliefs, we are going to use the rhythm method."

    C. "I am being refitted for a diaphragm with my doctor next week."

    D. "I will not need birth control until I stop breastfeeding."

4. Which of the following postpartum clients is at greatest risk for developing a puerperal infection?

    A. A client with an episiotomy that is erythematous and has extended into a third-degree laceration

    B. A client who does not wash her hands between perineal care and breastfeeding

    C. A client who is not breastfeeding and is using measures to suppress lactation

    D. A client with a cesarean incision that is well-approximated with no drainage

5. A nurse is providing discharge instructions to a postpartum client following a cesarean birth. The client reports leaking urine every time she sneezes or coughs. The nurse suggests the client perform which of the following exercises to help alleviate this problem?

      A. Sit-ups

      B. Pelvic tilt

      C. Kegel

      D. Crunches

Chapter 18: Discharge Teaching: Postpartal Care

Application Exercises Answer Key

1. A nurse is conducting a home health visit on a client who is 2 weeks postpartum and is breastfeeding. The client reports breast engorgement. Which of the following recommendations should the nurse make?

    A. Apply cold compresses between feedings.

    B. Take a warm shower right after feedings.

    C. Apply breast milk to the nipples and allow them to air dry.

    D. Use the various infant positions for feedings.

Cold compresses applied to the breasts between feedings can help with breast engorgement. Taking a warm shower prior to feedings, not immediately after, can assist with the letdown reflex and milk flow. Breast milk applied to the nipples with air drying and using various positions for feedings help with preventing nipple soreness but have no effect on breast engorgement.

2. A client who is 4 weeks postpartum should contact her primary care provider for which of the following client findings?

    A. Scant, non-odorous white vaginal discharge

    B. Uterine cramping during breastfeeding

    C. Sore nipple with cracks and fissures

    D. Decreased response with sexual activity

A sore nipple that has cracks and fissures is an indication of mastitis. Lochia alba, a white vaginal discharge, is normal from the eleventh day postpartum to approximately 6 weeks following birth. Oxytocin, which is released with breastfeeding, causes the uterus to contract and may cause discomfort. Physiological reactions to sexual activity may be slower and less intense for the first 3 months following birth.

3. A nurse is conducting a home visit with a client who is 3 months postpartum and breastfeeding her infant. Menses has not yet resumed. The client is discussing contraception with the nurse stating that she does not want to have another child for a couple of years. The nurse understands that this client needs further instruction if the client makes which of the following statements?

    A. "I have already started using oral contraceptives."

    B. "Because of our beliefs, we are going to use the rhythm method."

    C. "I am being refitted for a diaphragm with my doctor next week."

    D. "I will not need birth control until I stop breastfeeding."

Lactating does not prevent pregnancy, even if menses has not yet resumed. Oral contraceptives are a good form of birth control. The rhythm method is not as effective, but if that is what the couple chooses because of their belief system, this is their option. The client is correct in having her diaphragm refitted by her primary care provider, which should be done after a pregnancy and birth or a 7 kg (15 lb) weight change.

4. Which of the following postpartum clients is at greatest risk for developing a puerperal infection?

    A. A client with an episiotomy that is erythematous and has extended into a third-degree laceration

    B. A client who does not wash her hands between perineal care and breastfeeding

    C. A client who is not breastfeeding and is using measures to suppress lactation

    D. A client with a cesarean incision that is well-approximated with no drainage

The best prevention of infection is frequent handwashing. Not performing handwashing between perineal care and breastfeeding places the client at an increased risk for developing mastitis. Episiotomy, lacerations, and cesarean incisions all place the client at risk for infection, but not as great as that of not performing handwashing. A client who is suppressing lactation is also at risk for milk stasis providing a medium for bacterial growth, but again, not performing handwashing is still the greatest risk for developing an infection.

5. A nurse is providing discharge instructions to a postpartum client following a cesarean birth. The client reports leaking urine every time she sneezes or coughs. The nurse suggests the client perform which of the following exercises to help alleviate this problem?

        A. Sit-ups

        B. Pelvic tilt

        C. Kegel

        D. Crunches

Kegel exercises consist of the voluntary contraction and relaxation of the pubococcygeal muscle as if to start and stop the urine flow. This strengthens the pelvic muscles, which will assist the client in decreasing the stress incontinence that occurs with sneezing and coughing. Sit-ups and crunches are both abdominal exercises that should not be performed until the client's 6-week postpartum follow-up appointment. Pelvic tilt exercises consist of the alternate arching and straightening of the back to strengthen the back muscles and relieve back discomfort.

Unit 4   Newborn Care

Chapter 19:   Newborn Assessment

Contributor: Linda S. Wood, MSN, RN

NCLEX-RN® Connections:

Learning Objective: Review and apply knowledge within "**Newborn Assessment**" in readiness for performance of the following nursing activities as outlined by the NCLEX-RN® test plan:

Δ   Assess the newborn using Apgar scores, physical exam, physical measurements, and vital signs.

Key Points

Δ   **Adjustments to extrauterine life** occur as the neonate's **respiratory** and **circulatory** systems are required to **rapidly adjust** to life outside of the uterus.

Δ   The establishment of **respiratory function** with the cutting of the umbilical cord is the most critical extrauterine adjustment as air inflates the lungs with the first breath.

Δ   **Circulatory changes after birth** occur with the expulsion of the placenta and the cutting of the umbilical cord as the neonate begins breathing on her own. The **three shunts**, ductus arteriosus, ductus venosus, and foramen ovale, **functionally close** during the neonate's transition to extrauterine life with the oxygenation of blood in the lungs and readjustment of atrial blood pressure in the heart.

Δ   Assessments of the neonate include:

•   Initial assessment immediately after birth (Apgar score and quick review of systems).

•   Gestational age assessment within 2 hr.

•   Comprehensive physical exam within 24 hr.

Nursing Assessments

Δ   The newborn's initial assessments are performed immediately after birth and include **Apgar scoring** at 1 and 5 min (allowing the nurse to rapidly assess extrauterine adaptation) and a **brief physical exam** to rule out abnormalities.

Δ   **Apgar scoring** assigns values of 0 to 2 for each physiological assessment. Scored totals give an overall view of the neonate's well-being.

  •   0 to 3 indicates severe distress

  •   4 to 6 indicates moderate distress

  •   7 to 10 indicates no distress

Score	0	1	2
Heart rate	Absent	< 100	> 100
Respiratory rate	Absent	Slow, weak cry	Good cry
Muscle tone	Flaccid	Some flexion	Well-flexed
Reflex irritability	None	Grimace	Cry
Color	Blue, pale	Pink body, cyanotic hands and feet (acrocyanosis)	Completely pink

Δ   A nurse performs a **quick initial assessment** to **review systems** and to **observe** the neonate **for any abnormalities**. The assessment can be performed by observing while the infant is lying with the mother or when the nurse is drying and wrapping the infant.

  •   **External assessment** – skin color, peeling, birthmarks, nail length, foot creases, breast tissue, nasal patency, and meconium staining (may indicate fetal hypoxia).

  •   **Chest** – point of maximal impulse location, ease of breathing, auscultation for heart rate and quality of tones and respirations for crackles, wheezes, and equality of bilateral breath sounds.

  •   **Abdomen** – rounded abdomen and umbilical cord for one vein and two arteries.

  •   **Neurologic** – muscle tone and reflex reaction (Moro's reflex). Palpate the presence and size of fontanels and sutures, and assess fontanels for fullness or bulge.

  •   **Other observations** – inspect for any gross structural malformations.

Δ   A **gestational age assessment** is performed within 2 to 12 hr of birth. Neonatal morbidity and mortality are related to gestational age and birth weight. This assessment involves taking **measurements of** the newborn and the use of the *New Ballard Scale* which provides an estimation of gestational age and a baseline to assess growth and development.

- The normal ranges of **physical measurements** include:

  ◊ **Weight** – 2,500 to 4,000 g. The infant's weight should be obtained by placing a protective liner on the scale prior to weighing to protect the infant from heat loss. Weigh the infant at the same time daily.

  ◊ **Length** – 45 to 55 cm (18 to 22 in). The infant's length should be measured from the top of the head to the heel of the foot.

  ◊ **Head circumference** – 32 to 36.8 cm (12.6 to 14.5 in). The infant's head circumference is measured at the widest diameter, which is the occipitofrontal at the level of the infant's eyebrows.

  ◊ **Chest circumference** – 30 to 33 cm (12 to 13 in). The infant's chest circumference is measured at the nipple line and should be 2 to 3 cm less than the head circumference.

- *New Ballard Scale* – an infant maturity rating scale that assesses neuromuscular and physical maturity. Each individual assessment parameter displays at least six ranges of development along a continuum. Each range of development within an assessment is assigned a number value from -1 to 5. The totals are added to give a maturity rating in weeks gestation (e.g., a score of 35 indicates 38 weeks gestation).

  ◊ **Neuromuscular maturity** assesses:

    ° Posture ranging from fully extended to fully flexed (0 to 4).

    ° Square window formation with the neonate's wrist (-1 to 4).

    ° Arm recoil, where the neonate's arm is passively extended and spontaneously returns to flexion (0 to 4).

    ° Popliteal angle, which is the degree of the angle to which the knees can extend (-1 to 5).

    ° Scarf sign, which is crossing the neonate's arm over the chest (-1 to 4).

    ° Heel to ear, which is how far the neonate's heels reach to her ears (-1 to 4).

  ◊ **Physical maturity** assesses:

    ° Skin texture ranging from sticky and transparent to leathery, cracked, and wrinkled (-1 to 5).

    ° Lanugo presence and amount ranging from none, sparse, abundant, thinning, bald, or mostly bald (-1 to 4).

        °   Plantar surface creases ranging from < 40 to 50 mm to creases over the entire sole (-1 to 4).

        °   Breast tissue amount ranging from imperceptible to full areola with a 5 to 10 mm bud (-1 to 4).

        °   Eyes and ears for amount of eye opening and ear cartilage present (-1 to 4).

        °   Genitalia development ranging from flat smooth scrotum to pendulous testes with deep rugae for males (-1 to 4) and prominent clitoris with flat labia to the labia majora covering the labia minora and clitoris for females (-1 to 4).

- **Classification** of the newborn **by gestational age and birth weight** is then determined.

  ◊ **Large for gestational age (LGA)** – weight is above the 90th percentile.

  ◊ **Appropriate for gestational age (AGA)** – weight is between the 10th and 90th percentile.

  ◊ **Small for gestational age (SGA)** – weight is below the 10th percentile.

  ◊ **Low birth weight (LBW)** – a weight of 2,500 g or less at birth.

  ◊ **Very low birth weight (VLBW)** – weight of 1,500 g or less at birth.

  ◊ **Intrauterine growth restriction (IUGR)** – rate of growth does not meet expected norms.

  ◊ **Preterm or premature** – born prior to completion of 37th week of gestation.

  ◊ **Term** – birth between beginning of 38th week gestation and prior to the end of the 42nd week of gestation.

  ◊ **Postterm (postdate)** – born after the completion of 42 weeks gestation.

  ◊ **Postmature** – born after the completion of 42 weeks gestation with signs of placental insufficiency.

Δ   A **more extensive physical exam** is performed on the neonate **within 24 hr of birth.** Vital signs are then obtained. The physical assessment should progress cephalocaudal (head to toe). Neurological and behavioral assessments are completed by eliciting reflexes and observing neonatal responses. Laboratory data is monitored.

Δ   **Vital signs** are normally checked in the following sequence: respirations, heart rate, blood pressure, and temperature. The nurse should observe the respiratory rate first before the infant becomes active or agitated with the stethoscope, thermometer, and/or the blood pressure cuff.

- **Respiratory rate** increases from **30 to 60/min** with short periods of **apnea (less than 15 sec)** occurring most frequently during the rapid eye movement (REM) sleep cycle. Periods of apnea lasting longer than 15 sec need to be evaluated. Crackles and wheezing are symptoms of fluid or infection in the lungs. Grunting and nasal flaring are signs of respiratory distress.

- **Heart rate** should be **100 to 160 beats/min** with brief fluctuations above and below this range depending on activity level (e.g., crying, sleeping). **Apical pulse** rate should be obtained for a **full minute**, preferably when the infant is sleeping. The pediatric stethoscope head should be placed on the fourth or fifth intercostal space at the left midclavicular line over the apex of the neonate's heart.

- **Blood pressure** should be 60 to 80 mm Hg systolic and 40 to 50 mm Hg diastolic.

- **Temperature** should be 36.5 to 37.2° C (97.7 to 98.9° F) axillary. The neonate is at **risk** for **hypothermia** and **hyperthermia** until **thermoregulation** (ability to produce heat and maintain normal body temperature) stabilizes. If the neonate becomes **chilled (cold stress), oxygen demands can increase** and acidosis can occur. **Fetal hypoxia** results in **depressed respirations** rather than increased.

Δ   **Physical exam from head to toe**

- **Posture**

  ◊   The neonate should be lying in a curled-up position with his arms and legs in **moderate flexion**.

  ◊   The neonate should **be resistant** to **extension** of his extremities.

- **Skin**

  ◊   **Color** should be **pink** or **acrocyanotic** with **no jaundice** present on first day. Secondary to increased bilirubin, jaundice may appear on third day of life but then spontaneously decreases.

  ◊   **Turgor** should be good, showing the neonate to be well-hydrated. The skin should spring back immediately when pinched.

  ◊   **Texture** should be dry, soft, and smooth showing good hydration. Cracks in hands and feet may be present. In full-term infants, **desquamation (peeling)** occurs a few days after birth.

  ◊   **Vernix caseosa** (protective, thick, cheesy covering) varies in amount with more usually present in creases and folds.

  ◊   **Lanugo** (fine downy hair) varies in newborns regarding the amount present and is found over the shoulders, pinnas, and forehead of newborns.

◊ Normal deviations:

° **Milia** (small raised white spots on the chin, nose, and forehead) may be present. These spots disappear spontaneously without treatment (instruct the infant's parents not to squeeze or pop the spots).

° **Mongolian spots** (bluish purple spots of pigmentation) are commonly noted on the neonate's back, shoulders, and buttocks. These spots are frequently present on dark-skinned infants.

° **Telangiectatic nevi** (stork bites) are flat pink or red marks that easily blanch and are found on the neonate's upper eyelids, back of the neck, and middle of the forehead. They usually fade by the second year of life.

° **Nevus flammeus** (port wine stain) is a capillary angioma below the surface of the skin that is red or purple, varies in size and shape, is commonly seen on the face, and does not blanch or disappear.

° **Erythema toxicum** (erythema neonatorum) is a pink rash that appears suddenly anywhere on the body of a term neonate during the first 3 weeks. No treatment is required.

• **Head**

◊ The newborn's **head** should be 2 to 3 cm **larger** than her **chest** circumference. If the head circumference is greater than or equal to 4 cm larger than chest circumference, this can be an indication of hydrocephalus (excessive cerebral fluid within the brain cavity surrounding the brain). If the head circumference is less than or equal to 32 cm, this can be an indication of microcephaly (abnormally small head).

◊ The newborn's **anterior fontanel** should be palpated and approximately **5 cm on average** and **diamond shaped**. The posterior fontanel is smaller and triangle shaped. Both fontanels should be soft and flat. The fontanels may bulge when the infant cries, coughs, or vomits: nonelevated when the infant is quiet. **Bulging** fontanels may indicate **increased intracranial pressure**, **infection**, or **hemorrhage**. **Depressed** fontanels may indicate **dehydration**.

◊ The **sutures** of the newborn should be **palpable**, **unjoined**, and may be overlapping (molding), a normal occurrence resulting from head compression during labor.

◊ **Caput succedaneum** (localized swelling of the soft tissues of the scalp caused by pressure on the head during labor) is a normal finding that may be palpated as a soft fluctuant mass and may cross over the suture line. Caput succedaneum usually resolves in 3 to 4 days and does not require treatment.

◊ **Cephalohematoma** is a collection of blood between the periosteum and the skull bone that it covers. It does not cross the suture line. It results from trauma during birth such as pressure of the fetal head against the maternal pelvis in a prolonged difficult labor or forceps delivery. It appears in the first 1 to 2 days after birth and simultaneously resolves in 3 to 6 weeks.

- **Eyes**

  ◊ Assess for symmetry in size and shape.

  ◊ **Placement of the eyes**: Each eye and the space between the eyes should each equal one-third of the total distance between outer canthus of both eyes to rule out chromosomal abnormalities such as Down syndrome.

  ◊ The eyes of newborns are normally blue or gray.

  ◊ Permanent eye color is established within 3 to 12 months.

  ◊ Lacrimal glands are immature in a newborn resulting in tearless crying.

  ◊ Subconjunctival hemorrhages may result from pressure during birth.

  ◊ Pupillary and red reflex are present in newborns.

  ◊ Eyeball movement will demonstrate random, jerky movements.

- **Ears**

  ◊ **Placement of the ears**: An imaginary line through the inner to outer canthus of the eye to the ear should be even with the upper tip of the pinna of the of the newborn's ear. **Low set** ears can indicate a chromosome abnormality such as Down syndrome or a **renal disorder**.

  ◊ Cartilage should be firm and well-formed. Lack of cartilage indicates prematurity.

  ◊ The newborn should respond to voices and other sounds.

- **Nose**

  ◊ The newborn's nose should be midline, flat, and broad with lack of a bridge.

  ◊ Some mucus should be present but with no drainage.

  ◊ Neonates are **obligate nose breathers** and do not develop the response of opening the mouth with a nasal obstruction until 3 weeks after birth; therefore, a nasal blockage may result in flaring of the nares, cyanosis, or asphyxia.

  ◊ The newborn should sneeze to clear the nose.

- **Mouth**

  ◊ Assess for **palate closure** and **strength** of **sucking**.

◊ The lip movements of a newborn should be symmetrical.

◊ Gums should be pink.

◊ **Saliva** should be **scant**. Excessive saliva may indicate a tracheoesophageal fistula.

◊ **Epstein pearls** (small white cysts found on the gums and at the junction of the soft and hard palates) are normal in newborns. They result from the accumulation of epithelial cells and disappear a few weeks after birth.

◊ **Tongue** should move freely, be symmetrical in shape, and not protruding (a large and protruding tongue may be a sign of Down syndrome).

◊ **Soft** and **hard palate** should be intact. Anatomic grove to accommodate the nipple may be present and will disappear by 3 to 4 years of age.

◊ **Gums** and **tongue** should be **pink**. Gray-white patches on the tongue and gums can indicate thrush, a fungal infection caused by *Candida albicans*, sometimes acquired from the mother's vaginal secretions.

- **Neck**

  ◊ A newborn's **neck** should be **short**, **thick**, surrounded by **skin folds**, and exhibit no webbing.

  ◊ A newborn's **neck** should **move freely** from side to side and up and down.

  ◊ Absence of head control may indicate prematurity or Down syndrome.

- **Chest**

  ◊ The chest of a newborn should be **barrel-shaped**.

  ◊ **Respirations** are primarily **diaphragmatic** in newborns.

  ◊ Clavicles are intact.

  ◊ There are **no retractions**.

  ◊ **Nipples** should be **prominent**, well-formed, and symmetrical.

  ◊ **Breast nodule** is approximately **6 mm**.

- **Abdomen**

  ◊ The **umbilical cord** will have **two arteries and one vein**.

  ◊ Cord should be **odorless** and exhibit **no intestinal structures**.

  ◊ The **abdomen** should be **round**, **dome-shaped**, and non-distended.

  ◊ Bowel sounds should be present 1 to 2 hr following birth.

- **Anogenital**

  ◊ Anus should be present, patent, and not covered by a membrane.

  ◊ Male newborn **genitalia** should include **rugae** on the **scrotum**.

  ◊ **Testes** should have **descended** into scrotum.

  ◊ Male urinary meatus is located at penile tip.

  ◊ Female genitalia should include labia majora covering the labia minora and clitoris. Female genitalia are usually edematous.

  ◊ **Vaginal blood-tinged discharge** may occur in **female neonates,** which is caused by **maternal pregnancy hormones** and is normal.

  ◊ A hymenal tag should be present.

  ◊ **Urine should** be **passed within 24 hr after birth**. If the neonate does not urinate within the first 24 hr, this may be an indication of dehydration. **Uric acid crystals** will produce a **rust color** in the **urine** the first couple of days of life.

  ◊ **Meconium should be passed within 24 hr after birth.**

- **Extremities**

  ◊ A newborn should be assessed for **full range**, **symmetry of motion,** and **spontaneous movements.**

  ◊ **Extremities** should be **flexed.**

  ◊ Check for bowed legs and flat feet, which should be present because the lateral muscles are more developed than the medial muscles.

  ◊ **No click** should be heard **when abducting** the **hips** of a newborn.

  ◊ Gluteal folds should be even.

  ◊ **Soles** should be **well-lined over two-thirds** of a newborn's **foot.**

  ◊ Nail beds should be pink and there should be no extra digits present.

- **Spine**

  ◊ Spine should be **straight, flat**, and **easily flexed**.

- **Reflexes**

  ◊ **Sucking** – begins when a nipple or finger is placed in the mouth of a newborn.

  ◊ **Moro** – elicited by striking a flat surface the infant is lying on, or allowing the head and trunk of an infant in a semi-sitting position to fall backward to an angle of at least 30°. The infant's arms and legs symmetrically extend and then abduct while her fingers spread to form a "C".

◊ **Rooting** – when the cheek of a newborn is stroked, the newborn will turn his head in the direction of the stroke.

◊ **Tonic neck** – while the newborn lies in a supine position, his head is turned, causing his extremities on the same side to straighten and those on the opposite side to flex.

◊ **Babinski** – when the sole of the foot on the side of the newborn's small toe is stroked upward, the toes will fan upward and out.

◊ **Palmar grasp** – Infant will grasp object when palm is touched.

◊ **Plantar grasp** – Infant's toes will curl downward when sole of foot is touched.

◊ **Stepping** – when the newborn is held upright with her feet touching a flat surface, the newborn will respond with dancing or stepping movements.

◊ **Startle** – a loud noise such as a hand clap will elicit the newborn to abduct his arms and flex his elbows.

• **Senses**

◊ **Vision** – a neonate should be able to focus on objects 9 to 12 in away from his face. This is approximately the distance from the mother's face when the neonate is breastfeeding. The newborn's eyes are sensitive to light and they prefer dim lighting. Pupils are reactive to light and the blink reflex is easily stimulated. The neonate can track high contrast objects and prefers bright colors and patterns.

◊ **Hearing** – similar to that of an adult once the amniotic fluid drains from the ears. Neonates exhibit selective listening to the familiar voices and rhythms of intrauterine life. The neonate turns toward the general direction of a sound.

◊ **Touch** – the neonate should respond to tactile messages of pain and touch. The mouth is the most sensitive to touch in the neonate.

◊ **Taste** – the neonate can taste and prefers sweets over salty, sour, or bitter.

◊ **Smell** – neonates have a highly developed sense of smell, prefer sweet smells, and can recognize their mothers' smell.

Diagnostic and Therapeutic Procedures and Nursing Interventions

Δ **Cord blood** is collected from the newborn at birth. Laboratory tests are conducted on the blood to determine ABO blood type and Rh status. A complete blood count (CBC) may be done in the nursery by a capillary stick to evaluate for anemia, polycythemia, infection, or clotting problems. A glucose level may be done to evaluate for hypoglycemia.

Normal Laboratory Values

Hemoglobin	14 to 24 g/dL
Hematocrit	• 44 to 64%
Red blood cell count	• 4,800 to 7,100,000/mm³
Leukocytes	• 9,000 to 30,000/mm³
Platelets	• 150,000 to 300,000/mm³
Glucose	• 40 to 60 mg/dL
Bilirubin	• 0 to 6 mg/dL on day 1 • 8 mg/dL or less on day 2 • 12 mg/dL or less on day 3

NANDA Nursing Diagnoses

Δ   Ineffective airway clearance related to nasal obstruction

Δ   Impaired gas exchange related to amniotic fluid remaining in the neonatal lungs

Δ   Hypothermia or hyperthermia related to thermoregulation not yet stabilized

Δ   Deficient knowledge of the parents related to normal neonatal skin presentations

Nursing Interventions

Δ   **Select appropriate equipment for newborn assessment.**

• **Bulb syringe** – used for the suctioning of excess mucus from the newborn's mouth and nose.

• **Stethoscope with pediatric head** – used to evaluate the newborn's heart rate, breath sounds, and bowel sounds.

• **Axillary thermometer** – used to monitor the newborn's temperature and helps to avoid hypothermia. Rectal temperatures are avoided because they can injure the delicate rectal mucosa. A rectal temperature may be done once to evaluate for anal abnormalities.

• **Blood pressure cuff 2.5 cm wide** – (can use palpation or electronic method) for evaluation of the newborn's blood pressure. Blood pressure may be done in all four extremities if evaluating the newborn for cardiac problems.

• **Balance scale with paper in place** – scale should be at 0 before weighing newborn.

- **Tape measure with cm** – newborn should be measured from crown to rump for length. Measure the newborn's head circumference at greatest diameter (occipital to frontal). Measure the newborn's chest circumference beginning at the nipple line.

- **Clean gloves** – must be used for examining the newborn until he is given his first bath.

Δ **Provide education** to the mother and family about the **neonate's appearance,** and give reassurance about normal findings that the family may be concerned about (e.g., milia, Epstein's pearls, caput succedaneum).

Complications and Nursing Implications

Δ **Airway obstruction related to mucus**

- Monitor for obstruction of nares by alternately blocking one nare and observing for flaring of the other nare or cyanosis.

- If excess mucus exists, the newborn's mouth and nose should be suctioned with a bulb syringe. Gentle percussion over the newborn's chest can help loosen secretions.

Δ **Hypothermia**

- Monitor for an axillary neonatal temperature less than 36.5° C (97.7° F).

- If temperature is unstable, place the newborn in a radiant warmer and maintain skin temperature at approximately 36.5° C (97.7° F).

- Assess the newborn's axillary temperature every hour until it becomes stable.

- All exams and assessments should be performed on the newborn under a radiant warmer.

Δ **Inadequate oxygen supply related to obstructed airway, poorly functioning cardiopulmonary system, or hypothermia**

- Monitor respirations and skin color for cyanosis.

- Stabilize body temperature or clear airway as indicated, administer oxygen, and if needed, prepare for resuscitation.

Primary Reference:

Lowdermilk, D. L. & Perry, S. E. (2004). *Maternity & women's health care* (8th ed.). St. Louis, MO: Mosby.

Additional Resources:

NANDA International (2004). *NANDA nursing diagnoses: Definitions and classification 2005-2006*. Philadelphia: NANDA.

Pillitteri, A. (2003). *Maternal & child health nursing: Care of the childbearing and childrearing family*. (4th ed.). Philadelphia: Lippincott Williams & Wilkins.

Chapter 19: Newborn Assessment

Application Exercises

Scenario: A client has just given birth to her third child at 38 weeks. The newborn weighs 3,200 g and is in the 60th percentile for weight. Apgar scores are 6 and 9 at 1 and 5 min of age. Vital signs are as follows: temperature 36.8° C (98.2° F) axillary, heart rate 145 beats/min, respiratory rate 50/min, length 48.2 cm (19 in), head circumference 35 cm (14 in), and chest circumference 33 cm (13 in).

1. This neonate is classified as which of the following based on weight and gestational age?

    A. LBW

    B. AGA

    C. SGA

    D. LGA

2. What five areas are assessed during Apgar scoring?

3. Which of the following describes the head circumference of this infant?

    A. Hydrocephalic

    B. Microcephalic

    C. Normocephalic

    D. Encephalic

4. A rectal temperature is NOT the preferred method of temperature measurement in a newborn because

    A. axillary temperatures are more accurate.

    B. axillary temperatures are easier to obtain.

    C. rectal temperatures are painful for the newborn.

    D. rectal temperatures can injure delicate mucosa.

5. When performing a newborn assessment, which of the following is a good indication of adequate hydration?

      A. No urine output the first 24 hr

      B. A tense, bulging fontanel

      C. Soft, smooth skin

      D. Occasional spitting up

6. When assessing a newborn's mouth, the nurse observes small white nodules on the roof of the mouth. This finding is characteristic of which of the following conditions?

      A. Mongolian spots

      B. Milia spots

      C. Erythema toxicum

      D. Epstein's pearls

7. An initial assessment of a newborn's urine shows rust-colored streaks in the diaper. Which of the following factors is the probable cause?

      A. Uric acid crystals

      B. Birth trauma

      C. Cystitis

      D. Hematuria

8. One minute after birth, a newborn has a heart rate of 70 beats/min. Five minutes after birth his heart rate is 90 beats/min. Which of the following Apgar heart rate scores should the newborn receive?

      A. 0

      B. 1

      C. 2

      D. 3

9. A nurse is assessing the reflexes of a newborn. In checking for the Moro reflex, the nurse should perform which of the following?

      A. Make a loud noise such as clapping hands together over the infant's crib.

      B. Stimulate the pads of the newborn's hands with stroking or massage.

      C. Stimulate the soles of the newborn's feet on the outer lateral surface of each foot.

      D. Hold the infant in a semi-sitting position, then allow the infant's head and trunk to fall backward.

10. Which of the following signs pertaining to respirations indicate that a newborn is having no difficulty adapting to extrauterine life? (Select all that apply.)

_____ Expiratory grunting

_____ Respirations of 46/min

_____ Inspiratory nasal flaring

_____ Apnea for 10 sec periods

_____ Obligatory nose breathing

_____ Respirations of 26/min

_____ Crackles and wheezing

11. The mother of a newborn asks the nurse what the white pimple-like structures are on her newborn's nose. The nurse explains to the mother that the structures are

A. lanugo.

B. vernix.

C. Epstein's pearls.

D. milia.

12. A nurse is preparing to bathe a newborn and notices a bluish marking across the newborn's lower back. What is the significance of this finding?

A. The mark is frequently seen in dark-skinned infants.

B. The mark is abnormal and may indicate hyperbilirubinemia.

C. The mark may be a forceps mark from an operative delivery.

D. The mark is a sign of prolonged birth or trauma during delivery.

Chapter 19: Newborn Assessment

Application Exercises Answer Key

Scenario: A client has just given birth to her third child at 38 weeks. The newborn weighs 3,200 g and is in the 60th percentile for weight. Apgar scores are 6 and 9 at 1 and 5 min of age. Vital signs are as follows: temperature 36.8° C (98.2° F) axillary, heart rate 145 beats/min, respiratory rate 50/min, length 48.2 cm (19 in), head circumference 35 cm (14 in), and chest circumference 33 cm (13 in).

1. This neonate is classified as which of the following based on weight and gestational age?

   A. LBW

   B. AGA

   C. SGA

   D. LGA

   This neonate is classified as AGA because her weight is between the 10th and 9th percentile. A LBW neonate would weigh less than 2,500 g, a SGA neonate's weight is below the 10th percentile, and a LGA neonate's weight is above the 90th percentile.

2. What five areas are assessed during Apgar scoring?

   The five areas assessed when Apgar scoring a newborn are: heart rate, respiratory rate, muscle tone, reflex, and color irritability.

3. Which of the following describes the head circumference of this infant?

   A. Hydrocephalic

   B. Microcephalic

   C. Normocephalic

   D. Encephalic

   The newborn's head should be 2 to 3 cm larger than the chest circumference. If greater, this can be an indication of hydrocephalus. In this newborn's case, the head and chest circumference are both within normal parameters and the head is 2 cm larger than the chest. Encephalic means within the skull.

4. A rectal temperature is NOT the preferred method of temperature measurement in a newborn because

> A. axillary temperatures are more accurate.
>
> B. axillary temperatures are easier to obtain.
>
> C. rectal temperatures are painful for the newborn.
>
> **D. rectal temperatures can injure delicate mucosa.**

Rectal temperatures are avoided because they can injure the delicate rectal mucosa. A rectal temperature may be done once to evaluate for anal abnormalities.

5. When performing a newborn assessment, which of the following is a good indication of adequate hydration?

> A. No urine output the first 24 hr
>
> B. A tense, bulging fontanel
>
> **C. Soft, smooth skin**
>
> D. Occasional spitting up

Soft, smooth skin that has good turgor is a good sign of hydration. No urine output for 24 hr could indicate dehydration. A tense, bulging fontanel may be an indication of increased intracranial pressure. Spitting up a small amount is normal.

6. When assessing a newborn's mouth, the nurse observes small white nodules on the roof of the mouth. This finding is characteristic of which of the following conditions?

> A. Mongolian spots
>
> B. Milia spots
>
> C. Erythema toxicum
>
> **D. Epstein's pearls**

Epstein's pearls are small white nodules that appear on the roof a newborn's mouth. Mongolian spots are dark areas observed in dark-skinned newborns, and erythema toxicum is a transient maculopapular rash seen in newborns. Milia are small white bumps that occur on the nose due to clogged sebaceous glands.

7. An initial assessment of a newborn's urine shows rust-colored streaks in the diaper. Which of the following factors is the probable cause?

    A. Uric acid crystals
    B. Birth trauma
    C. Cystitis
    D. Hematuria

Uric acid crystals will produce a rust color in the urine the first couple of days of life. Cystitis, birth trauma, and hematuria are not normal findings in a newborn.

8. One minute after birth, a newborn has a heart rate of 70 beats/min. Five minutes after birth, his heart rate is 90 beats/min. Which of the following Apgar heart rate scores should the newborn receive?

    A. 0
    B. 1
    C. 2
    D. 3

Both 1 and 5 min heart rate scores would be 1 since the heart rate is less than 100.

9. A nurse is assessing the reflexes of a newborn. In checking for the Moro reflex, the nurse should perform which of the following?

    A. Make a loud noise such as clapping hands together over the infant's crib.
    B. Stimulate the pads of the newborn's hands with stroking or massage.
    C. Stimulate the soles of the newborn's feet on the outer lateral surface of each foot.
    D. Hold the infant in a semi-sitting position, then allow the infant's head and trunk to fall backward.

Moro is done by holding the infant in a semi-sitting position and then allowing the head and trunk to fall backward. Clapping hands will elicit the startle reflex. Stimulating the pads of the infant's hands will elicit the grasp reflex. Stimulating the outer lateral portion of the infant's soles will elicit a Babinski's reflex.

10. Which of the following signs pertaining to respirations indicate that a newborn is having no difficulty adapting to extrauterine life? (Select all that apply.)

_____ Expiratory grunting

__X__ **Respirations of 46/min**

_____ Inspiratory nasal flaring

__X__ **Apnea for 10 sec periods**

__X__ **Obligatory nose breathing**

_____ Respirations of 26/min

_____ Crackles and wheezing

Normal respiratory rate for a neonate increases from 30 to 60/min with short periods of apnea (less than 15 sec) occurring most frequently during the rapid eye movement (REM) sleep cycle. Periods of apnea lasting less than 15 sec are normal. Neonates are obligatory nose breathers. Grunting and nasal flaring are signs of respiratory distress. Crackles and wheezing are symptoms of fluid or infection in the lungs.

11. The mother of a newborn asks the nurse what the white pimple-like structures are on her newborn's nose. The nurse explains to the mother that the structures are

A. lanugo.

B. vernix.

C. Epstein's pearls.

D. milia.

Milia are clogged sebaceous glands on the nose. Lanugo is fine, downy hair. Vernix is a cheesy substance found in creases. Epstein's pearls are bumps found in the roof of the mouth.

12. A nurse is preparing to bathe a newborn and notices a bluish marking across the newborn's lower back. What is the significance of this finding?

A. The mark is frequently seen in dark-skinned infants.

B. The mark is abnormal and may indicate hyperbilirubinemia.

C. The mark may be a forceps mark from an operative delivery.

D. The mark is a sign of prolonged birth or trauma during delivery.

Mongolian spots are commonly found over the lumbosacral area of newborns of dark-skinned infants of African American, Asian, or Native American origin. Hyperbilirubinemia would be present as jaundice. Birth trauma would be present as ecchymosis, and forceps marks would most likely present as a cephalohematoma.

Unit 4   Newborn Care

Chapter 20:   Nursing Care of the Newborn

Contributor: Linda S. Wood, MSN, RN

NCLEX-RN® Connections:

Learning Objective: Review and apply knowledge within "**Nursing Care of the Newborn**" in readiness for performance of the following nursing activities as outlined by the NCLEX-RN® test plan:

Δ   Plan and implement interventions to ensure newborn security.

Δ   Assess the newborn and provide appropriate care.

Δ   Support and instruct client/family/significant others in care of the newborn.

Δ   Evaluate the client/family/significant others ability to provide appropriate newborn care.

Key Points

Δ   **Newborn care** can be divided into **three phases.**

- The **first phase** consists of **stabilization** and/or resuscitation to relieve **airway** obstruction if present and maintain adequate oxygenation and **thermoregulation** for the maintenance of body temperature.

- The **second phase** consists of **assessment completion** (e.g., Apgar score, physical examination, measurements, and monitoring laboratory studies).

- The **third phase** consists of **nursing interventions** and family **teaching** (e.g., umbilical cord care, prophylactic measures, newborn screening, infant feedings and bathing, facilitating parent-infant attachment).

Δ   Maintaining a **secure environment** to **minimize risk** of **infant abduction** is a high priority. After birth of the infant, a nurse immediately places **matching identification bracelets** on the newborn, mother, and significant other to protect the newborn. All facility staff who assist in caring for the newborn are required to wear picture identification badges.

Key Factors

Δ   Infants delivered by cesarean birth are more susceptible to fluid remaining in the lungs than infants delivered vaginally.

Δ   Infants with respiratory distress are at a higher risk for hypothermia.

Δ   Infants with mothers who are diabetic are at a higher risk for hypoglycemia.

Diagnostic and Therapeutic Procedures and Nursing Interventions

Δ   **Hemoglobin** and **hematocrit**

Δ   **Glucose** for hypoglycemia

Δ   **Newborn genetic screening** is mandated in all states. A capillary heel stick should be done 24 hr following birth. For results to be accurate, the newborn must receive formula or breast milk for at least 24 hr. If the newborn is discharged before 24 hr of age, the test should be repeated in 1 to 2 weeks.

   •   All states require testing for **phenylketonuria (PKU)**. PKU is a defect in protein metabolism in which the accumulation of the amino acid phenylalanine can result in mental retardation (treatment in the first 2 months of life can prevent retardation).

   •   Other genetic testing that may be done includes: **galactosemia, cystic fibrosis, maple syrup urine disease**, and **sickle cell disease**.

Δ   **Heel stick blood samples** are **obtained by** a **nurse.**

   •   Heel sticks are best done by **warming** the **newborn's heel** first to increase circulation and eliminate or decrease the pain associated with a heel stick.

   •   A **spring-activated lancet** is used so that the skin incision is made quickly and painlessly.

   •   The **outer aspect** of the **heel** should be used, and the lancet should go **no deeper than 2.4 mm** to prevent necrotizing osteochondritis resulting from penetration of bone with the lancet.

   •   **Three drops** of **blood** are drawn from the heel of the newborn and dropped onto a **filter paper** by a nurse.

   •   Apply pressure with **dry gauze (do not use alcohol as it will cause bleeding to continue)** until bleeding stops and cover with adhesive bandage.

   •   Cuddle and comfort the infant when the procedure is completed to reassure the infant and promote feelings of safety.

Δ   **Newborn hearing screening** is required in more than 30 states. Newborns are being screened in the nursery so that deafness can be detected and treated early.

Assessments, Nursing Diagnoses, and Nursing Interventions

Nursing Assessments

Δ **Vital signs** should be checked on admission/birth and every 30 min x 2, every 1 hr x 2, and then every 8 hr.

Δ **Weight, length, and head and chest circumference** should be assessed at birth and then daily weights.

Δ **Inspect** the **umbilical cord** for two arteries and one vein. Observe for any bleeding from the cord, and ensure the cord is clamped securely to prevent hemorrhage.

Δ **Observe for periods of reactivity** as the infant passes through periods of adjustment in the first 6 to 8 hr of life as body systems stabilize.

- **First period of reactivity** – The infant is alert and exhibits exploring activity, makes sucking sounds, and has a rapid heartbeat and respiratory rate. Heart rate may be as high as 160 to 180/min but will stabilize at a baseline of 100 to 120/min that lasts 15 to 30 min after birth.

- **Period of relative inactivity** – The infant will become quiet and begin rest and sleep. The neonate's heart rate and respirations will decrease and this period will last from 30 to 100/min after birth.

- **Second period of reactivity** – The infant reawakens, becomes responsive again, and often gags and chokes on mucus that has accumulated in his mouth. This period usually occurs 4 to 8 hr after birth and may last 10 min to several hours.

NANDA Nursing Diagnoses

Δ Risk for ineffective airway clearance related to excessive mucus in the infant's airway passages

Δ Risk for imbalanced body temperature related to ineffective thermoregulation

Δ Risk for infection related to improper umbilical cord care

Nursing Interventions

Δ **Stabilization and/or resuscitation of airway**

- **Monitor the infant for signs and symptoms of respiratory complications.**

  ◊ **Bradypnea** – respirations less than 25/min.

  ◊ **Tachypnea** – respirations greater than 60/min.

  ◊ **Abnormal breath sounds** – expiratory grunting, crackles, and wheezes.

  ◊ **Respiratory distress** – nasal flaring, retractions, chin tug, and labored breathing.

- **Interventions for stabilization and resuscitation of airway**

  ◊ Most secretions in air passages are cleared by the cough reflex in the infant. Routine **suctioning** of the **mouth** and **nasal passages with a bulb syringe** is done to remove excess mucus in the respiratory tract.

    ° Gentle percussion may be performed over the chest wall using a percussion cup to loosen secretions prior to suctioning.

    ° Support the infant by holding the head slightly lower than the body. Turn the infant's head to the side if the infant is coughing or choking on secretions to allow gravity to aid in drainage of secretions.

    ° Suction the infant's mouth first (prevents the infant from gasping as the nares are touched and inhaling pharyngeal secretions).

    ° Compress the bulb before insertion into the mouth and release bulb after insertion.

    ° Insert the bulb into one side of the infant's mouth and then the other side making sure to avoid the center of the infant's mouth, which could stimulate the gag reflex.

    ° The nasal passages are suctioned one nostril at a time.

    ° If these measures are unsuccessful, mechanical suction and/or back blows and chest thrusts may need to be used as well as the institution of emergency procedures.

    ° The bulb syringe should be kept with the infant, and the infant's family should be instructed on how to use it. Family members should be asked to perform a demonstration to show they understand bulb syringe techniques.

Δ **Thermoregulation** provides a neutral thermal environment that helps an infant maintain a normal core temperature with minimal oxygen consumption and caloric expenditure. A newborn has a relatively large surface-to-weight ratio, reduced metabolism per unit area, blood vessels closer to the surface, and small amounts of insulation. The newborn keeps warm by metabolizing brown fat, which is unique to newborns, but only within a very narrow temperature range. Becoming chilled (cold stress) can increase the newborn's oxygen demands and rapidly use up brown fat reserves. Therefore, monitoring temperature regulation is important.

- **Monitor for signs and symptoms of hypothermia in the infant.**

  ◊ Axillary temperature 36.5° C (97.7° F)

  ◊ **Cyanosis**

  ◊ Increased respiratory rate

- **Interventions to maintain thermoregulation**

  ◊ Core temperature varies within newborns, but it should be kept around 36.5° C (97.7° F). Heat can be lost by four mechanisms. Below is a summary of those mechanisms and how to avoid loss of heat.

    ° **Conduction** – loss of body heat resulting from direct contact with a cooler surface. The nurse should preheat a radiant warmer, warm a stethoscope and other instruments, and pad a scale with paper before weighing the newborn. The newborn should also be placed directly on the mother's abdomen and covered with a warm blanket.

    ° **Convection** – flow of heat from the body surface to cooler ambient air. The nurse should place the newborn's bassinet out of the direct line of a fan or air conditioning vent, swaddle the infant in a blanket, and keep the infant's head covered. Any procedure that must be done with the infant uncovered should be performed under a radiant heat source.

    ° **Evaporation** – loss of heat as surface liquid is converted to vapor. The nurse should gently rub the neonate dry with a warm sterile blanket (adhering to standard precautions and avoiding touching vernix caseosa) immediately after delivery. If thermoregulation is unstable, postpone the initial bath until the newborn's skin temperature is 36.5° C (97.7° F). When bathing the newborn, expose only one body part at a time, washing and drying thoroughly.

    ° **Radiation** – loss of heat from the body surface to a cooler solid surface that is close to, but not in direct contact. The nurse should keep the newborn and examining tables away from windows and air conditioners.

  ◊ The neonate's temperature stabilizes at 37° C (98.6° F) within 4 hr after birth if chilling is prevented.

Δ **Identification** is **applied immediately after birth** by the nurse. It is important because the newborn can be given to the wrong parents, switched, or kidnapped.

- The **mother**, **newborn**, and **significant other** are identified by **plastic identification wrist bands** with permanent locks that must be cut to be removed. Identification bands should include the newborn's name, sex, date, and time of birth. In addition, the newborn's footprints and mother's thumb prints are taken.

- Each time a **newborn** is taken to the parents, the **identification band** should be **verified against** the **mother's** identification band.

- The newborn is not to be given to anyone who does not have a **picture identification badge** distinguishing that person as **staff** of the facility maternal-newborn unit.

- Many hospitals have locked maternal-newborn units that require staff to permit entrance or exit from a unit. Some hospitals have a sensor device on the identification bands that sounds an alarm if the newborn is removed from the hospital.

Δ **Umbilical cord care** begins with the immediate clamping of the cord by the primary care provider after delivery. Two clamps are applied to the cord about 8 inches away from the infant's abdomen, and the cord is cut between the clamps. The cord may also be cut by the partner.

- After the infant is stabilized, a **disposable clamp** is applied and the **cord** is **cut shorter**.

- If **bleeding** from the cord vessels is **noted**, the **nurse** should **apply** a **second clamp**. If bleeding persists, the nurse should get assistance.

- After **assuring** the **clamp** is **secure** and there is no bleeding, the **cord** should be **kept clean** and **dry** to prevent infection.

- **Apply triple or antibiotic ointment** prescribed by the primary care provider to prevent infection and help enhance the drying and falling off of the cord.

- The **diaper** should be **folded** so it is **below** the **level of** the **cord** so that when it becomes wet the cord remains dry.

- **Only sponge** baths should be given **until** the **cord falls off**.

- The parents are taught cord care and reminded of the importance of keeping the cord clean and dry.

- Before discharge, the cord clamp is removed.

Δ **Prophylactic eye care** is the mandatory instillation of antibiotic ointment into the neonate's eyes to prevent ophthalmia neonatorum. Infections can be transmitted during descent through the birth canal. Ophthalmia neonatorum is caused by *Neisseria gonorrhoeae* or *Chlamydia trachomatis* and can cause blindness in the neonate.

- **Erythromycin** (E-Mycin) 0.5% ointment is the medication of choice.

- Use a single dose unit to avoid cross contamination between infants.

- Apply a 1 to 2 cm ribbon of erythromycin ointment to the **lower conjunctival sac** of each eye, starting from the inner canthus and moving outward

- Close the eye for about 5 sec and allow the ointment to spread across the conjunctiva. After about 1 min, wipe the excess ointment off.

- A possible **adverse reaction** is **chemical conjunctivitis,** which may cause redness, swelling, drainage, and temporarily blurred vision for 24 to 48 hr. This is a **normal** response to the medication. **Reassure** the newborn's **parents** that this **will resolve on its own**.

- **Application** may be **delayed for 1 hr after birth** to facilitate parent-infant bonding and eye contact during the first period of infant reactivity.

Δ **Vitamin K (AquaMEPHYTON) injection** is administered to prevent hemorrhagic disorders. Vitamin K is not produced in the gastrointestinal tract of the newborn until around day 8. Vitamin K is produced in the colon by bacteria that forms once formula or breast milk is introduced into the gut of the newborn.

- Administer 0.5 to 1 mg intramuscularly into the vastus lateralis (where muscle development is adequate) within 2 hr after birth.

Δ **Hepatitis B vaccinations** are recommended to be given to all infants.

- For infants born to healthy women, recommended dosage schedule is at birth, 1 month, and 6 months.

- For women infected with hepatitis B, hepatitis B immuno globulin (HBIG) along with the hepatitis B vaccine is given within 12 hr of birth. The hepatitis B vaccine is given alone at 1, 2, and 12 months.

- It is important **not to give** the **vitamin K** and the **hepatitis B injections in** the **same thigh**. Sites should be alternated.

Δ **Feedings** may be started immediately following birth.

- **Breastfeeding** is often **started shortly after birth** and promotes maternal-infant bonding.

- **Formula feeding** is usually started at about 2 to 4 hr of age. A few sips of sterile water may be given to assess sucking and swallowing reflexes and assure there are no anomalies such as tracheoesophageal fistula prior to starting formula feeding.

- The newborn is **fed on demand**, which is **normally every 3 to 4 hr** for bottle fed infants and more frequently for breastfed infants.

Δ **Sleep-wake states** are variations of consciousness in the newborn consisting of six states along a continuum comprised of: **deep sleep, light sleep, drowsy, quiet alert, active alert, and extreme irritability (crying)**.

- **Newborns sleep approximately 17 hr a day**, an average of 4 hr at a time. It is important that newborns are positioned supine (back). Studies have proven that the incidence of **sudden infant death syndrome (SIDS)** has dramatically decreased when newborns were no longer placed prone (on the stomach) in cribs (Hein & Petit, 2001; Pollack, H., & Frohna, J., 2002).

Δ **Elimination** needs to be monitored closely.

- Newborns should **void once within 24 hr** of birth. They should void 6 to 10 times a day after 4 days of life.

- **Meconium** should be passed **within** the **first 24 hr** after birth. The newborn will then continue to stool 3 to 4 times a day depending on whether he is being breastfed or bottle fed.

- **Stools** of **breastfed infants** may appear **yellow** and **seedy**. These stools are **lighter in color** and **looser** than the stools of formula fed infants.

Δ **Perineal care** is performed to keep the perineal area of the newborn clean and dry. The ammonia in the urine is very irritating to the skin of the newborn and can cause a diaper rash.

- After each diaper change, the newborn's perineal area should be washed with clear water or water with a mild soap. Diaper wipes with alcohol should be avoided. Pat dry. A&D ointment or petroleum jelly may be applied depending on hospital protocol.

Δ **Bathing of the newborn** can begin once the infant's temperature has stabilized to at least 36.5° C (97.7° F). A complete sponge bath should be given within the first 1 to 2 hr after birth under a radiant heat source to prevent heat loss. If necessary, the first bathing will be postponed until thermoregulation stabilizes.

- After the initial bath, the newborn's face, diaper area, and skin folds are cleansed daily. Complete bathing is performed 2 to 3 times a week.

- Bathing by immersion is not done until the umbilical cord has fallen off and the circumcision has healed on males.

- Gloves should be worn until the newborn's first bath to avoid exposure to body secretions.

- Provide parent teaching on bathing of the newborn (e.g., bathing should go from clean to dirty areas). *(For information, refer to chapter 24, Discharge Teaching: Newborn Care).*

Δ **Infection control** is essential in preventing cross contamination from newborn to newborn and between newborns and staff. All newborns are at risk for infection during the first few months of life because their immune systems are immature.

- Newborns should have their own bassinet equipped with a thermometer, diaper, shirt, and bathing supplies.

- All personnel caring for a newborn should scrub with antimicrobial soap from elbows to finger tips before entering the nursery. In between care of the newborn, hands should be washed. Cover gowns or special uniforms are used to avoid direct contact with clothes.

△ **Family education and promotion of parent-infant attachment**

- Provide family education while performing all nursing care. Encourage family involvement, allowing the mother and family to perform infant care with direct supervision and support by the nurse.

- Encourage mothers and family to hold the newborn so that they can experience eye-to-eye contact and interaction.

Complications and Nursing Implications

△ **Cold stress (complication of ineffective thermoregulation)** can lead to hypoxia, acidosis, and hypoglycemia.

- Monitor for signs and symptoms of cold stress (e.g., cyanotic trunk, depressed respirations).

- To prevent cold stress, avoid heat loss by any of the heat loss mechanisms. If cold stress does occur, the newborn should be warmed slowly over a period of 2 to 4 hr. Correct the hypoxia by administering oxygen. Correct the acidosis and hypoglycemia.

△ **Hypoglycemia** frequently occurs in the first few hours of life secondary to the use of energy to establish respirations and maintain body heat.

- **Monitor** for **signs** of **jitteriness**, irregular respiratory effort, cyanosis, a weak, high-pitched cry, lethargy, twitching, eye rolling, seizures, and a **blood glucose level less than 40 mg/dL** by heel stick.

- Give **oral glucose** or **infant formula immediately,** or have the **mother breastfeed** to elevate the infant's blood glucose. Brain damage can result if brain cells are completely depleted of glucose.

△ **Cord infection (complication of improper cord care)** can result if the cord is not kept clean and dry.

- Monitor for symptoms of a cord that is moist and red, has a foul odor, or has purulent drainage.

- Notify the primary care provider immediately if signs and symptoms of cord infection are present.

△ **Hemorrhage (complication of improper cord care)** due to the cord clamp not being tight enough.

- Monitor the neonate to assure that the clamp is tight and if seepage of blood is noted. Then, a second clamp should be applied.

- If the cord continues to bleed, notify the primary care provider immediately.

Primary Reference:

Lowdermilk, D. L. & Perry, S. E. (2004). *Maternity & women's health care* (8th ed.). St. Louis, MO: Mosby.

Additional Resources:

Hein, A. H., & Petit, F. S. (2001). Back to sleep: Good advice for parents but not for hospitals? *Journal of The American Academy of Pediatrics, 107,* 537-539.

NANDA International (2004). *NANDA nursing diagnoses: Definitions and classification 2005-2006.* Philadelphia: NANDA.

Pillitteri, A. (2003). *Maternal & child health nursing: Care of the childbearing and childrearing family* (5th ed.). Philadelphia: Lippincott, Williams, & Wilkins.

Pollack, A. H., & Frohna, G. J. (2002). Infant sleep placement after the back to sleep campaign. *Journal of The American Academy of Pediatrics, 109,* 608-614.

Springhouse (2003). *Maternal-neonatal nursing made incredibly easy!* (1st ed.). Philadelphia: Lippincott, Williams, & Wilkins.

Chapter 20: Nursing Care of the Newborn

Application Exercises

1. A nurse is instilling prophylactic eye treatment for ophthalmia neonatorum. Which of the following is the medication of choice to treat ophthalmia neonatorum?

    A. Gentamicin

    B. Nystatin

    C. Erythromycin

    D. Vitamin K

2. A nurse needs to maintain thermoregulation. What are the four methods of heat loss and what measures can the nurse use to avoid heat loss?

3. What is the single most important nursing measure that should be done to prevent newborn infection?

4. Why is it important to place an infant in a crib supine rather than prone?

5. A newborn is born to a mother who is infected with hepatitis B. What treatment should this newborn receive?

6. A newborn not completely dried immediately after delivery loses heat through which of the following mechanisms of heat loss?

    A. Conduction

    B. Convection

    C. Evaporation

    D. Radiation

7. When performing nursing care for a newborn after birth, which of the following nursing interventions is the highest priority?

    A. Obtaining glucose

    B. Giving the initial bath

    C. Giving the vitamin K injection

    D. Covering the newborn's head with a cap

8. A nurse is preparing to administer a vitamin K injection to a newborn. Which of the following is the best response by the nurse to the newborn's mother regarding why this medication is given?

    A. "Vitamin K assists with blood clotting."

    B. "Vitamin K assists the bowel in maturing."

    C. "Vitamin K is a preventative vaccination."

    D. "Vitamin K protects against excess fluid production."

9. When caring for a newborn's umbilical cord, a nurse should include which of the following nursing interventions?

    A. Cover the cord with petroleum jelly after bathing.

    B. Wash the cord with soap and water each day during a tub bath.

    C. Apply hydrogen peroxide to the cord with each diaper change.

    D. Keep the cord dry and clean with the diaper folded below it.

10. By keeping the nursery temperature warm and wrapping the newborn in warm blankets, the nurse is preventing which of the following types of heat loss?

    A. Conduction

    B. Radiation

    C. Convection

    D. Evaporation

11. Which of the following is appropriate when giving a newborn her first bath?

    A. Give an immersed tub bath.

    B. Use hexachlorophene soap.

    C. Use water and mild soap.

    D. Give it right after delivery.

12. The correct security measures that should be followed when bringing a newborn to the mother for breastfeeding include

    A. asking the mother to state her full name.

    B. looking at the name on the infant's bassinet.

    C. matching the mother's identification band with the newborn's.

    D. matching names on the bassinet and room number.

Chapter 20: Nursing Care of the Newborn

Application Exercises Answer Key

1. A nurse is instilling prophylactic eye treatment for ophthalmia neonatorum. Which of the following is the medication of choice to treat ophthalmia neonatorum?

> A. Gentamicin
>
> B. Nystatin
>
> **C. Erythromycin**
>
> D. Vitamin K

The medication of choice for ophthalmia neonatorum is erythromycin ophthalmic ointment 0.5%. This antibiotic is both bacteriostatic and bactericidal, thus providing prophylaxis against Neisseria gonorrhoeae and Chlamydia trachomatis. Gentamicin is an antibiotic also, but is not used for ophthalmia neonatorum. Nystatin is used for Candida albicans in oral yeast infections. Vitamin K is given to prevent hemorrhage in the neonate.

2. A nurse needs to maintain thermoregulation. What are the four methods of heat loss and what measures can the nurse use to avoid heat loss?

Heat loss occurs through four mechanisms. Conduction can be prevented by preheating the radiating warmer and linen, warming the stethoscope, and placing a paper towel over a scale before weighing the newborn. Convection can be prevented by placing the newborn's crib away from any air conditioning vents. Evaporation can be prevented by drying the newborn immediately after delivery and bathing. Radiation can be prevented by keeping the newborn and examining tables away from air conditioning vents and windows.

3. What is the single most important nursing measure that should be done to prevent newborn infection?

Handwashing is the single most important nursing intervention to prevent infection. The nurse must engage in a 3- to 5-min scrub from elbow to finger tips before entering the nursery and thereafter. Hands should be washed before and after contact with the newborn.

4. Why is it important to place an infant in a crib supine rather than prone?

Research studies have shown that the supine position dramatically decreases the incidence of sudden infant death syndrome in newborns (Hein & Petit, 2001; Pollack & Frohna 2002).

5. A newborn is born to a mother who is infected with hepatitis B. What treatment should this newborn receive?

If a newborn is born to a mother who is infected with hepatitis B, the newborn should receive the hepatitis B vaccine and hepatitis B immuno globulin vaccine. Both should be administered within 12 hr following birth. The hepatitis B vaccine induces protective antibodies in newborns who receive the recommended three doses. HBIG provides a high titer of antibody to hepatitis B surface antigen. The vaccine provides prophylaxis against infection of newborns born to mothers who carry or are infected with hepatitis B.

6. A newborn not completely dried immediately after delivery loses heat through which of the following mechanisms of heat loss?

       A. Conduction

       B. Convection

       C. Evaporation

       D. Radiation

Evaporation is the loss of heat that occurs when a liquid is converted to a vapor. In a newborn, heat loss by evaporation occurs as a result of vaporization of the moisture from the skin. Conduction is the loss of heat from the body surface area to cooler surfaces that the newborn may be in contact with. Convection is the flow of heat from the body surface area to cooler air. Radiation is the loss of heat to a cooler surface that is not in direct contact with the newborn.

7. When performing nursing care for a newborn after birth, which of the following nursing interventions is the highest priority?

      A. Obtaining glucose

      B. Giving the initial bath

      C. Giving the vitamin K injection

      D. Covering the newborn's head with a cap

Thermoregulation is a high priority in the stabilization of a newborn. Covering a newborn's head with a cap prevents cold stress due to excessive evaporative heat loss. A glucose test is not required right away unless there are risk factors. Initial baths aren't given until the newborn's temperature is stable. Vitamin K can be given immediately after birth, but is not as high a priority as the immediate stabilization of body temperature.

8. A nurse is preparing to administer a vitamin K injection to a newborn. Which of the following is the best response by the nurse to the newborn's mother regarding why this medication is given?

      A. "Vitamin K assists with blood clotting."

      B. "Vitamin K assists the bowel in maturing."

      C. "Vitamin K is a preventative vaccination."

      D. "Vitamin K protects against excess fluid production."

Vitamin K is deficient in a newborn because the colon is sterile. For vitamin K to be produced, there must be bacteria available. Once a newborn receives the first feeding, the bacteria will be produced. Until that point, a newborn is at risk of hemorrhagic disease. Vitamin K is required to activate clotting factors II, VII, IX, and X. Vitamin K does not assist the bowel to mature. Vitamin K is not part of the vaccinations that are administered. Vitamin K does not protect against excess fluid production.

9. When caring for a newborn's umbilical cord, a nurse should include which of the following nursing interventions?

      A. Cover the cord with petroleum jelly after bathing.

      B. Wash the cord with soap and water each day during a tub bath.

      C. Apply hydrogen peroxide to the cord with each diaper change.

      D. Keep the cord dry and clean with the diaper folded below it.

Keeping the cord dry and clean helps reduce infection and hastens drying. Folding the diaper below the cord prevents urine from the diaper penetrating the cord site. Petroleum jelly prevents the cord from drying and encourages infection. Newborns aren't given tub baths or completely immersed in water until the cord completely falls off. Triple dye and antibiotic ointment, not hydrogen peroxide, are applied to the cord site.

10. By keeping the nursery temperature warm and wrapping the newborn in warm blankets, the nurse is preventing which of the following types of heat loss?

      A. Conduction

      B. Radiation

      C. Convection

      D. Evaporation

Convection heat loss is the flow of heat from the body surface to cooler air. Conduction is the loss of heat from the body surface area to cooler surfaces in direct contact. Radiation is the loss of heat from the body surface area to cooler surfaces not in direct contact but in close proximity. Evaporation is the loss of heat that occurs when a liquid is converted to a vapor.

11. Which of the following is appropriate when giving a newborn her first bath?

      A. Give an immersed tub bath.

      B. Use hexachlorophene soap.

      C. Use water and mild soap.

      D. Give it right after delivery.

Only water and mild soap should be used to prevent drying out of the skin. Hexachlorophene soaps should be avoided because a newborn's neurological system can be damaged by them. Tub baths are delayed until the umbilical cord falls off. The initial bath is given when a newborn's temperature is stable.

12. The correct security measures that should be followed when bringing a newborn to the mother for breastfeeding include

      A. asking the mother to state her full name.

      B. looking at the name on the infant's bassinet.

      C. matching the mother's identification band with the newborn's.

      D. matching names on the bassinet and room number.

The mother, newborn, and significant other are identified by plastic identification wrist bands with permanent locks that must be cut to be removed. Identification bands should include the newborn's name, sex, date, and time of birth. Each time a newborn is taken to the parents, the identification band should be verified against the mother's identification band.

Unit 4   Newborn Care

Chapter 21:   Meeting the Nutritional Needs of Newborns
                Contributor: Linda S. Wood, MSN, RN

↻ NCLEX-RN® Connections:

Learning Objective: Review and apply knowledge within **"Meeting the Nutritional Needs of Newborns"** in readiness for performance of the following nursing activities as outlined by the NCLEX-RN® test plan:

Δ   Assist the client in meeting the nutritional needs of newborns.

📖 Key Points

Δ   Optimal growth and development during infancy is enhanced by **good nutrition**. Feeding the infant is a time for provision of nutrients and bonding between the mother and her infant. Whether the mother chooses to breast or bottle feed, nurses need to provide education and support.

Δ   Normal weight loss immediately after birth and weight gain with growth and development should be as follows:

Weight Loss/Gain
Loss of 5 to 10% immediately after birth (regain 10 to 14 days after birth)
Gain of 110 to 200 g/week for first 3 months

Δ   **Breastfeeding** is the optimal source of nutrition for newborns. Breastfeeding is recommended exclusively for the first 6 months of age by the American Academy of Pediatrics.

Δ   **Colostrum** is secreted from the mother's breasts during postpartum days 1 to 3 and contains the IgA immunoglobulin that provides passive immunity to the newborn.

Δ   **Formula feeding** can be a successful and adequate source of nutrition if the mother chooses not to breastfeed.

Δ   **Frequency of feedings** (beginning of one feeding to beginning of the next) is every 2 to 3 hr for breastfed infants and every 3 to 4 hr for formula fed infants. Parents should awaken the infant to feed at least every 3 hr during the day and at least every 4 hr during the night until the infant is feeding well and gaining weight adequately. Then, a feed-on-demand schedule may be followed.

Δ   Healthy newborns need a **fluid intake** of 100 to 140 mL/kg/24 hr. Newborns do not need to have water supplemented because they receive enough water from either breast milk or formula.

Δ   Adequate **caloric intake** is essential to provide energy for growth, digestion, physical activity, and maintenance of metabolic function. For the first 3 months the infant requires **110 kcal/kg/day**. From 3 to 6 months, the requirement decreases to **100 kcal/kg/day**. Both breast milk and formula provide **20 kcal/oz**.

Δ   **Carbohydrates should make up 40 to 50%** of the infant's total caloric intake. The most abundant carbohydrate in breast milk or formula is **lactose**.

Δ   At least **15%** of calories must come from **fat (triglycerides)**. The fat in human milk is easier to digest than fat in cow's milk. For that reason, the milk fat is removed and another fat such as corn oil is substituted.

Δ   For adequate growth and development to take place, a newborn must receive **2.2 g/kg of protein** per day.

Δ   All **vitamins** are contained in breast milk but have to be added to formulas. Vitamin D may be deficient in breast milk so supplementation may be necessary. Supplementation is recommended for breastfed infants who are dark-skinned with limited exposure to the sun and mothers who are vegetarians who exclude meat, fish, and dairy products.

Δ   The mineral content of commercial infant formula and breast milk is adequate with the exception of **iron and fluoride**.

   •   **Iron** is low in all forms of milk, but it is absorbed better from breast milk. Infants who are entirely breastfed for the first 6 months maintain adequate Hgb levels. Thereafter, they need to receive iron-fortified cereal and other foods rich in iron. Infants who are formula fed should receive iron-fortified infant formula until 12 months of age.

   •   **Fluoride** levels in breast milk and formulas are low. A fluoride supplement should be given to infants not receiving fluoridated water after 6 months of age.

Δ   **Solids** are **not introduced until 6 months** of age. If introduced too early, food allergies may develop.

Δ   **Nursing interventions** can help a new mother be successful in breastfeeding.

Δ   **Advantages of breastfeeding** – Parents should be presented with factual information about the nutritional and immunological needs of their newborn. The nurse should present information about both breastfeeding and bottle feeding in a nonjudgmental manner.

- Benefits of breastfeeding include:

    ◊ Reduces the risk of infection by providing IgA antibodies, lysozymes, leukocytes, macrophages, and lactoferrin that prevents infections.

    ◊ Promotes rapid brain growth due to large amounts of lactose.

    ◊ Provides protein and nitrogen for neurological cell building.

    ◊ Contains electrolytes and minerals.

    ◊ Easily digestible.

    ◊ Convenient and cheap.

    ◊ Improves newborn's ability to regulate calcium and phosphorus levels.

    ◊ Sucking associated with breastfeeding reduces dental problems.

    ◊ Colostrum provides IgA antibodies.

Key Factors

Δ Risk factors for **failure to thrive (infant)** can be related to ineffective feeding patterns of the infant or inadequate breastfeeding by the mother.

- **Newborn causes** include:

    ◊ Inadequate breastfeeding.

    ◊ Illness.

    ◊ Infection.

    ◊ Malabsorption.

    ◊ Other circumstances that increase newborn's energy needs *(For information, refer to Chapter 24, Discharge Teaching: Newborn Care).*

- **Maternal factors** include:

    ◊ Inadequate emptying of the breast.

    ◊ Pain with feeding.

    ◊ Inappropriate timing of feeding.

    ◊ Inadequate breast tissue.

    ◊ Maternal hemorrhage.

    ◊ Illness.

    ◊ Infections.

Assessments

Δ   **Monitor** the newborn **for adequate growth** and **weight gain**.

- **Weights** are done **daily** in the **newborn nursery** and then **at 2 weeks** of age for **breastfed** infants and **6 weeks** of age for **formula fed** infants. Growth is followed by placing the infant's weight on a growth chart. Adequate growth should be within the 10th to 90th percentile. Poor weight gain would be below 10% and too much weight gain would be above 90%.

- The infant's **length** and **head circumference** are also monitored closely.

Δ   **Assessment** of **newborn nutrition** begins during pregnancy and continues after birth by assessing the parents' attitudes and choices about their newborn's feeding. Breastfeeding is the preferred method. However, if the mother chooses not to breastfeed, she must not be made to feel guilty.

- **Newborn**

  ◊   Maturity level

  ◊   History of labor and delivery

  ◊   Birth trauma

  ◊   Maternal risk factors

  ◊   Congenital defects

  ◊   Physical stability

  ◊   State of alertness

  ◊   Presence of bowel sounds

- **Mother**

  ◊   Previous experience with breastfeeding

  ◊   Knowledge about breastfeeding

  ◊   Cultural factors

  ◊   Feelings about breastfeeding

  ◊   Physical features of breasts

  ◊   Physical/psychological readiness

  ◊   Support of family and significant others

Δ   **Assess** the **mother's ability** to **feed** her **infant**, whether by breast or bottle.

Δ   **Calculate the newborn's 24-hr intake**, if indicated, to assure adequate nutrition (1 oz is approximately equivalent to 30 mL).

NANDA Nursing Diagnoses

Δ   Health-seeking behaviors related to the infant's nutritional needs

Δ   Effective breastfeeding related to nursing interventions

Δ   Risk for ineffective breastfeeding related to deficient knowledge

Δ   Ineffective infant feeding patterns related to improper latching techniques

Δ   Imbalanced nutrition, less than body requirements (infant) related to difficulty feeding the infant

Nursing Interventions

Δ   Provide **client education** on **feeding-readiness cues exhibited by infants** and encourage the mother to begin feeding her infant upon cues rather than waiting until the infant is crying. Cues include:

- Hand-to-mouth or hand-to-hand movements.
- Sucking motions.
- Rooting.
- Mouthing.

Δ   **Nursing interventions** to promote successful **breastfeeding** include:

- Explaining breastfeeding techniques to the mother. Have the mother **wash her hands**, **get comfortable**, and **have fluids** to drink during breastfeeding.
- Explaining the **let-down reflex** (stimulation of maternal nipple releases oxytocin that causes the letdown of milk).
- Reassuring the client that **uterine cramps** are **normal** during breastfeeding, resulting **from oxytocin**.
- Expressing a few drops of **colostrum or milk** and **spreading it over** the **nipple** to lubricate the nipple and entice the infant.
- Showing the mother the **proper latch-on position**. Have the mother support the breast in one hand with the thumb on top and four fingers underneath and compress the breast. With the infant's mouth directly in front of the nipple, the infant can be stimulated to open its mouth by tickling the infant's lower lip with the tip of the nipple. The mother pulls the infant to the nipple with the infant's mouth covering part of the areola as well as the nipple.
- Explaining to the client that when her infant is latched on correctly, the infant's nose, cheeks, and chin will all be touching the breast.

- Showing the client how to **depress** the **breast tissue around** the **infant's nose** if necessary to create **breathing space** for the infant.

- Demonstrating the four **basic breastfeeding positions**: football, cradle or modified cradle, across the lap, and side-lying.

- Encouraging the mother to **breastfeed at least 15 min** or more **per breast** to ensure the newborn receives adequate fat and protein in rich hind milk.

- Explaining to the client that **newborns** will **nurse on demand**.

- Showing the mother how to insert a finger in the side of the infant's mouth to **break the suction** from the nipple **prior to removing** the **infant from** the **breast** to prevent nipple trauma.

- Showing the mother how to **burp** the infant in **between breasts**. The infant should be burped either over the shoulder or sitting upright with its chin supported. The parent should gently pat the newborn on the back to elicit a burp.

- Telling the mother to always **begin** the **next feeding with** the **breast** she stopped feeding the infant with in the previous feeding.

- Telling the mother how to tell if her newborn is receiving **adequate feeding** (**gaining weight, voiding 6 to 8 diapers a day**, and **contentness between feedings**).

- Explaining to the client that **loose, pale, yellow stools are normal with breastfeeding.**

- **Telling the client how to avoid nipple confusion** in the newborn by **not offering supplemental formula** feeding or pacifier.

- Telling the client to always **place** the **infant on his back** after feedings.

Δ **Nursing interventions** to promote successful **storage of breast milk** obtained by a breast pump:

- Inform the mother that breast milk can still be provided to the infant during periods of separation by using a **breast pump**.

  ◊ Breast pumps can be manual, electric, or battery-operated and pumped directly into a bottle or freezer bag.

  ◊ One or both breasts can be pumped, and suction is adjustable for comfort.

- Teach the parents that breast milk must be stored according to guidelines for proper containers, labeling, refrigerating, and freezing.

  ◊ Breast **milk** may be **safely stored** in the **refrigerator** for **up to 48 hr after expression** from the breast. Unused refrigerated breast milk should be discarded after 48 hr.

  ◊ Breast **milk** can be **stored** in the **freezer** for **up to 1 year.**

◊   **Thawing** the **milk** in the **refrigerator for 24 hr** is the best way to preserve the immunoglobulins present in the breast milk. It can also be thawed by holding the container **under running lukewarm water** or placing it in a **container of lukewarm water**. The bottle should be rotated often but not shaken when thawing in this manner.

◊   Thawing by **microwave** is **contraindicated** because it destroys some of the immune factors and lysozymes contained in the milk. Microwave thawing also leads to the development of uneven hot spots in the milk because of uneven heating which can burn the infant.

Δ   **Nursing interventions** to promote **successful bottle feeding** include:

- Teaching the parents how to prepare formula, bottles, and nipples.

- Teaching the parents about the different forms of formula (ready-to-feed, concentrated, and powder) and how to prepare each correctly.

- **Washing hands** and preparing bottles. Bottles can be washed in dishwater with hot soapy water or warm tap water.

- Teaching parents to wipe the lid clean on the concentrated can before opening it.

- Using tap water to mix concentrated or powder formula. If the water source is questionable, tap water should be boiled first.

- Instructing parents that prepared formula can be refrigerated for up to 48 hr.

- Teaching the parents to **check** the **flow of formula** from the bottle to assure it is not coming out too slow or too fast.

- Showing the parents how to **cradle** the **newborn** in their arms **in a semi-upright position**. The newborn should **not** be **placed in the supine position during bottle feeding** because of the danger of aspiration. Infants who bottle feed do best when **held close** and **at** a **45° angle**.

- Instructing the mother how to place the nipple on **top** of the **infant's tongue**.

- Keeping the **nipple filled** with **formula** to **prevent** the newborn from **swallowing** air.

- Always **holding** the **bottle** and **never propping it**.

- Newborns should be burped several times during a feeding, usually after each ½ to 1 oz of milk.

- **Placing** the **infant in a supine position** after feedings.

- Discarding any **unused formula** remaining in the bottle when the infant is finished feeding due to the possibility of **bacterial contamination**.

- Teaching the parents how to tell if their **newborn** is **being adequately fed (gaining weight, voiding 6 to 8 diapers per day**, and **contentness between feedings)**.

Complications and Nursing Implications

Δ   There may be **special considerations** when a newborn has difficulty receiving adequate nutrition. **Nursing interventions** can often help these newborns receive adequate nutrition.

- **Sleepy newborn**
    ◊   Unwrap the infant.
    ◊   Change the infant's diaper.
    ◊   Hold the infant upright and turn from side to side.
    ◊   Talk to the infant.
    ◊   Massage the infant's back, rub hands and feet.
    ◊   Apply a cool cloth to the infant's face.

- **Fussy newborn**
    ◊   Swaddle the infant.
    ◊   Hold the infant close, move, and rock gently.
    ◊   Reduce the infant's environmental stimuli.
    ◊   Place the infant skin to skin.

Δ   **Failure to thrive** is slow weight gain. A newborn usually falls below the 5th percentile on the growth chart.

- Breastfeeding newborns:
    ◊   Evaluate positioning and latch-on in breastfeeding.
    ◊   Massage the breast during feeding.

- Formula feeding newborns:
    ◊   Evaluate how much and how often the newborn is feeding.
    ◊   If the newborn is spitting up or vomiting a lot, the newborn may have an allergy or intolerance to cow-milk based formula and may require a switch to a soy-based formula.

Primary Reference:

Lowdermilk, D. L. & Perry, S. E. (2004). *Maternity & women's health care* (8th ed.). St. Louis, MO: Mosby.

Additional Resources:

NANDA International (2004). *NANDA nursing diagnoses: Definitions and classification 2005-2006.* Philadelphia: NANDA.

Pillitteri, A. (2003). *Maternal & child health nursing: Care of the childbearing and childrearing family.* Philadelphia: Lippincott, Williams, & Wilkins.

Springhouse (2003). *Maternal-neonatal nursing made incredibly easy!* Philadelphia: Lippincott, Williams, & Wilkins.

Chapter 21: Meeting the Nutritional Needs of Newborns

Application Exercises

Scenario: A newborn, whose weight is average for gestation, weighs 3.2 kg (7 lb) at birth. The mother plans to breastfeed.

1. Why is it important that the newborn breastfeed and receive the colostrum?

2. If the infant weighs 3.2 kg (7 lb), how many mL of fluid should the newborn receive in 24 hr?

3. How many kcal/kg should this newborn receive in 24 hr?

4. The mother asks the nurse, "How can I tell if my baby is receiving enough to eat?" What should the nurse tell the mother?

5. How often should the newborn be burped during breastfeeding?

6. A nurse is taking a newborn to her mother for her first breastfeeding. The mother tells the nurse that her breasts are small and she is concerned she will not be able to breastfeed. Which of the following statements by the nurse is most appropriate?

    A. "The size of your breasts does not affect your ability to breastfeed."
    B. "Your baby will probably have to be supplemented with formula."
    C. "It would be best to bottle feed so your baby receives adequate calories."
    D. "Drink lots of fluids so you can increase your milk production and breast size."

7. A nurse is giving instructions to a mother about how to breastfeed her newborn correctly. Which of the following actions by the mother indicates the need for additional teaching?

    A. The mother uses the thumb of her free hand to gently press the breast away from the newborn's nose.

    B. The mother inserts a finger in the side of the infant's mouth before removing the nipple from the newborn's mouth.

    C. The mother gently strokes the newborn's lips with her nipple when she is ready to breastfeed.

    D. The mother places a breast shield over her nipple before placing the nipple in the newborn's mouth.

8. Which of the following newborns is not adequately meeting nutritional needs?

    A. The infant who awakens during the night for feedings

    B. The infant who breastfeeds every 2 to 3 hr

    C. The infant who has two wet diapers a day

    D. The infant who has loose, pale, and yellow stools

9. A mother plans to use a concentrated formula at home. The nurse reviews formula preparation with the mother. Which of the following statements made by the mother indicates the need for additional teaching?

    A. "The formula must be used immediately after it is prepared."

    B. "Warm tap water can be used to dilute the concentrate."

    C. "The top of the can of formula must be wiped before opening."

    D. "Formula bottles can be washed in dishwater."

10. A nurse is teaching a group of new parents about proper techniques for bottle feeding. Which of the following instructions should the nurse provide?

    A. Burp the newborn at the end of the feeding.

    B. Hold the newborn close in a supine position.

    C. Keep the nipple full of formula throughout the feeding.

    D. Refrigerate any unused formula.

11. Six hours after admission to the nursery, a newborn is taken to his mother for his first feeding. The mother wants to bottle feed. The nurse reviews basic principles of bottle feeding with the mother. Which of the following observations by the nurse indicates that the mother has an incorrect understanding of the basic principles of bottle feeding?

   A. The mother burps the infant after each ½ to 1 ounce of formula taken.

   B. The mother places the newborn on its right side after feeding.

   C. The mother places the nipple on the tongue of the newborn.

   D. The mother places the newborn in a supine position during feeding.

12. A mother asks why it is important to keep the nipple full of formula when bottle feeding. The nurse explains that the nipple is always full of formula to

   A. prevent damaging the newborn's gums.

   B. keep the infant from getting too tired.

   C. keep the infant from regurgitating the formula.

   D. prevent the infant from swallowing air when sucking.

13. While listening to breastfeeding instructions, a new mother asks the nurse, "Why is colostrum so important for my baby?" The nurse explains that colostrum provides

   A. IgA.

   B. vitamin K.

   C. more iron.

   D. more fat.

14. How much weight is normal for a newborn to lose during the first 24 hr?

   A. None

   B. 5 to 10%

   C. 10 to 20%

   D. 15 to 20%

Chapter 21: Meeting the Nutritional Needs of Newborns

Application Exercises Answer Key

Scenario: A newborn, whose weight is average for gestation, weighs 3.2 kg (7 lb) at birth. The mother plans to breastfeed.

1. Why is it important that the newborn breastfeed and receive the colostrum?

    Colostrum is secreted during days 1 to 3 and contains the IgA immunoglobulin that provides passive immunity to the newborn.

2. If the infant weighs 3.2 kg (7 lb), how many mL of fluid should the newborn receive in 24 hr?

    A 3.2 kg (7 lb) newborn needs 320 to 448 mL per 24 hr of fluid (100 to 140 mL/kg/24 hr).

3. How many kcal/kg should this newborn receive in 24 hr?

    A 3.2 kg (7 lb) newborn will need 352 kcal/24 hr (110 kcal/kg/24 hr) during the first 3 months of age.

4. The mother asks the nurse, "How can I tell if my baby is receiving enough to eat?" What should the nurse tell the mother?

    A newborn is receiving adequate nutrition if the newborn is content between feedings, gains weight, and voids 6 to 8 diapers/day.

5. How often should the newborn be burped during breastfeeding?

    A newborn should be burped between breasts.

6. A nurse is taking a newborn to her mother for her first breastfeeding. The mother tells the nurse that her breasts are small and she is concerned she will not be able to breastfeed. Which of the following statements by the nurse is most appropriate?

> **A. "The size of your breasts does not affect your ability to breastfeed."**
> B. "Your baby will probably have to be supplemented with formula."
> C. "It would be best to bottle feed so your baby receives adequate calories."
> D. "Drink lots of fluids so you can increase your milk production and breast size."

Each breast consists of lobules that contain milk-secreting cells. The size of the breast is determined by the amount of adipose tissue, not the number of milk-secreting cells. Thus, the size of the woman's breast has nothing to do with her ability to breastfeed. The newborn should not be supplemented with formula as this will cause nipple confusion. There is no reason for the mother to bottle feed. Drinking adequate fluids will help with milk production, but this has no relationship to the size of the client's breast and the fact that breast size is irrelevant to successful breastfeeding.

7. A nurse is giving instructions to a mother about how to breastfeed her newborn correctly. Which of the following actions by the mother indicates the need for additional teaching?

> A. The mother uses the thumb of her free hand to gently press the breast away from the newborn's nose.
> B. The mother inserts a finger in the side of the infant's mouth before removing the nipple from the newborn's mouth.
> C. The mother gently strokes the newborn's lips with her nipple when she is ready to breastfeed.
> **D. The mother places a breast shield over her nipple before placing the nipple in the newborn's mouth.**

A breast shield is not routinely used for breastfeeding. A breast shield is worn when the nipples are flat or inverted or occasionally when the nipples are sore and cracked. All other techniques are appropriate for breastfeeding.

8. Which of the following newborns is not adequately meeting nutritional needs?

    A. The infant who awakens during the night for feedings

    B. The infant who breastfeeds every 2 to 3 hr

    C. The infant who has two wet diapers a day

    D. The infant who has loose, pale, and yellow stools

The newborn whose nutritional needs are not being met will have fewer than 6 to 8 wet diapers per day. The newborn is at risk for developing dehydration. It is normal for newborns to awake during the night for a feeding and to eat every 2 to 3 hr. Loose, pale, yellow stools are normal with breastfeeding.

9. A mother plans to use a concentrated formula at home. The nurse reviews formula preparation with the mother. Which of the following statements made by the mother indicates the need for additional teaching?

    A. "The formula must be used immediately after it is prepared."

    B. "Warm tap water can be used to dilute the concentrate."

    C. "The top of the can of formula must be wiped before opening."

    D. "Formula bottles can be washed in dishwater."

Prepared formula can be refrigerated up to 48 hr. Formula remaining in the bottle when the newborn has finished feeding should be discarded. Bottles can be washed in dishwater with hot soapy water or warm tap water. If the water source is questionable, tap water should be boiled first. Also, the lid of the formula can should be wiped before it is opened.

10. A nurse is teaching a group of new parents about proper techniques for bottle feeding. Which of the following instructions should the nurse provide?

    A. Burp the newborn at the end of the feeding.

    B. Hold the newborn close in a supine position.

    C. Keep the nipple full of formula throughout the feeding.

    D. Refrigerate any unused formula.

The nipple should always be kept full of formula to prevent the newborn from sucking in air during the feeding. The newborn should be burped after each ½ oz and the newborn should be cradled in a semi-upright position. Any unused formula should be discarded due to the possibility of bacterial contamination.

11. Six hours after admission to the nursery, a newborn is taken to his mother for his first feeding. The mother wants to bottle feed. The nurse reviews basic principles of bottle feeding with the mother. Which of the following observations by the nurse indicates that the mother has an incorrect understanding of the basic principles of bottle feeding?

A. The mother burps the infant after each ounce of formula taken.

B. The mother places the newborn on its right side after feeding.

C. The mother places the nipple on the tongue of the newborn.

D. The mother places the newborn in a supine position during feeding.

The newborn should not be placed in the supine position because of the danger of aspiration. Infants bottle feeding do best when held close and at a 45° angle. All other techniques are correct for bottle feeding the newborn.

12. A mother asks why it is important to keep the nipple full of formula when bottle feeding. The nurse explains that the nipple is always full of formula to

A. prevent damaging the newborn's gums.

B. keep the infant from getting too tired.

C. keep the infant from regurgitating the formula.

D. prevent the infant from swallowing air when sucking.

Positioning the bottle so the nipple remains full of formula throughout the feeding prevents the newborn from swallowing air. Keeping the nipple full of formula does not prevent damage to the newborn's gums nor will it prevent regurgitation. There is no indication that this technique prevents fatigue in the newborn either.

13. While listening to breastfeeding instructions, a new mother asks the nurse, "Why is colostrum so important for my baby?" The nurse explains that colostrum provides

A. IgA.

B. vitamin K.

C. more iron.

D. more fat.

Colostrum provides IgA, which is an immunoglobulin that provides passive immunity to the newborn. Vitamin K is produced in the colon once food is introduced into the newborn's gut. Additional fat or iron does not exist in colostrum.

14. How much weight is normal for a newborn to lose during the first 24 hr?

     A. None
     B. 5 to 10%
     C. 10 to 20%
     D. 15 to 20%

The normal weight loss after birth is 5 to 10%. Anything higher than that would put the newborn at risk for dehydration and failure to thrive. All newborns lose some weight after birth due to fluid loss.

Unit 4   Newborn Care

Chapter 22:   Circumcision
                Contributor: Linda S. Wood, MSN, RN

↻ NCLEX-RN® Connections:

Learning Objective: Review and apply knowledge within "**Circumcision**" in readiness for performance of the following nursing activities as outlined by the NCLEX-RN® test plan:

Δ   Assist and teach the client/family/significant others regarding newborn care following circumcision.

📖 Key Points

Δ   **Circumcision** is the **surgical removal** of the **foreskin** of the **penis.**

Δ   Circumcision is a personal choice made by the newborn's family for reasons of hygiene, religious conviction (e.g., Jewish male on eighth day after birth, tradition, culture, social norms). Parents should make a well-informed decision.

Δ   Contraindications for circumcision include newborns born with the congenital anomalies of **hypospadias** (abnormal positioning of urethra on ventral undersurface of the penis) and **epispadias** (urethral canal terminates on dorsum of penis) because the prepuce skin may be needed when the plastic surgeon repairs the defect.

Δ   Circumcision should not be done immediately following birth because the infant's level of vitamin K, which prevents hemorrhage, is at a low point and the neonate would be at risk for bleeding.

Δ   Another major reason circumcision is not done immediately after birth is because of the danger of cold stress.

Key Factors

Δ   The American Academy of Pediatrics does not recommend routine circumcision.

Δ   Advocates of circumcision state that circumcision promotes a penis with clean glans, minimizes the risk of phimosis later in life, and reduces the risk of penile cancer and cervical cancer in sexual partners.

Diagnostic and Therapeutic Procedures and Management

Δ   There are several surgical methods for removing the foreskin including the **Yellen, Mogen, and Gomco clamps, and Plastibell**.

Δ   Anesthesia is now mandatory for all circumcisions. **Types of anesthesia** include the ring block, dorsal penile nerve block, and topical anesthetic.

Δ   Yellen, Mogen, or Gomco clamp procedures

   • The primary care provider applies the Yellen, Mogen, or Gomco clamp to the penis, loosens the foreskin, and inserts the cone under the foreskin to provide a cutting surface for removal of the foreskin and to protect the penis.

   • The wound is covered with sterile petroleum gauze to prevent infection and control bleeding.

Δ   Plastibell procedure

   • The primary care provider slides the Plastibell device between the foreskin and the glans of the penis.

   • The provider ties a suture tightly around the foreskin at the coronal edge of the glans.

   • Foreskin distal to the suture becomes ischemic and atrophies.

   • After 5 to 8 days, the foreskin drops off with the Plastibell attached, leaving a clean, well-healed excision.

Nursing Assessments

Δ   Preprocedure, assess the infant for contraindications including:

   • Hypospadias or epispadias.

   • A history of bleeding tendencies in the family (hemophilia and clotting disorders).

   • Ambiguous genitalia (when the newborn has genitalia that may include both male and female characteristics).

   • An illness or an infection.

Δ   Postprocedure, assess for:

   • Bleeding every 15 min for the first hour and then every hour for 24 hr.

   • The first voiding.

NANDA Nursing Diagnoses

Δ   Risk for injury related to circumcision procedure

Δ   Acute pain related to surgical removal of prepuce

Δ   Risk for infection related to penile foreskin removal

Nursing Interventions

Δ   Preprocedure parent teaching:

- Explain the procedure to the parents and assuring them that an anesthetic will be administered to minimize pain.

- Explain that the newborn will not be able to be bottle feed for up 4 hr prior to the procedure to prevent vomiting and aspiration. Breastfed infants may nurse up until the procedure.

- Explain that the newborn will need to be restrained on a special board during the procedure.

Δ   A signed consent form should be on the newborn's chart prior to the procedure.

Δ   Gather and prepare supplies.

Δ   Assist with procedure by:

- Placing the newborn on the restraining board and restraining the newborn's arms and legs. Do not leave the newborn unattended.

- Assisting the primary care provider as needed and comforting the newborn as needed.

- Documenting in the nurse's notes:

    ◊   Circumcision type, date, and time.

    ◊   Parent teaching provided.

    ◊   Any excessive bleeding.

    ◊   Time newborn urinates before discharge.

Δ   Postprocedure care:

- Remove the newborn from the restraining board.

- Check the newborn for bleeding.

- Fan fold diapers to prevent pressure on the circumcised area.

Δ   Postprocedure parent teaching:

- Teach the parents to keep the area clean. Change the infant's diaper at least every 4 hr and clean the penis with warm water with each diaper change. With clamp procedures, apply petroleum jelly with each diaper change for at least 24 hr after the circumcision to keep the diaper from adhering to the penis. The diaper should be fan folded to prevent pressure on the circumcised area.

- Avoid wrapping the penis in tight gauze, which can impair circulation to the glans.

- A tub bath should not be given until the circumcision is completely healed. Until then, warm water should be gently trickled over the penis.

- Notify the primary care provider if there is any redness, discharge, swelling, strong odor, tenderness, decrease in urination, or excessive crying from the infant.

- Tell the parents a film of yellowish mucus may form over the glans by day 2 and it is important not to wash this off.

- Teach the parents to avoid using premoistened towelettes to clean the penis because they contain alcohol.

- Inform the parents that the newborn may be fussy or may sleep for several hours after the circumcision.

- Inform the parents that the circumcision will heal completely within a couple of weeks.

Complications and Nursing Management

Δ   Hemorrhage

- Monitor for **bleeding.**

- Provide gentle pressure using 4 x 4 gauze. Gelfoam powder or a sponge may be applied to stop bleeding. If bleeding persists, notify the primary care provider that a blood vessel may need to be ligated. Have a nurse continue to hold pressure until the primary care provider arrives while another nurse prepares the circumcision tray and suture material.

Δ   Cold stress/hypoglycemia

- Monitor for **excessive loss of heat** resulting in increased respirations and lowered body temperature.

- Provide a heat source during the procedure (heat lamp or radiant warmer) and swaddle and feed the newborn as soon as the procedure is over.

   Δ   Other complications

   • Advise the parents to monitor for **other complications** (e.g., **infection, urethral fistula, delayed healing** and **scarring, fibrous bands** that will likely not be seen until after discharge if they occur).

   • Provide adequate discharge instructions to the parents about signs and symptoms to observe for and how to report them to the primary care provider.

Primary Reference:

Lowdermilk, D. L. & Perry, S. E. (2004). *Maternity & women's health care* (8th ed.). St. Louis, MO: Mosby.

Additional Resources:

NANDA International (2004). *NANDA nursing diagnoses: Definitions and classification 2005-2006.* Philadelphia: NANDA.

Pillitteri, A. (2003). *Maternal & child health nursing: Care of the childbearing and childrearing family* (5th ed.). Philadelphia: Lippincott.

Springhouse (2003). *Maternal-Neonatal nursing made incredibly easy!* (1st ed.). Philadelphia: Lippincott, Williams, & Wilkins.

Chapter 22: Circumcision

Application Exercises

1. A newborn is being discharged 3 hr after a circumcision. The nurse instructs the parents about the action they should take first if they see active bleeding from the circumcised area. The nurse tells them to

        A. notify the primary care provider.

        B. apply gentle pressure with sterile gauze.

        C. fan-fold the infant's diaper.

        D. wrap the infant's penis with gauze.

2. A parent has been given instructions about care of a newborn following circumcision. Which of the following statements, if made by the parent, indicates a need for further clarification?

        A. "His circumcision will heal completely within a couple of weeks."

        B. "I do not need to remove the yellow exudate that will form."

        C. "I will clean his penis with each diaper change."

        D. "I will give him a tub bath within a couple of days."

3. A nurse is assessing an infant immediately following circumcision and notes that the circumcised area is red with a small amount of bloody drainage. Which of the following is the most appropriate nursing action?

        A. Document the findings.

        B. Contact the primary care provider.

        C. Reassess in 4 hr.

        D. Reinforce the dressing.

4. Two days after a circumcision, a nurse notes yellow exudate around the head of a newborn's penis. Which of the following is the most appropriate nursing intervention?

        A. Leave the area alone as this is a normal finding.

        B. Report the finding to the primary care provider and document it.

        C. Take the newborn's temperature because an infection is suspected.

        D. Try to remove the exudate with a warm washcloth.

5. Twenty-four hours after delivery, and just prior to discharge, an infant is about to undergo an elective circumcision. He has not been fed for several hours and is restrained on a circumcision board. The procedure will be done using a Gomco clamp. The nursery nurse will provide care for the infant after the circumcision and prior to discharge. Identify the priority nursing intervention that should be included in the infant's post circumcision care.

6. Why is a circumcision contraindicated in a male newborn with hypospadias or epispadias?

7. Which of the following statements made by a parent about caring for her son's circumcision indicates an understanding of the nurse's teaching?

    A. "I will cleanse the penis by squeezing warm water from a clean washcloth over it."

    B. "I will gently brush away any yellow crusts that form around the incision."

    C. "I will thoroughly cleanse my baby's penis if it has a foul odor."

    D. "I will wrap my baby's penis snugly with gauze to stop any bleeding."

8. A newborn has just been circumcised using a clamp procedure. Which of the following nursing interventions is part of the initial care of a circumcised neonate?

    A. Apply alcohol to the site.

    B. Keep the newborn in the prone position.

    C. Apply petroleum gauze to the site for 24 hr.

    D. Avoid changing the infant's diaper unless absolutely needed.

Chapter 22: Circumcision

Application Exercises Answer Key

1. A newborn is being discharged 3 hr after a circumcision. The nurse instructs the parents about the action they should take first if they see active bleeding from the circumcised area. The nurse tells them to

>A. notify the primary care provider.
>**B. apply gentle pressure with sterile gauze.**
>C. fan-fold the infant's diaper.
>D. wrap the infant's penis with gauze.

Applying gentle pressure to the wound should stop the bleeding. If the parents cannot control the bleeding with this measure, they must notify the primary care provider. Fan-folding the diaper reduces pressure on the penis, but it will not stop excessive bleeding after circumcision. Wrapping the penis in gauze will not stop bleeding unless it is wrapped tightly, which would be unsafe because pressure from wrapped gauze could impair circulation to the glans.

2. A parent has been given instructions about care of a newborn following circumcision. Which of the following statements, if made by the parent, indicates a need for further clarification?

>A. "His circumcision will heal completely within a couple of weeks."
>B. "I do not need to remove the yellow exudate that will form."
>C. "I will clean his penis with each diaper change."
>**D. "I will give him a tub bath within a couple of days."**

A tub bath should not be given until the circumcision is completely healed. All other answers show that the parent has a good understanding of the information taught.

3. A nurse is assessing an infant immediately following circumcision and notes that the circumcised area is red with a small amount of bloody drainage. Which of the following is the most appropriate nursing action?

    A. Document the findings.

    B. Contact the primary care provider.

    C. Reassess in 4 hr.

    D. Reinforce the dressing.

Document the finding as part of the normal healing process. There is no need to notify the primary care provider at this time, apply pressure, or reinforce the dressing. The circumcision should be assessed ever 15 min for the first hour and at least every hr for the first 12 hr.

4. Two days after a circumcision, a nurse notes yellow exudate around the head of a newborn's penis. Which of the following is the most appropriate nursing intervention?

    A. Leave the area alone as this is a normal finding.

    B. Report the finding to the primary care provider and document it.

    C. Take the newborn's temperature because an infection is suspected.

    D. Try to remove the exudate with a warm washcloth.

The yellow-white exudate is part of the granulation process and is a normal finding for a healing penis after a circumcision. The primary care provider does not need to be notified. There is no indication of an infection. The exudate should not be removed.

5. Twenty-four hours after delivery, and just prior to discharge, an infant is about to undergo an elective circumcision. He has not been fed for several hours and is restrained on a circumcision board. The procedure will be done using a Gomco clamp. The nursery nurse will provide care for the infant after the circumcision and prior to discharge. Identify the priority nursing intervention that should be included in the infant's post circumcision care.

Observe for bleeding by conducting checks every 15 min for 1 hr and then every hour for at least 12 hr.

6. Why is a circumcision contraindicated in a male newborn with hypospadias or epispadias?

In hypospadias and epispadias, the urethra is located somewhere other than the tip of the urethra, and the foreskin is needed for plastic surgery to repair the defect.

7. Which of the following statements made by a parent about caring for her son's circumcision indicates an understanding of the nurse's teaching?

> **A. "I will cleanse the penis by squeezing warm water from a clean washcloth over it."**
> B. "I will gently brush away any yellow crusts that form around the incision."
> C. "I will thoroughly cleanse my baby's penis if it has a foul odor."
> D. "I will wrap my baby's penis snugly with gauze to stop any bleeding."

The penis should be cleansed by allowing warm water to gently trickle over it. Wrapping the penis in gauze will not stop bleeding unless it is wrapped tightly, which would be unsafe because pressure from wrapped gauze could impair circulation to the glans. The yellow crust should not be cleansed away but allowed to fall away on its own. A foul odor or discharge is a sign of infection and should be reported to the primary care provider.

8. A newborn has just been circumcised using a clamp procedure. Which of the following nursing interventions is part of the initial care of a circumcised neonate?

> A. Apply alcohol to the site.
> B. Keep the newborn in the prone position.
> **C. Apply petroleum gauze to the site for 24 hr.**
> D. Avoid changing the infant's diaper unless absolutely needed.

Petroleum gauze is applied to the site for 24 hr to prevent the skin edges from sticking to the diaper. Newborns should never be placed prone for any reason. Diapers are changed more frequently to inspect the site. Alcohol is contraindicated for circumcision care due to the fresh wound.

Unit 4   Newborn Care

Chapter 23:   Assessment and Management of Newborn Complications
                Contributor: Linda S. Wood, MSN, RN

↻ NCLEX-RN® Connections:

> **Learning Objective**: Review and apply knowledge within "**Assessment and Management of Newborn Complications**" in readiness for performance of the following nursing activities as outlined by the NCLEX-RN® test plan:
>
> Δ   Assess the client for symptoms of newborn complications.
>
> Δ   Plan and provide care for the client who is experiencing newborn complications.

Newborn Complication: Preterm Infant

📖 Key Points

Δ   A **preterm infant** is one who is born after 20 weeks gestation and before the completion of 37 weeks gestation.

Δ   **Preterm newborns** are at **risk** for a **variety of complications** due to **immature organ systems.** The degree of complications depends on gestational age. The closer the newborn is to 40 weeks gestation, the less the chances are for complications.

•   **Respiratory distress syndrome (RDS)** – decreased surfactant in the alveoli regardless of birth weight.

•   **Bronchopulmonary dysplasia (BPD)** – causes the lungs to become stiff and noncompliant, requiring an infant to be placed on mechanical ventilation and oxygen. It is sometimes difficult to remove the infant from ventilation and oxygen after initial placement.

•   **Aspiration** – a result of the premature infant not having an intact gag reflex or the ability to effectively suck or swallow.

•   **Apnea of prematurity** – a result of immature neurological and chemical mechanisms.

•   **Intraventricular hemorrhage** – bleeding in or around the ventricles of the brain.

- **Retinopathy of prematurity** – disease caused by abnormal growth of retinal blood vessels and is a complication associated with oxygen administration to the neonate. It can cause mild to severe eye and vision problems.

- **Patent ductus arteriosus (PDA)** – occurs when the ductus arteriosus reopens after birth due to neonatal hypoxia.

- **Necrotizing enterocolitis (NEC)** – an inflammatory disease of the gastrointestinal mucosa due to ischemia. NEC results in necrosis and perforation of the bowel. Short gut syndrome may be the result secondary to removal of most or part of the small intestine due to necrosis.

- **Additional complications** include infection, hyperbilirubinemia, anemia, hypoglycemia, and delayed growth and development.

Key Factors

Δ **Preterm births** can be attributed to many **causes** including:

- Gestational hypertension.
- Multiple pregnancies.
- Adolescent pregnancy.
- Lack of prenatal care.
- Substance abuse.
- Smoking.
- Previous history of preterm delivery.
- Abnormalities of the uterus.
- Cervical incompetence.
- Premature rupture of the membranes (PROM).
- Placenta previa.

Diagnostic and Therapeutic Procedures and Nursing Interventions

Δ **Tests** are performed to **monitor** for **or treat** the many **complications** of preterm birth.

- Complete blood count (CBC) shows decreased hemoglobin and hematocrit as a result of the slow production of red blood cells
- Urinalysis and specific gravity
- Increased prothrombin time and partial thromboplastin time with an increased tendency to bleed
- Chest x-ray

- Arterial blood gas (ABG)

- Head ultrasounds

- Echocardiography

- Eye exams

- Serum glucose

- Calcium

- Bilirubin

Nursing Assessments

Δ   Monitor for **signs and symptoms** of a **preterm infant**.

- **Ballard assessment** shows a physical and neurological assessment totaling less than 37 weeks gestation

- **Periodic breathing** consists of 5 to 10 sec respiratory pauses, followed by 10 to 15 sec compensatory rapid respirations

- Signs of increased respiratory effort and/or respiratory distress

- Apnea (pause in respirations longer than 10 to 15 sec)

- Low birth weight

- **Minimal subcutaneous fat deposits**

- Head large in comparison to body

- Wrinkled features

- **Skin** that is thin, smooth, shiny, and may be translucent

- Veins clearly visible under thin, transparent epidermis

- **Lanugo** over the body

- **Soft, pliable ear cartilage**

- **Minimal creases** in the **soles** and **palms**

- Skull and rib cage feel soft

- Closed eyes if 22 to 24 weeks gestation

- **Few scrotal rugae**

- **Undescended testes**

- **Prominent labia** and **clitoris**

- **Flat areola without breast buds**

- Weak grasp reflex

- **Heels fully movable to** the **ears, posture extended and frog-like**

- **Inability to coordinate suck and swallow,** and a weak or absent gag, suck, and cough reflex; weak swallow

- **Hypotonic muscles**, decreased level of activity, weak cry for more than 24 hr

- Lethargy, tachycardia, and poor weight gain

- Signs of infection

Δ   Observe for **signs** of **dehydration or overhydration** (resulting from IV nutrition and fluid administration).

- **Dehydration**

  ◊   Urine output less than 1 mL/kg/hr

  ◊   Urine specific gravity more than 1.015

  ◊   Weight loss

  ◊   Dry mucous membranes

  ◊   Poor skin turgor

  ◊   Depressed fontanel

- **Overhydration**

  ◊   Urine output greater than 3 mL/kg/hr

  ◊   Urine specific gravity less than 1.001

  ◊   Edema

  ◊   Increased weight gain

  ◊   Rales

  ◊   Intake greater than output

Δ   **Assessments** for **premature infants** include:

- Performing rapid initial assessment.

- Monitoring the infant's vital signs and temperature.

- Observing for complications of prematurity.

- Assessing the infant's ability to consume and digest nutrients. Before a premature infant can feed by breast or nipple, the infant must have an intact gag reflex and be able to suck and swallow to prevent aspiration.

- Monitoring the infant's intake and output.

- Monitoring elimination patterns consisting of frequency, amount, color, and consistency.

- Monitoring the infant for weight and fluid loss as well as measuring and recording the infant's weight daily.

- Monitoring for bleeding from puncture sites and the gastrointestinal tract.

NANDA Nursing Diagnoses

Δ   Ineffective airway clearance related to neuromuscular dysfunction

Δ   Excess fluid volume related to intravenous nutrition

Δ   Sudden infant death syndrome related to prematurity of infant

Δ   Ineffective thermoregulation related to insufficient subcutaneous body fat

Δ   Risk for infection related to immature immune system

Δ   Risk for disorganized infant behavior related to prematurity of infant

Nursing Interventions

Δ   **Goals** include **meeting** the **infant's growth** and **development needs** and **anticipating** and **managing associated complications** such as respiratory distress syndrome and sepsis.

Δ   The **main priority** in **treating preterm newborns** is **supporting** the **cardiac** and **respiratory systems** as needed. Most preterm infants are cared for in a neonatal intensive care unit (NICU). Meticulous care and observation in the NICU is necessary until the newborn can receive oral feedings, maintain body temperature, and weighs approximately 2 kg (4.4 lb).

- Perform **resuscitative measures** if needed.

- Ensure **thermoregulation** (neutral thermal environment) to maintain the premature infant's body temperature

- Administer **respiratory support measures** such as surfactant and/or oxygen administration.

- Administer **parental or enteral nutrition and fluids** as prescribed (most premature infants less than 34 weeks will receive fluids either by IV or gavage feedings).

- Administer **medications** as prescribed.

- **Minimize stimulation**. Cluster nursing care. Touch the newborn very smoothly and lightly. Keep lighting dim and noise levels reduced.

- **Position** the infant in **neutral flexion** with **the extremities close to the body** to conserve body heat. **Prone and side-lying positions are preferred** to supine with body containment using blanket rolls, swaddling, and secure holding to provide secure boundaries. Prone position encourages flexion of the extremities.

- Provide for **non-nutritive sucking** such as using a pacifier while gavage feeding.

- Protect against infection.

- Keep parents informed and educated about the care of their preterm newborn.

Newborn Complication: Respiratory Distress Syndrome (RDS)

 Key Points

Δ **Respiratory distress syndrome (RDS)** occurs as a result of **surfactant deficiency** in the lungs and is characterized by **poor gas exchange** and **ventilatory failure**.

Δ **Surfactant** is a phospholipid that **assists** in **alveoli expansion.** Surfactant keeps alveoli from collapsing and allows gas exchange to occur.

Δ **Atelectasis** (collapsing of a portion of lung) **increases** the **work of breathing**. As a result, respiratory acidosis and hypoxemia can develop.

Δ **Birth weight alone** is **not** an **indicator** of **fetal lung maturity**.

Δ **Complications** from **RDS** are **related to oxygen therapy** and **mechanical ventilation**.

- Pneumothorax

- Pneumomediastinum

- Retinopathy of prematurity

- Bronchopulmonary dysplasia

- Infection

- Intraventricular hemorrhage

Key Factors

Δ **Risk factors** that contribute to **RDS** include:

- **Decreased gestational age** (preterm).

- Perinatal asphyxia (e.g., meconium staining, cord prolapse, and nuchal cord).

- Maternal diabetes.

- Premature rupture of membranes.

- Maternal use of barbiturates or narcotics close to birth.

- Maternal hypotension.

- Cesarean birth without labor.

- Hydrops fetalis (massive edema of the fetus caused by hyperbilirubinemia).

- Maternal bleeding during the third trimester.

Diagnostic and Therapeutic Procedures and Nursing Interventions

Δ   Newborns diagnosed with **RDS** require specific tests to evaluate their lung maturity, ability to exchange gases, and complications.

Δ   **ABGs** reveal **hypercapnia** (excess of carbon dioxide in the blood) and **respiratory or mixed acidosis.**

Δ   Chest x-ray

Δ   Culture and sensitivity of the blood, urine, and cerebrospinal fluid

Δ   Blood glucose and serum calcium

Nursing Assessments

Δ   Monitor for **signs** and **symptoms** of **RDS.**

- Increased respiratory rate greater than 60/min (tachypnea)

- Intercostal and substernal retractions

- Labored breathing

- Fine rales on auscultation

- Nasal flaring

- Expiratory grunting

- Cyanosis

- As RDS worsens, the infant may become unresponsive, flaccid, and apneic, with decreased breath sounds.

Δ   **Assessment** for **RDS** includes:

- Monitoring pulse oximetry.

- Monitoring nutrition.

- Monitoring vital signs closely.

- Monitoring IV.

NANDA Nursing Diagnoses

△ Impaired gas exchange related to deficient surfactant or underdeveloped alveoli

△ Risk for impaired parent-infant attachment related to RDS of infant requiring medical interventions

△ Impaired spontaneous ventilation related to decreased surfactant levels in the infant's alveoli

△ Dysfunctional ventilatory weaning response related to inability of the infant to breathe and/or complications associated with treatment of the disease

△ Ineffective cardiovascular tissue perfusion related to RDS

Nursing Interventions

△ **Factors that can accelerate lung maturation in the fetus while in utero** include increased gestational age, intrauterine stress, exogenous steroid use, and ruptured membranes.

△ **Nursing interventions** for **RDS** in the infant are mostly supportive.

• **Suction** the infant's mouth, trachea, and nose as needed.

• Maintain **thermoregulation**.

• Administer **medications** as prescribed (e.g., exogenous surfactant in prematurity, naloxone [Narcan] in maternal narcotic use).

• Provide **mouth** and **skin care**.

• **Correct respiratory acidosis** by ventilatory support.

• **Correct metabolic acidosis** by administering sodium bicarbonate.

• Maintain **adequate oxygenation**, prevent lactic acidosis, and avoid toxic effects of oxygen.

• **Decrease stimuli**.

• Offer emotional support to the parents.

Newborn Complication: Postterm Infant

 Key Points

△ **A postterm infant** is one who is born after the completion of 42 weeks of gestation. Postmaturity of the infant can be associated with either of the following:

- **Dysmaturity** from **placental degeneration** and **uteroplacental insufficiency** (placenta functions effectively for only 40 weeks) resulting in chronic **fetal hypoxia** and fetal distress in utero. The fetal response is **polycythemia, meconium aspiration,** and neonatal respiratory problems. Perinatal mortality is higher due to increased oxygen demands during labor not being met by the insufficient placenta.

- **Continued growth of the fetus in utero** because the placenta continues to function effectively and the infant becomes large for gestational age at birth. This leads to a difficult delivery, **cephalopelvic disproportion**, as well as high insulin reserves and insufficient glucose reserves at birth. The neonatal response can be **birth trauma**, perinatal asphyxia, a clavicle fracture, seizures, **hypoglycemia**, and temperature instability (cold stress).

Δ   A **postmature infant** may be either **small for gestational age (SGA) or large for gestational age (LGA)** depending on how well the placenta functions during the last weeks of the pregnancy.

Δ   Postmature infants have an **increased risk for aspirating the meconium** passed by the fetus in utero.

Δ   **Persistent pulmonary hypertension (persistent fetal circulation)** is a complication that can result from meconium aspiration. There is an interference in the transition from fetal to neonatal circulation, and the ductus arteriosus (connecting main pulmonary artery and the aorta) and foramen ovale (shunt between the right and left atria) remain open and fetal pathways of blood flow continue.

Key Factors

Δ   In most cases, the **cause** of an **infant** going **postterm** is **unknown**, but there is a **higher incidence** in **first pregnancies** and in **women** who have had a **previous postterm pregnancy**.

Diagnostic and Therapeutic Procedures and Nursing Interventions

Δ   Cesarean delivery

Δ   Chest x-ray to rule out meconium aspiration syndrome

Δ   Blood glucose levels to monitor for hypoglycemia

Δ   Arterial blood gases secondary to chronic hypoxia in utero due to placental insufficiency

Δ   Complete blood count may show polycythemia from decreased oxygenation in utero

Δ   Hematocrit elevated from polycythemia and dehydration

Nursing Assessments

Δ   Monitor **signs** and **symptoms** of **postterm infant.**

- Wasted appearance, **thin** with **loose skin**, having used some of the subcutaneous fat

- **Peeling, cracked, and dry skin**; leathery from decrease in protective vernix and amniotic fluid

- Long, thin body

- **Meconium** staining of fingernails

- **Hair** and **nails** may be **long**

- May demonstrate **more alertness** similar to a 2-week-old infant

- May have difficulty establishing respirations secondary to meconium aspiration

- Signs and symptoms of **hypoglycemia** due to insufficient stores of glycogen

- Signs and symptoms of **cold stress**

- Neurological symptoms that become apparent with the development of fine motor skills

- **Macrosomia**

Δ   **Nursing assessment** of the **postterm infant** includes:

- Observing for birth injury or trauma.

- Respiratory status.

- Reflexes.

- Monitoring vital signs and temperature.

- Monitoring intravenous fluids.

NANDA Nursing Diagnoses

Δ   Ineffective airway clearance related to meconium aspiration

Δ   Risk for aspiration related to the presence of meconium

Δ   Ineffective thermoregulation related to decreased subcutaneous fat

Nursing Interventions

Δ   **Nursing interventions** for the **postterm infant** include:

- Assisting with **surfactant lavages** during delivery to prevent meconium aspiration.

- **Suctioning meconium** from the neonate's mouth and nares before the first breath.

- Using mechanical **ventilation** if necessary.

- Administering **oxygen** as prescribed.

- Administering **intravenous fluids.**

- Preparing and/or assisting with **exchange transfusion** if hematocrit is high.

- Providing **thermoregulation** in an **incubator** to avoid cold stress.

- Providing early feedings to **avoid hypoglycemia.**

- Identifying and **treating** any **birth injuries.**

Newborn Complication: Large for Gestational Age Infant (LGA)/Macrosomic

Key Points

◊ **Large for gestational age (LGA)** is a neonate whose weight is **above the 90ᵗʰ percentile** or **weighing more than 4,000 g (8 lb, 12 oz)**. LGA neonates may be preterm, postterm, or full term. LGA does not necessarily mean postmature.

◊ **Macrosomic infants** are at **risk for birth injuries** (e.g., **clavicle fracture** or a **cesarean birth, hypoglycemia, polycythemia**).

◊ Uncontrolled **hyperglycemia** during pregnancy (leading risk factor for LGA) can lead to **congenital defects** with the most common being congenital heart defects, tracheoesophageal fistula, and central nervous system anomalies.

Key Factors

Δ **Contributing factors** of an **LGA** infant include:

- **Postterm infants.**

- **Maternal diabetes** during pregnancy. High glucose levels stimulate continued insulin production by the fetus.

- Fetal disorder of transposition of the great vessels.

- Genetic factors.

- Obesity.

- Multiparous mother.

Diagnostic and Therapeutic Procedures and Nursing Interventions

Δ **Cesarean** delivery if necessary

Δ **Chest x-ray** to rule out meconium aspiration syndrome

Δ **Blood glucose levels** to monitor closely for hypoglycemia (less than 40 mg/dL)

Δ Arterial blood gases may be prescribed due to chronic hypoxia in utero secondary to placental insufficiency

Δ CBC shows **polycythemia** (hematocrit greater than 65%) from in utero hypoxia

Δ **Hyperbilirubinemia** resulting from polycythemia as excessive red blood cells break down after birth

Δ Hypocalcemia may result in response to a long and difficult birth

Nursing Assessments

Δ Monitor LGA infants for:

- **Weight above 90th percentile (4,000 g).**

- **Plump** and **full-faced** (cushingoid appearance) from increased subcutaneous fat.

- Signs of **hypoxia.**

- **Birth trauma** (e.g., fractures, intracranial hemorrhage, and central nervous system injury).

- Sluggishness, **hypotonic muscles**, and hypoactivity.

- **Tremors** from **hypocalcemia.**

- Signs and symptoms of **hypoglycemia.**

- Signs and symptoms of respiratory distress from immature lungs or meconium aspiration.

Δ Nursing assessment for LGA infants include:

- Observing for injury.

- Reflexes.

- Early and frequent glucose levels.

- Monitoring vital signs and temperature.

- Auscultating lung sounds.

NANDA Nursing Diagnoses

Δ   Risk for injury such as a clavicle fracture related to birth trauma

Δ   Risk for peripheral neurovascular dysfunction related to injury sustained during birth

Δ   Impaired physical mobility related to paralysis of facial or brachial nerve sustained during birth injury

Δ   Ineffective tissue perfusion related to hypoglycemia

Nursing Interventions

Δ   **Nursing interventions** for an **LGA** infant include:

- Obtaining early and frequent **heel sticks** (glucose testing).

- Providing **early feedings** or **intravenous therapy** to **maintain normal glucose** levels.

- **Thermoregulation** with incubator care.

- Administering surfactant by endotracheal tube if indicated.

- Identifying and treating any birth injuries.

Newborn Complication: Hypoglycemia

 Key Points

Δ   **Hypoglycemia** is a serum glucose level of **less than 40 mg/dL**. Routine assessment of all newborns, especially LGA infants, should include observing for symptoms of hypoglycemia.

Δ   **Hypoglycemia** – differs for the preterm and term newborn. Hypoglycemia occurring in the first 3 days of life in the term newborn is defined as a blood glucose level of < 40 mg/dL. In the preterm newborn, hypoglycemia is defined as the blood glucose level of < 25 mg/dL.

Δ   **Untreated hypoglycemia** can result in **mental retardation**.

Key Factors

Δ   Maternal diabetes

Δ   Preterm infant

Δ   LGA

Δ   Stress at birth such as cold stress and asphyxia

Δ   Maternal epidural anesthesia

Diagnostic and Therapeutic Procedures and Nursing Interventions

Δ   Two consecutive low plasma glucose levels less than 40 mg/dL in the term infant, less than 25 mg/dL in the preterm infant

 Nursing Assessments

Δ   Monitor for **signs** and **symptoms** of **hypoglycemia**.

- Poor feeding

- Jitteriness/tremors

- Hypothermia

- Diaphoresis

- Weak shrill cry

- Lethargy

- Flaccid muscle tone

- Seizures/coma

Δ   **Nursing assessments** for **hypoglycemia** include:

- Monitoring blood glucose level closely.

- Monitoring IV if unable to orally feed.

- Monitoring for signs of hypoglycemia.

- Monitoring vital signs and temperature.

NANDA Nursing Diagnoses

Δ   Disproportionate growth of the neonate related to maternal diabetes

Δ   Imbalanced nutrition: Less than body requirements related to poor feeding

Δ   Risk for injury related to central nervous system complications of hypoglycemia

Nursing Interventions

Δ **Nursing interventions** for **hypoglycemia** include:

- Obtaining blood per **heel stick** for glucose monitoring.

- Frequent oral and/or gavage feedings or continuos parenteral **nutrition** is provided early after birth to treat hypoglycemia (untreated hypoglycemia can lead to seizures, brain damage, and death).

Newborn Complication: Small for Gestational Age Infant (SGA)/Intrauterine Growth Restriction (IUGR)

Key Points

Δ **Small for gestational age (SGA)** describes an infant whose birth weight is **at or below the 10th percentile**.

Δ **Common complications** of **SGA** infants are perinatal asphyxia, meconium aspiration, hypoglycemia, polycythemia, and instability of body temperature.

Key Factors

Δ **Factors** that **contribute** to a newborn being **SGA** include:

- Congenital or chromosomal anomalies.

- Maternal infections, disease, or malnutrition.

- Gestational hypertension and/or diabetes.

- Smoking, drug, or alcohol use.

- Multiple gestations.

- Placental factors (e.g., small placenta, placenta previa, decreased placental perfusion).

- Fetal congenital infections such as rubella or toxoplasmosis.

Diagnostic and Therapeutic Procedures and Nursing Interventions

Δ Chest x-ray to rule out meconium aspiration syndrome

Δ Blood glucose level for hypoglycemia

Δ CBC will show polycythemia resulting from fetal hypoxia and intrauterine stress

Δ ABGs may be prescribed due to chronic hypoxia in utero due to placental insufficiency

Nursing Assessments

Δ   Monitor for **signs** and **symptoms** of **SGA/IUGR.**

- **Weight below 10th percentile**
- Normal skull, but reduced body dimensions
- **Reduced subcutaneous fat**
- **Loose, dry skin**
- Decreased muscle mass particularly over the cheeks and buttocks
- **Drawn abdomen** rather than well-rounded
- Thin, dry, yellow, and dull umbilical cord rather than gray, glistening, and moist
- **Scalp hair sparse**
- **Wide skull sutures** from inadequate bone growth
- Signs of respiratory distress and hypoxia
- **Wide-eyed and alert attributed to prolonged fetal hypoxia**
- Signs of meconium aspiration
- Signs of hypoglycemia
- Signs of hypothermia

Δ   **Nursing assessments** for **SGA infants** include:

- Auscultating breath sounds.
- Pulse oximetry.
- Assessing axillary skin temperature every 4 hr.
- Cardiovascular circulation.
- Signs of fatigue or respiratory distress.
- Signs of skin break down.
- Monitoring vital signs and temperature.

NANDA Nursing Diagnoses

- Impaired gas exchange related to aspiration of meconium
- Ineffective thermoregulation related to decreased subcutaneous fat
- Imbalanced nutrition: Less than body requirements related to increased metabolic rate

Nursing Interventions

Δ   **Nursing interventions** for **SGA/IUGR** infants include:

- **Supporting respiratory efforts** and **suctioning** as necessary to maintain an open airway.

- Providing a neutral thermal environment (isolette or radiant heat warmer) to **prevent cold stress**.

- Initiating **early feedings** (SGA will have more frequent feedings).

- Parenteral nutrition if necessary.

- Administering a **partial exchange transfusion** to reduce viscosity of the blood if prescribed.

- Maintaining **adequate hydration**.

- Conserving a newborn's energy level.

- Preventing skin breakdown.

- Protecting from infection.

- Providing support to parents and extended family and encouraging them to participate in newborn care.

Newborn Complication: Hyperbilirubinemia

 Key Points

Δ   **Hyperbilirubinemia** is an **elevation of serum bilirubin levels** resulting in jaundice. Jaundice normally appears in a cephalocaudal manner, first being noticed in the head (especially the sclera and mucous membranes), and then progresses down the thorax, abdomen, and extremities.

Δ   **Jaundice can be either physiologic or pathologic**

- **Physiologic jaundice** is considered benign (resulting from normal newborn physiology of increased bilirubin production due to the shortened lifespan and breakdown of fetal RBCs and liver immaturity). The infant with physiological jaundice has no other symptoms and shows signs of **jaundice after 24 hr of age**.

- **Pathologic jaundice** is a result of an underlying disease. Pathologic jaundice appears **before 24 hr of age** or is **persistent after day 7**. In the term infant, bilirubin levels increase more than 0.5 mg/dL/hr, peaks at **greater than 13 mg/dL**, or is associated with anemia and hepatosplenomegaly. Pathologic jaundice is usually caused by a blood group incompatibility or an infection, but may be the result of RBC disorders.

Δ **Kernicterus** (bilirubin encephalopathy) can result from untreated hyperbilirubinemia with **bilirubin levels at or higher than 25 mg/dL**. It is a neurological syndrome caused by bilirubin depositing in brain cells. Survivors may develop cerebral palsy, epilepsy, or mental retardation. They may have minor effects such as learning disorders or perceptual-motor disabilities.

Key Factors

Δ **Factors that affect development of hyperbilirubinemia** include:

- Increased RBC production or breakdown.

- **Rh or ABO incompatibility.**

- Decreased liver function.

- Maternal enzymes in breast milk.

- Ineffective breastfeeding.

- Certain medications (aspirin, tranquilizers, and sulfonamides).

- Hypoglycemia.

- Hypothermia.

- Anoxia.

Diagnostic and Therapeutic Procedures and Nursing Interventions

Δ Laboratory testing includes:

- **Elevated serum bilirubin level** (direct and indirect bilirubin). Monitor the infant's bilirubin levels every 4 hr until level returns to normal.

- Blood group incapability between the mother and newborn.

- Hemoglobin and hematocrit.

- **Direct Coombs' test** reveals the presence of antibody-coated (sensitized) Rh-positive RBCs in the newborn.

- Electrolyte levels for dehydration from phototherapy.

Δ **Phototherapy** is the primary treatment of hyperbilirubinemia.

Nursing Assessments

Δ Monitor for **signs** and **symptoms** of **jaundice** differentiating between pathologic and physiologic jaundice.

- Note yellowish tint to skin, sclera, and mucous membranes.

- To verify jaundice, press the infant's skin on the cheek or abdomen lightly with one finger, then release pressure and observe skin color for yellowish tint as the skin is blanched.

- Note time of jaundice onset to distinguish between physiologic and pathologic jaundice.

- Assess the underlying cause by reviewing the maternal prenatal, family, and newborn history.

- Signs of hypoxia, hypothermia, hypoglycemia, and metabolic acidosis can occur as a result of hyperbilirubinemia and increase the risk of brain damage.

Δ Monitor for **signs** and **symptoms** of **kernicterus.**

- Yellowish skin

- Lethargy

- Hypotonic

- Poor suck

- If untreated, the infant will become hypertonic with backward arching of the neck and trunk

- High-pitched cry

- Fever

Δ **Nursing assessments** for **hyperbilirubinemia** include:

- Observing skin and mucous membranes for signs of jaundice.

- Monitoring vital signs.

Δ **Observe** for **side effects of phototherapy.**

- Bronze discoloration, not a serious complication

- Maculopapular skin rash, not a serious complication

- Development of **pressure areas**

- **Dehydration** (e.g., poor skin turgor, dry mucous membranes, decreased urinary output)

- **Elevated temperature**

Δ **Nursing assessments** during **phototherapy** include:

- Monitoring elimination and weighing daily, watching for signs of dehydration.

- Checking axillary temperature every 4 hr during phototherapy because temperature may become elevated.

NANDA Nursing Diagnoses

Δ   Risk for injury related to hemolytic disease and effects of phototherapy

Δ   Deficient knowledge (parents) related to hyperbilirubinemia and treatment

Nursing Interventions

Δ   **Nursing interventions** for **hyperbilirubinemia** include:

- **Feeding early** and **frequently** – every 3 to 4 hr. This will **promote bilirubin excretion** in the stools.

- Maintaining **adequate fluid intake** to prevent dehydration.

- Reassuring the parents that most newborns experience some degree of jaundice.

- Explaining hyperbilirubinemia, causes, diagnostic tests, and treatment to parents.

- Explaining that the newborn's **stool contains** some **bile** that will be **loose and green.**

- Setting up **phototherapy** if prescribed.

  ◊   Maintaining **eye mask** over the newborn's eyes for protection of corneas and retinas.

  ◊   Keeping the **newborn undressed** with the exception of a male newborn. A surgical mask should be placed (make like a bikini) over the genitalia to prevent possible testicular damage from heat and light waves. Be sure to remove the metal strip from the mask to prevent burning.

  ◊   **Not applying lotions or ointments** to the infant because they absorb heat and can cause burns.

  ◊   **Removing the newborn from phototherapy every 4 hr** and unmasking the newborn's eyes and checking for signs of inflammation or injury.

  ◊   **Repositioning the newborn every 2 hr** to **expose all of the body surfaces** to the phototherapy lights and **prevent pressure sores.**

  ◊   Turning off phototherapy lights before drawing blood for testing.

Δ   Administering an **exchange transfusion** for infants at risk for kernicterus.

Newborn Complications: Congenital Anomalies

 Key Points

Δ   Newborns can be born with a multitude of **congenital anomalies** involving all systems. These are often diagnosed prenatally. A nurse should provide emotional support to the parents who are facing procedures or surgeries to correct the defects.

Δ   **Congenital anomalies** are present at birth and can involve any of the body systems. Major anomalies causing serious problems include:

- **Congenital heart disease** (atrial septal defects, ventricular septal defects, coarctation of the aorta, tetralogy of Fallot, transposition of the great vessels, stenosis, atresia of valves).

- **Neurological defects** (neural tube defects, hydrocephalus, anencephaly, encephalocele, meningocele, or myelomeningocele).

- **Gastrointestinal problems** (cleft lip/palate, diaphragmatic hernia, imperforate anus, tracheoesophageal fistula/esophageal atresia, omphalocele, gastroschisis, umbilical hernia, or intestinal obstruction).

- **Musculoskeletal deformities** (clubfoot, polydactyly, developmental dysplasia of the hip).

- **Genitourinary deformities** (hypospadias, epispadias, exstrophy of the bladder).

- **Metabolic disorders** (phenylketonuria, galactosemia, hypothyroidism).

- **Chromosomal abnormalities** (e.g., Down syndrome, which is the most common trisomic abnormality with 47 chromosomes in each cell).

Key Factors

Δ   **Risk factors** for **congenital anomalies** include genetic and/or environmental factors.

- Maternal age greater than 40 years

- Chromosome abnormalities such as Down syndrome

- Viral infections such as rubella

- Excessive body heat exposure during the first trimester (neural tube defects)

- Medications and substance abuse during pregnancy

- Radiation exposure

- Maternal metabolic disorders (e.g., phenylketonuria, diabetes mellitus)

- Poor maternal nutrition such as folic acid deficiency (neural tube defects)

- Premature infants

- SGA infants

- Oligohydramnios or polyhydramnios

Diagnostic and Therapeutic Procedures and Nursing Interventions

Δ   **Prenatal diagnoses** of congenital anomalies are often made by amniocentesis, chorionic villi sampling, ultrasound, and alpha fetal protein.

Δ   **Routine testing** of newborns for **metabolic disorders** (inborn errors of metabolism)

- **Guthrie test** for phenylketonuria (PKU) showing elevations of phenylalanine in blood and urine. Not reliable until the infant has ingested sufficient amounts of protein.

- Blood and urine levels of **galactose** (galactosemia)

- **Thyroxine** measurement (hypothyroidism)

Δ   **Cytologic studies** (karyotyping of chromosomes) such as a buccal smear uses cells scraped from the mucosa from inside of the mouth.

Δ   **Dermatoglyphics** examines the patterns formed by the ridges in the skin on the digits, palms, and soles (Down syndrome).

Δ   Congenital anomalies are generally **identified soon after birth** by Apgar scoring and a brief assessment indicating the need for further investigation. Once identified, congenital anomalies are **treated in a pediatric setting.**

Nursing Assessments

Δ   Monitor for **signs** and **symptoms** of **congenital anomalies** including:

- **Cleft lip/palate** – failure of the lip or hard or soft palate to fuse.

- **Tracheoesophageal atresia** – failure of the esophagus to connect to the stomach, excessive mucous secretions and drooling, periodic cyanotic episodes and choking, abdominal distention after birth, and immediate regurgitation after birth.

- **Phenylketonuria (PKU)** – the inability to metabolize the amino acid phenylalanine; can result in mental retardation if untreated.

- **Galactosemia** – inability to metabolize galactose into glucose. Can result in failure to thrive, cataracts, jaundice, cirrhosis of the liver, sepsis, and mental retardation if untreated.

- **Hypothyroidism** – slow metabolism caused by maternal iodine deficiency or maternal antithyroid medications during pregnancy. Can result in hypothermia, poor feeding, lethargy, jaundice, and cretinism if untreated.

- **Neurologic anomalies (spina bifida)** – a neural tube defect in which the vertebral arch fails to close and there may be a protrusion of the meninges and/or spinal cord.

- **Hydrocephalus** – excessive spinal fluid accumulation in the ventricles of the brain causing the head to enlarge and the fontanels to bulge. Sun-setting sign is common in which the whites of the eyes are visible above the iris.

- **Patent ductus arteriosus (PDA)** – noncyanotic heart defect in which the ductus arteriosus connecting the pulmonary artery and the aorta fails to close after birth. Signs and symptoms consist of murmurs, abnormal heart rate or rhythm, breathlessness, and fatigue while feeding.

- **Tetralogy of Fallot** – cyanotic heart defect characterized by a ventricular septal defect, the aorta positioned over the ventricular septal defect, stenosis of the pulmonary valve, and hypertrophy of the left ventricle. Observe for signs of respiratory difficulties, cyanosis, tachycardia, tachypnea, and diaphoresis.

- **Down syndrome** – oblique palpebral fissures or upward slant of eyes, epicanthal folds, flat facial profile with a depressed nasal bridge and a small nose, protruding tongue, small low-set ears, short broad hands with a fifth finger that has one flexion crease instead of two, a deep crease across the center of the palm frequently referred to as a simian crease, hyperflexibility, and hypotonic muscles.

Δ **Nursing assessments** of infants with **congenital anomalies** include:

- Newborn's ability to take in adequate nourishment.

- Newborn's ability to eliminate waste products.

- Vital signs and axillary temperature.

- Infant-parental bonding, observing the parent's response to the diagnosis of a congenital defect, and encouraging the parents to verbalize concerns.

NANDA Nursing Diagnoses

Δ Risk for impaired parenting related to congenital anomaly of infant

Δ Risk for injury or death related to congenital anomaly

Δ Risk for infection related to congenital anomaly or its treatment

Δ Dysfunctional grieving related to the birth of an infant with a congenital anomaly

Δ Deficient knowledge related to congenital anomaly and its treatment

Nursing Interventions

Δ Nursing interventions for congenital anomalies are dependent upon the type and extent of the anomaly.

- **Neurologic anomalies (spina bifida)**

    ◊ Protect membrane with sterile covering and plastic to prevent drying.

    ◊ Observe for leakage of cerebrospinal fluid.

    ◊ Handle newborn gently by positioning prone or to the side to prevent trauma.

    ◊ Prevent infection by keeping free from contamination by urine and feces.

    ◊ Measure the circumference of the head to identify hydrocephalus.

    ◊ Assess for increased intracranial pressure.

- **Hydrocephalus**

    ◊ Frequently reposition the infant's head to prevent sores.

    ◊ Measure the infant's head circumference daily.

    ◊ Assess the infant for signs of increased intracranial pressure such as vomiting and a shrill cry.

- **PDA**

    ◊ Educate the parents about the treatment of surgery.

- **Tetralogy of Fallot**

    ◊ Conserve the infant's energy to reduce the workload on the heart.

    ◊ Administer gavage feedings or give oral feedings with a special nipple.

    ◊ Elevate the infant's head and shoulders to improve respirations and reduce the cardiac workload.

    ◊ Prevent infection.

    ◊ Place the infant in a knee-chest position during respiratory distress.

Δ **Nursing interventions** for **congenital anomalies** include:

- Establishing and maintaining adequate **respiration**.

- Establishing extrauterine **circulation**.

- Establishing good **thermoregulation**.

- Providing adequate **nutrition.**

    ◊ **Cleft lip/palate** – determine the most effective nipple for feeding. Feed the infant in the upright position to decrease aspiration risk. Feed slowly, burping frequently secondary to tendency to swallow air. Cleanse the mouth with water after feedings.

◊ **Tracheoesophageal atresia** – withhold feedings until the determination of esophageal patency. Elevate the head of the crib to prevent gastric juice reflux. Supervise the first feeding of all newborns to observe for this anomaly.

◊ **PKU** – special synthetic formula in which phenylalanine is removed or reduced. Restriction of meat, dairy products, diet drinks, and protein. Aspartame must be avoided.

◊ **Galactosemia** – give infant a milk substance because galactose is present in milk.

- Administering **medications** as prescribed such as thyroid replacement for hypothyroidism.

- **Educating** the parents regarding preoperative and postoperative treatment procedures.

- Encouraging the parents to hold, touch, and talk to their newborn.

- Ensuring that the parents provide consistent care to the newborn.

Newborn Complication: Birth Trauma or Injury

Key Points

Δ **Birth injury** consists of a **physical injury sustained** by a newborn **during labor and delivery**. Most injuries are minor and resolve rapidly. Other injuries may require some intervention. A few are serious enough to be fatal.

Δ **Types of birth injuries include:**

- Scalp (e.g., caput succedaneum, cephalohematoma).

- Skull (e.g., linear fracture, depressed fracture).

- Intracranial (e.g., epidural or subdural hematoma, cerebral contusion).

- Spinal cord (e.g., spinal cord transaction or injury, vertebral artery injury).

- Plexus (e.g., total brachial plexus injury, Klumpke paralysis).

- Cranial and peripheral nerve (e.g., radial nerve palsy, diaphragmatic paralysis).

Key Factors

Δ **Maternal, intrapartum, obstetric birth techniques, and newborn factors may predispose the newborn to injuries**. These include:

- Fetal macrosomia.

- Abnormal or difficult presentations.

- Uterine dysfunction leading to precipitate or prolonged labor.

- Cephalopelvic disproportion.

- Multifetal gestation.

- Congenital abnormalities.

- Internal FHR monitoring.

- Forceps or vacuum extraction.

- External version.

- Cesarean birth.

Diagnostic and Therapeutic Procedures and Nursing Interventions

Δ **Birth injuries** are normally diagnosed by CT scan, x-ray of suspected area of fracture, or neurological exam to determine paralysis of nerves.

Nursing Assessments

Δ Monitor the newborn for **signs** and **symptoms** of **birth injuries,** which include:

- Irritability, seizures, and depression. These are all signs of a **subarachnoid hemorrhage**.

- Facial flattening and unresponsiveness to grimace that accompanies crying or stimulation, and the eye remaining open are symptoms to assess for **facial paralysis**.

- Weak or hoarse cry, which is characteristic of **laryngeal nerve palsy** from excessive traction on the neck.

- Flaccid muscle tone, which may signal **joint dislocations and separation** during birth.

- Flaccid muscle tone of the extremities, which is suggestive of **nerve plexus injuries** or **long bone fractures.**

- Limited motion of an arm, crepitus over a clavicle, and absence of Moro reflex on the affected side, which are symptoms of **clavicular fractures**.

- Flaccid arm with the elbow extended and the hand rotated inward, absence of the Moro reflex on the affected side, sensory loss over the lateral aspect of the arm, and intact grasp reflex, which are symptoms of **Erb-Duchenne paralysis (brachial paralysis).**

- Localized discoloration, ecchymosis, petechiae, and edema over the presenting part. These are seen with **soft tissue injuries**.

Δ **Nursing assessments** for **birth injuries** include:

- **Reviewing maternal history** and looking for factors that may predispose the newborn to injuries.

- **Apgar scoring** that might indicate a possibility of birth injury. Neonates in need of immediate resuscitation should be identified.

- **Initial head to toe physical assessment** and **continued assessment** upon each contact with the neonate.

- **Vital signs** and temperature.

NANDA Nursing Diagnoses

Δ Injury related to birth trauma

Δ Impaired physical mobility related to brachial plexus injury

Δ Impaired gas exchange related to diaphragmatic paralysis

Δ Acute pain related to injury

Nursing Interventions

Δ **Nursing interventions** for **birth injuries** include:

- Administering **treatment** to the newborn **based on** the **injury** and according to the primary care provider's prescriptions.

- **Preventing further trauma** by **decreasing stimuli** and movement.

- Educating the infant's parents and family regarding the injury and the management of the injury.

- Promoting parent-newborn bonding.

Newborn Complication: Neonatal Infection/Sepsis (Sepsis Neonatorum)

 Key Points

Δ **Infection** may be contracted by the newborn before, during, or after delivery. Newborns are more susceptible to micro-organisms because of their limited immunity and inability to localize infection. The infection can therefore spread rapidly into the bloodstream.

Δ **Neonatal sepsis** is the presence of micro-organisms or their toxins in the blood or tissues of the infant during the first month after birth. Signs of sepsis are subtle and may resemble other diseases; the nurse often notices them during routine care of the infant.

Δ **Prevention of infection and neonatal sepsis** starts perinatally with maternal screening for infections, prophylactic interventions, and the use of sterile and aseptic techniques during delivery. Prophylactic antibiotic treatment of the eyes of all newborns and appropriate umbilical cord care also help to prevent neonatal infection and sepsis.

Key Factors

Δ **Risk factors** for **infection/sepsis** of the newborn include:

- Premature rupture of the membranes.

- TORCH (toxoplasmosis, rubella, cytomegalovirus, and herpes).

- Chorioamnionitis.

- Premature birth.

- Low birth weight.

- Substance abuse.

- Maternal urinary tract infection.

- Meconium.

- Human immunodeficiency virus (HIV) transmitted from the mother to the newborn perinatally through the placenta and postnatally through the breast milk.

Diagnostic and Therapeutic Procedures and Nursing Interventions

Δ **Complete septic workup** includes:

- CBC.

- Blood, urine, and cerebrospinal fluid cultures and sensitivities.

Δ **Positive blood cultures**, usually polymicrobial (more than one pathogen) indicates the presence of infection/sepsis.

- Organisms frequently responsible for neonatal infections include: *Staphylococcus aureus, S. epidermidis, Escherichia coli, Haemophilus influenza, and group B Streptococcus.*

Δ **Chemical profile** shows a **fluid and electrolyte imbalance.**

Nursing Assessments

Δ   Monitor for **signs** and **symptoms** of **neonatal infection/sepsis,** which include:

- Temperature instability.

- Suspicious drainage (e.g., eyes, umbilical stump).

- Poor feeding pattern, such as a weak suck or decreased intake.

- Vomiting and diarrhea.

- Poor weight gain.

- Abdominal distention, large residual if feeding by gavage.

- Apnea, sternal retractions, grunting, and nasal flaring.

- Decreased oxygen saturation.

- Color changes such as jaundice, pallor, and petechiae.

- Tachycardia or bradycardia.

- Poor muscle tone and lethargic.

Δ   **Nursing assessments** for **neonatal infection/sepsis** include:

- Assessing infection risks (review maternal record).

- Monitoring for signs of opportunistic infection.

- Monitoring vital signs continuously.

- Axillary temperature.

- Pulse oximetry.

- Assessing for weight loss.

- Monitoring fluid and electrolyte status.

- Monitoring visitors for infection.

NANDA Nursing Diagnoses

Δ   Infection related to maternal infection, need for indwelling intrauterine devices, or neonatal contact with pathogen

Δ   Ineffective thermoregulation related to infection

Δ   Impaired tissue integrity related to invasive procedures

Nursing Interventions

Δ **Nursing interventions** for **neonatal infections/sepsis** include:

- **Obtaining specimens** (blood, urine, and stool) to assist in identifying the causative organism.

- Initiating and maintaining **IV therapy** as prescribed to administer electrolyte replacements, fluids, and medications.

- Administering **medications** as prescribed (e.g., broad-spectrum antibiotics prior to cultures being obtained).

- Initiating and maintaining **respiratory support** as needed.

- Providing newborn care to **maintain temperature**.

- Maintaining standard precautions.

- Cleaning and sterilizing all equipment to be used.

- Providing family education on infection control, which includes:

  ◊ Instructing the family on the use of clean bottles and nipples for each feeding.

  ◊ Not storing leftover formula.

  ◊ Supervising handwashing.

- Providing emotional support to the family.

Newborn Complication: Maternal Substance Abuse During Pregnancy

 Key Points

Δ **Maternal substance abuse during pregnancy** consists of any use of alcohol or drugs during pregnancy. Intrauterine drug exposure can cause anomalies, neurobehavioral changes, and signs of withdrawal. These changes depend on specific drug or combination of drugs used, dosage, route of administration, metabolism and excretion by mother and fetus, timing of drug exposure, and length of drug exposure.

Δ **Substance withdrawal** in the newborn occurs when the mother uses illicit drugs while pregnant.

Δ **Fetal alcohol syndrome (FAS)** results from the chronic or periodic intake of alcohol during pregnancy. Alcohol is considered teratogenic, so the daily intake of alcohol increases the risk of FAS.

Δ   Newborns with **FAS** are at risk for specific congenital physical defects, along with long-term complications including:

- Feeding problems.

- Central nervous system dysfunction (e.g., mental retardation, cerebral palsy).

- Behavioral difficulties such as hyperactivity.

- Language abnormalities.

- Future substance abuse.

- Delayed growth and development.

- Poor maternal-infant bonding.

Key Factors

Δ   **Risk factors** for **maternal substance abuse during pregnancy** include:

- Mother using substances prior to knowing she is pregnant.

- Maternal substance abuse and addiction.

Diagnostic and Therapeutic Procedures and Nursing Interventions

Δ   **Drug screen** of urine or meconium to reveal the agent abused by the mother.

Δ   **Chest x-ray** for FAS to rule out congenital heart defects.

Δ   **Blood tests** should be done to **differentiate between neonatal drug withdrawal and central nervous system irritability**. Tests should include:

- CBC.

- Blood glucose.

- Calcium.

- Magnesium.

- TSH, T_4, T_3.

- ABS.

Nursing Assessments

Δ Monitor for **signs** and **symptoms** of **neonatal abstinence syndrome** (withdrawal) in the neonate using the **neonatal abstinence scoring system** that assesses for and scores the following:

- **Central nervous systems** – irritability, tremors, high-pitched, shrill cry, incessant crying, hyperactive with increased Moro reflex, increased deep tendon reflexes, increased muscle tone, increased wakefulness, excoriations on the knees and face, and convulsions.

- **Metabolic, vasomotor, and respiratory** – nasal congestion with flaring, tachypnea, sweating, frequent yawning, skin mottling, tachypnea greater than 60/min, temperature greater than 37.2° C (99° F).

- **Gastrointestinal** – poor feeding, vomiting, regurgitation (projectile vomiting), diarrhea, and excessive, uncoordinated, and constant sucking.

Δ **Opiate withdrawal** can last for 2 to 3 weeks.

- Signs and symptoms of neonatal abstinence syndrome include rapid changes in mood, hypersensitivity to noise and external stimuli, dehydration, and poor weight gain.

Δ **Heroin withdrawal**

- Signs and symptoms of neonatal abstinence syndrome include low birth weight and SGA, decreased Moro reflexes (rather than increased), and hypothermia or hyperthermia.

Δ **Methadone withdrawal**

- Signs and symptoms of neonatal abstinence syndrome include an increased incidence of seizures, higher birth weights, and higher risk of sudden infant death syndrome.

Δ **Marijuana withdrawal**

- Signs and symptoms include preterm birth and meconium staining.

Δ **Amphetamine withdrawal**

- Preterm or SGA, drowsiness, jitters, respiratory distress, frequent infections, poor weight gain, emotional disturbances, and delayed growth and development.

Δ **Fetal alcohol syndrome**

- Facial anomalies include eyes with epicanthal folds, strabismus, and ptosis; mouth with a poor suck, cleft lip or palate, and small teeth

- Deafness

- Abnormal palmar creases and irregular hair

- Many vital organ anomalies such as heart defects including atrial and ventricular septal defects, teratology of Fallot, and patent ductus arteriosus

- Developmental delays and neurologic abnormalities

- Prenatal and postnatal growth retardation

- Sleep disturbances

Δ **Tobacco**

- Prematurity, low birth weight, increased risk for sudden infant death syndrome, increased risk for bronchitis, pneumonia, and developmental delays

Δ **Nursing assessments** for **maternal substance abuse** and **neonatal effects or withdrawal** include:

- Apgar scoring.

- Head to toe physical assessment.

- Eliciting and assessing reflexes.

- Monitoring infant's ability to feed and digest intake.

- Monitoring fluids and electrolytes such as skin turgor, mucous membranes, fontanels, and I&O.

- Observing the infant's behavior.

- Vital signs and temperature.

- Measuring and weighing of the neonate.

- Observing parent-infant bonding.

NANDA Nursing Diagnoses

Δ Risk for injury related to hyperactivity or seizures

Δ Altered nutrition: Less than body requirements related to poor suck reflex

Δ Risk for deficient fluid volume related to vomiting and diarrhea

Nursing Interventions

Δ   **Nursing interventions** for the **effects on the neonate of substance abuse during pregnancy** or **substance withdrawal** include:

- Administering **medications** as prescribed to **decrease central nervous system irritability** and **control seizures.**

- **Reducing external stimulation.**

- **Swaddling** the newborn snuggly to reduce self stimulation and protect the skin from abrasions.

- **Frequent, small feedings** of high-calorie formula – may need gavage feedings.

- **Elevating** the infant's **head** during and following feedings, and **burping** the infant well to reduce vomiting and aspiration.

- Trying **various nipples** to compensate for a poor suck reflex.

- Having **suction available** to reduce the risk for aspiration.

- For **cocaine addicted infants, avoiding eye contact** and using **vertical rocking** and a pacifier.

- Preventing infection.

- Referring mother to a drug and/or alcohol treatment center.

Primary Reference:

Lowdermilk, D. L. & Perry, S. E. (2004). *Maternity & women's health care* (8th ed.). St. Louis, MO: Mosby.

Additional Resources:

NANDA International (2004). *NANDA nursing diagnoses: Definitions and classification 2005-2006.* Philadelphia: NANDA.

Pillitteri, A. (2003). *Maternal & child health nursing: Care of the childbearing and childrearing family* (5th ed.). Philadelphia: Lippincott.

Springhouse (2003). *Maternal-neonatal nursing made incredibly easy!* (1st ed.). Philadelphia: Lippincott, Williams, & Wilkins.

Chapter 23: Assessment and Management of Newborn Complications

Application Exercises

Scenario: A nurse is called to the birthing room to assist with the assessment of a 32-week gestation newborn and to provide care to the mother postpartum. The infant's birth weight is 1,100 g. The infant's Apgar scores are 3 at 1 min and 7 at 5 min. The infant is experiencing nasal flaring, grunting, and substernal and intercostal retractions. He is flaccid and lying in a frog-like position. The infant is covered with a thick, cheesy substance (vernix caseosa), and lanugo is widely distributed over his body.

1. Which of the following are characteristics of a preterm infant that the nurse may see at this birth? (Select all that apply.)

    _____ Large head in comparison to body
    _____ Lanugo
    _____ Long hair
    _____ Long nails
    _____ Weak grasp reflex
    _____ Translucent skin
    _____ Plump face

2. What assessment findings indicate that a complication may be developing for this newborn?

3. Why is this infant at risk for ineffective thermoregulation?

4. A nurse is caring for an infant with a high bilirubin level who is receiving high intensity light treatments (phototherapy). The nurse's highest assessment priority in monitoring this infant is to check frequently and carefully for signs of which of the following common and potential serious complications of phototherapy?

    A. Retinal damage
    B. Bronze skin discoloration
    C. Dehydration
    D. Maculopapular skin rash

5. A nurse assesses a term newborn delivered less than 1 hr ago. The nurse suspects a problem based on the infant's

        A. relaxed posture.

        B. clenched fists.

        C. startle reaction.

        D. stepping movements.

6. A multiparous woman at 40 weeks of gestation has just given birth to her newborn. After prolonged pushing in the second stage, a forceps-assisted birth was necessary. The newborn weighs 9 lb, 8 oz (4,318 g). The newborn has marked caput succedaneum and marked bruising about the face, head, and shoulders. How would a nurse characterize this infant? (Select all that apply.)

      _____   Preterm

      _____   Term

      _____   Postterm

      _____   LGA

      _____   SGA

      _____   AGA

7. A nurse is examining an infant who was just delivered to a woman at 41 weeks gestation. Which of the following characteristics indicates that this infant is postterm?

        A. Abundant lanugo

        B. Flat areola without breast buds

        C. Heels movable fully to the ears

        D. Leathery, cracked, wrinkled skin

8. To evaluate the efficacy of synthetic surfactant given to a preterm infant diagnosed with RDS, the nurse's first priority in assessment is monitoring the infant's

   A. oxygen saturation.
   B. body temperature.
   C. bilirubin levels.
   D. heart rate.

9. A nurse should consider the possibility of neonatal withdrawal syndrome if a newborn

   A. has decreased muscle tone.
   B. has a continuous high-pitched cry.
   C. sleeps for 2 hr after feeding.
   D. has mild tremors when disturbed.

10. The parent of a postterm infant is concerned because his infant's skin is dry and peeling. Which of the following responses by the nurse is most appropriate?

   A. "This type of skin is an expected finding in babies born after 42 weeks of gestation."
   B. "It would be best for you to ask the pediatrician about the condition of your baby's skin."
   C. "Peeling skin is common in some families. Have you seen this in other infants in your family?"
   D. "Don't worry. We have several skin preparations we can apply to help resolve this condition."

11. A newborn is delivered at 39 weeks. The neonatal nurse plots the infant's weight and finds it to be in the 8th percentile for weight. This infant would be classified as

   A. term and AGA.
   B. preterm and LGA.
   C. term and SGA.
   D. postterm and SGA.

12. Which of the following nutritional problems should the nurse observe for in a preterm neonate?

   A. Hypoglycemia
   B. Hyperglycemia
   C. Anemia
   D. Galactosemia

Chapter 23: Assessment and Management of Newborn Complications

Application Exercises Answer Key

Scenario: A nurse is called to the birthing room to assist with the assessment of a 32-week gestation newborn and to provide care to the mother postpartum. The infant's birth weight is 1,100 g. The infant's Apgar scores are 3 at 1 min and 7 at 5 min. The infant is experiencing nasal flaring, grunting, and substernal and intercostal retractions. He is flaccid and lying in a frog-like position. The infant is covered with a thick, cheesy substance (vernix caseosa), and lanugo is widely distributed over his body.

1. Which of the following are characteristics of a preterm infant that the nurse may see at this birth? Select all that apply.

__X__	**Large head in comparison to body**
__X__	**Lanugo**
____	Long hair
____	Long nails
__X__	**Weak grasp reflex**
__X__	**Translucent skin**
____	Plump face

Characteristics of a preterm infant include large head in comparison to body, lanugo over the body, a weak grasp reflex, and skin that is thin, smooth, shiny, and may be translucent. Long hair and nails are signs of a postterm infant. A plump face would be seen in a macrosomic infant.

2. What assessment findings indicate that a complication may be developing for this newborn?

Nasal flaring, grunting, and substernal and intercostal retractions indicate that the infant is experiencing respiratory distress. The frog-like position, vernix caseosa, and lanugo are the usual assessment findings for a premature newborn at 32 weeks gestation.

3. Why is this infant at risk for ineffective thermoregulation?

The infant's low birth weight and gestational age mean that it has little glycogen stored in its liver and little brown fat available for producing heat. The preterm infant lacks subcutaneous fat to insulate his body and his flaccid muscle tone does not allow him to take a flexed position to prevent heat loss.

4. A nurse is caring for an infant with a high bilirubin level who is receiving high intensity light treatments (phototherapy). The nurse's highest assessment priority in monitoring this infant is to check frequently and carefully for signs of which of the following common and potential serious complications of phototherapy?

    A. Retinal damage

    B. Bronze skin discoloration

    C. Dehydration

    D. Maculopapular skin rash

Infants receiving phototherapy lose more water and have loose stools due to increased bilirubin excretion. This increases their risk of dehydration, a serious and sometimes life-threatening complication in an infant. Supplemental oral or intravenous fluids are given as needed to prevent this complication. It is not known whether or not phototherapy causes retinal damage; nevertheless, it is standard procedure to protect the infant's eyes by closing them and then covering them with eye patches while the infant is exposed to phototherapy. Due to the confinement of the patches, it is important for the nurse to assess the infant's eyes between therapy sessions for signs of conjunctivitis. However, the nurse would not be able to detect signs of retinal damage during routine assessments. Some infants who have elevated direct serum bilirubin levels develop a bronze discoloration as a side effect of phototherapy. This is not a serious complication. Infants can also develop a maculopapular skin rash as a side effect of phototherapy. Again, this is not a serious complication. Because the infant's opportunities to be held are limited, the nurse must assess the infant's skin carefully for development of pressure areas and must change the infant's position at least every 2 hr.

5. A nurse assesses a term newborn delivered less than 1 hr ago. The nurse suspects a problem based on the infant's

> **A. relaxed posture.**
>
> B. clenched fists.
>
> C. startle reaction.
>
> D. stepping movements.

A relaxed position indicates hypotonia, which is a possible result of hypoxia in utero or medications received by the mother. The nurse would expect to find fist clenching in a newborn. Straightened legs that are not flexed at the knees are an expected finding following a breech presentation. The nurse should review the delivery record before concluding that this finding represents a problem. It is expected that a newborn's legs would move one at a time as though the infant were pedaling a bicycle.

6. A multiparous woman at 40 weeks of gestation has just given birth to her newborn. After prolonged pushing in the second stage, a forceps-assisted birth was necessary. The newborn weighs 9 lb, 8 oz (4,318 g). The newborn has marked caput succedaneum and marked bruising about the face, head, and shoulders. How would a nurse characterize this infant? (Select all that apply.)

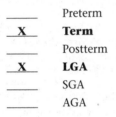

	Preterm
X	**Term**
	Postterm
X	**LGA**
	SGA
	AGA

The infant is term (40 weeks) and LGA (greater than 90th percentile in weight). Preterm is prior to 37 weeks gestation and postterm is after the completion of the 42nd week of gestation. SGA is an infant that is at or below the 10th percentile in weight. AGA is between the 10th and 90th percentile for weight.

7. A nurse is examining an infant who was just delivered to a woman at 41 weeks gestation. Which of the following characteristics indicates that this infant is postterm?

    A. Abundant lanugo

    B. Flat areola without breast buds

    C. Heels movable fully to the ears

    D. Leathery, cracked, wrinkled skin

Leathery, cracked, and wrinkled skin is seen in a postterm newborn due to placental insufficiency. Abundant lanugo, flat areolas without breast buds, and heels movable fully to ears are found in preterm newborns.

8. To evaluate the efficacy of synthetic surfactant given to a preterm infant diagnosed with RDS, the nurse's first priority in assessment is monitoring the infant's

    A. oxygen saturation.

    B. body temperature.

    C. bilirubin levels.

    D. heart rate.

Surfactant contains surface-active phospholipids, specifically lecithin and sphingomyelin, that are critical for alveolar stability. Surfactant therapy stabilizes the alveoli and prevents collapse, thereby increasing lung compliance and maintaining or improving oxygen saturation. Surfactant would not have a direct effect on body temperature, thus it would not reflect the efficacy of this treatment. However, cold stress increases the amount of oxygen the newborn needs. Hypothermia in a newborn can lead to metabolic acidosis, hypoxia, and shock. The nurse must provide a neutral thermal environment for this infant and monitor body temperature continuously. Surfactant does not have a direct effect on bilirubin levels; however, preterm infants are prone to hyperbilirubinemia and so this parameter must be monitored and treated as needed. However, serum bilirubin level is not a reflection of the efficacy of surfactant. It is important to monitor the heart rate of any preterm infant, as well as any infant who has RDS. Since surfactant can cause bradycardia, this is an especially important assessment parameter for this infant. However, heart rate is not a reflection of the efficacy of surfactant therapy.

9. A nurse should consider the possibility of neonatal withdrawal syndrome if a newborn

    A. has decreased muscle tone.

    B. has a continuous high-pitched cry.

    C. sleeps for 2 hr after feeding.

    D. has mild tremors when disturbed.

Symptoms of withdrawal from maternal substance abuse include central nervous system disturbances such as an excessive or continuous high-pitched cry and a markedly hyperactive Moro reflex. An infant withdrawing from narcotics or other substances abused maternally is likely to have an increased muscle tone along with other central nervous system disturbances. Most newborns sleep for varying amounts of time after feeding. Symptoms of withdrawal from maternal substance abuse include difficulty moving through various sleep stages. These infants might only sleep for very short periods of time. This sleep pattern disturbance is related to central nervous system excitation secondary to drug or alcohol withdrawal. Many newborns have mild tremors when they are disturbed. What distinguishes infants who have neonatal abstinence syndrome from this normal pattern is that they have moderate to severe tremors when they are undisturbed.

10. The parent of a postterm infant is concerned because his infant's skin is dry and peeling. Which of the following responses by the nurse is most appropriate?

    A. "This type of skin is an expected finding in babies born after 42 weeks of gestation."

    B. "It would be best for you to ask the pediatrician about the condition of your baby's skin."

    C. "Peeling skin is common in some families. Have you seen this in other infants in your family?"

    D. "Don't worry. We have several skin preparations we can apply to help resolve this condition."

Peeling skin is a normal condition seen in postterm newborns due to dehydration from placental insufficiency. There is no need to ask the primary care provider as this is a normal finding in postterm newborns. A condition of peeling skin in the family would not show up as early as the newborn period. Lotions will not help with the peeling because it is due to lack of nutrition. The peeling will resolve once the newborn receives adequate nutrition and fluids.

11. A newborn is delivered at 39 weeks. The neonatal nurse plots the infant's weight and finds it to be in the 8th percentile for weight. This infant would be classified as

  A. term and AGA.

  B. preterm and LGA.

  C. term and SGA.

  D. postterm and SGA.

This newborn is term, between 37 and 42 weeks gestation, SGA, and below the 10th percentile.

12. Which of the following nutritional problems should the nurse observe for in a preterm neonate?

  A. Hypoglycemia

  B. Hyperglycemia

  C. Anemia

  D. Galactosemia

A preterm neonate is at risk for hypoglycemia because it has not built up glycogen reserves yet. A preterm infant will have polycythemia and excessive red blood cells rather than anemia. Galactosemia is the inability of the neonate to convert galactose to glucose and is an inborn error of metabolism.

Unit 4   Newborn Care

Chapter 24:   Discharge Teaching: Newborn Care

Contributor: Linda S. Wood, MSN, RN

NCLEX-RN® Connections:

Learning Objective: Review and apply knowledge within "**Discharge Teaching: Newborn Care**" in readiness for performance of the following nursing activities as outlined by the NCLEX-RN® test plan:

Δ   Support and instruct the client/family/significant others in the care of the newborn.

Δ   Evaluate the client/family/significant others ability to provide appropriate newborn care.

Δ   Provide instruction and evaluate the client's correct use of infant car seats.

Key Points

Δ   Prior to discharge a nurse should provide **anticipatory guidance** to prepare new parents to care for their infant at home. Mothers and newborns are normally discharged once the newborn is 6 to 48 hr old. Serious complications can result if improper discharge instructions are not given to the parents prior to taking the infant home.

Δ   A nurse should inquire about the **family's current experience** and **knowledge** regarding **infant care**, anticipate the client's learning needs, and assess the client's readiness for learning in order to provide education on infant care.

Δ   Parents need to be made aware of some general guidelines about **infant behavior and care.** These guidelines include causes of crying in the newborn, quieting techniques, sleeping patterns, and feeding, bathing, and clothing the infant.

Δ   Parents need to be aware of the importance of **well-infant checkups**, **immunization schedules**, and when to call the primary care provider for **signs** of **illness**.

Δ Providing a **safe protective environment** at home should be stressed to the new parents and should include instruction about **proper car seat usage**, which is a very important part of discharge instruction.

Assessments, Nursing Diagnoses, and Nursing Interventions

 Nursing Assessment

Δ Assessment of the family's readiness to care for the infant at home should include:

- Previous infant experience and knowledge.

- Parent-infant attachment.

- Adjustment to the parental role.

- Social support.

- Educational needs.

- Sibling rivalry issues.

- Readiness of the parents to have their home and lifestyle altered to accommodate their newborn.

- Parents' ability to verbalize and demonstrate infant care following teaching.

NANDA Nursing Diagnoses

Δ Readiness for enhanced family coping related to bringing home the newborn

Δ Health-seeking behaviors related to newborn care

Δ Risk for impaired parenting related to deficient knowledge

Nursing Interventions

Δ Through verbal discussion, pamphlets, and demonstration, the nurse should provide education to the client and family regarding **infant behavior, quieting techniques, infant care, signs of infant well-being and illness,** and issues of **infant safety**.

Δ **Crying**

- Inform the parents that infants cry when they are hungry, need to be burped, are overstimulated, wet, cold, hot, tired, or bored. Assure the mother that in time, she will learn what her infant's cry means. The mother should be instructed not to feed the infant every time it cries. Overfeeding can lead to stomachaches and diarrhea. It is okay to let an infant cry for short periods of time.

Δ   **Quieting techniques include:**

- Carrying the infant in a front or back pack.

- Swaddling the infant.

- Preheating the infant's crib sheets with a hot water bottle or heating pad, which is removed before placing the infant in the crib.

- Providing rhythmic monotonous noises to simulate utero sounds.

- Providing movement (e.g., ride in the car, vibrating chair, infant swing, rocking infant).

- Placing the infant on its stomach across a holder's lap while bouncing legs.

- Close skin contact with the infant.

- En face.

- Stimulating the infant if it is bored.

Δ   **Sleep Wake Cycle**

- Reinforce to the parents that placing the infant in **the supine position** for sleeping greatly **decreases** the **risk** of **SIDS**.

- Most infants sleep **16 out of every 24 hr** the first week at home and sleep **2 to 3 hr at a time**.

- Many parents believe that adding solid food to the infant's diet will help with sleep patterns. The parents should be instructed **not to add cereal** to the infant's formula or feed the infant solid foods **until 4 to 6 months of age**. Most infants will sleep through the night without a feeding by 4 to 5 months of age.

- Keep things quiet and dark at night.

- The **infant** should **never sleep** in the **parents' bed** (suffocation).

- Most infants get their days and nights mixed up. Provide basic suggestions for **helping** the parents **develop** a **predictable routine**. Bring the infant out into the center of action in the afternoon and keep the infant there for the rest of the evening. Bathe the infant right before bedtime so the infant feels soothed. Give the infant its last feeding around 11 p.m. and then place it into a crib or bassinet.

- For **nighttime feedings** and **diaper changes**, keep a **small night light** on to avoid having to turn on bright lights. **Speak softly** and handle the infant gently so the infant goes back to sleep easily.

Δ   **Oral and Nasal Suctioning**

- Teach the parents to use a bulb syringe to suction any excess mucus from the nose and mouth.

- Parents should suction the mouth first and then the nose, one nostril at a time.

- The bulb should be compressed before inserting it into the infant's mouth or nose.

- When suctioning the infant's mouth, always insert the bulb on the sides of the infant's mouth, not in the middle, and do not touch the back of the throat to avoid the gag reflex

Δ **Positioning and Holding of Newborn (Support Head)**

- Teach the parents that the infant has minimal head control. The head must be supported whenever the infant is lifted, especially since the infant's head is larger than the rest of the body.

- Four basic ways to hold the infant:

  ◊ **Cradle hold** – newborn's head is cradled in the bend of the elbow. This permits eye-to-eye contact (good for feeding).

  ◊ **Upright position** – hold the infant upright and facing the holder while supporting the infant's head, upper back, and buttocks (good for burping).

  ◊ **Football hold** – half of the infant's body is supported by the holder's forearm with the head and neck resting in the palm of the hand (good for shampooing and breastfeeding).

  ◊ **Colic hold** – place the infant facedown along the holder's forearm with the hand firmly between the infant's legs and the infant's cheek should be by the holder's elbow on the outside. The infant should be able to see the ground. The holder's arm should be close to their body, using it to brace and steady the infant (good for quieting a fussy infant).

Δ **Bathing**

- Teach the parents proper infant bathing techniques by a demonstration. Have the parents return the demonstration. The infant's face and perineal area should be cleansed daily. Completely bathe the newborn 2 to 3 times a week using mild soap.

- Bathing should take place before a feeding to prevent spitting up or vomiting.

- Organize all equipment so that the infant is not left unattended in the water (safety). Never leave the newborn alone in the tub or sink.

- Make sure the hot water heater is set at 49° C (120.2° F) or less. The room should be warm and bath water should be 37° to 38° C (98.6° to 100.4° F). Test the water for comfort on inner wrist prior to bathing the infant.

- Avoid drafts or chilling of the infant and expose only the body part being bathed (convection). Dry the infant thoroughly (evaporation).

- Sponge bathing is adequate until the infant's cord falls off and the umbilical area is healed. Move from the cleanest to dirtiest part of the infant's body, beginning with the infant's eyes, face, and head; and proceed to the chest, arms, and legs; and wash the groin area last.

- The infant's eyes should be cleaned using a clean portion of the wash cloth and clear water for each eye, moving from the inner canthus to the outer canthus.

- Each area of the newborn's body should be washed, rinsed, and dried, with no soap left on the skin.

- Wash the area around the cord, taking care not to get the cord wet.

- Soap used should be mild and not contain hexachlorophene.

- The easiest and safest way to shampoo the newborn's head is in the bassinet.

- Rinse shampoo from the infant's head by holding the infant in a football-hold over a basin.

- Dry the newborn's hair to avoid chilling.

- In male newborns, to cleanse an uncircumcised penis, gently pull back the foreskin, wash with soap and water, rinse, and replace the foreskin. The foreskin should not be forced back or constriction may result.

- In female newborns, wash the vulva by wiping from front to back to prevent contamination of the vagina or urethra from rectal bacteria.

- Do not use lotions, oils, or powders, because they can alter an infant's skin and provide a medium for bacterial growth or cause an allergic reaction.

- Inform the parents that if powder is used, it should be placed in the parent's hands and then smoothed onto the infant's skin rather than dusted directly onto the infant, which can cause respiratory problems if inhaled.

Δ **Feeding/Elimination**

- Feeding for a breastfeeding infant should be on demand or every 2 to 3 hr. Formula fed infants should also be fed on demand or every 3 to 4 hr. Breastfed infants will average 20 to 30 min per breast.

- Infants should have 6 to 8 wet diapers a day with adequate feedings and may have 3 to 4 stools per day.

- **Burping** in the middle of a formula feeding or between breasts prevents gas build-up in the infant and decreases the risk of the infant vomiting.

- Most infants spit up a little after feedings. Keep the infant upright and quiet for a few minutes after feedings. *(For information, refer to chapter 21, Meeting the Nutritional Needs of Newborns.)*

- Infants should sleep on their back.

Δ   **Cord Care**

- The cord should be cleansed 2 to 3 times daily with the prescribed agent.

- Keep the cord dry and keep the top of the diaper folded underneath the cord.

- Avoid submerging the infant in water until the cord falls off at 7 to 10 days after birth.

- Any foul smelling, purulent drainage, or redness at the cord site should be reported to the primary care provider.

Δ   **Circumcision Care**

- Use petroleum jelly on the penis for at least the first 24 hr after circumcision to promote healing and prevent sticking of the diaper to the circumcision site.

- Report any frank bleeding, foul smelling drainage, or lack of voiding immediately to the primary care provider.

Δ   **Diapering**

- To avoid diaper rash, the diaper area should be kept clean and dry. Diapers should be changed frequently and the perineal area cleaned with warm water or wipes and dried thoroughly to prevent skin breakdown.

Δ   **Clothing**

- Instruct the parents on how to properly clothe their infant. The best clothing is soft and made of cotton. Clothes should be washed separately with mild detergent and hot water. Dress lightly for indoors and on hot days. Too many layers of clothing or blankets can make the infant too hot. On cold days, cover the infant's head when outdoors. A general rule is to dress the infant as the parents would dress themselves.

Δ   **Swaddling**

- Swaddling the infant snuggly in a receiving blanket helps the infant to feel more secure. Swaddling brings the infant's extremities in closer to its trunk similar to the intrauterine position. Parents should be shown how to swaddle their newborn.

    ◊   Fold the top corner of the blanket down.

    ◊   Place the infant on the blanket with the infant's neck near the fold.

    ◊   Pull one side of the blanket across the infant's body and tuck the corner under the other side.

    ◊   Bring the bottom portion of the blanket up to the infant's chest.

    ◊   Pull the remaining side of the blanket across the infant and tuck the blanket under the infant.

Δ   **Safety**

- Provide community resources to clients who may need additional and ongoing assessment and instruction on infant care (e.g., adolescent parents).

- Never leave the infant unattended with pets or other small children.

- Keep small objects (coins) out of the reach of infants (choking hazard).

- Never leave the infant alone on a bed, couch, or table. Infants move enough to reach the edge and fall off.

- Never provide an infant a soft surface to sleep on (e.g., pillows and waterbed). The infant's mattress should be firm. Never put pillows, large floppy toys, or loose plastic sheeting in a crib. The infant can suffocate.

- Never place the infant on its stomach to sleep during the first few months of life. The back-lying position is the position of choice.

- When using an infant carrier, always be within arm's reach when the carrier is on a high place such as a table. If possible, place the carrier on the floor near you.

- Do not tie anything around the infant's neck. Check the infant's crib for safety. Slats should be no more than 2.5 inches apart. The space between the mattress and sides should be less than 2 fingers widths.

- Keep a crib or playpen away from window blinds and drapery cords. Infants can become strangled in them.

- The bassinet or crib should be placed on an inner wall, not next to a window, to prevent cold stress by radiation.

- Eliminate potential fire hazards. Keep a crib and playpen away from heaters, radiators, and heat vents. Linens could catch fire if in contact with heat sources.

- Smoke detectors should be on every floor of a home and should be checked monthly to assure they are working. Batteries should be changed yearly. (Change batteries when daylight savings time occurs).

- Provide adequate ventilation. Control the temperature and humidity of the infant's environment.

- Avoid exposure to cigarette or cigar smoke in a home or elsewhere. Passive exposure increases the infant's risk of developing respiratory symptoms and illnesses.

- Be gentle with the infant. Do not swing the infant by his arms or throw the infant up in the air.

- All visitors should wash their hands before touching the newborn.

- Any individual with an infection should be kept away from the newborn.

Δ **Car Seat**

- Always use an approved car seat when traveling. Parents should be instructed about the proper installation of an approved car safety seat.

- The infant should always be in a rear-facing car seat from birth to 9.1 kg (20 lb) or 1 year of age, after which, a toddler seat should be used.

- The infant car seat should be secured in the rear seat of the car.

- The shoulder straps should be snug enough so they do not fall off the infant's shoulders.

Δ **Infant Wellness Checkups**

- Parents should be advised that their infant will require **well-infant checkups** at **2 to 6 weeks of age**, and then **every 2 months until 6 months of age**.

- The **schedule for immunizations** should be reviewed with the parents and the nurse should stress the importance of receiving these immunizations on a schedule for the infant to be protected against diphtheria, tetanus, pertussis, hepatitis B, *Haemophilus influenzae*, polio, measles, mumps, rubella, and varicella.

Δ **Signs of Illness to Report**

- Parents should be instructed regarding the signs of illness and to report them immediately. These signs include:

  ◊ A fever above 38° C (100.4° F) or a temperature below 36.6° C (97.9° F).

  ◊ Poor feeding or little interest in food.

  ◊ Forceful vomiting or frequent vomiting.

  ◊ Diarrhea or decreased bowel movements.

  ◊ Decreased urination.

  ◊ Labored breathing with flared nostrils or an absence of breathing for greater than 15 sec.

  ◊ Cyanosis.

  ◊ Jaundice.

  ◊ Lethargy.

  ◊ Difficulty waking.

  ◊ Inconsolable crying.

  ◊ Bleeding or purulent drainage around umbilical cord or circumcision.

  ◊ Drainage developing in eyes.

Δ Parents should be **instructed in relieving airway obstruction and performing CPR.**

Complications and Nursing Implications

Δ   Complications stemming from improper discharge instructions include:

- Infected cord or circumcision from improper cord care or tub bathing too soon.

- Falls, suffocation, strangulation, burns resulting in injuries, fractures, aspiration, or even death due to improper safety precautions.

- Respiratory infections due to passive smoke or inhaled powders.

- Improper or no use of a car seat resulting in injuries or death.

- Serious infections due to lack of noncompliance with immunization schedule.

Primary Reference:

Lowdermilk, D. L. & Perry, S. E. (2004). *Maternity & women's health care* (8th ed.). St. Louis, MO: Mosby.

Additional Resources:

NANDA International (2004). *NANDA nursing diagnoses: Definitions and classification 2005-2006*. Philadelphia: NANDA.

Pillitteri, A. (2003). *Maternal & child health nursing: Care of the childbearing and childrearing family* (5th ed.). Philadelphia: Lippincott.

Springhouse (2003). *Maternal-neonatal nursing made incredibly easy!* (1st ed.). Philadelphia: Lippincott, Williams, & Wilkins.

Chapter 24: Discharge Teaching: Newborn Care

Application Exercises

1. To ensure infant safety prior to discharge, the nurse must make sure that the parents

    A. have arranged a babysitter trained in infant CPR.

    B. are prepared to intervene if any of the infant's siblings show signs of jealousy or resentment.

    C. know how to use a rectal thermometer to take the infant's temperature if signs of illness are evident.

    D. have an approved infant car seat for transporting the newborn and know how to secure it in a vehicle.

2. A postpartum client is preparing herself and her infant for discharge. The mother asks how warmly she should dress her infant. Which of the following is the best response by the nurse?

    A. "A simple rule of thumb is to dress the baby as you would dress yourself, adding or subtracting layers of clothes as needed."

    B. "Your baby will need to be double-wrapped for the first 2 weeks because sufficient warmth is very important."

    C. "Whenever you are outside, cover your baby with a blanket to reduce exposure to ultraviolet rays."

    D. "The baby's hands and feet should be pink and warm when dressed appropriately."

3. A nurse on a postpartum unit has just completed teaching a parenting class for six couples. Which of the following statements made by the father indicates to the nurse that the parent has understood a major concept of the class?

    A. "This is a lot of work. We are going to have to stay organized."

    B. "Having a schedule every day is extremely important so that we can bathe the baby at the same time daily."

    C. "My baby is breastfeeding so there will not be much for me to do."

    D. "Staying with the baby and maintaining safety precautions is a top priority."

4. A nurse is providing instructions to the parents of an infant regarding car travel and safety seats prior to discharge. Which of the following is the most appropriate information related to car seat safety for the infant?

    A. Restrain the infant in a car seat in the front seat in a semi-reclined, rear-facing position.

    B. Restrain the infant in a car seat in the front seat in a semi-reclined, forward-facing position.

    C. Restrain the infant in a car seat in the back seat in a semi-reclined, rear-facing position.

    D. Restrain the infant in a car seat in the back seat in a semi-reclined, forward-facing position.

5. A nurse is reinforcing umbilical cord care instruction for a couple whose newborn is being discharged. The nurse should make sure they understand that they must

    A. apply an antibiotic ointment to the surrounding area.

    B. use alcohol on the cord.

    C. wash the cord only as needed with warm soapy water.

    D. keep the cord dry until it falls off.

6. Which of the following statements made by a client indicates the client has a good understanding of how to use a bulb syringe to suction excess mucus from the infant's airway?

    A. The mother states that the infant's mouth should be suctioned before the nose.

    B. The mother states that the infant's nose should be suctioned before the mouth.

    C. The mother states that the bulb syringe should reach to the back of the infant's mouth.

    D. The mother states that the bulb syringe should be compressed after it is placed in the infant's mouth or nose.

7. A nurse is providing instructions to a new mother regarding cord care for her infant. Which of the following statements made by the mother indicates a need for further instruction?

    A. "I should cleanse the cord two or three times a day."

    B. "The cord will fall off in 1 to 2 weeks."

    C. "Triple antibiotic ointment may be used to clean the cord."

    D. "I need to fold the diaper above the cord to prevent infection."

Chapter 24: Discharge Teaching: Newborn Care

Application Exercises Answer Key

1. To ensure infant safety prior to discharge, the nurse must make sure that the parents

    A. have arranged a babysitter trained in infant CPR.

    B. are prepared to intervene if any of the infant's siblings show signs of jealousy or resentment.

    C. know how to use a rectal thermometer to take the infant's temperature if signs of illness are evident.

    D. have an approved infant car seat for transporting the newborn and know how to secure it in a vehicle.

    The parents must have an approved car seat and know how to use it correctly to assure the infant's safety. All other answers are not related to safety concerns.

2. A postpartum client is preparing herself and her infant for discharge. The mother asks how warmly she should dress her infant. Which of the following is the best response by the nurse?

    A. "A simple rule of thumb is to dress the baby as you would dress yourself, adding or subtracting layers of clothes as needed."

    B. "Your baby will need to be double-wrapped for the first 2 weeks because sufficient warmth is very important."

    C. "Whenever you are outside, cover your baby with a blanket to reduce exposure to ultraviolet rays."

    D. "The baby's hands and feet should be pink and warm when dressed appropriately."

    New parents often overdress the newborn, and then the infant becomes overheated and irritable. A good rule of thumb is to dress the infant in the same layers of clothing that the parents would dress themselves and add or remove clothing as needed.

3. A nurse on a postpartum unit has just completed teaching a parenting class for six couples. Which of the following statements made by a the father indicates to the nurse that the parent has understood a major concept of the class?

    A. "This is a lot of work. We are going to have to stay organized."

    B. "Having a schedule every day is extremely important so that we can bathe the baby at the same time daily."

    C. "My baby is breastfeeding so there will not be much for me to do."

    D. "Staying with the baby and maintaining safety precautions is a top priority."

The infant should never be left alone to prevent injuries. Organization is important, but both parents need to be involved in the care of the newborn. A schedule is not needed for bathing. Infants can be bathed any time of the day or night and do not necessarily need a bath every day. The face and perineal area should be washed every day.

4. A nurse is providing instructions to the parents of an infant regarding car travel and safety seats prior to discharge. Which of the following is the most appropriate information related to car seat safety for the infant?

    A. Restrain the infant in a car seat in the front seat in a semi-reclined, rear-facing position.

    B. Restrain the infant in a car seat in the front seat in a semi-reclined, forward-facing position.

    C. Restrain the infant in a car seat in the back seat in a semi-reclined, rear-facing position.

    D. Restrain the infant in a car seat in the back seat in a semi-reclined, forward-facing position.

Infants who weigh up to 9.1 kg (20 lb) should be restrained in a car seat in a semi-reclined, rear-facing position in the back seat of the car.

5. A nurse is reinforcing umbilical cord care instruction for a couple whose newborn is being discharged. The nurse should make sure they understand that they must

    A. apply an antibiotic ointment to the surrounding area.

    B. use alcohol on the cord.

    C. wash the cord only as needed with warm soapy water.

    D. keep the cord dry until it falls off.

The cord should be kept clean and dry so it will fall off in 10 to 14 days.

6. Which of the following statements made by a client indicates the client has a good understanding of how to use a bulb syringe to suction excess mucus from the infant's airway?

    A. The mother states that the infant's mouth should be suctioned before the nose.

    B. The mother states that the infant's nose should be suctioned before the mouth.

    C. The mother states that the bulb syringe should reach to the back of the infant's mouth.

    D. The mother states that the bulb syringe should be compressed after it is placed in the infant's mouth or nose.

When suctioning the infant with a bulb-syringe, the bulb should be compressed before it is placed in the infant's mouth or nose. The infant's mouth should be suctioned before the nose to prevent aspiration during the gasp response. Also, the back of the infant's throat should not be touched when suctioning the mouth because the gag reflex may be stimulated. The bulb syringe should be compressed before inserting it into the infant's mouth.

7. A nurse is providing instructions to a new mother regarding cord care for her infant. Which of the following statements made by the mother indicates a need for further instruction?

    A. "I should cleanse the cord two or three times a day."

    B. "The cord will fall off in 1 to 2 weeks."

    C. "Triple antibiotic ointment may be used to clean the cord."

    D. "I need to fold the diaper above the cord to prevent infection."

The infant's cord should be kept clean and dry to decrease bacterial growth. The diaper should be folded below the cord to keep urine away from it. The cord should be cleansed 2 to 3 times a day with the prescribed agents. Cord care is required until the cord dries up and falls off between 7 and 14 days.